Exploring America
Part 1

Columbus Through Reconstruction

Exploring America Part 1: Columbus Through Reconstruction
Ray Notgrass

ISBN 978-1-60999-066-4

Copyright © 2014 Notgrass Company. All rights reserved.
No part of this material may be reproduced without permission from the publisher.

This book is licensed for sale only in the United States of America.

Previous Page: *Declaration of Independence*, John Trumbull (American, 1818)

Front Cover Images—Top: *American Frigate* Chesapeake *HMS* Shannon by R. Dodd. Portraits (L to R): *Old Sachem,* Sarony, Major & Knapp; *A Fair Puritan,* E. Percy Moran; *John Adams,* John Singleton Copely; Union Soldier, Ferd. Mayer & Co.; African American Sailor, Ball & Thomas Photographic Art Gallery.
Back Cover Image—Pamunkey River by William McIlvaine. All images courtesy the Library of Congress.
Author Photo—Mary Evelyn McCurdy

All product names, brands, and other trademarks mentioned or pictured
in this book are used for educational purposes only.
No association with or endorsement by the owners of the trademarks is intended.
Each trademark remains the property of its respective owner.

Unless otherwise noted, Scripture quotations taken from the New American Standard Bible,
Copyright 1960, 1962, 1963, 1971, 1972, 1973, 1975, 1977, 1995
by the Lockman Foundation. Used by permission.

Cover design by Mary Evelyn McCurdy
Interior design by John Notgrass

Printed in the United States of America

Notgrass Company
975 Roaring River Road
Gainesboro, TN 38562
1-800-211-8793
www.notgrass.com

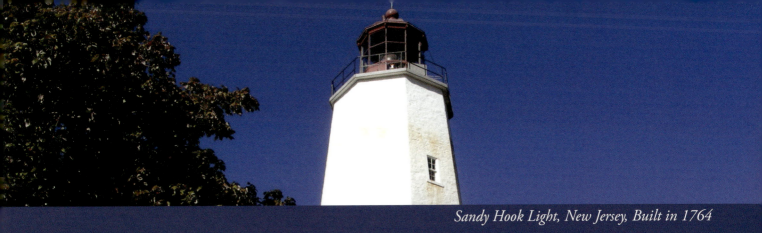

Sandy Hook Light, New Jersey, Built in 1764

Table of Contents

How to Use This Curriculum   vii

Advice on Writing   x

Assigned Literature   xvi

1 This Is Our Country   1

1 - Why Study History?   3
2 - Themes in American History   7
3 - 1491   11
4 - Columbus and the Spanish   16
5 - Bible Study: How You See the World Makes a Difference   21

2 English Settlement of America   25

6 - The Reformation   27
7 - England on the Rise   32
8 - English Colonies in America   36
9 - Life in the Colonies   44
10 - Bible Study: The Shape of Religion in the Colonies   50

3 English Colonies in the 1700s   55

11 - The Enlightenment   57
12 - The Experiment of Self-Government   62
13 - The French and Indian War   66
14 - The Growing Conflict   71
15 - Bible Study: The Great Awakening   77

4 Revolution   81

16 - The War Begins   83
17 - The Declaration of Independence   87
18 - The Revolutionary War   91
19 - Society and Government After the Revolution   97
20 - Bible Study: God Is Sovereign   101

5 The Constitution 105

21 - From Confederation to the Constitution 107
22 - Basic Principles and the U.S. Congress 114
23 - The Presidency, the Federal Judiciary, and Other Matters 121
24 - Amendments to the Constitution 126
25 - Bible Study: The Bible as Spiritual Constitution 131

First Page of the U.S. Constitution, 1787

6 The New Nation 135

26 - The First President 137
27 - Conflicts Foreign and Domestic 141
28 - The Man from Massachusetts 145
29 - The End of a Revolutionary Century 149
30 - Bible Study: Religion in the New Nation 153

7 An Expanding Nation 159

31 - Expanding Democracy 161
32 - The Expanding Power of the Supreme Court 168
33 - The War of 1812 172
34 - The Era of Good Feelings? 179
35 - Bible Study: The Second Great Awakening 185

8 Growing Pains 189

36 - The Missouri Compromise 191
37 - The Monroe Doctrine 195
38 - John Quincy Adams 199
39 - Andrew Jackson Before the Presidency 204
40 - Bible Study: Nineteenth Century Religious Movements 209

9 Democrats and Whigs 215

41 - Jackson's Issues 217
42 - Van Buren and the Whigs 225
43 - Moving Westward 232
44 - Polk, Texas, and Mexico 239
45 - Bible Study: Protest 245

Table of Contents

Four Generations of a Slave Family in Beaufort, South Carolina, 1862

10 Challenges and Changes 249

46 - Slavery 251
47 - Abolition 257
48 - The Growth of Cities and Industry 263
49 - Immigration and Other Changes 269
50 - Bible Study: God Defines Success 274

11 A Time of Crisis 279

51 - Sectionalism 281
52 - Trouble in the Territories 287
53 - Twilight of the Giants 294
54 - Stumbling Toward War 299
55 - Bible Study: Differences 305

12 The Nation Divides 309

56 - 1860: Election and Secession 311
57 - 1861: Inauguration and Fort Sumter 316
58 - North and South 321
59 - Early Battles 325
60 - Bible Study: War 332

13 The Terrible Conflict 337

61 - 1862 339
62 - 1863 343
63 - 1864-1865 347
64 - Costs of the Conflict 353
65 - Bible Study: Faith on the Front Lines 359

Envelope Mailed During the Civil War

Exploring America Part 1

14 Reconstruction 363

- 66 - Off to a Rocky Start   365
- 67 - Congressional Reconstruction   371
- 68 - The Impeachment and Trial of Andrew Johnson   376
- 69 - Life Goes On   381
- 70 - Bible Study: Nehemiah's Reconstruction   387

15 Moving Forward 391

- 71 - The Grant Presidency   393
- 72 - Postwar Life in the United States   400
- 73 - The Transcontinental Railroad   407
- 74 - The Election of 1876   412
- 75 - Bible Study: What Is Progress?   418

Image Credits   C-1

"East and West shaking hands at laying last rail," Union Pacific Photographer Andrew Russell, 1869

Wesley Biddle Notgrass, Governor's Island, New York (1942)

How to Use This Curriculum

My dad served in the U.S. Army during World War II. He endured the German bombing of Bristol, England, where he was stationed before the D-Day invasion. His unit landed on Utah Beach on the northern coast of France the day after D-Day. As the Allied army was advancing through France, the Germans bombed the train station where Dad was sleeping one night. On another occasion, as he stood on a small balcony, a German pilot fired at him and just missed him. Dad suffered through the bitter cold weather that occurred during the Battle of the Bulge.

My father participated in history. If you had suggested to him that the experience of millions of soldiers in World War II, as well as the experience of all those on the home front, was boring and irrelevant because it was history, I think he would have been confused and hurt. For him, history was literally a life and death story.

This curriculum will guide you through the story of our country from the first European explorers to the present. We place great emphasis on original documents and speeches because these allow the participants in history to tell the story from their own perspective. This curriculum also introduces some of the great literature that Americans have produced: novels, short stories, autobiographies, memoirs, essays, poems, hymns, and other kinds of writing. The written and spoken word has a profound ability to move hearts and minds.

This course also explores the significance of faith with regard to history. Faith is connected with history in two ways. First, people have often been motivated to act because of their faith in God. For instance, faith motivated the Pilgrims on the *Mayflower* to seek a new land in which to live. Faith caused people to oppose slavery. Faith has been expressed often in the speeches and documents that Americans have produced. We recognize and highlight the importance of faith throughout the American story.

A second way that faith should be connected to history is by looking at the overall story of American history through the eyes of faith. We encourage students to think about the faith lessons that they can learn from people and events in history. For instance, many God-fearing Americans owned slaves and had a strong prejudice against blacks. We need to understand what caused those Christian people to be blinded by their culture and how they missed the example of Jesus and the teaching of Scripture about this issue (see John 4:7-9, Galatians 3:28, and Ephesians 2:19). This might help us realize cultural blindnesses we suffer today. A study of history can inform, challenge, and strengthen our own faith.

How It Works

This curriculum provides credit in three high school subjects: American history, English, and Bible. The 150 lessons are divided into thirty units of five lessons each. Since a typical school year has thirty-six weeks, you have some flexibility in completing the course. You can take two weeks to complete a unit when you find a topic particularly interesting or when your schedule is especially busy. Families are free to choose how they want to schedule the course, but many families choose to begin a unit on Monday and finish it on Friday.

On the first day of a unit, you and a parent should read the unit introduction. Here you will find a brief overview of the unit; a list of lessons for that unit; a Bible passage to memorize; a list of books used with that unit; choices for a project for that unit; and, when a literature title is begun, an introduction to that book.

After reading the introduction, choose a project to complete by the end of the unit and make a schedule for how to complete it. Find the memory work for the week in the Bible translation of your choice.

Complete the following each day:

- Read one lesson.

- Complete each of the Bible, *American Voices*, and Literature assignments for the lesson.

- Work on your Bible memorization and on your chosen project.

- If you are using the optional *Student Review*, complete the assignment(s) for that lesson.

On the last day of each unit, you will recite or write your memory work and complete your project for the unit. An assignment checklist is available as a free download on our website (notgrass.com/ealinks). We recommend that students keep their completed assignments in a three-ring binder used exclusively for *Exploring America*.

Student Review

The optional *Student Review Pack* has daily review questions; a history quiz for each unit; and comprehensive exams in history, English, and Bible every five units. Reminders to do these are included in the list of daily assignments. The *Student Review* also offers literary analysis for the twelve full-length works of literature.

Tips on Memorization

Each unit of *Exploring America* gives a Bible passage to memorize. Here are some tips on memorization. Pay attention and internalize what the verses mean. You can more easily memorize thoughts that you understand than a string of words that have no meaning to you. Write the verses on an index card or divide them between several index cards. Keep these handy to use when you have a spare moment. Copying out the verses is a good exercise, especially if you learn visually.

Draw pictures illustrating the verses. Ask another person to read the verses to you. Ask another person to listen to you and correct your recitation. Working on memorization consistently in small chunks of time over several days works much better than last-minute cramming.

Unit Projects

Each unit has three choices for a project. Your choices always include a writing assignment. Discuss with a parent how many writing assignments you need to complete to fulfill the English requirement as you study *Exploring America*. We recommend that you choose the writing assignment as your project a minimum of six times throughout the course. The other project choices include a wide variety of activities: building models, cooking, field trips, volunteer opportunities, and more, all of which will enhance and expand what you are learning in the course.

How to Use This Curriculum

The projects relate to the material in the unit. Where applicable, the lesson from which the project is drawn is noted. You should choose your project at the beginning of the unit and work on it throughout the unit. Don't wait until the end of the unit or until you reach the lesson noted. You might need to look ahead at the relevant section of the lesson to get started on your project.

As you choose your project unit by unit, take the opportunity to try new things and expand your skills. If you have never made a model out of STYROFOAM™, or seldom do any cooking, or don't know how to make a video, this is your chance!

You are expected to complete each project at a high school level. Some of these assignments could be given to an elementary school student and the results would be on an elementary school level. Your work should be performed with care and research and with attention to accuracy, creativity, and excellence. Throwing something together in a haphazard fashion is not appropriate. Whether you spend your time writing an essay or building a model, use your mind and hands to create something you can be proud of.

How We Present Scripture

The most important material in this course are the studies from God's Word. Understanding history and literature is important, but how we live before God is the most important issue before each one of us. We want to help you as you do that by digging into spiritual trends and issues in American history.

We believe in the inspiration and authority of the Bible, and our desire is to present the Bible in all of its truth, wisdom, and power. We strive in all we do simply to be Christians. We are on a quest to understand the truth that God has provided in His Word. We believe that eternal truth does exist, but we do not claim to know it all.

In this curriculum we have sought to present a fair analysis of American history, highlighting various people, viewpoints, and denominations. If you read something in this curriculum that differs from what your family believes, take the opportunity to discuss the issue and search the Scriptures together. We welcome your feedback. If you believe that we have written something in error, please e-mail us so that we can learn together the truth that will set us free.

Thanks

Like all Notgrass history curriculum, this new edition of *Exploring America* has been a family project. I updated the lesson content. My wife Charlene proofread with me and provided valuable input. Our son John searched for the new color illustrations and photographs and did the page layout. Our daughter Mary Evelyn designed the covers, and our daughter Bethany developed the unit activities. Our son-in-law Nate updated the *Student Review* questions.

We have been richly blessed by the positive feedback we have received from homeschooling families all across the country regarding the first two editions of this curriculum. I thank the Father, who put me in this great country, gave me a wonderful family, and blesses me in countless other ways. Any criticism should be directed toward me; give Him all the praise.

God has blessed us with a beautiful and fascinating country. He has given us the freedom to know Him and the opportunity to serve Him in our country. Knowing where we have been will help us know where we should be going by the grace of God as individuals, as families, and as a nation. Thank you for joining with us in the exciting adventure of *Exploring America*.

Ray Notgrass
Gainesboro, Tennessee
ray@notgrass.com
June 2014

Underwood Typewriter from the Early 1900s

Advice on Writing

Composition is part of most high school English courses. It usually involves learning how to express ideas, write themes, and do research papers. Practicing writing helps you to develop your style and skill, just as practicing any activity will help you to be better at it. I make my living by writing, so I appreciate the importance of this skill.

One goal of high school composition is to prepare you for college composition. I have taught college students who never learned to construct a good sentence, let alone a good paragraph. However, learning to write just for high school and college composition assignments is a limited goal. Life does exist beyond school.

You will probably have many occasions to engage in research and to prepare your thoughts on a vital subject such as abortion or capital punishment. You will have numerous opportunities to write: letters to friends and family, journals, letters to the editor, advertisements for your business, and reviews and articles for periodicals, to mention just a few. The Internet has created new possibilities for sharing your ideas in written form. Desktop publishing has made getting a book published within the reach of many people who might not get a contract from a big-name publisher.

Writing helps you express what you understand about a subject. If you can't explain something to another person, you probably don't understand it well yourself. The writing assignments in this course will help you learn to pull your thoughts together.

Good writing style is important in getting your ideas across to other people. Writing skills will be helpful in your job or in conducting your own business. You will bless your spouse and children if you write thoughtful letters to them often. You can help others by expressing yourself well in writing.

Three ways to improve your writing are to read good writing, to write often yourself, and to receive criticism of your writing with humility and a desire to do better. Reading and applying the guidance in good books on writing will also help you refine your technique. I recommend *The Elements of Style* by William Strunk Jr. and E. B. White.

Writing Assignments in This Course

Each week you do a writing assignment (instead of one of the other suggested projects), you will have two possible topics from which to choose. Some of the assignments ask you to imagine you were living at the time and write a journal entry, speech, or article to express your perspective on something related to that unit. The other assignments ask you to write an essay about a particular person, idea, or other topic.

How to Use This Curriculum

A basic way to compose an essay is to write five paragraphs: an opening paragraph that states your purpose, three paragraphs that develop three different points or arguments, and a closing paragraph that summarizes your position or topic. If you are floundering on a particular assignment, using this outline can get you started.

The usual target length of your writing projects for this course is 300 to 500 words, which is about two or three typed, double-spaced pages.

Writing Tips to Implement

Here are some tips I have learned that have helped my writing.

Write with passion. Believe in what you are saying. People have plenty to read, so give them something that will grip them. If you don't believe deeply in what you are saying, you give others no reason to do so either. This raises an issue that is related to many writing assignments. Assigned writing is like assigned reading: we often approach it as a chore. Deep emotion and a passion for convincing others are difficult to express in a theme on "The American Interstate System" or "How I Spent My Summer Vacation."

If a writing assignment in this curriculum does not excite you, change it or select one about which you can write passionately. If you ever do write about the American Interstate system, approach it in a way that makes it personal and compelling.

Writing with passion means that you should not soft-pedal what you say. Phrases such as "It seems to me," "I think that it would be good if," or "My personal opinion, for what it is worth," take the fire out of your message. It is your piece, so we know it is your opinion. Just state it. Related to this is the common use of quotation marks to highlight a word. Save quotation marks for when you are actually quoting something.

Develop your paper in an orderly and logical way. Using an outline helps me to structure what I am writing. Identify the major points you want to make, the order in which you need to make them, and what secondary points you want to include to support your major points. Be sure that each paragraph has one main point, expressed in a topic sentence, with the other sentences supporting that point. In a narrative, tell what happened first before you tell what happened later. In an essay, make your points in the order of their importance to your overall theme.

Don't try to put everything you believe into one piece. Trust that you will have the opportunity to write again, and stay focused on your topic. Your challenge is to narrow your topic sufficiently to be able to cover it completely.

Use short, simple sentences. Longer sentences do not necessarily show greater intelligence or convey ideas more effectively. You are trying to teach or convince a reader who perhaps has not been thinking about the topic the way you have. He or she will need to see your ideas expressed simply and clearly. Shorter sentences generally stay with people longer: "These are the times that try men's souls." "The only thing we have to fear is fear itself."

Writing Habits to Avoid

Avoid these habits that weaken your writing.

Do not begin sentences with "There is" or "There are." Find a more forceful way to cast the sentence. Compare "Four score and seven years ago our fathers brought forth upon this continent a new nation" to "There was a country begun by our ancestors 87 years ago."

Do not habitually begin sentences with "and" or "but." This practice has become a trendy habit in informal writing, but the grammar books tell you never to do this.

Avoid the word "would." Such usage is an attempt to soft-pedal, to indicate customary behavior, or to describe something that is not a reality. "That would be a good idea" is less powerful than "That is a good idea." "Americans would often violate the terms of treaties made with Native Americans" is not as sharp as "Americans often violated the terms of the treaties."

Don't imitate someone else's style. That person didn't become a good writer by copying someone else's style; he or she developed his or her own style. You might become enamored with the writing of a favorite author and want to write the way he or she does. Learn from that author, but be yourself.

Additional Suggestions

C. S. Lewis had good suggestions about writing (*Letters of C. S. Lewis*, edited by W. H. Lewis, first published in 1966; this edition New York: Harcourt Brace, revised edition 1988; pp. 468-9, 485):

- Write with the ear. Each sentence should read well aloud.
- Don't say something is exciting or important. Prove that it is by how you describe it.
- Turn off the radio (in our day, he might say the iPod and television).
- Read good books and avoid nearly all magazines.

A key to good writing is rewriting. Writing is hard work, and you shouldn't let anyone tell you otherwise. You will not get every word and phrase just right the first time you put them down on paper or type them on the computer. Great, famous, well-paid writers have to rewrite their work and often have editors who revise and critique what they write. Don't be impatient, and don't wait until the last minute. Write something; then go back and rewrite it; then go back a day or two later to consider it again. This is where another pair of loving and honest eyes is helpful. People who have read my writing and who were willing to point out the faults in it have often helped me (although I admit that I have winced inside when I heard their criticism).

Find someone who is willing to take a red pen to your work; a favorite uncle or grandparent might not be that person. You might know exactly what you mean by a particular statement, but someone else might not understand what you said at all. I have often found that when someone doesn't understand a statement I have written, it is because I have tried to say something without really saying it. In other words, I have muddied what should have been a clear statement; and that fuzzy lack of commitment showed through.

Your writing will improve with practice, experience, and exposure to good writing. I hope that in ten years you will not write the same way you do now. The only way you can get to that point is to keep writing, keep learning, and keep reading. I hope that this course helps you on your journey.

Writing a Research Paper

We recommend that you write a research paper of eight to ten typed double-spaced pages (about 2,000-2,500 words) over a four-week period of your choice while you are studying *Exploring America*. Waiting until the second semester will give you time to prepare and to practice writing shorter papers for your weekly special projects.

This section guides you step-by-step through the process. You and your parents should discuss whether you think a research paper assignment is appropriate for you. Also discuss with your parents whether you should reduce or eliminate the special projects for each unit during the time you are working on your research paper.

When you are ready to begin, refer to this section. If you feel a need for more detailed guidance, we recommend the section on research papers in *Writer's Inc.* by Great Source. You can also find sample research papers online. The Purdue University Online Writing Lab (OWL) has a sample. (Visit notgrass.com/ealinks for more details.)

Research Paper Basics

A research paper combines the work of investigation with the task of writing. Choosing your topic is the first step. When you write a research paper, you must define your topic as clearly as possible. You might have to do some general research before you can define your topic. Topics such as "The Colonial Period" or "The Impact of the Civil War" are too broad for a research paper. "Commerce in the Colonial Period" or "Women in the Civil War" are more defined and manageable.

Next comes research. Research involves finding legitimate, authoritative sources on the subject and gathering information from those sources. The modern researcher has a wealth of material available to him, some good and some worthless. Sources include books, periodicals, encyclopedias, scholarly articles, and original sources. Original or primary sources are materials written or developed at the time of history you are investigating. A diary written by a sailor on a trading vessel during the Victorian Era is an example of an original source. You probably will not be able to hold the actual document in your hands, but many transcriptions of original source materials can be found in print and online. Secondary sources are materials written later about the subject in question.

Use caution with online sources, as many are not authoritative. A comment by a reader on a blog about the Roman Empire is not necessarily based on fact, and you cannot use information gathered from such a source in a research paper. It might give you an idea about something to research yourself, but just because someone posted it online doesn't make it accurate or relevant. Wikipedia is the classic example of a non-authoritative source for research. A great deal of the material found on Wikipedia is accurate; but because of the way in which the articles are created and edited, Wikipedia cannot be relied upon as an authoritative source. Websites maintained by universities, government entities, and reputable publishers of reference materials are good sources for online research. Google Books and Project Gutenberg have many historic books available in their entirety online.

Do not neglect print resources for information. A good old-fashioned one-hour visit to the library might provide much more valuable material than hours of sifting through material online. However, you need to be sure that your print sources are reliable also. Encyclopedias and books published by large publishers are your best sources.

The researcher must give proper credit to her sources. Plagiarism is using someone else's words or ideas without giving proper credit to that source. The Internet contains information that you could simply copy and paste into your paper. Though this might be tempting, it is absolutely wrong. Plagiarism is at once lying, stealing, and cheating. You do not have to cite a source for basic information, such as the fact that Columbus sailed across the Atlantic in 1492. However, you do need to cite sources for detailed information and for unique perspectives about a topic. As you take notes while doing research, indicate clearly what is a direct quote and what is your paraphrase of another person's writing. Do not copy another person's exact words into your paper without showing that you are quoting and giving credit to the source.

A research paper is a big project that can seem overwhelming. Divide the project into manageable steps. We have provided a schedule that will help you do this. You might need extra time on some steps while you breeze quickly through others. You must stay on track to meet your deadline. Look ahead to the finished product and take it step-by-step.

Your paper should be based on historical fact and should not primarily be an opinion piece. Sometimes differentiating between the two is difficult. A simple list of facts that can be found elsewhere is not interesting. Your paper should have a point, and you should bring your own thoughts to bear on the facts you gather in your research. Your paper will be dull if you do not draw interesting conclusions. Noting how nineteenth century American painting expressed American ideals is excellent; on the other hand, listing reasons why you like American painting is irrelevant to this paper. Your task for your research paper is to provide information, make observations, and draw conclusions on the topic in an interesting, readable format that is worth someone's time to read.

Four-Week Schedule (see further explanation for each day below)				
Day 1	**Day 2**	**Day 3**	**Day 4**	**Day 5**
Investigate possible topics.	Choose a topic and write a purpose sentence.	Research sources, make preliminary outline.	Learn how to give credit.	Make a research plan.
Day 6	**Day 7**	**Day 8**	**Day 9**	**Day 10**
Begin research.	Continue research.	Continue research.	Finish research.	Finalize outline.
Day 11	**Day 12**	**Day 13**	**Day 14**	**Day 15**
Begin writing.	Work on first draft.	Work on first draft.	Work on first draft.	Finish first draft.
Day 16	**Day 17**	**Day 18**	**Day 19**	**Day 20**
Work on final draft.	Work on final draft.	Work on final draft.	Finish final draft.	Polish and turn it in!

Day 1: Read "Research Paper Basics" (on the previous two pages) and all daily assignments below. Make a list of at least seven ideas for topics. Discuss ideas for topics with a parent. Select topics that you would like to spend the next few weeks studying and writing about. The index of this curriculum is a source for possible topics.

Day 2: Investigate possible sources for your top three topic ideas to make sure you will be able to find enough material. Choose your topic and write a one-sentence summary of your purpose for the paper. Don't say, "This paper is about how the United States transformed international relations." Instead, state the substance of your paper: "The United States transformed international relations in trade, politics, economics, and science."

Day 3: Gather possible sources for research. Make a list of places to look. You can bookmark websites, visit the library, and look through relevant periodicals. Develop a preliminary outline for your paper.

Day 4: Learn how to cite your sources properly. Your research paper should follow MLA (Modern Language Association) guidelines for source citations. Your paper needs to have footnotes or in-text citations for your sources of information and a separate Works Cited page at the end of your paper. Look online for the most up-to-date MLA

How to Use This Curriculum

guidelines. We recommend Purdue University's Online Writing Lab (OWL).

Practice some example citations. Whether you use note cards, copy and paste to a computer document, or a combination of these approaches, be consistent and accurate in your in-text and bibliography citations. Look over the guidelines and your examples with a parent to make sure you are on the right track.

Day 5: Make a general outline for your paper to help guide your research. Make some notes about what you want to say in your paper, questions you hope to answer in your research, and ideas for the main point of your paper. This plan will enable you to make the most of your research time. You want to immerse yourself in the topic you will be writing about. Your final paper will not include every bit of information you read, but you want to write from a position of overflow instead of scraping together just enough facts to fill up your paper.

Day 6: Begin your research. Develop a system to stay organized, keeping track of the source for every quote or fact. For example, if you are using the book *John Adams* note which facts and quotations come from that specific work and the relevant page numbers. You need to know clearly where every item of information came from: book, website, article, etc. Use a minimum of six different sources for your paper.

Day 7: Continue your research.

Day 8: Continue your research.

Day 9: Finish your research. Where do you want this paper to go? What do you want to say? Decide what information you gathered in your research is relevant and what isn't. Highlight key findings in your research. Set aside (but don't throw away) information that does not seem relevant to what you want to say. Talk about your general ideas for your paper with a parent.

Day 10: Work on the final outline for your paper. Jot down the points you want to make in the introduction, the main sections of your paper, what you want to include in each section, and what you

want to emphasize in the conclusion. Organize these into an outline. Your research might have shown you that you need to emphasize a point that you had not previously realized was important, or you might not be able to find much information about what you thought was a main idea.

Look through the information you gathered in your research to make sure you didn't leave anything important out of your outline. Finalize your outline and talk about it with a parent. A good, detailed outline will ease your writing process significantly.

Day 11: Re-read "Advice on Writing" on pages x-xii of this book. Begin writing your paper, starting with your introduction and conclusion. Your introduction should give a general idea of what your paper is about and the main points you will make. Your conclusion will re-emphasize your main points. Include proper citations as you go, both in-text and on your Works Cited page.

Day 12: Continue work on your first draft.

Day 13: Continue work on your first draft.

Day 14: Continue work on your first draft.

Day 15: Finish the first draft of your paper. Check your in-text source citations and Works Cited page against your research notes and make sure your formatting is correct. Proofread your paper and make corrections. Give your paper a title. Ask a parent to read and correct your paper and make suggestions for improvement.

Day 16: Discuss the paper with your parent. Think about improvements that you can make. Begin working on the final draft of your paper. Fix mistakes and polish your style.

Day 17: Continue working on your final draft.

Day 18: Continue working on your final draft.

Day 19: Finish writing your final draft. Read your paper carefully for spelling and grammatical errors.

Day 20: Read your paper aloud. Make any final corrections. Save it, print it off, and turn it in. Good work!

Section of U.S. Highway 221 in North Carolina

Assigned Literature

Units 2-3	*The Scarlet Letter*	Nathaniel Hawthorne
Units 6-7	*Narrative of the Life of David Crockett*	David Crockett
Unit 8	*Narrative of the Life of Frederick Douglass*	Frederick Douglass
Units 9-11	*Uncle Tom's Cabin*	Harriet Beecher Stowe
Units 12-13	*Co. Aytch*	Sam Watkins
Units 15	*Humorous Stories and Sketches*	Mark Twain
Units 16-17	*In His Steps*	Charles Sheldon
Unit 18	*Up From Slavery*	Booker T. Washington
Unit 19	*Mama's Bank Account*	Kathryn Forbes
Units 20-21	*Miracle in the Hills*	Mary T. Martin Sloop and LeGette Blythe
Units 22-23	*To Kill a Mockingbird*	Harper Lee
Unit 27	*The Giver*	Lois Lowry

The Stow Minutemen Company of Massachusetts on Memorial Day (2014)

1 This Is Our Country

History plays an important part in every person's life. History is not just names and dates and wars; history is personal because persons make history and are affected by history. We see central themes that arise repeatedly throughout the story of our nation. Our perspectives on both history and the contemporary world are influenced by our worldview, so we want to be sure that our worldview is Biblically based.

Lesson 1 - Why Study History?
Lesson 2 - Themes in American History
Lesson 3 - 1491
Lesson 4 - Columbus and the Spanish
Lesson 5 - Bible Study: How You See the World Makes A Difference

Memory Work	Memorize Acts 17:26-28 by the end of this unit.
Books Used	The Bible *American Voices*
Project (choose one)	1) Write 300 to 500 words on one of the following topics:

- Write a summary of your worldview, giving specific citations from Scripture to support your beliefs. Include the following ideas: your view of God and how He works in the world, the value and purpose of human beings, the basis on which you determine right and wrong, how your worldview affects what you believe and do, the influences that have affected your worldview, and an example of your perspective on a current or historical event. See Lesson 5.

- Write about a time when you experienced discrimination because someone treated you with prejudice, or a time you felt prejudice toward someone else. See Lesson 2.

2) Design a poster that communicates—through any combination of words, pictures, or symbols—the themes in American history as given in Lesson 2.

3) Choose one of the explorers discussed in Lesson 4 and dramatize a scene of the discovery of America into the form of a play. You may need to do additional research.

Vietnam Veterans Memorial, Washington, D.C.

Lesson 1

Why Study History?

Millions of Americans know it simply as "The Wall." Two dark slabs of marble form a wall that cuts a wide V into the ground on the Capitol Mall in Washington, D.C. The marble wall is short at one end, cuts more deeply into the ground at the middle, and then becomes short again at the other end. The surface of The Wall is covered with names: thousands of names, tens of thousands of names—the names of those who died in Vietnam. Along the base of The Wall are flower arrangements and notes from children to their daddies. Legless men in wheelchairs sit before The Wall. Some of them merely stare while others fight back tears.

This is the scene at the Vietnam Veterans Memorial, The Wall. The veterans who come to The Wall and the people whose names are carved into it have participated in history. The Wall is symbolic. Just like its physical structure, our involvement in Vietnam was small at first, then it became deeper and deeper, and then after several years we began pulling out until our involvement ended. In addition, when you understand how Vietnam tore into our country the way that those marble slabs tear into the Capitol Mall, you will understand the impact of Vietnam on our national consciousness. You will also begin to understand why we study history—and why we must study history.

History might seem irrelevant in today's fast-paced world. After all, we are barely able to keep up with the events and changes taking place around us. Modern issues demand our best efforts at finding immediate resolution to them. The information that is available to us is growing at an astounding rate, and we feel a need to access that information quickly. With all of this dominating the present, we must have good reasons to study the people and events of the distant past. Here are four reasons why we study history.

Reason 1: History Is Our Story

Each of us has meaningful connections with history. One man whose name is on the Vietnam Veterans Memorial was in my Boy Scout troop when I was growing up. My wife is a descendant of the first white settler in what became Nashville, Tennessee. My great-great-grandfather was killed in the Civil War. We knew a man who was a direct descendant of one of the passengers on the *Mayflower*.

Not only does everyone have these connections with history, but these connections influence who we are today. Many Americans are descendants of immigrants who left everything for a new start in this country. We are influenced by the section of the country in which we live and the events that happened there in years gone by. Your grandparents lived during the Cold War, and their experiences influenced your parents, who influenced you.

Besides these direct personal connections, history affects us deeply in other ways. Our thought world is influenced by ideas that were seriously considered and widely discussed before we were born. Concepts developed in Greek and Roman thought, ideas from the Enlightenment, and the theory of evolution all influence our thinking. We are ennobled by the stories of heroes, pathmakers, and inventors; we are convicted by the stories of charlatans, brutes, and turncoats. We stand on the shoulders of the successes and struggles of previous generations. Knowing where we have been helps us know who we are. To know history is to know ourselves better.

U.S. Marine in Da Nang, Vietnam, 1965

Reason 2: History Helps Us Understand the Present

C. S. Lewis said that a knowledge of history will help a person be immune to "the great cataract of nonsense that pours from the press and the microphone of his own age."* In other words, history helps us to discern what is nonsense and what is lasting truth.

The voices that clamor for our attention today are loud, insistent, and attractive. For instance, if you only listen to today's media and secular scholars, you might conclude that faith has never been a significant factor in American life. A fair-minded study of history, however, will show that faith has played a vital role in our history. In addition, the media would have us think that today's crises are the most monumental we've ever faced, today's products are the most important we could ever buy, and today's thinkers are the most brilliant that the world has ever known. A study of history, however, gives a larger context for today's headlines. We have faced and survived many other serious crises, many seemingly vital products of yesterday are but dim memories today, and what appears to be today's brilliance may prove to be tomorrow's nonsense.

Some of the basic assumptions that many people have today, such as the nature and worth of human beings and the proper role of government action, are different from the assumptions that Americans shared a century or two ago. If it seems that today's government programs aren't working, it could be that these programs are based on assumptions that are less reliable and less true than assumptions held in times past. If we listen to the past, perhaps we can develop approaches for today that really work.

---

* From "Learning in War Time," a sermon Lewis gave in 1939, originally published in 1949 in *The Weight of Glory and Other Addresses*; this edition New York: Macmillan, 1980, p. 29.

Lesson 1 - Why Study History?

College Students at a March for Life, 2012

Reason 3: History Helps Us Learn From the Past

In one of the best-known comments ever made on the value of studying history, George Santayana wrote, "Those who cannot remember the past are condemned to repeat it." A desire to avoid repeating the mistakes of history can motivate what happens today. For instance, whenever American troops are deployed in a foreign crisis, government leaders are quick to assure us that this is not going to be another Vietnam. Nobody wants another Vietnam, but we must understand what happened in the Vietnam War to keep it from happening again.

We can learn from the past in positive ways also. In the first half of the 1800s, those who called for the abolition of slavery were few in number and were considered extremists. In the 1860s, slavery was abolished in the United States. This illustrates how a view that begins as extreme can become mainstream. Those who want to see an end to abortion today can learn something from the approach that the abolitionists took. Perhaps the pro-life position, seen as extreme by many today, can someday become government policy.

History tells us inspiring stories about people who have acted on the basis of their faith, many times going against the tide of the times; and who have accomplished great good. We read about people who have overcome great hardships and setbacks, who have taken great risks for the good of others, and who have followed a vision that led them to new lands or new inventions. When we encounter hardships, face difficult choices, or consider new possibilities, history helps us go through these situations with victory.

Reason 4: God Teaches Us That History Is Important

We can tell from the way God created the world that He is a God of physics, mathematics, and art. In the same way, we can tell from Scripture that God is a God of history. The Lord included several summaries of history in Scripture.

- As the Israelites ended their forty years of wandering in the desert, Moses reminded them of events they had experienced during their journey (Deuteronomy 1-4).

- After the death of Moses, Joshua led the Israelites into the Promised Land. The Israelite army conquered the land God had given them. Before the individual tribes settled down onto their own separate lands, Joshua reminded them of the history of their nation (Joshua 24).

- Many years later, when the Israelites returned from the captivity which had resulted from their sins, the people gathered in Jerusalem. As the people listened, the Levites prayed to God, recounting His working from Creation through their current situation (Nehemiah 9).

- Jewish leaders persecuting the early church arrested Stephen. When they asked him to defend himself against the charges made against him, Stephen recounted the history of the Israelites from Abraham through the murder of Jesus to prove that his accusers were just as stiff-necked as the opponents of God's servants had been in previous generations (Acts 7).

God wanted Israel to remember their history through the yearly festivals of Passover, Pentecost, and Tabernacles. These festivals made Israel's history personal for each generation (Exodus 12:26-27). If the Israelites forgot their history, they risked becoming unfaithful to God (Deuteronomy 4:9, 6:10-25, and 8:10-20). Much of the Old Testament is historical narrative which teaches the meaning of faith in everyday human life.

Jesus came not "once upon a time" but at a specific point in history (see Luke 1:5 and 3:1-2 and Galatians 4:4). Jesus gave the Lord's Supper to Christians as a reminder of that specific event in history when Jesus purchased their redemption by His own death (Matthew 26:26-28).

God has a plan for human history, and He is working it out in His wisdom and power until time on earth ends and eternity begins. God is working today to bring His people to a better future, and as He does this He wants us to learn from the past for our own spiritual good.

This is why we study history.

*But when the fullness of the time came,
God sent forth His Son . . .
Galatians 4:4*

★ Assignments for Lesson 1 ★

American Voices — Read the speech "Knowing History and Knowing Who We Are" by David McCullough (pages 394-400).

English — Read the section titled "Advice on Writing" (pages x-xii).

Bible — Start memorizing Acts 17:26-28.

Project — Choose your project for this unit and start working on it.

Student Review — Optional: Answer the questions for Lesson 1.

Idaho Farm

Lesson 2

Themes in American History

I love the United States of America. I get a lump in my throat when I watch the Olympics and an American wins a gold medal. When that happens, I feel a thrill as the American flag is raised and the national anthem is played once again. I love old black-and-white movies directed by Frank Capra, such as *Mr. Smith Goes to Washington* and *You Can't Take It With You*, that unashamedly promote the ideals that have made this country great.

I love the United States with its varied and beautiful landscape. My family has been blessed to see the rocky Oregon coast, the multifaceted beauty of Yellowstone, the awesome vista of the Grand Canyon, the vast sweep of a Kansas sunflower field, and the picturesque villages of New England.

I love the stories of brave men and women who risked everything to come to a new land, who carved out homesteads in the wilderness, and who became successful after starting with almost nothing. The citizen-soldiers who moved out across the globe to fight oppression in two world wars and in many smaller conflicts inspire me. I fear we do not appreciate enough the price that has been paid for our freedom to worship God and to spread His message without undue hindrance and persecution.

I love the United States, but I have to be objective enough to see her faults. The enslavement of four million blacks before the Civil War is a shameful legacy, as is the record of prejudice, discrimination, and violence toward their descendants that has occurred since 1865. Our political system has seen far too much corruption and dishonesty. We are becoming increasingly materialistic and secular, and our families are suffering as a result.

American history is a rich story because it tells of some of the best and some of the worst deeds that people can do. It is a story of promises and hopes that have been fulfilled to an amazing degree but that can be fulfilled even more. Because the story of America is our story, it can teach us, inspire us, and rebuke us.

As you study American history, you will see certain themes repeated. The most important overarching theme is that the hand of God has been guiding, blessing, protecting, and sometimes chastening us. We will see many evidences of this reality, and it is still true even when we do not see it. Here are four other threads that weave through the story of America.

Expansion

America has expanded geographically, culturally, intellectually, and in terms of personal rights. A noted historian of the late nineteenth and early twentieth centuries, Frederick Jackson Turner, developed the idea that the attraction of the frontier has been a major influence in American history. This frontier idea is an example of the theme of expansion.

However, that expansion has often come at a cost to other people. For instance, as Europeans expanded their control of more and more of the continent, Native Americans were treated shamefully. In another example, a major part of America's economic expansion before 1860 came at the expense of slaves. In the twentieth century, the influence of the United States expanded to affect events around the world; but again that expansion came at a cost. We need to understand both expansion and the cost of expansion in the story of America.

Power and Control

People want to control their own destinies. This is why millions of people have immigrated to the United States and why millions of Americans today own their own property and their own businesses. However, some people also want to control others. The desire by whites to control society is why blacks had few rights after the Civil War. Most political campaigns are carried out because political parties want to control the reins of government.

John Dyson of Maryland, born into slavery in the 1850s, was photographed in 1940.

One way in which the desire for power and control shows up repeatedly involves the economic motivation behind events. For instance, the desire by American colonists for economic success led to their willingness to use (control) black Africans as slaves. The desire for power and money influenced the growth of industry in America in the late nineteenth century. You will see over and over how the desire for power and control has influenced what people do.

A Mixture of Good and Bad

As you study history, you will see that most people and events are a mixture of good and bad. President Bill Clinton oversaw unprecedented economic growth but was a moral failure. Industrial growth gave us a better material life but caused many workers to suffer. We would like to think that everything and everybody is either clearly good or clearly bad, but this is not the case.

You and I are not completely good or completely evil; we are a mixture. People who do great things have clay feet. Presidents and generals have strong points and weak points. Events that bring progress have side effects. We must learn to distinguish between the good and the bad—often in the same person, institution, or event.

Ethnocentricity

Most Americans believe that our way of doing things is right and that other ways are wrong. This includes how we dress, how we talk, how we eat, and many other things that we believe and do. This tendency is called ethnocentrism. When Catholic immigrants from Ireland and Europe came to largely Protestant America in the early 1800s, many Protestant Americans were suspicious of them and prejudiced against them simply because they were different and had different beliefs. People in different sections of the country—the South, the North, the Midwest, and the West—can also be ethnocentric

This 1882 political cartoon shows Uncle Sam (lower right) using immigrants to the U.S. from other countries to build a wall to keep out the Chinese. Meanwhile, Chinese in the background tear down a wall, indicating their growing openness to international trade and communication.

---

about the way they live as compared to the ways of people who live in other sections of the country.

This tendency to think that one's own ways are best influences international relations. The leaders of a particular nation's government believe that they have to defend and strengthen their own country because they cannot count on other nations to do so. British self-interest led to Britain's developing a world-wide empire. The Marshall Plan to rebuild Europe after World War II certainly helped that devastated continent, but one major motivation for the U.S. in implementing the plan was to avoid another costly involvement of American forces in yet another European war. American involvement in Korea, Vietnam, and the Middle East was partly out of concern for other people but primarily because such involvement was seen as protecting our country's own national interests. Because each nation is made up of human beings, each nation tends to be ethnocentric. Conflicts arise when countries approach an issue with differing interests.

Some people believe that the United States is God's new chosen people. Certainly God has richly blessed America. We can see His guiding hand in our history. However, God Himself has not declared that America is His chosen people. When God established a covenant with Israel and declared them to be His chosen people, He did it through Moses on Mount Sinai (Exodus 19). The new covenant in Christ, by which believers are God's new chosen people, is set forth in the inspired New Testament (Hebrews 9:6-15). But no one has ever received an equivalent revelation from God declaring that America is God's new covenant people.

A better understanding of God's relationship with the United States is that He blesses and guides our country just as He does all the world. Christians in America have a stewardship from God to use well the blessings He has given us. We have a charge from God to take advantage of our freedom to live for Him and to communicate His Word.

The Fabric of History

Lives and events do not happen in isolation; they are connected with what happened yesterday, and they influence what will happen tomorrow. The Civil War did not just erupt in the mid 1800s; turmoil about slavery and states' rights had been brewing since the writing of the Constitution.

However, some aspects of history have more direct influence on our lives today than do others. For instance, the American Civil War has influenced us more than the Spanish conquest of the Aztecs. Interestingly, today we are seeing a growing influence on American life from the Hispanic cultures to our south. Perhaps the Spanish conquest of the Aztecs will come to have more influence on Americans than even the Civil War does.

Does history repeat itself? Yes and no. As we have been saying, certain themes do repeat themselves in American history. Americans have repeatedly fought foreign aggressors whose tactics and philosophies bear a striking similarity to each other. Hitler was just Lenin with a swastika, and Osama bin Laden was just Hitler without a government. We see the same issues over and over in history because people are the same as they have always been. This is why we can and should learn from history.

But at the same time, every situation is different in some ways. Aggressors in previous generations rattled sabres; today North Korea and Iran rattle nuclear weapons. Many politicians have always wanted to spend other people's money (called taxes) to promote themselves. Today, though, they propose to do it in terms of billions instead of mere millions of dollars. To understand and to live well in today's world, we must learn from the patterns of history; we must also grasp the unique situation in which God has placed us today.

He made from one man every nation of mankind to live on all the face of the earth, having determined their appointed times and the boundaries of their habitation.
Acts 17:26

★ Assignments for Lesson 2 ★

Bible   Read Paul's sermon that he gave in the synagogue at Pisidian Antioch, which is recorded in Acts 13:15-43. Note how Paul used history to make his point.

Work on memorizing Acts 17:26-28.

Project   Work on your project.

Student Review   Optional: Answer the questions for Lesson 2.

The Cotswolds in England

Lesson 3

1491

Life in the English village of Notgrove had not changed much in the thousand years before 1491. Every day Geoffrey the shepherd tended the flock that belonged to the lord of the manor. He and his wife and children worked the small patch of land that the lord allowed them to use to feed their family. The other people of the village worked at their jobs and tended their gardens day in and day out as well. Much of life was devoted simply to survival.

Most of the people who lived in the village were born there and died there. Many infants who had lived only a few days were buried in the churchyard. Occasionally a young man walked from Notgrove to nearby Gloucester and became apprenticed to a craftsman in a shop. People still talked about Thomas, the son of the cooper, who a few years earlier had gotten tired of making barrels and went all the way to Bristol on the western coast, fifty miles away, to work at the docks. A few people had made the ninety-mile trip to London; and the lord's steward had crossed the English Channel once to bring back some new, expensive dinnerware from France.

The horizon of possibilities for the people of Notgrove was limited. It seemed as though what was had always been and would always be. William, Lord of Notgrove, had inherited the manor from his father; and he planned to pass it on to his first-born son at his own death. The people who worked on the manor were the sons and grandsons of men who had worked there in previous years. Everyone considered himself to be a member of the Church headed by the pope in Rome. On Sundays everyone attended mass at the small stone building that served the Catholic parish.

The Late Middle Ages

Notgrove is a real English village in the Cotswolds. This description of life there in 1491 is based on what we know to have been generally true about life in England in the late fifteenth century. In fact, most of Europe in 1491 was like Notgrove. The majority of people lived in rural areas. Few large cities had developed. The accepted classes of royalty, nobility, and peasantry gave the world stability and security.

The most powerful agent of control and stability was religion—in particular the Roman Catholic Church. The Church had an extensive hierarchy that stretched from Rome to local parishes. It controlled all religious teaching and practice and therefore controlled most of the era's life and thought. The threat of excommunication (declaring someone to be unqualified to take communion and thus, in their minds, incapable of receiving grace) gave the

Church control over kings and lords. The threat of heresy trials gave the Church control over possible critics. The Church had become wealthy through the land and other gifts donated to it by its members.

Most people accepted the fact that God was ruler over the world. They believed that He set kings on their thrones and that He sent both rain and drought, blessings and difficulties.

How Life Was Beginning to Change

Notgrove in the Year of Our Lord 1491 was much like it had always been, but that was about to change. When Thomas Cooper walked from Notgrove to Bristol, he left the world that was passing away and entered the world that was developing. In many places throughout Europe, new possibilities were emerging. The thought world was changing from one of accepting and defending what had always been to one of exploring what could be. The change in Europe was the change from a settled mind to an inquisitive mind, from an attitude of self-sufficiency to a desire to reach out.

In a significant way, people were changing their view of God's will. The prevailing attitude had been that the settled order of things was God's will. The new attitude said that searching for possibilities was God's will. This attitude of exploration and discovery ushered in the period that later came to be called the Renaissance, which means rebirth.

Many areas of life changed during the Renaissance. In the mid-1400s in Germany, Johann Gutenberg developed a printing process that used movable type. This meant that in the 1490s more books were becoming available at lower cost, which meant that knowledge could be shared more widely and more easily than ever before. The arts were changing also. In Italy, Leonardo da Vinci (born in 1452) and Michelangelo (born in 1475) were demonstrating artistic talents that went far beyond those of the artists who came before them.

The Crusades of the 11th to 13th centuries, in which Europeans sought to take control of the Holy Land away from the Muslims, introduced Europeans to the geography, cultures, and riches of the East. In the late 1400s, international trade by many countries in Europe increased. Italian merchants, for instance, established trade with China and other countries in the Far East. This trade took place along overland routes through the Middle East and Asia.

Portugal also began looking outward. It was wealthy, unified, and strategically located to develop trade contacts by sea with other nations. Portugal's Prince Henry (sometimes called Henry the Navigator) encouraged exploration both to develop trade and to take the Christian message to other lands. In the late 1400s, courageous Portuguese sea captains sailed further and further down the western

Tripoli, a major Crusader stronghold in modern-day Lebanon, fell to the Turks in 1289.

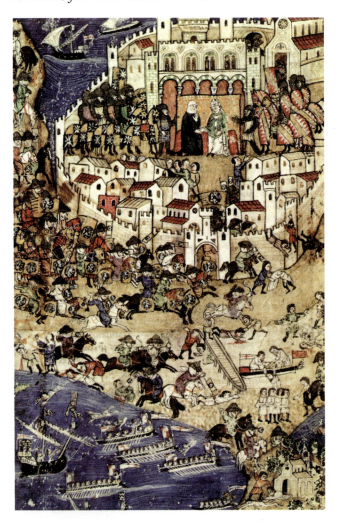

coast of Africa. Unfortunately, part of their business involved the slave trade, as African tribal rulers sold prisoners of war to the Europeans as slaves.

Wealthy Europeans enjoyed spices and other luxuries that came from India and China, but European traders did not like dealing with Arabs who served as middlemen (and sometimes highwaymen) on overland trade routes to the East. Some Europeans wondered if it was possible to get to the East without going through Arab lands. The Portuguese captain Bartholomew Diaz reached the southern tip of Africa in 1486 and envisioned going all the way to India. Vasco Da Gama finally sailed around Africa to India in 1498.

Some people had heard reports of carved objects and branches from unknown trees floating to the European coast from the west. As Europe experienced a Renaissance of learning and an expansion of its horizons, a few people wondered about a bold new idea, one that had intriguing possibilities for increased trade, exploration, knowledge, and evangelism. What would happen if someone left Europe and sailed west?

In America

Moluk lived peacefully on an island in the Caribbean Sea with his family and fellow villagers. The people lived off of fish and the abundant fruit that grew on the island. The weather was always warm. Moluk's oldest brother had been killed some time back when he had tried to defend his sister from men who had come from another island to take women for themselves. Another brother had been lost when his boat was swamped by a huge storm that had come up quickly. No one on the island wore any clothes. Moluk never thought to question or to wonder about his way of life. He assumed that the gods his people believed in controlled the world in which he lived.

Moluk is a fictional representative of the indigenous peoples who lived on the Caribbean islands in 1491, before Columbus came. They had

Harbour Island, The Bahamas

a culture, as did the Europeans; and their culture was also about to be transformed, just as European culture was changing. In fact, the cultures of the Caribbean were about to change because European culture was changing.

Our knowledge of indigenous peoples in the Americas before 1500 is not as extensive as what we know about Europeans living at the same time. The generally accepted explanation for how their ancestors came to the western hemisphere is that they walked across the Bering Strait from Asia to Alaska, either on ice or on a land bridge that no longer exists. From there they spread throughout North, Central, and South America over an undetermined length of time.

However, we have no record of any eyewitnesses to these commonly-accepted events. The Bering Strait theory is a guess; and, as C. S. Lewis wrote, "If you make the same guess often enough it ceases to be a guess and becomes a Scientific Fact."* Mankind began with Adam and Eve, and people were scattered after the Tower of Babel. Beyond this, we do not know for sure how people first came to the western hemisphere. They might have come by boats from other parts of the world.

---

* *The Pilgrim's Regress*, originally published 1933; this edition Grand Rapids: Eerdmans, 1992, p. 22.

Indigenous Peoples of the Americas

Archaeologists and anthropologists are still discovering information about the indigenous peoples of the Americas. The following ideas are generally accepted at this time.

The tribes in Central and South America developed more complex cultures than those in North America in terms of the size of their cities, the engineering of their buildings, and the nature of their societies. The Maya, for example, who lived in Central America before 900 AD, built pyramids, had a written language, and practiced accurate astronomy. They were taken over by the Toltecs, who ruled the area until about 1200 AD. Then the Aztecs emerged in what is now Mexico around 1300 AD. Meanwhile, the Incas developed a powerful and advanced civilization in what is now Peru in South America.

The idea that all indigenous tribes were kind, peace-loving people who were destroyed by cruel Europeans does not do justice to the facts. Many Central American tribes often engaged in battle. The Aztecs practiced human sacrifice on a large scale in their religious rituals. This does not justify what the European conquerors did to them, but we can understand the Spaniards' shock when they encountered the Aztecs.

By contrast, most North American tribes were smaller, more scattered, and more diverse.

Native tribes created thousands of petroglyphs (rock drawings), such as these in Petrified Forest National Park, Arizona.

The Toltec people carved large statues in the form of warriors. These examples from Tula in modern Mexico are fifteen feet tall.

Some tribes in North America lived a nomadic life during the time Central American peoples were living in settled communities. North American tribes developed varying types of social communities and implemented various methods of food production. Some tribes had elaborate social structures and built large mounds as worship or burial sites. Some followed migrating buffalo, deer, and elk, while others settled into farming villages. These early Native Americans built their homes with the materials they found in their surroundings, as indicated by the Anasazi cliff dwellings at Mesa Verde in Colorado and the frame longhouses in what is now the northeast United States.

Moluk's world, and the world of all the peoples who lived in the western hemisphere, was about to be turned upside down. People were coming who had never been to Moluk's island or even to his part of the world. Just as the Europeans' understanding of the world was expanding, Moluk's understanding was going to expand as well. Cultures met and clashed. European cultures soon dominated the existing cultures in the Americas.

Lesson 3 - 1491

People Movements

Historians and archaeologists speak of "push and pull" forces that bring about immigration and people movements. A push is a force in the originating country that prompts people to leave, such as war, famine, or political or religious persecution. A pull is an opportunity in another country that draws people toward it, such as the chance for cheap land, the discovery of gold, or the possibility of freedom.

The island of Britain was invaded many times by various ethnic groups. Galatia in Asia Minor was settled by people from Gaul (what is now France). The apparent movement of people from Asia into the western hemisphere (who descendents became the indigenous Americans) was another people movement. The British settlement of North America was a people movement. A people movement is occurring now as many Hispanic people move into the United States.

Chaco Culture National Historical Park in New Mexico preserves elaborate homes and buildings, such as the one pictured above. The Native Americans who used these structures moved elsewhere around the 13th century.

*The earth is the Lord's, and all it contains,
The world, and those who dwell in it.
Psalm 24:1*

★ Assignments for Lesson 3 ★

Bible — Read the speech that Paul gave in the Areopagus on Mars Hill, which is recorded in Acts 17:16-34. Note how Paul wrestled with the Greek culture that he was encountering.

Work on memorizing Acts 17:26-28.

Project — Work on your project.

Student Review — Optional: Answer the questions for Lesson 3.

Christopher Columbus Monument in Puerto Rico

Lesson 4

Columbus and the Spanish

Cristoforo Columbo was born in the Italian seaport of Genoa in 1451. The son of a weaver, he became interested in sea travel at an early age. When he was 25, he took part in a trading expedition to England. Columbus (the English version of his name) settled in Portugal and began studying possible sea routes to the Far East. Educated people in that day knew that the earth was round. The idea that people of the 15th century thought the earth was flat is a myth.

Columbus became convinced that a ship could reach China, Japan, and India more easily by sailing west than by sailing around Africa; but he made two major miscalculations. First, he thought the earth was smaller than it really is; and second, he did not know about any additional land masses between Europe and the Far East.

The eager and determined Columbus tried to find a sponsor for his proposed voyage. Columbus hoped for riches for himself, but he also wanted to spread the gospel of Christ and to bring honor and wealth to his sponsoring country. He made a proposal to the king of Portugal but was turned down. Columbus then went to Spain, which was becoming a rival to Portugal in international trade. In early 1492, the various ethnic regions of Spain became unified under the rule of King Ferdinand and Queen Isabella. Also that year, Spanish armies defeated Muslim invaders at Granada and the Catholic government expelled Jews from Spain. Since Ferdinand and Isabella wanted Spain to continue to grow in power, wealth, and influence, and because of Columbus' persistent requests, Spain's rulers gave the Genoan the financial backing he needed for his voyage.

Columbus Discovers the New World

Early on the morning of August 3, 1492, Columbus left Palos, Spain, with three small vessels, the *Santa Maria*, the *Niña*, and the *Pinta*. Problems developed with the rudder of the *Pinta*, and it took about a month of work in the Canary Islands for the rudder to be repaired. Finally the three ships headed west. Columbus kept two logs during the journey, one to be made public and another to be kept secret. The Admiral recorded shorter distances in the public one so that the crew would not become discouraged at traveling long distances without reaching land.

However, the crew did become discouraged and even angry. As Columbus grew fearful that they would have to turn back, the crew began seeing fresh branches in the water and birds in the air, evidence that land was near. Early on October 12, the crew sighted land, one of the islands in the Bahamas. Columbus went ashore later that day and claimed the land for Spain in the name of the Lord. He believed

Lesson 4 - Columbus and the Spanish

that he had arrived in the Far East. Since the islands near Asia were called the Indies, Columbus called the people he saw on the island Indians.

Columbus treated the Indians kindly at first and hoped that they would become Christians. However, Columbus and his men later were cruel to the natives. They abused the women and took several of the natives back to Spain as slaves. Columbus made three other voyages, exploring various Caribbean islands as well as the South American coast. He had an ever-growing desire for gold and other wealth. On his third voyage, he mishandled a situation with Spanish troops and was taken back to Spain in chains.

Columbus died in 1506. Late in his life, Columbus referred to the lands he had found as a new world. However, he probably always believed that he had simply discovered a new part of Asia.

The Legacy of Columbus

Columbus' legacy is mixed. On the positive side, it opened the western hemisphere to European exploration and settlement. Many members of indigenous tribes heard the gospel of Jesus and became believers. However, the European invasion also resulted in the abuse and death of thousands of other natives.

Columbus did not even receive the honor of having the new lands named for him. A later Italian explorer, Amerigo Vespucci, published in 1507 a description of the lands he had seen in the western hemisphere. A mapmaker wrongly credited Amerigo with discovering South America and suggested that it be named for him. Thus, all of the New World came to be called America.

Spain Explores the New World

The discoveries of Columbus encouraged Spain to send other explorers west. However, the growing rivalry between Spain and Portugal appeared to put those two countries on a collision course if they tried to claim and explore the same areas. In 1493 Pope Alexander VI declared a line of demarcation that went around the world north to south one hundred leagues (about three hundred miles) west of the Canary Islands off of Africa. The pope, who was himself Spanish, gave Spain the right to control lands west of the line. The Portuguese king did not like this arrangement and negotiated a treaty with Ferdinand and Isabella of Spain, signed in 1494, that placed the line further west and gave control of non-Christian lands east of the line to Portugal.

The treaty line cut through what is now Brazil. Explorer Pedro Cabral claimed Brazil for Portugal in 1500. This is why Brazil today speaks Portuguese and why Portugal continued to develop trade with the Far East by going around Africa. Spain, on the other hand, took advantage of its right to explore west of the line. This is why the Spanish conquered most of South and Central America and controlled much of what later became the southwest United States, without rivalry from Portugal.

The explorations of the Spanish, especially their incursions into North and South America during the 1500s, were the first European ventures to have a lasting impact on America. Consider the explorers and their travels listed on the next page.

This map shows the lines of demarcation negotiated between Spain and Portugal, including a later line set in the Pacific. Neither country was able to enforce control based on these arbitrary lines, however. For instance, Portugal claimed portions of Brazil west of the line in South America while Spain took over the Philippine Islands, which were in Portugal's hemisphere.

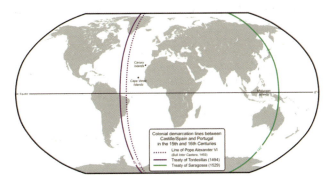

Leif Ericson Discovers North America
Christian Krohg (Norweigian, 1893)

Norwegian explorers sailed to Iceland, Greenland, and, apparently, the North American continent around 1000 AD. Eric the Red sailed from Iceland to Greenland, and his son Leif Ericson is thought to have landed on the eastern coast of what would become Canada. Although these excursions predated Columbus by several centuries, their ventures did not have the impact on Europe and America that the Spanish-sponsored explorations did.

- In 1513 Juan Ponce de Leon landed in and explored what became Florida. He was the first European known to set foot on what later became the United States. That same year, Vasco de Balboa crossed the isthmus of Panama from the east and became the first European known to see the Pacific Ocean from the Americas.

- Ferdinand Magellan led a crew to explore that part of the world reserved for Spain by the treaty. He began in 1519 and sailed around the tip of South America and across the Pacific. Magellan landed in the islands which were later named the Philippines for the Spanish prince who became King Philip II. Magellan was killed in a battle with the natives there. His crew continued on their journey and arrived back in Spain three years after their trip began.

- Also in 1519, Hernando Cortes (or Cortez) of Spain began an expedition against the

Unit 1 - This Is Our Country

Aztecs. The Aztec nation was centered in Mexico and ruled by Montezuma. Cortes strengthened his forces by gaining the loyalty of rival tribes in the area who hated the Aztecs. The Spanish forces took control of the Aztec capital Tenochtitlan (the site of present-day Mexico City) in 1521. Ten years later, Francisco Pizarro defeated the Incas in Peru, which led to Spanish domination of South America.

- In 1539 Spanish explorer Hernando de Soto began to lead his soldiers through what later became the southeast United States. De Soto was the first European known to see the Mississippi River. He died in 1542, and his body was lowered into the Mississippi.

- Francisco Coronado led an expedition that traveled across what became the panhandle of Texas and into Kansas (1540-1542). An officer under his command was the first European known to see the Grand Canyon.

- In 1565 Spain established St. Augustine, the first permanent settlement in the area that would become the United States. It is now in the State of Florida.

Castillo de San Marcos is the Spanish fort at St. Augustine.

Lesson 4 - Columbus and the Spanish

Spanish Strategy in the New World

The goal of these early expeditions by Spain was not primarily to settle or develop the new lands. Instead, Spain had other ideas. First, the Spanish wanted to control the areas, so they established forts to defend against Indian attacks. In Mexico and what became the southwestern United States, Spanish *conquistadors* (conquerors) established dominance over the land and over the native peoples who lived there. The natives were granted full Spanish citizenship, but this meant that they were expected to pay taxes to the Spanish throne.

Second, the Spanish wanted to extract whatever gold or other riches they could find and send it back to Spain. Coronado was searching for the fabled Seven Cities of Cibola, which supposedly were paved with gold. De Leon hoped to find the Fountain of Youth in Florida and in this way transform human life for Europeans.

Third, the Spanish wanted to find a water route to the Far East. European focus was still on developing trade routes with China, Japan, and India. For the accomplishing of this goal, the Americas were seen as a roadblock.

Finally, Catholic priests sought to convert the native peoples to Christianity. Some became sincere believers in Jesus. In many cases, the dominant religion became a mixture of Catholic doctrines and native beliefs.

Spain was the dominant European power in North America until well after the start of English colonization in 1607. By 1574 an estimated 160,000 Spaniards lived in the New World, including about 15,000 in Mexico City alone. The Spanish empire stretched from what is now the western United States, through Central America, and across most of South America. Spain ruled parts of these lands for over three hundred years. English culture eventually dominated the United States as a whole; but in Florida, Texas, and the Southwest, the Spanish presence has had a strong influence on culture, architecture, and language.

The Northwest Passage

*For many years, explorers continued to believe that they could find a way from Europe to Asia by sailing west. They searched for a water passage through the American land mass to the Pacific. One goal of the Lewis and Clark Expedition of 1803-1805 was to find such a route. This painting by English artist John Everett Millais expresses British frustration at not finding a water route around Canada (*The North-west Passage, *1874).*

The explorer Roald Amundsen finished a three-year voyage from east to west through the Arctic waters north of Canada in 1906. Arctic ice made this Northwest Passage dangerous, so it was not suitable for commercial shipping. No practical water passage through the Americas existed until the Panama Canal was completed in 1914. Diminished Arctic ice in the 2000s allowed several vessels to pass successfully north of Canada. The crew of a small yacht, led by Eric Forsyth, completed a circumnavigation of North America in 2009.

Cultural Exchange

European and indigenous American cultures had a complex interchange as a result of this exploration of the Americas. Europeans saw many plants and animals in the New World that they had not seen before, such as turkeys, bison, corn, and potatoes. Over the next several decades, Europeans spread American crops around the world.

New words entered the Europeans' vocabulary, such as tobacco, raccoon, and tepee. The Europeans brought firearms and horses, which they used to defeat the Indians in battle. The explorers also brought diseases such as smallpox and measles to which the native peoples had no immunity. As a result of warfare and disease, the indigenous population was greatly reduced in a relatively short time.

The world of Notgrove and the world of Moluk were changing, and they were never going to be the same. A zeal for control and for wealth, tempered by expressions of Christian faith, led adventurers and pioneers from the Old World to establish outposts in these new lands.

It is He who sits above the circle of the earth,
And its inhabitants are like grasshoppers.
Isaiah 40:22a

★ Assignments for Lesson 4 ★

Bible — Our view of life and the world around us is affected by our knowledge and experience. Write down three ways that the spiritual worldview of Europeans might have been affected by the explorations of Columbus. (Keep your responses to this and future Bible assignments in your *Exploring America* notebook or discuss them with your parents.)

Work on memorizing Acts 17:26-28.

Project — Work on your project.

Student Review — Optional: Answer the questions for Lesson 4.

Boys Going to Work at a Cigarette Factory in North Carolina, 1911

Lesson 5 - Bible Study

How You See the World Makes a Difference

The same historical event can have different interpretations depending on the outlooks of the persons doing the interpreting.

- The Protestant Reformation led by Martin Luther is seen by millions of believers as a fresh wind of spiritual freedom. To Catholics, however, the Reformation was a tragic division that destroyed the unity of the one Church.

- Child labor laws enacted at the end of the nineteenth century and the beginning of the twentieth century were hailed by reformers as a necessary protection for children, while many businessmen condemned them as an unnecessary intrusion of the government into the workplace.

- The 1973 Supreme Court decision *Roe v. Wade* declared certain state laws restricting abortion unconstitutional. To abortion opponents (such as this author), the decision was a tragedy for human life; for abortion advocates, it was a victory for women's rights.

- The coming of Columbus to the New World in 1492 is one of those pivotal events that is seen differently by different people. Based on your interpretation of that event, you might believe that Columbus was a bold, heroic explorer who initiated the exciting development of European-based culture in America; or you might believe that he was a cruel villain who caused the tragic destruction of indigenous cultures; or you might conclude that he was a mixture of both. The difference in how you view what Columbus did is based on your worldview.

Differing Worldviews

A worldview is just that: a person's understanding of the world in which that person lives. Everyone has a worldview, and one's worldview is shaped by his culture, training, experience, family background, political persuasion, and faith in God (or lack of it). A person's worldview provides a framework by which he or she evaluates the meaning of the events that take place and by which he or she makes decisions about what he or she will do.

People in different times and places have had and continue to have different worldviews. For example:

- Many cultures throughout history have understood humans to be the pawns of cruel or disinterested gods. People in these cultures would see a devastating thunderstorm as punishment from the gods.

- Today, millions of people see humans as strictly physical objects without any spiritual nature. They believe that we happened into existence by evolutionary chance and that what takes place in the world is simply what occurs when atoms and molecules come together. This view of human life and of man's purpose is different from that of someone who believes that God made man in His image.

- Many Eastern cultures believe in a cyclical view of history. In this worldview, people, plants, and animals are born; they live; and they die. That which dies becomes the soil from which new life springs. What has happened before will happen again. A belief in reincarnation is sometimes part of a cyclical view of life.

Burning a Draft Card During the Vietnam War (1968)

Your Worldview Makes a Difference In How You Interpret Historical Events

Our worldview is the result of our beliefs, experiences, and ideals. This influences not only how we see the world around us but also how we understand events in history. A Marxist university professor in the United States, for instance, will likely portray the period of Communist domination in Russia differently from the way a Russian preacher who spent years in prison for his faith would see it. The idea of gay marriage might be discussed one way by a television commentator and quite differently by your parents. Think about how different worldviews affect how people see these issues in history:

- Were women oppressed until the twentieth century, and only then were they able to receive the first elements of real personhood? Or was the way women lived before the twentieth century closer to God's ideal for them, and were the changes in the twentieth century dangerous steps away from God's plan?

- Was the civil rights movement an attempt by Communist agents to undermine American society, or was it the desperate effort of longsuffering Americans to claim the rights that they believed should be theirs?

- Were the young people who protested the Vietnam War dangerous subversives who wanted to overthrow the United States government, or were they simply exercising their American freedoms in an attempt to bring home the troops from a war our leaders had never decided to win?

Your answer to these questions will depend on your worldview.

Lesson 5 - Bible Study: How You See the World Makes a Difference

Your Worldview Affects How You Live Every Day

Worldview is not an idle, theoretical topic. A person's worldview has significant impact on his or her everyday decisions.

- Should a pregnant but unmarried woman have an abortion, or should she have the baby and either rear it herself or give it up for adoption?

- Should a father accept a promotion that promises higher pay, regardless of the consequences to his family, or should he consider other factors besides money?

- How should people care for the earth: as our "mother" with a spiritual life and identity of its own, or as a stewardship from God?

What you think is right in these situations will depend on your worldview: what you value, what you believe to be the truth, the worth you give to people, what you believe is God's will, and other factors that help you give meaning to life.

We Look At History With a God-Centered Worldview

This curriculum approaches history with the belief that God created the heavens and the earth and that He continues to guide the events of the world. We believe that humankind is a special creation by God in His image and that humans have unique worth before God and a spiritual identity in the soul. We believe that what happens in our world is not the result of blind chance; instead, events are the result of a combination of God's sovereignty and the autonomy God gives us to choose, succeed, and fail. We believe that God's purpose for the created world is to give honor to Christ. Colossians 1:16-17 says that, "[B]y Him (Christ) all things were created,

Times Square, New York

both in the heavens and on earth . . . all things have been created through Him and for Him. He is before all things, and in Him all things hold together." We believe that God has given mankind standards of right and wrong and that He will hold all of mankind accountable one day in the Judgment. We believe that the ultimate will of God will be accomplished despite what people might do. This faith in God is the overriding factor in our worldview.

In your study of history, you need to recognize the worldview that you have which serves as the glasses through which you see historical events. Be sure to base your worldview on a fair and accurate understanding of God's truth.

*But we preach Christ crucified, to Jews a stumbling block
and to Gentiles foolishness, but to those who are called,
both Jews and Greeks, Christ the power of God
and the wisdom of God.*
1 Corinthians 1:23-24

★ Assignments for Lesson 5 ★

American Voices — Read the excerpts from "The Meaning of July Fourth for the Negro" by Frederick Douglass (pages 177-182).

Bible — The Apostle Paul was aware of how different people had different worldviews. Read again the account of Paul's sermon to Jews in the synagogue in Pisidian Antioch in Acts 13:16-41 and the account of his speech to Gentiles in the Areopagus (on Mars Hill) in Acts 17:16-34. Notice that in the Jewish synagogue he refers extensively to the Old Testament, whereas in the pagan Areopagus he does not quote any Scripture. In fact, in the Areopagus Paul quotes two pagan writers in verse 28 (Epimenides of Crete and Aratus of Cilicia). The Jews in the synagogue had a strong belief in God and in the revelation of His word in Scripture. The people to whom Paul spoke in Athens, by contrast, had a limited understanding of God and dabbled in ideas and beliefs from various sources.

How might you use the approach Paul used in Acts 17 to communicate the gospel to the secular world today? Remember that most Americans believe in God but do not accept the Bible as God's authoritative Word. Many if not most Americans do not believe in absolute truth. Also, many do not know about Jesus or only heard stories about Him in their childhood. What are three points you think might be effective in opening the door to sharing the gospel with an unbeliever?

Recite or write Acts 17:26-28 from memory.

Project — Complete your project for the unit.

Student Review — Optional: Answer the questions for Lesson 5 and take the quiz for Unit 1.

Old Ship Church, Built in 1681 in Hingham, Massachusetts

2 English Settlement of America

The Protestant Reformation revolutionized spiritual thinking and also influenced concepts of political freedom. A century later, English settlers colonized the eastern coast of North America. While some came for economic gain, others came to be able to worship God and to guide their lives and communities under His hand as they saw fit. The principles of dependence on God, religious freedom, and democratic participation in civic life were firmly established in the colonies. Life was hard for the settlers, but they developed a distinctive American culture of which we today are the heirs.

Lesson 6 - The Reformation
Lesson 7 - England on the Rise
Lesson 8 - English Colonies in America
Lesson 9 - Life in the Colonies
Lesson 10 - Bible Study: The Shape of Religion in the Colonies

Memory Work Memorize Psalm 146:3-5 by the end of this unit.

Books Used The Bible
American Voices
The Scarlet Letter

Project (choose one)

1) Write 300 to 500 words on one of the following topics:
   - Write a summary of the ways in which religion was involved in the founding of the English colonies.
   - In Lesson 3 we read about an imaginary English family, the Coopers, from the village of Notgrove. Imagine that one of Thomas Cooper's descendants, named Samuel, settled in Boston in the mid-1600s. Write a letter from Samuel to his family in Bristol, England. What was life like for him? What work did he do? How was he affected by the religious life of the colonies?
2) Draw a map of the original thirteen American colonies. Don't copy a modern map showing the current borders of these states, rather consult a historically accurate map showing the borders of the original colonies.
3) Create a three-dimensional model of a Colonial-era farm or village. Research first so you can make your model historically accurate. Use the material of your choice (e.g., wood, cardboard, clay, STYROFOAM™, LEGO® bricks).

Literature

The Scarlet Letter

Nathaniel Hawthorne was born in Salem, Massachusetts, in 1804 and died in 1864. His ancestors were among the Puritan settlers of Massachusetts Bay. One ancestor was a judge in the infamous Salem witch trials. *The Scarlet Letter*, published in 1850, is set in the Massachusetts Bay colony (Boston) in the mid-1600s. Hester Prynne, after being publicly punished for the sin and crime of adultery, is scorned by many in the community.

Hawthorne explores what can happen when sin enters a community that is founded on faith. Certainly what Hester did was wrong, but hers was not the only wrong that was committed. Hester refuses to tell who the father of her child is. The father does not step forward, and his identity seems to be unimportant to the community. As other members of the community heap ridicule on her, they reveal their own sins of pride and judgmental attitudes. Often they are simply wrong in how they treat her and in their views of other people. Meanwhile, Hester is humble and contrite. She takes the responsibility for rearing and supporting her child.

The other main characters in the book are Arthur Dimmesdale, the young minister; Roger Chillingsworth, Hester's former husband who had been thought to be dead; and Pearl, the child born to Hester. Be sure to read the introductory essay, "The Customs House," which sets the mood and tone for the novel. Plan to finish the book by the end of the next unit.

Immanuel Lutheran Church, Elk Point, South Dakota

Lesson 6

The Reformation

Jesus said, "My kingdom is not of this world" (John 18:36). The early church was a simple community of faith in which members shared what they had with each other, focused on the apostles' teaching, and encouraged each other in their new lives in Christ (Acts 2:44-45). The Church of the Middle Ages, however, had a different organization from that described in the New Testament.

For instance, the New Testament makes no mention of church facilities. Christians met in homes (Romans 16:3-5, 1 Corinthians 16:19, and Colossians 4:15) and in public places such as the temple. The medieval Catholic Church, on the other hand, met in elaborate and expensive cathedrals that were the centerpiece of its religious practice.

The church in the New Testament had elders who shepherded local congregations of Christians (see Acts 14:23 and Titus 1:5). As far as we know, there was no organizational structure beyond the local congregation. In the Catholic Church, bishops and cardinals held administrative positions over large regions. Everyone in the Catholic Church answered ultimately to the pope.

In the New Testament, government authorities were often opposed to the church (see Acts 4:1-3, 16:22-24, and chapters 22-26). In Europe in the Middle Ages, by contrast, the Catholic Church was the primary influence over the secular government.

Catholic Practices

The Roman Catholic Church during the Renaissance was different in many ways from the church described in the New Testament. The Catholic Church was a wealthy, powerful institution

St. Peter's Basilica was constructed in Rome, Italy, by the order of Roman emperor Constantine in the mid-300s. The cross-section below shows the inside of the building. This church was in use until the 16th century, when a new and much more elaborate building was constructed. It retained the same name.

that exerted considerable influence over kings and politics. Power in the Church was centered in the pope, and an extensive hierarchy of clergy controlled Church life. Some elements of Catholicism, such as certain orders of monks, were examples of self-sacrifice and a desire to teach the gospel to others. However, many Church leaders were corrupt, and many Church practices differed from Scripture.

One of the greatest abuses was the selling of indulgences. The Catholic Church taught that when someone made a donation to the Church, the gift released the soul of a loved one from purgatory. (The Catholic Church teaches that purgatory is the place of punishment after death until a person has suffered enough for his sins and can then go to heaven.) This doctrine had no Scriptural basis, but in that day most people did not know the Bible. They were simply told by Church leaders that this was true. The selling of indulgences brought in vast amounts of wealth to the Church. After all, who would want to leave a loved one suffering in purgatory when the giving of a mere coin could release him? The practice also reinforced the belief that salvation is dependent on good works which earn the favor of God.

Luther's Revolt

Martin Luther was a Catholic priest and scholar in Germany in the early 1500s. He eagerly sought peace with God but could not find it on the basis of works. In preparation for taking on a teaching position, Luther did an unusual thing: he started reading the Bible. As he did, he came to see the wide differences between what the Bible said and what the Catholic Church practiced. Luther was increasingly disturbed at what he saw to be the corrupt practices of the Catholic Church. In 1517 he announced ninety-five theses (or points of debate) that challenged many Catholic doctrines and practices, including the practice of selling indulgences. At the time, the indulgences were being sold to raise money to build the new St. Peter's Basilica in Rome.

The Catholic hierarchy opposed Luther and put him on trial for heresy. Luther stood his ground and the Catholic Church excommunicated him, but the government leader of his district in Germany protected Luther from harm. Luther was not the first person to dissent from Catholic doctrine and practice, but he was successful because of the support he received in Germany. Luther gained many followers who gradually developed into a separate fellowship of believers. They eventually came to be called Lutherans. Luther's actions began what we know as the Protestant Reformation (a protest against what the Catholic Church was doing wrong and a movement to reform the Church to be more in keeping with the Scriptures).

Luther strongly believed that a person is saved by faith in Christ without having to perform good works to earn salvation. He also disapproved of the Catholic clergy taking on the role of mediating between God and man. Luther believed that

This 1521 woodcut illustration depicting the pope signing indulgences is by German artist Lucas Cranach the Elder, a friend of Martin Luther.

Lesson 6 - The Reformation

The Luther Monument in Worms, Germany, was built in 1868. A statue of Martin Luther stands in the center. Seated around Luther are four men who had called for reform in the Church in previous centuries: Peter Waldo, John Wycliffe, Jan Hus, and Girolamo Savonarola. On the outside corners are other German political leaders and scholars.

every individual could approach God on his own. Luther encouraged people to look to the Bible, not to Church doctrine and tradition, as the basis for their beliefs. His translation of the Bible into German helped accomplish this. For centuries the Scriptures had been available only in Latin. Luther's translation made it possible for more people to read and understand the Bible.

Martin Luther and other reformers opened the door to a new way of practicing Christianity. Within a generation, the movement that Martin Luther began significantly challenged the power and dominance of the Roman Catholic Church. The Catholic Church no longer had exclusive control over the spiritual lives of Europeans. In some countries (such as Spain), Protestants met fierce opposition and Catholicism continued to be the official religion.

In other countries (such as the Netherlands and the Scandinavian countries), Protestants became the majority. Sometimes religious wars broke out because many believers continued to use religion as a political weapon. The Protestant-Catholic conflict influenced national and international politics for many years.

The Reformation led to many groups being formed to express their faith in new ways. John Calvin, for example, was an influential Reformed theologian in Switzerland who rose to prominence in the mid-1530s. As the years passed, new leaders arose who differed with both Luther and Calvin and who started still more new groups. Europeans found that once the door to freedom and change is opened, closing it is hard.

The English Reformation

In England, the Reformation was the result of a different set of circumstances; but it also stemmed from a challenge to the authority of the pope. King Henry VIII of England broke with the Catholic Church in 1534 and had himself declared the leader of the Church of England, which is also called the Anglican Church. Henry challenged the authority of the pope primarily so that he could divorce his wife and marry another woman (we'll talk more about this in the next lesson). At first the new Church's practices were much like those of the Catholic Church. Henry's purpose for breaking with Rome was not to bring spiritual reformation but mostly to dispense with papal authority.

Henry VIII declared himself to be the head of all Christians in England. However, other believers in England followed Henry's example of rejecting the control of a hierarchy over believers and congregations. These believers wanted to follow God as they saw fit. As a result, numerous groups emerged over the succeeding decades. Conflict among Catholics, Anglicans, Scottish Presbyterians, Puritans, Separatists, and other groups in England continued for many years and took many forms.

Catherine of Aragon was a Spanish princess and the first wife of Henry VIII. English artist Henry Nelson O'Neil painted The Trial of Catherine of Aragon *in the 19th century, showing Henry seeking approval from Church officials for his divorce.*

Lesson 6 - The Reformation

The Political Impact of the Protestant Reformation

The religious upheavals in Europe affected the pattern of colonial development in the New World. Since Spain remained Catholic, the areas of the New World that it controlled were Catholic. Since England had many different religious groups, the areas of English settlement in the New World saw a diversity of religious expression.

The Protestant Reformation also changed political thought. As people were no longer willing simply to submit to the existing religious system, they came to reject the idea of simply submitting to the existing political systems. People wanted the freedom to govern themselves as they saw fit. The Protestant Reformation honored the individual's right to determine his own relationship with God. In the same way, people wanted the right to think for themselves politically and to have a say in the government to which they answered.

The Reformation changed the religious fabric of Europe. As it did so, it also changed the political landscape and the worldview that people held. This affected the colonization of America, the way those colonies were governed, what the colonists believed, and the later course of American history.

And having been made perfect, He became to all those who obey Him the source of eternal salvation.
Hebrews 5:9

★ Assignments for Lesson 6 ★

Literature — Begin reading *The Scarlet Letter*. Plan to finish it by the end of Unit 3.

Bible — Start memorizing Psalm 146:3-5.

Project — Choose your project for this unit and start working on it.

Student Review — Optional: Answer the questions for Lesson 6.

Devon Coast, Southwest England

Lesson 7

England on the Rise

In 1497, five years after Columbus' first voyage, King Henry VII of England hired the Italian sea captain Giovanni Caboti (John Cabot in English) to sail to the New World on behalf of England. Cabot left from Bristol on England's west coast and arrived in what he called a "new founde lande," now known as Newfoundland in Canada. On this and later journeys, Cabot explored the North American coast, perhaps going as far south as Chesapeake Bay.

In the 1990s, a replica of Cabot's ship, the Matthew, *was constructed in England. In 1997 a crew sailed it from Bristol to Newfoundland to celebrate the 500th anniversary of Cabot's voyage.*

Cabot's explorations in the name of England gave that country a claim to at least part of North America. However, unlike Spain, which capitalized quickly on Columbus' discoveries, over a century passed before England was able to secure a permanent foothold in the new-found land. This delay occurred because much royal and national energy was spent during the 1500s within England itself dealing with issues of royal succession and related Protestant-Catholic questions.

Henry VIII

Henry VII, of the House of Lancaster, became king of England in 1485 after he defeated the House of York to end the War of the Roses. He established his rule as the House of Tudor. Henry's son, Henry VIII, wanted a male child to keep the Tudor family on the throne. Henry VIII thought that a queen would not be a strong enough leader to maintain the Tudor dynasty. The first wife of Henry VIII bore him one child who survived infancy, a daughter named Mary. Since Henry had no male heir, he wanted to put his wife away and marry again. Henry asked the pope for an annulment of their marriage, a declaration by the Church that their marriage never existed in the eyes of the Church.

Lesson 7 - England on the Rise

Since the pope would not agree to an annulment of the marriage, Henry broke with the Catholic Church in 1534 and had Parliament declare him to be head of the Church in England. Henry then had his first marriage annulled through the new Anglican Church.

The second wife of Henry also gave birth to a daughter. Henry accused her of adultery and had her beheaded. His third wife died after giving birth to the male heir that Henry so desperately wanted. However, the son, Edward VI, was a sickly child. Henry married three more times but no child resulted from any of these unions.

> Henry the Eighth
> To six wives was wedded —
> One died, one survived,
> Two divorced, two beheaded.
>
> — Anonymous

Edward VI and Mary

Henry's son, Edward VI, came to the throne when he was only nine years old; and he died when he was fifteen. Royal advisors actually ran the country during his brief reign. Edward's death meant that Mary, Henry's daughter by his first marriage, became queen.

"Bloody Mary" ruled from 1553 to 1558. She was Catholic like her mother and ruthlessly sought to re-establish Catholic control in the country by executing or imprisoning many of her Anglican opponents. She died without an heir; so the English throne passed to her half-sister, Elizabeth I, the daughter of Henry VIII and his second wife.

Elizabeth I and Colonization

Elizabeth I reigned for 45 years (1558-1603) and is generally considered one of England's best and strongest rulers. She restored the Church of England as the state religion. To expand England's power and wealth, Elizabeth encouraged attempts to establish colonies in North America. Sir Walter Raleigh sponsored a group that settled on Roanoke Island off North Carolina in 1587. The governor of the colony returned to England for supplies but was not able to get back to Roanoke until 1590. When he arrived, he found that the settlement had been abandoned. The only clue to the settlers' fate was the word "Croatoan," the name of a nearby friendly Indian tribe, carved on a tree. No one knows whether the settlers died from illness or Indian attack or whether they moved to or were carried off to another location.

Also during Elizabeth's reign, a significant change in international relations enabled England to increase its influence in the world. Spain was the dominant European power through most of the 1500s. Since Spain was a Catholic nation, its rulers did not want to see Protestant England become

The Hampden Portrait *(of Elizabeth I)*
Steven van der Muelen (Dutch, c. 1563)

powerful. As tension increased between the two countries, the powerful Spanish naval fleet, called the Armada, sailed to England in 1588 to defeat the much smaller English navy. However, by skilled seamanship and with the help of a storm, the English defeated the Spanish Armada. This broke Spain's domination of international trade and exploration and allowed England to become a strong force in the New World.

Elizabeth I never married; thus she was called the Virgin Queen. At her death in 1603, the question again arose as to who would be ruler of England. The throne passed to a great-great-grandson of Henry VII, King James VI of Scotland, who became James I of England. James I began the rule of the English House of Stuart.

King James I of England and VI of Scotland
Daniël Mijtens (Dutch, 1621)

James I and His Legacy

James was a strong leader. He believed in the divine right of kings, the idea that since God places a king on his throne, the king is answerable only to God and not to the people he rules. In addition the king of England was seen as Defender of the Faith. At the request of Church leaders, James approved the production of a new English translation of the Bible, which appeared in 1611. It is sometimes called the Authorized Version because it was authorized by King James.

James I encouraged Protestants from Scotland to settle in the northern part of Catholic Ireland to increase the population there of subjects loyal to the British throne. This was the beginning of the Scots-Irish ethnic group. It was also the beginning of the Protestant majority in Northern Ireland, which has been a factor in the recurring strife between Protestants and Catholics in Ireland.

During James' rule, the first permanent English settlements were established in North America. Several developments in England's economy encouraged this colonization. First, trading companies pursued increased commerce with other nations. These companies were usually joint-stock ventures, in which several investors pooled their resources to finance foreign exploration and trade. They were not directly funded by the throne. Joint-stock companies founded the first colonies in America.

Second, the economic philosophy of mercantilism developed throughout Europe during this time. Under mercantilism, the government encouraged and assisted private businesses, especially those involved in foreign trade. One element of mercantilism that helped build national wealth was the encouragement of foreign colonies. These colonies provided natural resources for the home country and created new markets for products made in the home country.

Lesson 7 - England on the Rise

Third, a major change in English agriculture was the enclosure movement, which consolidated many small land holdings into large estates. This drove many poorer people off of the land and into cities. The establishment of colonies was seen as a way for these displaced persons to start a new life.

In the early 1600s, therefore, England had defeated Spain; it had a strong and stable king on the throne; and its government encouraged business, exploration, and trade. England was now poised to take advantage of John Cabot's claims to North America that had been made over a century earlier.

> *"For I hate divorce," says the Lord, the God of Israel,*
> *"and him who covers his garment with wrong," says the Lord of hosts.*
> *"So take heed to your spirit, that you do not deal treacherously."*
> *Malachi 2:16*

★ Assignments for Lesson 7 ★

Literature — Continue reading *The Scarlet Letter*.

Bible — Read Mark 7:1-23. The scene in Mark 7 involves Jesus' criticism of the traditions of the Pharisees that violated God's commandments. Traditions are not necessarily wrong. They are wrong if they cause us to violate God's clear teachings. List three ways in which you believe that traditional beliefs or practices of some churches are not in keeping with God's commandments.

Work on memorizing Psalm 146:3-5.

Project — Work on your project.

Student Review — Optional: Answer the questions for Lesson 7.

Re-enactors at the Celebration of the 350th Anniversary of Jamestown

Lesson 8

English Colonies in America

Jamestown, Virginia

In 1606 James I granted a charter to a group of businessmen that allowed them to plant a colony in the region of North America that was called Virginia. The area was named for the late Virgin Queen, Elizabeth I. On May 24, 1607, three ships carrying 120 men (no women) landed on the Virginia coast. They established the settlement of Jamestown at the mouth of what they called the James River.

The men in this first party were primarily adventurers who were interested in acquiring wealth as quickly as possible. They were neither farmers nor hunters; and as a result of difficult conditions, many did not survive.

As time went on, the men of the settlement established trade with the nearby Indians and learned to hunt and fish and to plant and harvest crops. One man in the party of settlers, John Smith, had some experience in exploring new lands, and he took it upon himself to instill discipline in the men. Much of the credit for the colony's success belongs to Smith's leadership.

Excerpt from the First Virginia Charter - April 10, 1606
(presented in its original spelling)

James, by the grace of God King of England, Scotland, France, and Ireland, Defender of the Faith, etc. Whereas our loving and weldisposed subjects, Sir Thomas Gates and Sir George Somers, Knightes; Richarde Hackluit, Clarke, Prebendarie of Westminster; and Edwarde Maria Winghfeilde, Thomas Hannam and Raleighe Gilberde, Esquies; William Parker and George Popham, Gentlemen; and divers others of our loving subjects, have been humble sutors unto us that wee woulde vouchsafe unto them our licence to make habitacion, plantacion and to deduce a colonie of sondrie of our people into that parte of America commonly called Virginia, and other parts and territories in America either appartaining unto us or which are not nowe actuallie possessed by anie Christian prince or people, scituate, lying and being all along the sea coastes between fower and thirtie degrees of northerly latitude from the equinoctiall line and five and fortie degrees of the same latitude and in the maine lande betweene the same fower and thirtie and five and fourtie degrees, and the ilandes thereunto adjacente or within one hundred miles of the coaste thereof. . . .

Wee, greatly commending and graciously accepting of theire desires to the furtherance of soe noble a worke which may, by the providence of Almightie God, hereafter tende to the glorie of His Divine Majestie in propagating of Christian religion to suche people as yet live in darkenesse and miserable ignorance of the true knowledge and worshippe of God and may in tyme bring the infidels and salvages living in those parts to humane civilitie and to a setled and quiet govermente, doe by theise our lettres patents graciously accepte of and agree to theire humble and well intended desires. . . .

The state-supported Anglican Church was the religious presence in Jamestown. Although the Virginia Charter recognized the opportunity the colony had for spreading the Christian religion, the primary interest of most of the first settlers was economic gain.

Despite the difficulties and the loss of life, the Jamestown settlement was deemed to be a success. During the next several years, other colonies were established further up the James River away from the coast. By 1650 about 15,000 English colonists lived in Virginia.

In 1619 the governor of Virginia, who was appointed by the king, called for a yearly meeting of two representatives called burgesses from each settlement to oversee the governing of the entire colony. The Virginia House of Burgesses was the first representative assembly in America and set a pattern for American government that continues to this day.

Another far-reaching event took place in the Virginia colony in 1619. A Dutch trading ship landed with about twenty Africans who had come by way of the West Indies. The Dutch traded the Africans to the colonists in exchange for goods.

Pocahontas / Rebecca Rolfe

John Smith wrote in his journal about being taken captive by the Indians and being saved from execution by Pocahontas, daughter of Powhatan the chief. Historians today think that the incident was a bit of play-acting by the Indians, designed to make Powhatan appear merciful and generous and to make the colonists feel dependent on him.

In 1614 Pocahontas married another Jamestown settler, John Rolfe, and converted to the Anglican Church. The marriage improved relations between settlers and the Indians. Pocahontas took the name Rebecca. With her husband and their son, she visited England and was a sensation with the English people.

Rebecca died from smallpox in 1617 and was buried in England. Rolfe and their son returned to Virginia, where the Rolfe family is still prominent.

The Marriage of Pocahontas
Henry Brueckner (American, 1855)

The historical record is not clear whether these blacks were sold permanently as slaves or for a limited time as indentured servants. Whatever the details, this was the first time blacks were treated as commodities in what became the United States.

The Pilgrims of Plymouth

After Henry VIII's break with the Roman Catholic Church, the religious landscape of England became diverse. Some were not satisfied with what they saw as the worldliness and the Catholic-like practices of the Church of England. Those who wanted to purify the Church came to be called Puritans. Others wanted no part of the Anglican system and sought to be separate and independent. These people were called Separatists. Both Separatists and Puritans were involved in the next major emigration of English settlers to America.

The Anglican Church was founded because Henry VIII wanted freedom from Rome; but the Anglican establishment was not willing to give other groups the same freedom from Anglican control. Those who refused to recognize Anglican authority were sometimes imprisoned or even executed. One group of Separatists left England in 1608 to live in the freer religious climate of the Netherlands. However, they did not like living there and were concerned about their children growing up learning the Dutch language and culture. The Separatists returned to England and made plans to resettle in America. In the fall of 1620 about one hundred people crowded onto the *Mayflower*. The second ship they had hoped to use proved not to be seaworthy. Less than half of those on board were part of the Separatist group; the rest were seamen and adventurers.

These Pilgrims, as they have come to be called, set sail for the northern part of Virginia. They were blown off course far to the north, however. They landed in December 1620 in what became Massachusetts. Since their landing site left their official status in question, before they got off the *Mayflower* these new Americans drew up the first document of government in America, the Mayflower Compact. This set the pattern in America for drawing up a guiding written document whenever people established a new government.

The Pilgrims and the others on the *Mayflower* named their settlement Plymouth after the city in England from which they had departed. Landing in barren New England as winter approached, without shelter or crops, they faced a difficult lot. About half of the Plymouth settlers died during the first year. Local Indians, especially Samoset and Squanto, taught the settlers how to plant corn and carry out other necessary tasks. Providentially, Squanto had been to Europe and had learned English. After their first year at Plymouth, the settlers gave a feast of thanksgiving in November 1621, when they thanked God for His blessings and for sustaining them through their difficulties.

William Bradford (1590-1657) was governor of the Plymouth colony for thirty one-year terms. He had been part of the Separatist group that lived in the Netherlands for several years, and he was a signer

According to tradition, the Pilgrims stepped onto a large rock when they landed at Plymouth. The first written mention of such a rock came about one hundred years later. When the large "Plymouth Rock" was being moved, it split into two pieces. What remains on the Plymouth shore under a protective portico today is a small portion of that rock. The date of 1620 was chiseled into the rock in 1880.

Lesson 8 - English Colonies in America

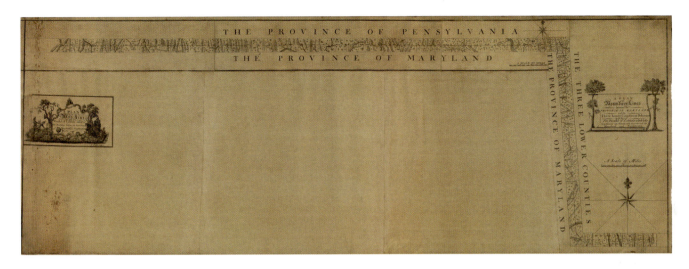

Charles Mason and Jeremiah Dixon surveyed the boundary line between Pennsylvania and Maryland in the 1760s. The boundary became known as the Mason-Dixon Line. Pennsylvania eventually outlawed slavery while Maryland maintained it until the Civil War. The Mason-Dixon Line came to be a symbol of the division between the slave and non-slave portions of the United States. The 1768 illustration above is by Charles Mason.

of the Mayflower Compact. Bradford's history, *Of Plymouth Plantation*, is a reliable original source of information about the settlement. He provided able, godly leadership for the colony.

The Puritans of Massachusetts Bay

Ten years later, in 1630, a group of Puritans founded a separate colony a few miles north of Plymouth. It was called Massachusetts Bay and eventually became Boston and the surrounding cities. The governor, John Winthrop, received a royal charter in which the king gave control of the colony to the members of the founding company who lived in New England, not to any group or person in England. This was a significant step toward self-government in America.

Over the next ten years, Massachusetts Bay became the most populous English colony in America. Its congregational Puritanism had a profound influence in New England and in the rest of English America. Their hard work and pursuit of learning (characterized by the founding of Harvard College to train ministers in 1636) also set important patterns for the country that was being formed along the coast of North America.

Plymouth, Massachusetts Bay, other nearby settlements, and Maine were merged into the single colony of Massachusetts in 1691. Maine continued to be part of Massachusetts until it was admitted into the Union as a separate state in 1820.

Rhode Island

The Puritan leaders of Massachusetts Bay wanted the freedom to worship God as they saw fit; but, as we have seen in other situations, they did not want to give the same freedom to those who disagreed with them. Roger Williams, a minister in nearby Salem, believed that government should be separate from the practice of religion. This was a new idea to many people. Most Puritans believed that the church and the government should be closely related and should influence each other. Williams also believed that settlers should buy the land they wanted from the Indians instead of simply taking it from them. Williams thought himself purer than the rest of the Puritans and questioned whether any others in the settlement were really faithful to God. He was banished from Massachusetts Bay in 1635 on the charge of being a heretic. Williams eventually settled on land he purchased from the Indians in the area that became known as Rhode Island. The colony of Rhode Island, founded in 1636, developed a clear policy and a strong tradition of religious toleration.

Anne Hutchinson was another dissenter who got into trouble with the Puritans. Hutchinson began holding Sunday afternoon meetings in her home, in which she discussed (and often questioned) the sermon presented earlier in the day. She appeared to claim direct inspiration from God for her ideas. Hutchinson was convicted of heresy in 1637 and banished from Massachusetts Bay. She moved first to Rhode Island and eventually to Long Island, New York. She was killed in an Indian raid in 1642.

Connecticut and New Hampshire

England eventually established thirteen colonies along the Atlantic coast of North America. The first, Virginia, was founded at Jamestown in 1607; the last, Georgia, was begun in 1733. All of the American colonies shared significant cultural similarities; but the colonies also had important differences in their origin, lifestyle, and economies. This pattern has influenced the diverse nature of American life to the present day.

Other offshoots of Massachusetts Bay began more peacefully than the Rhode Island colony started by Roger Williams. Thomas Hooker led the formation of the colony of Connecticut in 1637, which was made up of people who left Massachusetts Bay on friendly terms. In 1639 the Connecticut

The French in North America

During this period, several other European nations were establishing colonies around the world, but the only significant challenge to England for control of the eastern half of North America came from France. Giovanni da Verrazano, an Italian, explored the east coast of North America on behalf of France in 1524. Jacques Cartier sailed up the St. Lawrence River to the present location of Montreal, Canada, and established a colony near Quebec in 1542. Samuel de Champlain established colonies in Acadia and a more permanent one at Quebec. The French had two main interests in North America: (1) to establish trade with the Indians, especially for animal furs that were in great demand in France, and (2) to take the Christian message to the Indians.

In 1673 trader Louis Joliet and Jesuit priest Jacques Marquette paddled down the Mississippi River from its source to a point south of Memphis. Nine years later, Robert de La Salle made it all the way to the mouth of the Mississippi. New Orleans was founded in 1718. France thus controlled Canada and the most important river route in North America. However, England successfully challenged French control of Canada later in the 18th century, and the westward march of the United States eventually eliminated French control of the Mississippi.

Père Marquette and the Indians
Wilhelm Lamprecht (German, 1869)

General Court drew up the Fundamental Orders of Connecticut, which established laws for the governing of the colony. New Hampshire separated from Massachusetts in 1679.

Maryland and the Carolinas

Jamestown, Plymouth, and Massachusetts Bay were founded by joint-stock companies. Later colonies were headed by proprietors, who were individuals or groups that received charters from the king to start colonies. Sir George Calvert (the first Lord Baltimore) received a charter from King Charles I (the son of and successor to James I) in 1632 to create a colony just north of Virginia. Calvert was a Catholic, and his plan was to create a refuge for English Catholics who felt persecuted by Anglicans. After Calvert's death, his sons established the colony and made themselves lords of the land. Protestants were also encouraged to settle in Maryland (named for the Catholic Queen Mary). Protestants were always in the majority there, although most of the wealthier families were Catholic. Maryland guaranteed religious freedom for all Christian faiths.

Charles II in 1663 gave eight proprietors a large land grant south of Virginia. They named it Carolina in honor of Charles (Carol is the French form of Charles). The first charter of government, which was soon abandoned, was a document written in part by philosopher John Locke. The charter created a complicated society, including distinct social classes and an almost medieval social and economic system. Because of the large land area that the colony covered, continuous turmoil in the colony, and the two distinct population centers that developed, North and South Carolina were formed in 1729.

New York and New Jersey

In 1609 the Englishman Henry Hudson sailed to America on behalf of the Netherlands and explored up the Hudson River. The Dutch claimed the area, and Dutch trading companies founded the colony of New Netherlands. New Amsterdam was established on Manhattan Island in 1624. Dutch settlers created huge estates along the Hudson River, but not many Dutch were interested in coming to the New World.

The Flag of Maryland, adopted in 1904, is the only U.S. state flag based on English heraldry (designs representing specific people or families). The Flag of Maryland is the heraldic banner of George Calvert.

The English government believed that it had rightful claim to the colony of New Netherlands. In 1664 Charles II named his brother, the Duke of York, proprietor of the area. The Dutch surrendered to an English expedition without a shot being fired, and New Netherlands became New York.

Also in 1664, the Duke of York granted control of the area between the Hudson River and the Delaware River to two of his friends, who established the colony of New Jersey. For a time, this area was divided into East and West Jersey; but the two parts were re-combined into the colony of New Jersey in 1702.

Pennsylvania, Delaware, and Georgia

George Fox of England founded a new religious group, the Society of Friends, in 1674. He believed in direct individual inspiration (which he called the Inner Light), opposed formal clergy, and urged pacifism and simplicity of lifestyle. The Friends' meetings were simple affairs in which anyone who was moved to speak could do so. Because the Friends trembled (sometimes literally) at God's Word and were sometimes overcome with emotion in their meetings, they were called Quakers by those who wanted to ridicule them.

In 1681 the wealthy Quaker William Penn received a charter from Charles II for a large colony just south of New York. It was called Pennsylvania (Penn's Woods) in honor of Penn's father. William Penn viewed the colony as a holy experiment. He actively recruited settlers for it. Penn insisted on religious toleration, and people from many backgrounds (Mennonite, Amish, Baptist, and other non-Quakers) moved to the colony from France, Northern Ireland, Germany, and other countries. Penn also insisted upon purchasing land from the Indians instead of simply seizing it. He even learned to speak Indian languages so that he could carry on negotiations with the Native Americans, although Penn himself did not spend much time in the colony. The area of Delaware was given to Penn in 1682, and it became a separate colony in 1701.

Edward Hicks (1780-1849) was an American painter and a member of the Society of Friends (Quakers). He painted dozens of variations of an image he called the Peaceable Kingdom, using imagery from Isaiah 11. This version (c. 1834) depicts William Penn in the background making a treaty with the Indians in Pennsylvania.

Lesson 8 - English Colonies in America

Georgia was founded by Sir James Oglethorpe in 1733 and was overseen by trustees in England. The colony served many purposes. In addition to being an economic venture for investors, it was a buffer zone between the other English colonies and Spanish-controlled Florida. The colony's original leaders planned for it to be a social experiment, creating a model society and giving former debtors in England a new start in life. It also was intended to provide a haven for victims of religious persecution in Europe.

Because of these high ideals, and also to lessen potential Spanish influence that might encourage a revolt, slavery was not allowed in Georgia for the first several years. However, the ban on slavery was widely ignored; and the development of plantation agriculture led to slavery being allowed officially in 1749.

*And the wolf will dwell with the lamb,
And the leopard will lie down with the young goat,
And the calf and the young lion and the fatling together;
And a little boy will lead them.
Isaiah 11:6*

★ Assignments for Lesson 8 ★

American Voices — Read the excerpt from "A Description of New England" by John Smith, the Mayflower Compact, the excerpts from "A Model of Christian Charity" by John Winthrop, and the Preamble to the Fundamental Orders of Connecticut (pages 1-5).

Literature — Continue reading *The Scarlet Letter*.

Bible — What are three ways in which English colonists could have shown respect for Native Americans while seeking to evangelize them?

Work on memorizing Psalm 146:3-5.

Project — Work on your project.

Student Review — Optional: Answer the questions for Lesson 8.

Reconstructed Plimoth Plantation in Massachusetts

Lesson 9

Life in the Colonies

The American colonies were settled and made successful not only by the handful of leaders whose names we recognize, but also by thousands of individuals and families who took the risk of crossing the Atlantic Ocean and were determined to survive and prosper.

The colonies were begun by individual initiative. None were started directly by officials in the English government. Colonial founders had a wide variety of motivations and approaches, as indicated in the previous lesson. Settlers also had many different motivations for coming. The most common reason was the chance to start a new life and the possibility of accomplishing more with their lives in America than they ever could have expected in England or in any other country of origin.

Another common reason for moving to the New World was the desire to enjoy religious freedom. The colonies offered a haven for many believers. Such havens were rare in the world of that day. A relatively smaller number of those who came to American shores sought power and wealth, or they sought to exercise in the colonies the power and wealth they already possessed. Still others came against their will. African slaves were brought either directly from Africa or, more commonly, through the British West Indies.

Most of the immigrants to the thirteen colonies were from England, and most were young men in their early twenties. One estimate is that families made up about one-third of the immigrants; the rest were single adults. Another large group who came besides the English were the Scots-Irish from Scotland and Northern Ireland. Many of them eventually migrated into the Appalachian highlands. Smaller numbers of Dutch and German immigrants came also.

The differences in speech accents that Americans have today stem from the settlement patterns of the original colonists. Britain is a small country, but its different regions have markedly different accents. The accents that developed in America came about because, generally speaking, those who moved to New England came from one area of England, those who moved to the southern colonies came from another area, and so forth. They brought their accents with them, and the different ways of speaking the same language continue today.

The settlers brought various national and ethnic backgrounds with them, but as they took up residence in the new land they created a new identity: American. The settlers maintained their ethnic identity to a great degree, but they also changed as a result of living in America.

Lesson 9 - Life in the Colonies

Ease for Some, Hardship for Most

Most of the settlers lived in a relatively narrow area along the Atlantic coast. Only gradually did Europeans populate the regions further inland. Some cities in the colonies became large for their day; for a time, for instance, Philadelphia was the second largest city in the British Empire. A few families in the cities enjoyed a prosperous way of life. However, most people lived in small communities and endured difficult frontier conditions. Life was precarious for many; famine, sickness, economic downturn, and Indian attacks all took their toll.

Colonial Farmers and Craftsmen

The vast majority of settlers were farmers who worked their own land to eke out a living for their families. Often, the sons of original settlers moved further west to start their own farms. As the population grew, opportunities developed for tradesmen, such as blacksmiths and joiners (furniture-makers), to establish businesses. Young men often were apprenticed to master craftsmen and spent several years learning a trade before becoming journeymen (hiring their skills out to others) and eventually reaching the level of craftsmen themselves. As trade grew within the colonies, and especially as trade with England and other countries increased, the job of merchant became more common. Shipbuilding and seagoing trades were of great importance in port cities on the Atlantic coast.

Obtaining Land and Work

In England, land was relatively scarce and labor was plentiful. As a result, opportunities for significant advancement were limited. In America, by contrast, land was plentiful and labor was relatively scarce. This meant that many more people had the opportunity to get ahead and to succeed financially.

Dutch influence is still seen in New York through family names such as Roosevelt and certain words. For instance, "kill" is the Dutch word for creek; the Catskill Mountains are pictured below. The Dutch are related ethnically to the Germans, just as the word Dutch is related to the word the Germans use for themselves, Deutsch.

The success of some was built on the labor of others. In addition to slaves, indentured servants were common. Indentured servants sold their papers (indentures) to sea captains, who then sold them to people in the colonies. An indentured servant worked for the person who owned his indentures for a set period of time (often three, five, or seven years). At the end of the term, the indentured servant was usually given fifty acres of land to start out on his own. The indenture system provided cheap labor and gave those who were patient the opportunity for a new start.

Life in Families

Men were almost universally accepted as heads of households. Many men worked at home, either as farmers or as shopkeepers in the same buildings where they lived. Most married women accepted their role as housewife and deferred to their husbands. Women understood the importance of their work in the home and carried it out diligently. Women were not able to vote, preach, hold office, or go to college. They had few legal rights. Married women generally did not own property apart from their husbands, and they were not allowed to sit on juries or testify in trials. A few women worked outside of the home setting, such as in taverns.

American colonists had a higher birthrate and a lower death rate than the rates that existed in England and Europe at the time. Most people were relatively younger when they got married, so they were healthier and had more childbearing years. America suffered little famine and had less exposure to disease than did the crowded and unsanitary cities in Europe. As a result, the population of the English colonies in America grew rapidly.

Regional Differences

The colonies developed differences related to their regions. New England (Massachusetts, Rhode

Early American Writing

The first English writings from and about America were journals, such as those written by John Smith, William Bradford, and John Winthrop. Many of these were not published until much later. The journals of John Winthrop, governor of the Massachusetts Bay Colony, were kept in the building of the Old South Church in Boston for many years. After the Revolutionary War, two volumes were found in the possession of a member of the Winthrop family in Connecticut; the third was discovered in the Old South Church. They were published in 1825-1826.

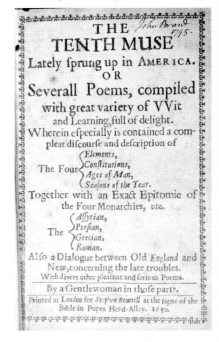

The first literature written in America was poetry. Anne Bradstreet was the first person living in America to have literary works published. The title page of her poetry collection, published in London in 1650, is shown at right. Michael Wigglesworth was a Puritan minister who wrote long, convicting poems. "The Day of Doom" describes the judgment day in clear terms. It sold 1,800 copies in its first year of publication (1662) and was eagerly read and reread. Perhaps half of the population of New England read the poem. Another poem by Wigglesworth, "God's Controversy With New England," explained that a drought which had come upon them was God's punishment because they had abandoned God's ways.

Lesson 9 - Life in the Colonies

English vs. British

Though people use the terms England and Britain interchangeably, this is not accurate. The island of Britain, or Great Britain, contains the countries of England, Scotland, and Wales. Wales came under English rule in 1284 and was incorporated into England by the Act of Union of 1536. James I governed both England and Scotland, but the two countries were not officially united until the Act of Union in 1707. From that point on it is accurate to call the united country Britain or Great Britain.

Since England is the most politically powerful part of Britain, it is usually accurate to refer to the government and society in general as English, but only if you are clearly not talking about Scotland or Wales specifically. You might get by with calling a Scotsman or a Welshman British, but you should never refer to one of them as English. Many Scots and Welsh resent England's rule over them. English is the language of business and everyday life throughout Britain. The Scottish Gaelic and Welsh languages are still alive, although fewer and fewer people speak them.

An Act of Union passed by Parliament in 1801 incorporated Ireland into the United Kingdom. Ireland declared itself a free state in 1921, but the six northern counties of Ireland remained politically aligned with Great Britain and are called Northern Ireland. The most accurate name for the nation today is the United Kingdom of Great Britain and Northern Ireland, which is abbreviated UK. London, England, is the capital of the UK. Many in Ireland (which is predominantly Catholic) want Northern Ireland to be part of Ireland. Most people in Northern Ireland (which is predominantly Protestant) want to remain part of the UK. In the late twentieth century the British government gave greater autonomy to Wales, Scotland, and Northern Ireland by allowing provincial assemblies to form and to decide on local matters.

Island, Connecticut, and New Hampshire) was home to many small farmers. The rocky soil did not encourage large plantations. Relatively more New Englanders were engaged in trade, fishing, and shipping professions.

New England settlers were interested in education. They believed that schools should teach not only academic subjects but also spiritual truths to counter the influence of Satan. Massachusetts passed what came to be called the Old Deluder Law in 1647. It required that every town of any size establish a school. The law said that "One chief point of that old deluder, Satan, [was] to keep men from a knowledge of the Scriptures." Thus the schools taught reading primarily so that people could read and understand the Bible.

The land in the southern colonies (Maryland, Virginia, North and South Carolina, and Georgia) encouraged large plantations that produced cash crops, mostly tobacco but also rice and lumber (not cotton as yet). Since plantations were more labor-intensive, they were more dependent on slavery,

Slavery in Virginia, Late 1600s

although slavery was legal and practiced in all of the colonies. The scattered population of the South made the founding of schools more difficult than in the small New England communities.

The middle colonies (New York, New Jersey, Pennsylvania, and Delaware) developed a mixture of what was found in the other two regions. Most people were small farmers, but towns and cities provided a market for the work of craftsmen and those engaged in overseas commerce. Some landholdings in the middle colonies were quite large.

Relations with Native Americans

English colonists set a pattern in their relationships with Native Americans that was followed many times both during the colonial period and after the United States became an independent country. French traders wanted to cultivate business with the Indians and therefore generally treated them with respect. However, many English settlers wanted to get the Indians out of the way and therefore treated them with contempt.

The response to settlers by Native Americans varied. Some Native Americans helped the early settlers, while some tribes accommodated themselves to the presence of the Europeans. A few even became dependent on the colonists. Other tribes, however, opposed the whites fiercely. When Indian tribes attempted to resist English advancement, they were routinely defeated and sometimes destroyed. Conflicts such as the Pequot War (1637) and King Philip's War (1675-1676) in New England and the Yamasee War (1715-1717) in the South resulted in the defeat of the Indians and the loss of their land to the whites. Victorious colonists transported many defeated Native Americans to the West Indies to be sold or traded as slaves.

Metacomet (c. 1639-1676) was leader of the Wampanoag tribe in New England. He took the English name Philip and attempted to maintain good relations with the English. As the English settlements continued to expand, hostilities broke out in 1675. King Philip was killed in battle the next year. The engraving below was made many decades later by Paul Revere.

Lesson 9 - Life in the Colonies

Native tribes often fought among themselves, and both French and English settlers played tribes against each other for their own benefit. Diseases brought by the Europeans also took a heavy toll among the Indians. The Iroquois League of Indian nations in New York State provided stronger resistance than other groups did, but eventually they also were defeated by the whites' superior firepower.

Some English settlers sought to teach the Indians the gospel and to demonstrate the love of Christ. John Eliot (1604-1690) translated the Bible into the language of the Massachusetts tribes and spent his life seeking to teach them the way of Christ. However, the number of English who treated the Indians with respect was far less than the number who abused and took advantage of them.

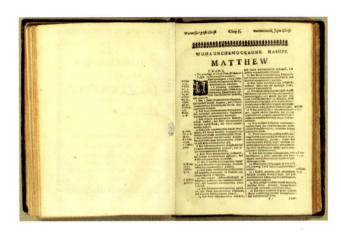

The first complete Bible printed in America was John Eliot's translation into the Algonquian language. The Bible was published in 1663. Eliot also published The Indian Grammar in 1666 "for the Help of such as desire to Learn the same, for the furtherance of the Gospel among them." The image above is from a second edition of Eliot's Bible, published in 1685.

Be diligent to present yourself approved to God as a workman who does not need to be ashamed, accurately handling the word of truth.
2 Timothy 2:15

★ Assignments for Lesson 9 ★

American Voices — Read the poems by Anne Bradstreet (page 7).

Literature — Continue reading *The Scarlet Letter*.

Bible — Work on memorizing Psalm 146:3-5.

Project — Work on your project.

Student Review — Optional: Answer the questions for Lesson 9.

Great Friends Meeting House in Newport, Rhode Island, Established in 1699

Lesson 10 - Bible Study

The Shape of Religion in the Colonies

The religious beliefs and practices of the colonists influenced the course of American history and continue to have a role in American religious practices today. As we study the practice of religion in the colonies, we are challenged to rethink the meaning of faith in our own lives.

The Influence of Religion

Religion was of utmost importance in the colonies. Faith in God defined the nature and practice of the Plymouth, Massachusetts Bay, Maryland, and Pennsylvania colonies and had a strong influence in all of the early English settlements. Most of those who came brought their religious traditions with them and continued to practice what they had known in their homelands.

The overwhelming consensus in the colonies was that the church should have the primary influence in defining what was acceptable behavior for all people in society. In the Massachusetts Bay colony, for instance, church membership (which was based on having a conversion experience) was a requirement for being able to vote and take part in government. Church leaders didn't want unconverted sinners in positions of authority or even taking part in elections.

Today, many in our society are uncomfortable when perspectives of faith are included in the consideration of public policy. For most colonists, however, the idea of faith being separated from community and governmental activities would have been a strange notion. They believed that community life and government were precisely where faith needed to be practiced if church members were going to be faithful to God's covenant with them as His people. The role of the church in today's society has become quite different from the role it played in the early colonies.

The Influence of the World

However, the early colonies did have a significant number of secular residents who were not church members. We cannot know their exact numbers; but the presence of worldly influences, even in Plymouth and Boston, was a serious concern for church leaders.

In addition, the level of faith shown by the original settlers did not always continue in later generations. Not every member of one generation effectively passed his faith on to the next generation. Not all of the children and grandchildren of the first generation of colonists gave evidence of their conversion; as a result, they were not able to receive full church membership. Moreover, only church members were able to have their children baptized. Church leaders became concerned that church membership would shrink and church influence in the community would be threatened.

In 1662 the ministers in Boston agreed to what was called the Half-Way Covenant. This allowed the children of people who had not become members to have a kind of half-way membership in the church. The children of non-members could be baptized, and parents were expected to teach their children the church's standards; but no one could participate in communion without having a conversion experience. This transformed church membership into a social status in the community that was separate from a person's individual faith. This in turn changed how some viewed the identity and purpose of the church in America.

Calvinist Theology, Anglican Practice

The dominant theology in the colonies was Calvinism. Theologian John Calvin (1509-1564) had emphasized the absolute sovereignty of God and the absolute depravity of man. He believed that only the working of God could arouse a human heart to conversion and that God had already predestined those whom he would choose to save (Calvin called these the elect). An individual was expected to be able to give a testimony of his conversion experience if he was indeed saved. Good works were evidence that the conversion had taken place.

Calvin also emphasized God's working by means of covenants, such as the Old Testament covenant with Israel and the New Testament covenant through Christ. God had a covenant relationship with his church, Calvin emphasized, and believers were expected to have a covenant relationship with each other for the conduct of everyday life. A community was to operate on the basis of this commitment or covenant among its members.

While the predominant theology was Calvinist, the predominant form of religious practice was Anglican. Puritans saw themselves as Anglican, but they practiced congregational autonomy instead of submitting to the Anglican hierarchy in England. The practices of the simple New England congregations were not as formal as those of the Anglican Church in England. Southern colonies, on the other hand, were more accepting of traditional Anglican practices, since many of the planters had been upper-class Anglicans in England. However, a significant number of colonists were members of non-Anglican fellowships.

Some of the colonies had official, established churches. This meant that those churches (often the Church of England) received financial support from the tax revenues of those colonies. Having a state-supported religion seems odd to us today, but this merely reflected the practice that most colonists had known in Europe. Countries began to have state churches in the fourth century AD, so having

Anglicans created Bruton Parish in Virginia in 1674. The current building in Colonial Williamsburg was completed in 1715.

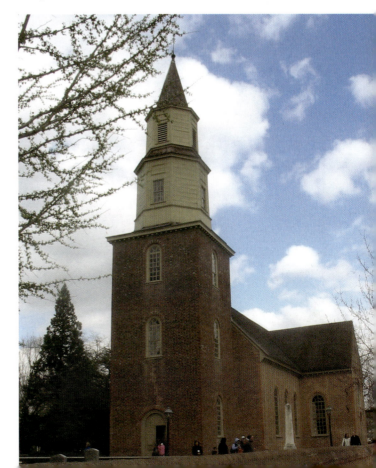

a state church in the 1600s seemed normal to many. Roger Williams and William Penn were among the few who insisted on not having an established religion and urged official equality (usually called toleration) of all religious beliefs.

Many people in America eventually reacted to the strict teachings of Calvinism by adopting a more liberal faith, particularly as taught in Congregationalist Churches. This trend of liberal theology has continued to be a major influence in American thought. The trend away from official recognition of faith has also continued, to the point that now many believe that any religious expression in a public context is unconstitutional.

This illustration of a witch trial in Salem comes from an 1876 book on American history.

Allegations of Witchcraft

The desire to maintain pure Christian doctrine led to church leaders being on the lookout for any possible heresies or false teachings. One particular problem in Massachusetts was the practice of witchcraft. Apparently, a slave from the West Indies influenced a few young girls in Salem, Massachusetts, to dabble in the practices of witchcraft that she had known in her homeland. When community leaders confronted the girls, the girls made accusations about other people in Salem being involved in witchcraft, perhaps to divert attention from themselves. Accusations and suspicions grew, and in 1692 a number of people in Salem were put on trial for witchcraft. In the atmosphere of fear and suspicion that prevailed, twenty people were found guilty. Nineteen persons were hanged and one was crushed to death with stones; none were burned at the stake.

Some people might have been practicing witchcraft in Salem, but colonial leaders overreacted in their attempt to deal with it. One judge who was involved—an ancestor of Nathaniel Hawthorne—later publicly repented of his participation in the trials and regretted his actions for the rest of his life.

Modern "Witch Hunts"

The Salem witch trials have had an influence on American politics. To "go on a witch hunt" is a phrase that has come to mean trying to find wrongdoers on scanty evidence and creating an atmosphere of fear and intimidation. In the early 1950s, Senator Joseph McCarthy charged that some officials in the U.S. State Department were Communists. He produced no evidence, and not a single government employee was found to be a Communist by McCarthy's work. However, he raised questions about people and equated suspicion with guilt. This fear of Communism also affected the entertainment industry, where actors and writers were accused of being Communists and sometimes lost their jobs just by being accused. Many people at the time said that McCarthy was on a witch hunt.

McCarthy at a Senate Subcommittee Meeting

Upheavals in England

Religion played a significant part in two major political upheavals in England that affected the American colonies during the 1600s. King Charles I was an arrogant Anglican who offended the Puritans in control of Parliament at the time. A civil war broke out in 1642 between the forces of the king (called Cavaliers or Royalists) and the forces supporting Parliament and the Puritans (called Roundheads because of their simple haircuts). The Puritan Parliamentarians were led by Oliver Cromwell. Cromwell and the Puritans defeated the Royalists. Charles was eventually taken prisoner and was beheaded in 1649. Cromwell became Lord Protector of England and imposed Puritan values on the country. While many English did not care much for Charles I, they were horrified by his execution. In some ways England has never gotten over this internal conflict, just as the United States has not yet gotten over its own Civil War. As with the practice of witchcraft in Salem, the Parliamentarians tried to solve a bad situation with a bad solution.

When Cromwell died, he was succeeded by his son Richard. Richard Cromwell, however, was not the forceful leader that his father was; and he resigned in 1659. Charles II assumed the throne; but he was a poor leader in the pattern of his father. On his deathbed, Charles II professed the Catholic faith. His son and successor, James II, was also a Catholic. The Anglican leaders of Parliament sought to depose James II to stop the Catholic domination of the monarchy. James II abandoned the throne and fled to Catholic-controlled France. In 1688 Parliament invited William, Protestant prince of the Netherlands, and his Protestant wife Mary to come to England to be king and queen. Their ascension to the English throne was justified by the fact that William was the grandson of Charles I and Mary was the daughter of James II.

English Civil War Re-enactors

This change in leadership is called the Glorious or Bloodless Revolution. The move insured that the English monarchy would be Protestant, but it also had political significance. The monarch now ruled at the request of Parliament, which represented the people. The Glorious Revolution of 1688 changed the role of the monarch in English government and greatly increased the power and prestige of Parliament.

The American colonies were still being settled during all this upheaval. When the government in England changed, the American colonies had to be sure that their position with the new rulers was secure. The political changes in Britain affected the American colonies on a long-term basis in at least two ways. First, as the colonies matured, colonial leaders got tired of dealing with a changeable and often disagreeable British monarchy. Second, the Americans learned something about taking power into their own hands in order to be rid of a king they did not like. In 1776, almost a century after the Glorious Revolution, the representatives of the American colonies did just that. They threw off the rule of the English king and formed a new government for the people of the United States of America.

Set your mind on the things above, not on the things that are on earth. For you have died and your life is hidden with Christ in God.
Colossians 3:2-3

★ Assignments for Lesson 10 ★

American Voices — Read the excerpts from the *Bay Psalm Book* and the *New England Primer* (pages 6, 8, and 9).

Literature — Continue reading *The Scarlet Letter*.

Bible — Read Acts 2:37-41 and 1 Corinthians 12:13. On what is membership in the Lord's church to be based?

Read Galatians 5:19-21 and 6:1-4. What should Christians and church leaders do when they discover that church members are practicing witchcraft or committing other sins?

Recite or write Psalm 146:3-5 from memory.

Project — Complete your project for the unit.

Student Review — Optional: Answer the questions for Lesson 10 and take the quiz for Unit 2.

Strong-Porter House, Coventry, Connecticut (c. 1730)

3 English Colonies in the 1700s

The Enlightenment worldview put man and reason at the center of the universe and pushed to the side (in the minds of some) God's role as Sustainer of the universe. This questioning of traditional thought and authority extended into the political sphere. The culture that Great Britain and her American colonies shared did not outweigh the oppressive nature of British relations with the colonies and the growing reality of a distinct American existence. The Great Awakening was a spiritual revival in the colonies during this period that had a wide influence at the time.

Lesson 11 - The Enlightenment
Lesson 12 - The Experiment of Self-Government
Lesson 13 - The French and Indian War
Lesson 14 - The Growing Conflict
Lesson 15 - Bible Study: The Great Awakening

Memory Work Memorize Colossians 2:8-10 by the end of this unit.

Books Used The Bible
American Voices
The Scarlet Letter

Project (choose one)

1) Write 300 to 500 words on one of the following topics:

- How do you reconcile (1) belief in an all-powerful God who rules the universe, (2) that universe operating on the basis of natural law, and (3) the Biblical teaching that God is a personal God who responds to our prayers? Give your response to Enlightenment thinking as it compares to traditional Christian teaching. See Lesson 11.

- Write an essay responding to Jonathan Edwards' sermon, "Sinners in the Hands of An Angry God" (read in Lessons 11-12). Discuss what you agree with and what you disagree with. How is it good to hear lessons such as this one, and how is it counterproductive? What would be the effect of this sermon in your church?

2) Make a video "public service announcement" as if made in the 1760s that tries to convince your fellow colonial Americans to boycott British goods. Give at least three arguments to justify this action. Your video should be at least three minutes long. See Lesson 14.

3) Prepare a Cajun meal for your family. See Lesson 13.

Detail from Celestial Map by Frederik de Wit (Dutch, 17th Century)

Lesson 11

The Enlightenment

Thomas Cooper, a colonist in Plymouth, Massachusetts, was sure about what made the world go around, just like his ancestors in Notgrove, England, had been almost three hundred years earlier. He knew that God held the universe in His hands and brought about everything that happened according to His divine will. If he ever stopped to think about it, Thomas realized that he knew little about the motion of the stars, what caused weather developments, and how new life was created. He knew God, however, and he believed that was all he needed to know. Thomas was not aware of anyone who did not assign the operation of the world to the work of God.

Although Thomas Cooper was certain about his own worldview, the thought world around him was changing. The eighteenth century saw the development of a new worldview that put man—not God—at the center of science and world affairs. This period is called the Enlightenment because many scientists and philosophers of the day believed that they were being enlightened as to the true nature of the world. Their studies and speculations changed the way people have viewed the world from that day to this.

Background of the Scientific Revolution

The foundation for the Enlightenment was the Scientific Revolution of the sixteenth and seventeenth centuries. The work of three scientists illustrates the changes that took place in that earlier era. First, the Polish astronomer Nicolaus Copernicus published *On the Revolution of Heavenly Bodies* in 1543. Copernicus said that the sun was the center of the universe and that the earth revolved around the sun. This was in direct contradiction to the official Catholic doctrine that the earth was the center of the universe and that all heavenly bodies rotated around it. Copernicus could have been charged by the Catholic Church with heresy, but he died soon after his work was published and so he escaped that fate.

Second, the Italian astronomer Galileo Galilei confirmed the work of Copernicus in the early 1600s. Galileo, however, had the misfortune of living long enough to be denounced as a heretic by the Catholic Church.

Third, the English scientist Isaac Newton published his landmark *Principia Mathematica (Mathematical Principles)* in 1687. In this work

Newton discussed his studies of gravity and other aspects of the physical world. He demonstrated that the universe operates on the basis of regular, predictable natural laws. The period of the Enlightenment is generally seen as beginning with the publication of Newton's work and continuing until the beginning of the French Revolution in 1789.

The ideas of Copernicus, Galileo, and Newton were radical in their day, but today we do not question whether the earth revolves around the sun or whether the operation of gravity is regular and predictable. We accept these as established facts. The revolution has endured.

The Enlightenment and the Role of God

These scientific findings did not just provide insights into how the universe works. For some, they also had far-reaching philosophical and spiritual implications. Some scientists and philosophers interpreted these discoveries to mean that scientific laws were the real basis for the operation of the universe, not the will of God. Most of the scientists in the Enlightenment believed in God and believed that natural law honored God, but the door had been opened for people to move the study of God to the sidelines and to emphasize the study of the physical world alone as the key to understanding the universe.

The change in outlook brought on by the Enlightenment was the change from a religious and metaphysical (beyond the physical) outlook on the world to an outlook based on scientific study of the physical world. It was a change reflected by the experts that were respected by society in general. In earlier times, theologians and clergymen were looked to for wisdom and answers; now scientists began to assume that role. We should not think that this change took place immediately among everyday people on farms and in the shops. The change took place first in the academic world and eventually trickled down to influence the thinking of the average person.

This science-based study of the world gave rise to the eighteenth-century religion of Deism. Deists tried to balance their belief in God with their scientific understandings. Deism held that God created the world but then stepped back from its on-going operation and allowed it to function by means of natural law. It is sometimes claimed that Deism was the predominant religion of the eighteenth century, but this is not the case. Some educated people, including some of the Founding Fathers of the United States, were Deists; but the large majority of Americans maintained a more traditional belief in God as Creator and Sustainer of the universe.

Reason and Human Society

Enlightenment philosophers attempted to apply reason and natural law to human society. Englishman John Locke, in his *Essay Concerning Human Understanding* (1690), said that the nature of society

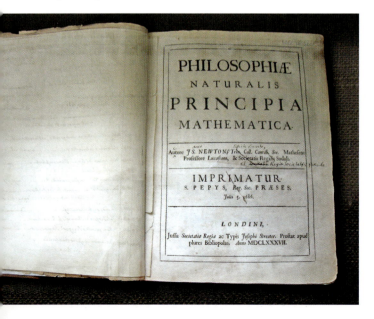

This is Isaac Newton's personal copy of the first edition of his book. It contains his handwritten corrections and updates for the second edition.

Lesson 11 - The Enlightenment

and the lives of individuals are not predetermined by God but can be changed by education and the application of reason. In another publication from the same year, *Two Treatises on Government*, Locke said that political authority came from what he called social contracts made among a people, not from kings receiving authority from God. These social contracts are the way that a society determines the kind of government it wants. The contracts might not be on a piece of paper but they are nonetheless real and binding. Locke said that ultimate political power rested with the people, not with kings, and that majorities can change governments.

Locke applied natural law to the understanding of society and government by saying that society and government were not the result of unquestioned tradition but were instead the result of the rational application of laws concerning human existence. It was no longer acceptable, in Locke's view, for a government action to be taken or a political position to be held because the Church said so or because the king said so. A growing number of influential people wanted to see a reason behind a particular action or position.

The date of Locke's publications is significant: 1690, two years after the Glorious Revolution of 1688, when Parliament invited William and Mary to assume the throne of England. Parliament's action put the monarchy on notice that it, not the crown, actually ruled England. Locke's writings were to a great degree a justification of the Glorious Revolution.

Much later, Jean-Jacques Rousseau wrote in *The Social Contract* (1762) that democracy was the best and most reasonable form of government because in it people worked together for the common good on the basis of what was virtuous. This approach, Rousseau said, led to a better society. It was a radical idea to suggest that the people, not the king, were the basis for a healthy society and government.

Jean-Jacques Rousseau, *Allan Ramsay (British, 1766)*

Questions Raised by the Enlightenment

The change in worldview brought about by the Enlightenment was a major shift in many ways.

- The Enlightenment questioned the role of kings. Monarchy was no longer seen as having a rational basis. Why did someone deserve to be king just because he was the son of a king? Why would that person necessarily be the most qualified person to rule a country? In addition, monarchy had no basis in the will of the people since kings were not voted into office.

- Enlightenment thinking questioned the role of religion. Faith came to be seen by many as not being scientific or rational. The Catholic Church, in fact, had been in error about the earth being the center of the solar system. The various Christian denominations with their conflicting interpretations of Scripture appeared to be approaching truth in a subjective and irrational way. A reasoned approach to Scripture, some said, should not result in conflicting interpretations. In addition, the Enlightenment was seen by some as an aid to bringing about heaven on earth. Mankind no longer had to wait for heaven to have a better life; such a life was possible on earth if people simply followed the laws of reason.

- The Enlightenment questioned the role of God. What role did a personal God have in a universe that operated on the basis of fixed natural law? What was the purpose of prayer, since in many cases prayer was apparently a request for God to suspend natural law? The change in worldview brought on by the Enlightenment was reflected in the way that people answered the simple question of what made the world go around. Was it the will of God, or was it natural law?

- The Enlightenment elevated the role of man. The reasoning ability of man, rather than tradition or faith, was becoming the basis for human understanding and action. Man no longer had to find his place within the workings of the mind of God; instead, for Enlightenment thinkers, God had to fit within the workings of the mind of man.

Enlightenment rationalism swept the field of scientific and philosophical inquiry. It became the common way for educated people to see the world. Rationalism continues to dominate much philosophical and scientific thinking today, although new scientific insights and the wrenching political calamities of the twentieth century seriously challenged the view that reason is the only key needed to understand man and his world. How is it rational, for instance, to believe that the material world is made up of atoms, when we cannot know for certain where the electrons of those atoms are at any given moment? How does one rationally explain the fact that the vast majority of our material universe consists of nothing material, merely empty space? What is the rational, materialistic basis of such realities as love, joy, and hope in the face of obstacles? How can reason explain the irrational horrors of World War I, the Holocaust, and Communism that destroyed the lives of millions of people in the supposedly enlightened twentieth century? Rationalism cannot adequately explain these realities.

We must realize that rationalism is a kind of faith. It is a statement of belief that the world operates in a certain way. Some scientists believed that rationalism would provide ultimate answers about our world and our lives, but we have discovered that it does not. We must look elsewhere for ultimate answers. The laws of gravity and other aspects of the natural world can be proven, but this does not answer the question of whether the physical world is all that exists, nor does it identify the purpose of the created world. These deeper questions remind us that spiritual reality is part of our world also. By coming to know the reality of God and His mind, we will find the ultimate answers for our lives.

Marie-Thérèse Rodet Geoffrin (1699-1777) was a wealthy Paris patron of the arts and sciences who hosted meetings in her home. This 1812 painting by French artist Anicet-Charles-Gabriel Lemonnier depicts guests gathered to hear a reading from a book by French author Voltaire (1694-1778).

Lesson 11 - The Enlightenment

The heavens are telling of the glory of God;
And their expanse is declaring the work of His hands.
Psalm 19:1

★ Assignments for Lesson 11 ★

American Voices — Begin reading "Sayings from Poor Richard's Almanack" by Benjamin Franklin (pages 10-14). You will read the rest of the sayings tomorrow.

Begin reading Jonathan Edwards' sermon, "Sinners in the Hands of an Angry God" (pages 20-23). You will read the rest of the sermon tomorrow. You might try reading Edwards' sermon aloud. Remember, however, that he did not shout, wave his hands, or walk about the platform when he delivered it. The force of his words was in the message itself.

Literature — Continue reading *The Scarlet Letter.* Plan to finish it by the end of this unit.

Bible — Start memorizing Colossians 2:8-10.

Project — Choose your project for this unit and start working on it.

Student Review — Optional: Answer the questions for Lesson 11.

The Proprietary House, Home of the Last Royal Governor of New Jersey (1764)

Lesson 12

The Experiment of Self-Government

As the British colonies in America developed, many political leaders in the colonies were influenced by the Enlightenment worldview. It did not seem reasonable or right to them for the colonies to be governed by a hereditary king who lived thousands of miles away and had no concept of what life in America was like. The key issue that eventually led to the separation of the American colonies from Britain was this issue of power and control: who should hold political power in the colonies and how the colonies should be governed. Through a combination of circumstances in England, circumstances in the colonies, powerful individuals, and significant decisions on both sides of the Atlantic, the American colonies developed a pattern of thinking and of government that led them away from oversight by Britain and toward independence.

We need to understand two important facts about the American Revolution to grasp how it happened. One, it did not happen overnight. It was the culmination of developments that took place over many years in the colonial experiment of self-government. Two, the outcome was not clear or obvious at any point in the process. The success of the American Revolution is sometimes thought of as being inevitable. However, public opinion and the thinking of the leaders were often sharply divided about what was the best course to take. American civil and military leaders had to use their best judgment to make decisions under challenging circumstances and to take great risks. We believe that the hand of God was guiding the process, as He does all of history, but the eventual outcome was not obvious to the people involved at the time.

Colonial Government

When a royal colony was founded, the king named a governor as his direct representative. In proprietary colonies, the governor held office with the approval of the proprietor. In Rhode Island and Connecticut, the elected assembly had the right to choose the governor.

Each governor had a council of advisors. The council was made up of a small group of wealthy colonists who were appointed by the king. Council members were expected to support the policies of the king, but in reality they had their own economic interests at heart. The council often differed with official royal policy when council members believed that such policy interfered with their interests. This council served as a rough equivalent to the House of Lords in England or to the upper house of a legislature.

Lesson 12 - The Experiment of Self-Government

Each colony also had a representative assembly elected by free males who each owned a certain amount of property. Property ownership requirements were higher for elected officials. The general belief of the day was that those who owned property had a greater interest in the stability and well-being of the colony. Men who did not own property were not considered stable enough to make wise political decisions.

The pattern of local government in America came directly from England. For example, the most important local enforcement official and tax collector in the American colonies was the sheriff. The county judge or justice of the peace decided cases involving local disputes. These roles of sheriff and justice of the peace came from English county government. This 1940 photo shows a deputy sheriff in Mongolion, New Mexico.

Colonial Assemblies Gain Power

At first the British king and the appointed governors held ultimate political authority in the colonies. During the 1700s, however, colonial assemblies exercised greater powers. They gained the right to initiate legislation instead of only being able to vote on bills proposed by the governor. Assemblies also became able to judge the qualifications of their members and to choose their own speakers (chairmen), which was a change from the policy of having the governor decide those matters. Colonial legislatures dealt with such issues as land questions, the creation of colonial currency (each colony had its own), and relations with the Indians.

The British government held the position that colonial assemblies were merely permitted by the king and could be limited in their powers or even dismissed at any time. The colonists, on the other hand, saw the powers of the assemblies as being derived from the consent of the people they governed. This basic difference in the understanding of who held political power resulted in conflict between the British throne and colonial governments over the power of the colonial assemblies.

As colonial assemblies developed more power and the English crown became more concerned about controlling life in the colonies, the governors were often caught in the middle. The conflict between a colonial legislature and a governor showed up most often in issues regarding money and appropriations. If the majority of an assembly differed with a policy or decision, the assembly might refuse to appropriate money or it might withhold the salaries of royal officials.

Events in England

In addition to these developments in the colonies, events in England affected relations between the colonies and the government in London. Colonies founded in the 1600s were chartered by the king. In 1675 the king established the Lords of Trade,

The trial of John Peter Zenger for seditious libel in 1735 established the principle of freedom of the press in America. Zenger had criticized the governor of New York in his newspaper and had been put in prison for ten months. Printing negative comments about governing officials was against the law. Zenger's defense was that what he had published was true, but the law didn't make any allowance for that. The jury found Zenger not guilty, and as a result newspaper editors felt more free to criticize the government in their publications. By 1745 the colonies had twenty-two newspapers, fairly evenly spread among the regions, and the press continued to grow in influence during the century.

a council that sought to exercise more direct control over the colonies. The Lords of Trade demonstrated their power in 1686 by creating the Dominion of New England, which combined all of the New England colonies into one government. New Englanders resented this intrusion into their affairs and especially resented the poorly qualified governor that the king appointed to oversee the Dominion.

With the Glorious Revolution in 1688, the colonial governments of New England rejected the Dominion as the failed policy of a deposed king. The governor was imprisoned, and the colonies resumed their previous methods of governing themselves individually. This strengthened the hand of the American colonies in disputes with England. The Lords of Trade were replaced with the Board of Trade in 1696; but England was so preoccupied with its new king, and Parliament was so concerned about defining and exercising its growing powers, that the colonies did not receive much official attention.

Changing World, Unchanging Policy

As the 1700s unfolded, the colonies changed and England changed; but British policy toward the colonies did not change to reflect the new developments. The economies of the colonies were still strongly tied to England (a fact which sometimes

Lesson 12 - The Experiment of Self-Government

helped and sometimes irritated the colonists), but the colonies developed a thriving economy and a rich cultural diversity of their own. This, coupled with the lively political life in the colonies and the growing desire there for self-government, led to increasing conflicts between London and the American colonies. Mistakes in British policies dealing with the colonies encouraged this desire for American independence and eventually led to the Revolution of 1776.

The desire for self-rule sometimes expressed itself violently, as in one conflict that related to official policy about the western frontier. As settlers moved west, Native Americans often resisted their advances. A dispute on the Virginia frontier between settlers and Indians led to one farmer's worker being killed by the Indians in 1675. White settlers took revenge by killing several Indians, some in cold blood. Angered natives then attacked frontier settlements. In one Indian attack the overseer of Nathanael Bacon's property was killed.

In 1676 Bacon organized a group of vigilantes to do battle against the Indians. When the governor ordered him to stop, Bacon threatened to take action against the governor. Bacon led an assault on Jamestown and had the town burned. However, he died of swamp fever a month later and the revolt dissipated. Bacon's Rebellion highlights three significant elements of colonial life: the constant threat of Indian attack, conflict over western settlement policy, and the growing willingness of colonists to defy governmental authority.

Loyalty and truth preserve the king,
And he upholds his throne by righteousness.
Proverbs 20:28

★ Assignments for Lesson 12 ★

American Voices — Finish reading "Sayings from Poor Richard's Almanack" by Benjamin Franklin (pages 15-19).

Finish reading "Sinners in the Hands of an Angry God" by Jonathan Edwards (pages 24-29).

Literature — Continue reading *The Scarlet Letter*.

Bible — Work on memorizing Colossians 2:8-10.

Project — Work on your project.

Student Review — Optional: Answer the questions for Lesson 12.

Re-enactors at the 250th Anniversary of the Siege of Fort William Henry (2007)

Lesson 13

The French and Indian War

England and France became enemies after the Normans (descendants of Vikings in northern France) conquered England in 1066. The Norman kings of England also claimed land in France, which led to protracted wars and intrigues between the French and English monarchs. From the mid-1500s on, one additional element of the conflict was the fact that France was predominantly Catholic and Great Britain was mostly Protestant.

Both Britain and France grew stronger and wealthier during the 1700s, largely because of their overseas colonies. Each claimed various parts of the world as being under their authority. As Europeans began settling North America, the two countries competed to control different parts of the continent. Beginning in 1689, England, France, and other European countries fought a series of wars that primarily involved political alliances in Europe; but these conflicts spilled over into North America.

The major conflict in North America in the 1750s and 1760s became known as the French and Indian War. In Great Britain, it was called the Great War for Empire because English and French forces fought in several places around the world. In Europe the conflict was called the Seven Years' War because it lasted there from 1756 until 1763.

Conflict in the West

Great Britain established control of the eastern seaboard in North America with her thirteen colonies. France controlled most of Canada and the Mississippi River. One area over which the two countries disputed was the territory between the Ohio River and the Great Lakes. Both countries wanted to control that region and the opportunities it offered to trade with Native Americans.

One way that both France and Britain tried to gain control of the region was to make alliances with Native American tribes. These tribes promised to fight with the armies of one country against the other (and against the tribes loyal to the other country). The British could also call on the colonial militias for additional troops. Militia members were not professional soldiers but were farmers and shopkeepers who took up arms when the need arose. Once the fighting was finished, the militiamen returned to their farms and shops.

To stake their claims in the Ohio River region, each country built forts where the Allegheny and Monongahela Rivers combine to form the Ohio River in western Pennsylvania. The French built Fort Duquesne (pronounced Doo-KANE) and the British built Fort Necessity. The governor of Virginia

66

Lesson 13 - The French and Indian War

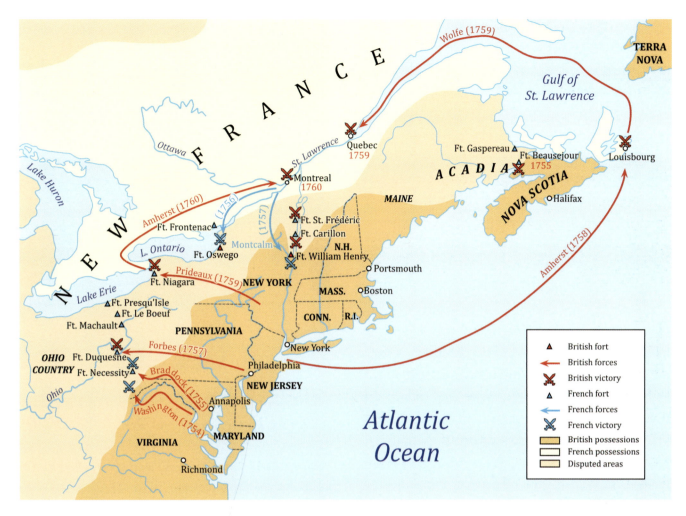

Troop Movements and Battles in the French and Indian War

sent the young militia officer George Washington and a small band of troops to Fort Necessity to push the French out of the region. However, Washington was defeated on July 4, 1754, and had to withdraw. This battle marked the beginning of the French and Indian War. Since British colonies were part of the British Empire, the American colonies found themselves at war with France.

A Slow Start for the British

The war went badly at first for the British and for their colonies and allied Indian tribes. British military commanders did not prove to be good leaders and the British soldiers did not fight well. Then William Pitt became leader of the British government in 1757 and turned things around. He put better officers in charge, and those men created effective armies made up of British regular troops and American militiamen. Pitt urged a more aggressive war effort and assured the colonies that they would be reimbursed for the expenses they incurred in fighting the war.

In the face of a British attack, the French burned and abandoned Fort Duquesne in 1758. The British then built Fort Pitt on the site, which later became the city of Pittsburgh. In other decisive battles the British captured the French Canadian cities of Quebec (1759) and Montreal (1760).

Results of the War

England and France finally agreed to negotiate a treaty; and war ended with the Treaty of Paris, signed in 1763. By the terms of the treaty, France gave control of Canada to Britain. Spain, which had been an ally of France, had to give control of Florida to Britain. During the conflict, France had given Spain control of the Louisiana Territory in exchange for Spain's entering the war against Britain. Thus, France had lost control of the Louisiana Territory as well. The defeat of France in the war made Britain the unquestioned colonial power in North America. France lost all her territories in North America as well as many of her colonies around the world, including India. From this point, France was no longer the major international power it had been.

However, the victory was a costly one for Britain. It emerged from the war deeply in debt. To help pay for the war's expenses, it placed new taxes on the colonies. The colonists resented this move, and their resentment was a major step toward the American Revolution. Also, Britain had a huge area in North America to oversee, and the oppressive way that Britain tried to govern and control the region also helped bring about the Revolution in the American colonies.

The war had a significant impact within France as well. Defeated in North America, France tried to weaken Britain by helping the new American nation in its revolution against Great Britain a few years later. The combined expenses of the French and Indian War and the American Revolution led to serious financial troubles in France, which helped spark the French Revolution in 1789.

The Albany Plan of Union

A sidelight to the conflict between Britain and France was the first consideration given to a unified government for the thirteen British colonies. Because of the threat posed by France, the British government ordered representatives from several of the colonies to meet in Albany, New York, in 1754 to develop a policy of greater unity among the colonies. Britain's purpose was to make sure that the colonies fought together under the leadership

One British victory early in the war was the capture of Acadia in the French-held area of Nova Scotia, Canada. About 5,000 to 7,000 French-speaking residents were forced to leave, and these refugees were scattered down the Atlantic coast. Many found their way to New Orleans (the closest French-speaking haven). This is how the Acadians from Canada came to be the Cajuns in Louisiana. The sad tale of this forced emigration is told in the narrative poem Evangeline: A Tale of Acadie *by Henry Wadsworth Longfellow. Marcel Rebecchini's statue of Evangeline, shown above, is located in St. Martinville, Louisiana.*

of the king. At the meeting, a committee headed by Benjamin Franklin proposed a new general government for the American colonies. Many of the ideas in the Albany Plan of Union were the basis for the national government that was formed later under the Articles of Confederation and later still under the Constitution of the United States.

The executive proposed by the plan was called the President-General, a title similar to the title of President in the Constitution. The President-General was to approve of all laws and to see that they were carried out. The President-General was also to conduct relations with Indian tribes. These roles were similar to those given to the President in the Constitution. Representatives from the colonies to the Grand Council were to be selected by colonial assemblies, not by direct popular vote. This is how the Constitution originally called for U.S. Senators to be chosen.

The number of representatives from each colony depended on the population. Each colony had between two and seven elected members. These were the same limits on representation set by the Articles of Confederation. The chairman of the Grand Council was called the Speaker, which was the title given to the chairman of the House of Representatives in the Constitution. All of the actions of the proposed government were to be approved by the Crown.

The Albany proposal recognized the authority of the British monarchy over the colonies and was not a revolutionary form of government. However, all of the colonies either rejected or ignored the Albany Plan of Union. The British government rejected the idea, too.

What Else Was Happening?

1685-1750   *Life of Johann Sebastian Bach.*

1719   *Daniel Defoe publishes* Robinson Crusoe.

1741   *Danish navigator Vitus Bering discovers the strait between Alaska and Russia that now bears his name.*

1752   *Benjamin Franklin invents the lightning rod after flying a kite in a storm. Lightning rods help protect buildings.*

1752   *Britain finally adopts the Gregorian calendar. The Julian calendar, in use since the days of Julius Caesar, was too long at 365 and 1/4 days. In 1582 Pope Gregory XIII ordained that 10 days be dropped one time from that year to rectify the situation and that years ending in hundreds be leap years only if they are divisible by 400. When England and the colonies adopt the change, another day is dropped. Thus, the day after September 2 is declared to be September 14.*

1753   *Pennsylvania Dutch introduce covered (Conestoga) wagons to travel on the frontier. The painting at right is by Newbold Hough Trotter (American, 1883).*

1756-1791   *Life of Wolfgang Amadeus Mozart*

1762   *During a long gambling session in London, the Earl of Sandwich orders meat and cheese between slices of bread so that he can eat with one hand and continue gambling with the other. The resulting dish now bears his name.*

1767   *Daniel Boone makes his first trip through the Cumberland Gap.*

1769   *Scottish scientist James Watt perfects the steam engine.*

*But I say to you who hear, love your enemies,
do good to those who hate you . . .*
Luke 6:27

★ Assignments for Lesson 13 ★

American Voices — Read the Albany Plan of Union (pages 30-31).

Literature — Continue reading *The Scarlet Letter*.

Bible — God is a God of righteousness and always does what is right. He is willing to punish and condemn, but He is also a God of love. We should have a proper fear of God, but God chose to draw people to Himself by a demonstration of suffering love in Jesus on the cross rather than by sending His Son to scorch people with thunderbolts. As you think about Jonathan Edwards' sermon, write down how these passages either support or differ from Edwards' main point:

- Micah 7:18
- Matthew 7:22-27
- Mark 9:42-50
- John 3:16
- Romans 1:18
- Hebrews 12:25-29

Work on memorizing Colossians 2:8-10.

Project — Work on your project.

Student Review — Optional: Answer the questions for Lesson 13.

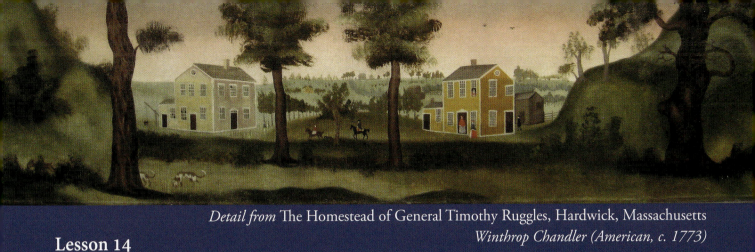

Detail from The Homestead of General Timothy Ruggles, Hardwick, Massachusetts
Winthrop Chandler (American, c. 1773)

Lesson 14

The Growing Conflict

Britain's victory in the French and Indian War eliminated the threat of a French attack on the British colonies in America, but it created other problems for Britain. Some of these problems were self-inflicted because of the way the royal government dealt with the colonies. The result of these problems was that, twenty years after acquiring a huge amount of North American real estate from France and Spain, Britain lost its thirteen North American colonies and the land that stretched west of them to the Mississippi River.

Similarities and Differences

Britain's colonies in America had much in common with their British homeland. Most of the colonists (or their parents or grandparents) came from Britain, bringing with them the language and culture they had known. Many of the professional trades as well as the social classes that the colonists recognized had been transplanted from England. A good number of upper class American offspring received their education in England. From England the colonists had gotten their concepts about representative government and the rights of individuals. The colonists practiced the English legal system. Great Britain was by far the colonies' largest trading partner. The hundreds of thousands of colonists born in America thought of themselves as subjects of the crown.

Yet the American colonial experience, even though it was linked to Britain, was decidedly different from the life that both the common people and the governing class in Britain knew. The colonies had no royalty. While people in Britain generally accepted their class distinctions and their respective lots in life, Americans saw new possibilities for their lives and envisioned how things could be different. The frontier that had beckoned the English and the Scots-Irish had become the American colonies; now the colonists had their own frontier to the west that drew them on. The pioneer life of log cabins, coonskin caps, and Indian skirmishes was quite different from life in English country villages.

In addition to these cultural differences, British and American policies and politics were going in different directions. The basis of these differences was that Britain wanted more control over the colonies while many colonists wanted more freedom. After the French and Indian War, Britain stationed a standing army in the colonies. The official explanation given by London was that the army was there to guard against an enemy attack, but to many Americans it looked like a police force designed to quell any domestic unrest in the colonies. British law allowed for troops to be quartered in private homes in the colonies. This was insulting enough to the colonists; but in addition, arrogant and undisciplined British troops showed the worst side of Britain to the already resentful colonists.

Control of the Colonies

The central issue confronting Britain's colonial system in the last third of the eighteenth century involved determining the best way for the king to govern the colonies. Over one hundred fifty years had passed since the colonies had begun. British policy toward the colonies in the 1600s and early 1700s had been inconsistent, with changes in London's control or laxity largely depending on attitudes and issues within the British government instead of conditions and needs in the colonies. However, the overall desire by Britain to exercise tight control over the colonies had not changed, and this desire increased as the eighteenth century wore on. Meanwhile, Americans had gained a great deal of experience in self-government and in coping with life in the New World.

Britain did not fully appreciate the good market that had developed for its products in America. In 1700 the estimated population of the colonies was about 250,000; by 1750, around one million people lived in the thirteen colonies. As of 1775, the British population in America was approximately 2.5 million, which was about one-third of the population of England itself. America was a force to be reckoned with, and Britain did not reckon with it well. The crown took a controlling, condescending attitude toward the colonies and virtually ignored the talent and intellect that had developed there.

During the time that the colonies were being settled and developed, a crucial debate brewed within England over the relative powers of the throne and Parliament. At the time Jamestown was settled in 1607, the king was a virtual dictator. The two revolutions in England during the 1600s changed that, and during that period Parliament increased its power in the government. The colonies

Illustration of British Redcoats from a 1916 Book

had begun with charters issued by the king, but increasingly the Americans had to deal with restrictive laws passed by Parliament.

To whom did the colonies answer—the king or Parliament? In addition, the nature of colonial government was another subject of debate, as was mentioned in a previous lesson. Were the colonial governments merely permitted by the king and therefore subject to change or withdrawal at any time, or was self-government an inalienable right of man that could not be withdrawn by either royal or parliamentary decree?

New Laws for the Colonies

After the French and Indian War, the British government enacted numerous laws that put more restrictions on the colonies. For instance, the crown now had to approve laws passed by colonial

Lesson 14 - The Growing Conflict

assemblies and confirm judges appointed to the bench in the colonies. Writs of assistance, which allowed searches of homes and business for illegal goods, were now permitted. The colonies were not allowed to print money. All of these restrictions chafed at the colonial consciousness, especially since the new laws followed a period when the crown had generally let the colonies go their own way.

In addition, the West became an issue again, but in a different way from when it was a factor in the French and Indian War. One reason that the war had been fought was the dispute between France and Britain over who would control the territory between the Ohio River and the Great Lakes. Following the war, Indian attacks on colonists erupted again in several places along the western colonial boundaries. In an attempt to avoid angering the Indians and to limit western settlement for a time, the King issued a proclamation in 1763 forbidding any new English settlement west of the Appalachian Mountain crest. This frustrated the colonists. They thought that they had fought the French and Indian War to open up the frontier for settlement, but now it was closed to them.

To help pay for the war and the army now stationed in the colonies, Parliament imposed new taxes on the colonies. Some of these taxes were created by the Sugar Act of 1764 and the Stamp Act of 1765. The Stamp Act was especially hated by the colonists because it required a revenue stamp to be purchased and applied to newspapers and to many kinds of documents used in everyday business. Most colonists agreed that Parliament had the right to regulate the colonies' trade with Britain and with other countries; but imposing taxes on domestic activities within the colonies was a new step—one that many Americans believed to be improper and illegal.

The Stamp Act and the Boston Massacre

Sons of Liberty groups were formed in some colonies as vigilantes that made sure the revenue stamps were not used. Representatives from the colonies met in what came to be called the Stamp Act Congress of 1765 to protest the Act and to declare their grievances over what they saw to be taxation without their having any representation in Parliament. The British replied that the colonists had virtual representation in Parliament, since the members of Parliament were supposedly looking out for the colonists' well-being. In addition, the British government said, the colonists were no different from many people in Great Britain itself who did not have the right to vote for members of Parliament. Why should the colonists have more say in the British government than many Britons themselves?

Parliament repealed the Stamp Act in 1766; but at the same time, it passed the Declaratory Act, which stated that Parliament did indeed have the authority to regulate and tax the colonies. As if to prove this authority, Parliament passed several new revenue

In the October 31, 1765, issue of his newspaper, Philadelphia publisher William Bradford announced: "I am sorry to be obliged to acquaint my readers, that as the Stamp Act, is feared to be obligatory upon us after the First of November ensuing, (the fatal tomorrow) the Publisher of this Paper unable to bear the burden, has thought it expedient to stop awhile." He also expressed the wish that his readers who were late in paying their subscriptions "would immediately discharge their respective arrears."

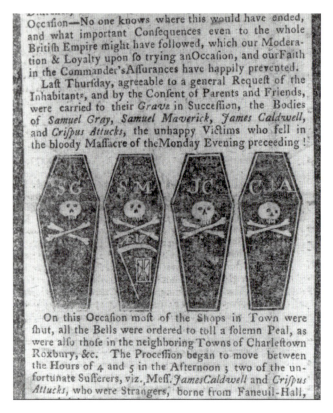

A Boston newspaper published this story about the Boston Massacre on March 12, 1770, with an illustration of four coffins. A fifth victim, Patrick Carr, died on March 14. Carr was an innocent bystander. According to the doctor who treated Carr's wounds, Carr believed that the soldiers had fired in self-defense after enduring a great deal of abuse. Carr forgave the unknown soldier who had mortally wounded him.

laws over the next few years. In response, prominent colonial leader John Dickinson published a series of "Letters from a Farmer in Pennsylvania" that denied Parliament's right to lay taxes on the colonies.

Resistance to the taxes was strong, especially in New England. Roving bands intimidated businesses and bureaucrats and enforced a boycott of British goods. On March 5, 1770, a mob encountered British troops that had been sent to Boston to keep the peace. Insults were exchanged, rocks and snowballs were thrown, shots were fired; and in the end five colonists were dead and eight more were wounded. One of the dead was Crispus Attucks, a runaway slave of mixed race who had worked for some years on ships coming in and out of Boston.

Now blood had been shed in the conflict between Britain and the colonies. The patriot cause had martyrs to remember and villains to denounce. In backing away from the confrontation, Parliament repealed the taxes on trade. However, as a symbolic gesture of its authority, Parliament maintained the tax on tea.

The murder trial of British soldiers involved in what came to be called the Boston Massacre was a tense confrontation between royal authority and colonial defiance. John Adams took the difficult role of defense attorney for the soldiers. Adams blamed the trouble on the "motley rabble" that started the incident and on the British policy of enforcement by confrontation. The soldiers, he said, should not be made to be scapegoats to carry the blame for those really at fault. During the trial Adams said, "Facts are stubborn things; and whatever may be our wishes, our inclinations, or the dictates of our passion, they cannot alter the state of facts and evidence."

This 1888 monument on the Boston Common commemorates those who died in the Boston Massacre.

Lesson 14 - The Growing Conflict

Illustration of the Boston Tea Party from The History of North America *(1789)*

In the end, all but two of the soldiers were acquitted, and those two were only convicted of manslaughter and were branded on their thumbs. Some colonists resented Adams' efforts, but on the whole he gained respect for being willing to stand up for truth and justice. The fair trial that the soldiers received probably did more for American liberty and justice than if the soldiers had been convicted and had themselves become martyrs.

Tea Controversy

In 1773 Parliament passed the Tea Act, which permitted the East India Company to sell its surplus tea in the colonies cheaply and to have its own agents control those sales. Thus, the frustration felt by the colonists was not that tea was becoming too expensive, but that it had become too cheap. Many Americans feared that the colonies would become dependent on this naked attempt by a British company to monopolize the American tea market. In many ports throughout the colonies, tea shipments were refused or were locked up. In Boston, on the evening of December 16, 1773, patriots thinly disguised as Indians boarded three ships and dumped the tea into the harbor while crowds on shore cheered.

Parliament responded by punishing Massachusetts and trying to make it an example for the other colonies. The British government passed the Coercive Acts (called the Intolerable Acts in the colonies) in 1774, severely restricting trade in and out of Boston and tightening British control over colonial life. Other colonies took notice of Massachusetts' situation; but instead of backing down, they banded more tightly together. If these Intolerable Acts could pass Parliament, patriot leaders mused, what might be next?

A Continental Congress of delegates from twelve of the colonies met in Philadelphia in September 1774 and passed resolutions condemning the Coercive Acts. Meanwhile, some colonists were not content to talk and pass resolutions. They began stockpiling weapons and ammunition to defend themselves and their property against whatever the British government and army might do. The powder keg was set; only a spark was needed for an explosion.

This map shows the thirteen colonies along the Atlantic Coast in 1775. After the French and Indian War, the Spanish had yielded control of Florida to the British, and the French had yielded control of their claims west of the Mississippi River to the Spanish.

When the righteous increase, the people rejoice,
But when a wicked man rules, people groan.
Proverbs 29:2

★ Assignments for Lesson 14 ★

American Voices   Read "Letters from a Farmer in Pennsylvania" (excerpts from Letter 2) by John Dickinson (pages 32-33).

Literature   Continue reading *The Scarlet Letter*.

Bible   In tomorrow's lesson we will be studying the Great Awakening, which was a spiritual revival that took place in the American colonies during the mid-1700s. Today, read Nehemiah Chapter 8, which describes the renewal of the covenant after the exiles returned to Jerusalem following the captivity in Babylon. List three things that the Jews either had to change or needed to restore in order to return to God's pattern.

Work on memorizing Colossians 2:8-10.

Project   Work on your project.

Student Review   Optional: Answer the questions for Lesson 14.

Listening to a Sermon by George Whitefield

Lesson 15 - Bible Study

The Great Awakening

Isaiah Wilkinson worked on the docks in Philadelphia. He heard the coarse language that the other workers used, and he knew about their hard-drinking evenings. Most of the people who lived in Philadelphia went to church services on Sunday, but to Isaiah churches were nothing but hypocrisy. He watched church-going businessmen defraud their customers every day of the week.

Many people like Isaiah Wilkinson were ambivalent about religion. They thought it might be good for some people but thought it wasn't necessary for them. However, a great change took place in the religious life of the colonies in the mid-1700s that had a profound effect on thousands of people. We call this change the Great Awakening.

The Need for Revival

As the American colonies grew wealthier, religious interest declined. Many churches became merely social institutions. The Half-Way Covenant in Massachusetts (mentioned in Lesson 10) had the effect of separating church membership from genuine religious commitment. Many settlements in the western parts of the colonies had a rough-and-tumble lifestyle where religion played only a small role. The colonies, many of which were founded on religious conviction, saw a marked decrease in the importance placed on spiritual matters.

One of the most important religious figures in the colonies in the 1730s was Jonathan Edwards. Edwards was a Congregationalist minister in Northampton, Massachusetts, in the western part of the colony. The lack of spiritual fervor he saw in his church and community disturbed him. Edwards had studied theology deeply and presented brilliant, eloquent sermons; but a shroud of cold formalism lay over the congregation and the town was largely unaffected by his work. He believed that religion ought to mean more to people and ought to have a deeper effect in their lives. He began preaching to bring about conviction in the hearts of his hearers. As he did so, a revival began that affected both the church and the town.

Edwards was by no means the only preacher who fanned the flames of religious commitment during this period. Many lesser known men throughout the colonies had great influence in various communities. Traveling evangelists as well as local ministers encouraged the spiritual revival.

The Influence of George Whitefield

In England, a fervent preacher named George Whitefield (pronounced WHIT-field) also preached in a way that encouraged spiritual renewal. He influenced John Wesley to take the unorthodox step of preaching in the open air. This was a controversial move because the accepted understanding in the Anglican Church in that day was that sermons were only to be preached in a church building. Wesley began preaching in fields and anywhere else he could, and the positive response was overwhelming.

Whitefield conducted preaching tours in the American colonies in 1739 and 1740. Whitefield had an unusual ability to move audiences with his powerful oratory. Thousands came to hear him as he preached in Philadelphia, Georgia, and New England. Isaiah Wilkinson attended Whitefield's service in Philadelphia, along with 10,000 others; and the young dockworker was brought to faith by the English evangelist's preaching. Jonathan Edwards heard Whitefield preach and was also profoundly affected.

A series of small revivals in a few localities became a sweeping movement throughout the colonies. The Great Awakening had a huge impact on the practice of Christianity in America. By one estimate about ten percent of the population of New England joined churches over a period of just a few years. Many of those who were convicted by the revivalist preaching they heard became Presbyterians, Baptists, and Methodists; and these conversions helped those denominations grow in America.

Jonathan Edwards became known as the leading preacher of his day. In 1741 he preached the convicting sermon, "Sinners in the Hands of An Angry God," to a congregation in Enfield, Connecticut. By all reports he presented it in a soft, quiet voice without excitement or much visible emotion; but the hearers were overcome with conviction at their spiritual need.

Reaction to the Renewal

At first most churches welcomed the revival and the renewed spiritual interest it generated. However, as time went on negative responses arose to the Great Awakening. Many leaders in established churches saw the new movement as a threat. Evangelists who were part of the Awakening criticized lifeless churches and denounced many of the clergy as unconverted themselves. Denominations suffered splits between those who embraced the new movement and those who defended the status quo.

In reaction to the evangelical fervor, theological liberals embarked on new paths. One such liberal trend developed into Unitarian and Universalist churches, where orthodox Christian teaching was replaced by new, man-made ideas about God and Christ. Unitarian doctrine holds that God is one and does not manifest Himself in three persons (hence the name *uni*-tarian, meaning one). Universalist teaching denies that Christ is the exclusive means of salvation and holds that all will be saved.

Illustration of George Whitefield from Memoirs of the Life of the Reverend George Whitefield *(1774)*

Lesson 15 - Bible Study: The Great Awakening

The Influence of Jonathan Edwards

A number of the descendants of Jonathan Edwards (pictured at left) and his wife, Sarah, achieved great prominence and accomplished much good. They included over a dozen college presidents, over sixty college professors, dozens of military officers, many judges and other civil officials, and about one hundred ministers and missionaries.

Other genealogical research has shown that alcoholism, crime, and poverty tend to run in families when children grow up seeing that example. Having godly ancestors does not ensure that someone will be godly, nor does having ungodly ancestors prevent someone from following Christ. Aaron Burr Sr. married a daughter of the Edwards, and their son was also named Aaron Burr. The younger Burr became Vice President of the United States but lived a checkered life personally and politically. All of us have both good and bad examples in our family trees. Each of us must decide how to live his or her life.

The Great Awakening led to the establishment of several denominational colleges for the training of ministers. Only a small minority of Americans pursued a college education, and many of those who did go to college were candidates for the ministry. A few colleges had been founded before the Great Awakening. Harvard College had begun in 1636 for the express purpose of training the next generation of Puritan clergy. William and Mary College was begun in 1693 to serve the same purpose for Anglicans. Yale College was founded in Connecticut in 1701 when Puritans there believed that Harvard was not maintaining its original vision.

As a result of the Great Awakening, the College of New Jersey was begun in 1746 to educate Presbyterian ministers. It later became Princeton University. Other educational institutions that were established included King's College of New York (1754, later Columbia University, for Anglicans); the College of Rhode Island (1764, which became Brown University); Queen's College in New Jersey (1766, the basis of Rutgers University); and Dartmouth College (1769, founded by Congregationalists).

The Great Awakening helped mold a particularly American expression of the Christian faith:

- Revivalist preaching, although it began in England, has continued to be a major part of American church life, much more than in England.

- The Great Awakening helped to create a multifaceted American Christianity, marked by many groups, sects, beliefs, and practices. After this period, no one church or theology ever predominated in America.

- The movement encouraged individuals to decide their spiritual direction for themselves and to act on individual conviction instead of deferring to an elite clergy or denominational tradition. This new idea extended into the political realm as well, and many people began to want more personal power in their political lives.

- The widespread nature of the revival served to unite the colonies in a way that had not been the case before. A new sense of an American identity permeated the thoughts and lives of many in the colonies.

- Finally, the Awakening led to the hope and belief that the New World might usher in the millennium as God's Promised Land, freed from the social burdens and religious traditions of the Old World. This millennial dream has surfaced many times in American history and continues to be a major part of the teaching of many churches.

The Great Awakening also demonstrated the fact that not everyone in the colonial period was a faithful churchgoer. As evangelists such as George Whitefield toured the colonies, they saw a great deal of worldliness that concerned them. Even Puritan New England had plenty of unrighteousness of which people needed to repent. The general influence of Christianity was stronger in American society at that time than it is today. However, even those "good old days" still had plenty of temptation, worldliness, and superficial religion.

The spiritual revival known as the Great Awakening can challenge all believers to make sure that their commitment to Christ is heart-felt and not just the result of family or church tradition. We need to be sure that our loyalty to Christ goes beyond engaging in religious activities and includes a genuine difference in the way that we live.

Then we shall not turn back from You;
Revive us, and we will call upon Your name.
Psalm 80:18

★ Assignments for Lesson 15 ★

Literature — Finish reading *The Scarlet Letter*. Literary analysis available in *Student Review*.

Bible — Recite or write Colossians 2:8-10 from memory.

Project — Complete your project for the unit.

Student Review — Optional: Answer the review questions for Lesson 15 and for *The Scarlet Letter* and take the quiz for Unit 3.

Revolutionary War Re-enactors (2012)

4 Revolution

The War for American Independence set this country on the political course that it maintains to this day. Key principles of political and personal freedom that Americans still cherish were established in the Declaration of Independence. The American victory in the war enabled the country to turn westward to settle new lands and to continue its growth. The Articles of Confederation was the first attempt at a national government and showed the need for a stronger union among the states. The American Revolution reminds us of the sovereignty of God over the affairs of men.

Lesson 16 - The War Begins
Lesson 17 - The Declaration of Independence
Lesson 18 - The Revolutionary War
Lesson 19 - Society and Government After the Revolution
Lesson 20 - Bible Study: God Is Sovereign

Memory Work

By the end of this unit, memorize the portion of Leviticus 25:10 that is inscribed on the Liberty Bell: "Proclaim liberty throughout all the land unto all the inhabitants thereof" (King James Version).

Books Used

The Bible
American Voices

Project (choose one)

1) Write 300 to 500 words on one of the following topics:

- Write a summary of the reasons Americans desired independence.

- Write about what the Christian's relationship to the government should be in the United States today and what it should be for a Christian living in Communist China today.

2) Make a portfolio of at least ten weapons that were used by the British and Americans during the War for American Independence. Include a detailed description and a drawing or photograph of each one.

3) Make an audio recording or video of yourself singing or playing at least five songs that were popular during the War for American Independence.

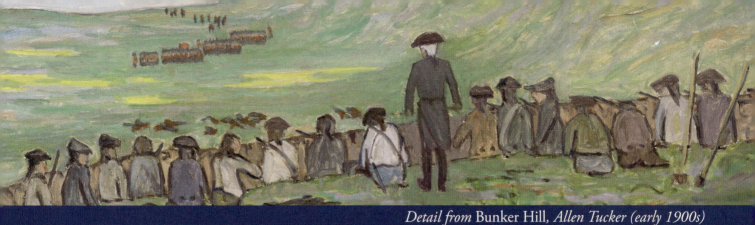

Detail from Bunker Hill, *Allen Tucker (early 1900s)*

Lesson 16

The War Begins

"The New England colonies are in a state of rebellion," declared King George III in late 1774. "Blows must decide whether they are to be subject to this country or independent." Events in America showed how correct the king's appraisal of the situation was.

Political Maneuvers

As the culmination of the colonies' resistance to the laws and policies of the British government, the First Continental Congress convened in Philadelphia in September of 1774. Representatives of twelve colonies (Georgia did not participate at first) passed resolutions condemning British actions, organized boycotts of British goods, and discussed questions of political philosophy and human rights. In response, the British Parliament declared the colony of Massachusetts to be in rebellion. The British government forbade any trade by the American colonies with nations outside of the British Empire and prohibited American fishing in the North Atlantic.

Meanwhile, the colonies prepared for war. Each colony organized a militia. Minute Man units were formed that were prepared for quick action. More and more people clamored for war and independence. On March 23, 1775, Patrick Henry addressed the Virginia House of Burgesses and eloquently stated the patriot cause in his "Give Me Liberty or Give Me Death" speech. Throughout the growing crisis with the colonies, the British government consistently refused to consider any policy or gesture of a conciliatory nature toward the colonies. In their arrogance, the British believed that any military confrontation with the colonists would be minor and brief and would end decisively in Britain's favor.

Lexington and Concord

In April of 1775, the royal governor of the colony of Massachusetts, Thomas Gage, received instructions from London to put an end to the rebellion that was taking place in the colony. The governor issued orders for troops to arrest Samuel Adams and John Hancock in the nearby town of Lexington and then to seize the patriot stockpile of weapons in Concord further away. British troops stationed in Boston left the city by boat during the evening of April 18, 1775, to carry out these orders. They landed outside of the city and started their march toward the nearby villages. Patriots learned of the British advance and sent Paul Revere and William Dawes into the countryside to warn Adams, Hancock, and the local militias. Dr. Samuel

Amos Doolittle, an engraver, and Ralph Earl, a painter, were soldiers from Connecticut under the command of Captain Benedict Arnold in 1775. They visited Massachusetts after the battles in April, and later that year published four illustrations based on their interviews and research. This one shows the Battle of Lexington.

Prescott joined the riders in Lexington. Revere and Dawes were stopped by British patrols, but Prescott got through to Concord.

In a confrontation in Lexington early on the morning of April 19, British soldiers killed several Minute Men. At Concord, however, the militiamen killed fourteen British troops and forced the British to withdraw toward Boston. As they did, patriots along the road, hiding behind rocks, fences, and barns, shot at the retreating soldiers. When the British finally returned to Boston, they had killed or wounded about one hundred Americans but had suffered about 250 casualties themselves. These skirmishes, especially the confrontation at Concord's North Bridge, came to be called collectively "the shot heard round the world." The American Revolutionary War, also known as the War for Independence, had begun. The British quickly realized that they were in for a hard fight.

The Second Continental Congress met in Philadelphia in May of 1775 and began functioning as a national government. It appointed George Washington of Virginia to be commander of a yet-unformed Continental Army. Washington had military experience from the French and Indian War, and he had gained wide respect as a person and as a leader.

Bunker (Breed's) Hill

Meanwhile, British troops had taken control of the city of Boston. Patriot forces outside of Boston laid a siege against the city. On the day Washington was commissioned by Congress, British forces moved against the patriot siege position on Breed's Hill (near Bunker Hill) outside of Boston. The American commander, Israel Putnam, ordered his troops not to fire until they could see the whites of the British soldiers' eyes. In other words, they were to use their scarce ammunition carefully and only shoot at the British at close range.

The British mounted three assaults against the colonists and finally ousted them from their position, but the victory came at a cost of over 1,000 British casualties. The British won the Battle of Bunker Hill, as it became known; but British General Sir Henry Clinton realized that "another such [victory] would have ruined us." Scattered fighting took place in southern Canada and in other parts of the colonies over the course of the next year.

Declaration of Causes

On July 5 and 6, 1775, the Continental Congress approved two resolutions, both written largely by John Dickinson. The first, called the "Olive Branch Petition," assured the king of the colonies' continued loyalty and pleaded for no further hostile action until the standing issues could be resolved. It said in part:

> Attached to your Majesty's person, family, and Government, with all devotion that principle and affection can inspire; connected with Great Britain by the strongest ties that can unite societies, and deploring every

event that tends in any degree to weaken them, we solemnly assure your Majesty, that we not only most ardently desire the former harmony between her and these Colonies may be restored, but that a concord may be established between them upon so firm a basis as to perpetuate its blessings, uninterrupted by any future dissensions, to succeeding generations in both countries, and to transmit your Majesty's name to posterity, adorned with that signal and lasting glory that has attended the memory of those illustrious personages, whose virtues and abilities have extricated states from dangerous convulsions, and by securing the happiness to others, have erected the most noble and durable monuments to their own fame.

The Minute Man Statue in Concord, Massachusetts, commemorated the 100th anniversary of the American Revolution. It became the basis for the logo of the National Guard of the United States. Its sculptor Daniel Chester French later created the statue of Abraham Lincoln in the Lincoln Memorial in Washington, D.C.

The second resolution, entitled the "Declaration of the Causes and Necessity of Taking Up Arms," took a different tone. It explained why the colonies were justified in standing up for their rights while resisting the actions of the British government:

Our cause is just. Our union is perfect. Our internal resources are great, and, if necessary, foreign assistance is undoubtedly attainable. We gratefully acknowledge, as signal instances of the Divine favour towards us, that his Providence would not permit us to be called into this severe controversy, until we were grown up to our present strength, had been previously exercised in warlike operation, and possessed of the means of defending ourselves. With hearts fortified with these animating reflections, we most solemnly, before God and the world, declare, that, exerting the utmost energy of those powers, which our beneficent Creator hath graciously bestowed upon us, the arms we have been compelled by our enemies to assume, we will, in defiance of every hazard, with unabating firmness and perseverance, employ for the preservation of our liberties; being with our mind resolved to dye Freemen rather than live Slaves.

In response to this declaration, King George III issued an official proclamation of rebellion and declared the colonies to be "open and avowed enemies." He began hiring German mercenary soldiers, most of whom came from the Hesse-Kassel region. This is why the German mercenaries came to be called Hessians.

The military situation in the colonies worsened for the British over the next few months. Under the threat of possible American attack, British troops withdrew from Boston to Nova Scotia in March of 1776. At this point no significant area of the thirteen American colonies remained under British control.

Thus far, the conflict constituted a civil war. Many Americans merely wanted to obtain more recognition of their rights as British citizens. A growing number, however, had a different goal in mind: complete separation from the British government.

> *They have healed the brokenness of My people superficially,*
> *Saying, "Peace, peace," but there is no peace.*
> Jeremiah 6:14

★ Assignments for Lesson 16 ★

American Voices Read Patrick Henry's "Give Me Liberty or Give Me Death!" speech (pages 36-37).

Read "Paul Revere's Ride" by Henry Wadsworth Longfellow (pages 139-142). This poem, written in 1860, had much to do with increasing the reputation of Paul Revere and his role in the Revolution, despite its historical inaccuracies.

Read "Concord Hymn" by Ralph Waldo Emerson (page 137). This poem was published in 1837 and gave us the phrase "the shot heard round the world."

Bible Read Romans 13:1-7 and Acts 5:29. Many ministers in the colonies assured their congregations that the Revolution was a noble and righteous cause. Were the American colonies right to rebel against the British monarch? Should they have remained subject to the British throne and tried to resolve their issues peacefully? What is the proper role of American Christians toward our government when it takes actions that are counter to the Christian faith? List an argument for and an argument against the American Revolution based on Scripture. List three ways that God brought good out of the Revolution.

Start memorizing the assigned portion of Leviticus 25:10.

Project Choose your project for this unit and start working on it.

Student Review Optional: Answer the questions for Lesson 16.

Detail from The Declaration of Independence of the United States of America, July 4, 1776
Charles Édouard Armand-Dumaresq (French, c. 1873)

Lesson 17

The Declaration of Independence

He was an Englishman who had failed in just about everything he had attempted in his adult life. At thirty-seven years of age, he had come from England to the colonies to get a new start. When he came, he brought with him a letter of recommendation from Benjamin Franklin, who was in England at the time.

This man planned to edit a magazine in Pennsylvania. He had been in America for less than a year when, in January of 1776, he anonymously published a pamphlet in Philadelphia which sold a phenomenal 100,000 copies in three months. His identity was eventually revealed; and the man's name, Thomas Paine, became widely known.

Paine had a skill for picking up an idea and expressing it in memorable terms. The pamphlet, "Common Sense," was an eloquent and moving call for the independence of the American colonies from Great Britain. Paine said that the king had acted as a brute toward the colonies and that everything in reason and nature declared "'Tis time to part." Paine focused his attention on the actions of the king instead of Parliament. Although the resolutions adopted by Congress in July of 1775 gave assurances that the colonies did not want to separate from Britain, Paine's words increased the desire of many Americans for the colonies to declare their independence.

"These Colonies Ought to Be Free"

Paine's pamphlet both reflected and furthered the growing sentiment for independence. On June 7, 1776, Richard Henry Lee of Virginia proposed a resolution in the Continental Congress which stated that "these united colonies are, and of right ought to be, free and independent states." The resolution was debated, and then a committee was named to draft a formal declaration of independence. The committee was composed of Benjamin Franklin, John Adams, Thomas Jefferson, Robert Livingston of New York, and Roger Sherman of Connecticut. Jefferson and Adams were asked to produce the draft, and Adams deferred to Jefferson for the task because Adams thought Jefferson was the better writer. Jefferson completed his first draft in a matter of a few days.

Then Jefferson's draft was debated and edited by the Congress. Lee's original resolution passed Congress on July 2, 1776. Rejoicing over the vote, John Adams predicted that July 2 would become the most remembered date in American history.

Actually, that honor was given to July 4, 1776, when Jefferson's Declaration, as amended by the delegates, was adopted by the Congress. Representatives from all thirteen colonies signed the Declaration.

"We Hold These Truths To Be Self-Evident"

In the Declaration, Jefferson provided the best statement to that point of the political philosophy that led the colonial leaders to declare the colonies' independence from Britain. It is a classic statement of Enlightenment thinking, appealing to "the Laws of Nature and of Nature's God" and enumerating truths that rational men held to be "self-evident."

Writing the Declaration of Independence, 1776
Jean Leon Gerome Ferris (American, c. 1900)

The Declaration gives a long list of wrongs committed by George III against the colonies. The colonists' grievances were against the actions of the king as head of the government and not against Parliament. Even with the growth of the powers of Parliament in previous decades, the king was still the head of the British government. The document concludes with a declaration of the United States' independence from Britain taken from Lee's original resolution. The signers, relying on "the protection of Divine Providence," pledged to each other "our lives, our fortunes, and our sacred honor."

Jefferson's closing words were not just flowery eloquence. When the colonies embarked upon this course, they did indeed risk everything. The British government considered colonial leaders to be rebels and traitors. If the cause for independence failed, they could expect to be treated as such and face execution. As Benjamin Franklin put it, the colonists had to hang together or they would hang separately. Despite the dangers they faced, the patriots had great confidence in the strength and correctness of their cause.

Divided Colonies

The colonists as a whole, however, were not united in a desire for independence. Many members of the upper class, for instance, saw great dangers in independence; and they decided to remain loyal to Britain. Although exact numbers cannot be known, John Adams estimated that perhaps one third of the colonists strongly favored independence, one third favored remaining a part of the British Empire, and the other one third was open to being persuaded one way or the other.

As time went on, that critical third portion of the colonial population developed the desire to become independent. This gave the independence movement the public support it needed to grow

Lesson 17 - The Declaration of Independence

Tories and Whigs

The names of the two largest political parties in England at the time came from derogatory labels given to them by their opponents. The Tory Party generally supported the king. The word Tory comes from the Irish Gaelic word toraidhe, *which means a robber or a pursued man. It was first used for the supporters of King James II, who were largely the land-owning aristocrats. The term came to be applied to anyone who supported the throne, and it has since developed the broader meaning of a conservative.*

The opposition party was called the Whigs. The term Whig is from the Scottish word whiggamore, *which means cattle driver. It was applied to Scottish dissenters in the 17th century and later came to be used for the land-owning gentry that supported Parliament against the throne. In relative terms the Whigs were the more liberal party. Two things that English political leaders did not want to be called were Irish robbers and Scottish cattle drivers, so that is precisely what their opponents called them. The terms came to be used in the colonies as well: people loyal to Britain were called Tories, while patriots were often called Whigs.*

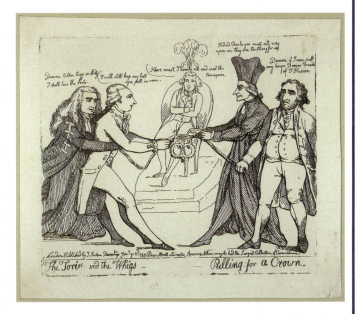

"The Tories and the Whigs Pulling for a Crown" (1789 Political Cartoon)

from being a small band of revolutionaries to being the majority of the colonists.

When independence was declared, almost 170 years had passed since the first English colony had been established in North America. What began as a few tiny outposts had become a strong nation. A growing sense of American identity, a history of insensitive policies by the British government, and the widespread acceptance of Enlightenment thinking on the nature of civil government led to the colonists declaring their independence. Now they had to fight the strongest army in the world to defend that declaration.

The Continental Congress met in a room borrowed from the Pennsylvania legislature. The Assembly Room, where they declared independence from Britain, is shown at right. The room has been restored with antique furnishings to resemble its appearance in the 1770s. This building in Philadelphia is now known as Independence Hall.

What Else Was Happening?

1774   *English minister and scientist Joseph Priestley discovers oxygen. He calls it dephlogisticated air.*

1775   *The Barber of Seville, an opera by Gioachino Rossini, debuts featuring the famous character Figaro.*

1776   *The book The Wealth of Nations by Adam Smith (pictured at left) promotes capitalism by encouraging governments to allow private citizens to pursue business unhindered by regulations.*

1783   *The first manned balloon flight takes place in Paris.*

For you were called to freedom, brethren;
only do not turn your freedom into an opportunity for the flesh,
but through love serve one another.
Galatians 5:13

★ Assignments for Lesson 17 ★

American Voices   Read the excerpts from *Common Sense* by Thomas Paine (pages 38-42).

Read the Declaration of Independence (pages 43-46).

Read the poems by Phillis Wheatley (pages 34-35).

Bible   Work on memorizing the assigned portion of Leviticus 25:10.

Project   Work on your project.

Student Review   Optional: Answer the questions for Lesson 17.

Detail from Surrender of General Burgoyne, *John Trumbull (American, 1821)*

Lesson 18

The Revolutionary War

Great Britain was the most industrialized nation in the world. Its strong economy was growing in large part because of its overseas trade and its colonies, primarily the American colonies. The British navy ruled the waves; its army was experienced, used to winning, and in fact won several major battles during the Revolutionary War. At one time or other during the war, British forces controlled the cities of Boston, New York, Philadelphia, Charleston, and Savannah.

On the other hand, the population of the American colonies was a fraction of Britain's population. The colonies had no standing army, a tiny navy, colonial militias that received minimal training, and limited resources for conducting a war. The Continental Congress was not a strong central government, and many of the individual colonial governments were also weak. The new nation did not have a unified national currency. Many soldiers were paid only with the promise of receiving land grants after the war—if the colonies won.

Initial Actions

The Americans embarrassed the British at Lexington and Concord and inflicted severe losses on the Redcoats at Breed's Hill. Soon British forces withdrew completely from Boston. Following these initial events, only scattered military activity took place for a time. Colonial forces invaded Canada in the hope of bringing it into the conflict on their side, but the attempt stalled and came to nothing.

The two-part British strategy for defeating the Revolution called for (1) seizing the largest American cities and (2) dividing New England from the rest of the colonies. One place that accomplished both of these ends for the British was New York City. On July 2, 1776, a British force of 32,000 men began landing in New York harbor. George Washington led a force of about 19,000 Continental Army soldiers and militiamen to oppose them. Successful British advances forced Washington to withdraw from the area, and the American commander led his army to a position near Philadelphia. British forces controlled New York City for the rest of the war.

Until the American Revolution, European armies traditionally fought battles by having soldiers line up and advance toward the enemy while shooting and reloading. As troops were killed or wounded, the lines reformed and made another advance. This led to huge numbers of casualties. The American forces introduced a different way of fighting. They preferred making surprise attacks and firing from behind trees, rocks, and other cover. The British thought this was an unmanly way to fight, but it was an effective way to win battles.

Nathan Hale was a captain in the Continental Army who served as a spy behind British lines on Long Island, New York. He was captured by the British on September 21, 1776, and hanged the next day. His last words were, "I only regret that I have but one life to lose for my country."

The statue of Hale shown above is located at Yale University, which Hale had attended from age fourteen to eighteen, graduating in 1773. Flanking the statue are two Yale soldiers from World War I.

"The Crisis"

The outlook for the Americans in the latter half of 1776 was bleak. One of the volunteers in Washington's colonial army was the writer Thomas Paine. In late 1776 he composed a new pamphlet, "The Crisis," that was published in December of that year. The pamphlet encouraged Americans to stay the course and to believe in the justness of their cause.

General Washington appreciated Paine's pamphlet and ordered that it be read aloud to his discouraged troops. Soon the fortunes of the American forces improved. On Christmas night, 1776, Washington led his men across the icy Delaware River and made a surprise attack on 1,500 Hessians at Trenton who were not expecting any military activity that night. The attack was a decisive victory for the patriots. Washington's men then pushed back Redcoat regiments at Princeton, New Jersey, and made winter camp in northern New Jersey.

The next major engagements took place in the fall of 1777. British troops moved on Philadelphia and captured that city. Washington led his men from New Jersey to counterattack, but the Americans' efforts failed. The British controlled Philadelphia and enjoyed a comfortable winter in the city. Meanwhile, the Continentals set up camp in Valley Forge, just outside of Philadelphia, and endured the harsh winter of 1777-1778 with insufficient food and scant clothing. Washington feared that his army might starve or disband, so he requested immediate assistance from the Continental Congress, which had fled from Philadelphia before the advancing British forces.

Saratoga

Meanwhile, the turning point of the war occurred further north. British General John "Gentleman Johnny" Burgoyne led a force south from Canada with plans to invade the Hudson River valley and thus sever New England from the rest of the colonies. However, the British invasion bogged down in the dense New York woods. The mobile Americans launched several successful attacks and forced Burgoyne to surrender at Saratoga on October 17, 1777. It was a decisive and embarrassing defeat for the British.

The American victory at Saratoga was important for patriot morale and for international relations. News of the victory led the French government to recognize the United States as a sovereign nation and to enter the war on America's side. France had already provided a small amount of assistance; but the formal alliance brought more money, ammunition, and even some troops to the American cause. The French government enjoyed the opportunity to embarrass and potentially to defeat the British forces that had defeated them in the French and Indian War a few years earlier.

Action in the West

During 1778, Americans achieved several victories on the western frontier. British forces had made alliances with Indian tribes in an attempt to control the region west of the thirteen colonies. American frontiersman George Rogers Clark led successful surprise attacks on British positions at Kaskaskia (in present-day Illinois) and Vincennes (in what is now Indiana).

The next year, American General John Sullivan led a decisive attack on the Iroquois at what is now Elmira, New York. Daniel Boone held off several British-backed Indian attacks against American settlements in Kentucky. These victories dissolved any effectiveness of the British-Indian alliance in the West and enabled more rapid settlement of the region after the war.

Southern Battles

As the war worsened for the British, they concentrated greater efforts on the southern colonies. The British hoped that influential Southerners would feel loyalty to England and stem the tide of American success. The invading army also tried to play on racial divisions in the South by enlisting blacks into the king's forces.

The British took control of Charleston and Savannah, then moved inland to seize additional areas. A British force under General Lord Charles Cornwallis decisively defeated an American army at Camden, South Carolina. Then on October 7, 1780, at the battle of King's Mountain on the border of North and South Carolina, American forces defeated the British in what was the turning point of the war in the South. The British lost again at Cowpens in South Carolina in early 1781. In addition, the loyalist uprising in the South for which the British had hoped did not materialize.

Benedict Arnold

When Benedict Arnold accepted his commission as a major general in the Continental Army, he signed the oath of allegiance shown at right. He renounced his allegiance to King George III and committed himself to supporting the cause of the United States. Arnold served that cause with distinction and developed a close relationship with George Washington.

However, Arnold was prideful and undisciplined and received a reprimand from Washington. Needing money to support his extravagant lifestyle, Arnold initiated contact with the British and offered to help them in exchange for a large sum of money. In 1780 Arnold was commander of the American post at West Point, New York, north of New York City. He planned to turn the post over to the British, but his scheme was discovered. Arnold escaped to the British side and became a general in the royal army. The British officer who served as Arnold's contact, John Andre, was captured by the Americans and hanged as a spy.

In September 1779, American Commodore John Paul Jones led a small fleet to England where he approached a British ship, Serapis. *The British attacked Jones' fleet and demanded that he surrender, but Jones replied, "I have not yet begun to fight." His own ship sank, but Jones escaped to another vessel and captured the* Serapis. *This is considered one of the greatest naval victories in American history. The portrait of Jones above is by Charles Willson Peale (American, c. 1781).*

British Surrender

Cornwallis retreated to the Chesapeake Bay, hoping to gain control of that strategic area. To counter his move, Washington led his army south from New York, linked up with a new French force, and moved toward Cornwallis' position. Meanwhile, a French naval fleet sailed into position off the Virginia coast. Cornwallis knew that his army was trapped; and on October 19, 1781, he surrendered his army to Washington at Yorktown, Virginia. At the surrender, American Army musicians joyfully played "Yankee Doodle," while the British band mournfully played an English tune, "The World Turned Upside Down." The British government realized that further military efforts would be futile and in early 1782 agreed to negotiate a treaty of peace. America had defeated Britain.

The Outcome of the War

The Treaty of Paris, signed in 1783, formally ended the war that had begun in 1775. The Treaty of Paris opens with these words:

> In the name of the most holy and undivided Trinity. It having pleased the Divine Providence to dispose the hearts of the most serene and most potent Prince George the Third, by the grace of God, king of Great Britain, France, and Ireland, defender of the faith, duke of Brunswick and Lunebourg, arch-treasurer and prince elector of the Holy Roman Empire etc., and of the United States of America, to forget all past misunderstandings and differences that have unhappily interrupted the good correspondence and friendship which they mutually wish to restore. . . .

Great Britain recognized the existence of the United States of America as a new and separate nation. The Mississippi River was agreed upon as the nation's western border. The United States was interested in obtaining Canada; but Britain was determined to keep it, and the United States backed off and recognized British control of Canada. Britain wanted the return of loyalist property in the U.S. to British subjects and the settlement of American debts owed to British individuals, but the treaty made no guarantees about these issues.

France used its influence in the treaty negotiations to weaken England as much as possible. The French government hoped one day to regain territory in North America that it had lost to England as a result of the French and Indian War. Because of Spain's alliance with France on behalf of the United States, Spain eventually received Florida back from Britain. Spain also continued its control of the area of Louisiana which lay west of the Mississippi.

Factors in the Conflict

The American David defeated the British Goliath because of several factors. George Washington's leadership, especially his character and courage, inspired the Army and the nation. Washington defeated the British forces primarily by wearing them down over time instead of forcing confrontations which the Americans might well have lost. The American forces fought better than the British and had the advantage of fighting on their own soil. The developing consciousness of Americans as a separate people gave them a cause for which they were willing to fight. Assistance from France proved to be a major help to the American effort.

On the other hand, Britain's military suffered from poor leadership by its generals. In addition, fighting a war on several fronts far from home proved difficult. To maintain their supply lines, British forces had to stay close to the Atlantic coast. But perhaps the major failing of the British was in its overall political relationship with the colonies. When questions arose involving control of the colonies, the British answer was usually to crack down. This did not win much loyalty from the Americans. The British have used this approach many times in dealing with their colonies, in places such as India and Ireland. The American colonies simply decided not to put up with it any longer.

Several other nations supported the colonists to a greater or lesser degree. Spain began helping France in 1779, and the Netherlands allied itself with the United States in 1780. A Prussian, Baron von Steuben, helped train and discipline American troops at Valley Forge in the spring of 1778.

Thomas Paine

Following his significant influence during the American Revolution, Thomas Paine left the U.S. for Europe in 1787. He divided his time between Britain and France, mostly working on inventions. He supported the French Revolution of 1789, and his book The Rights of Man *(1791-1792) was an eloquent statement of the philosophical basis for the overthrow of the French monarchy. The portrait of Paine at right is by French artist Laurent Dabos (c. 1791).*

Paine hoped for such a revolution in Britain as well, and his stance made him an outcast in that country. In 1792 Paine became a French citizen and was elected to the French National Assembly, even though he could not speak French. However, he condemned the execution of Louis XVI. This and his alignment with one of the factions in the Revolution caused him to become suspect by another faction, and he was imprisoned in late 1793 for almost a year. During his imprisonment, he worked on his next significant book, The Age of Reason *(1794-1795). This book announced his rejection of Christianity and the church, his denial of the authority of Scripture, and his proposal for the adoption of Deism. This stance cost Paine much of what popularity he had left. Later, Paine criticized Napoleon for his dictatorial rule. President Thomas Jefferson invited Paine to return to the U.S., which he did in 1802. Paine died in 1809.*

The Continental Congress commissioned the Marquis de Lafayette of France as a major general at the age of twenty, and he served with distinction on Washington's staff. Lafayette participated in several military campaigns and also used his influence in France to encourage the French government to provide more assistance to the Americans. Casimir Pulaski of Poland fought with the Americans as a brigadier general. He was killed in a British attack on Savannah, Georgia, in October of 1779.

The American Revolution was a landmark event in the history of the world. It established the principles of individual freedom and government by the consent of the governed. It inspired revolutions in France a few years later, in Europe and South America in the first half of the 1800s, and in Africa in the twentieth century.

Key Dates in the American Revolution

Fighting began in 1775.

Independence was declared in 1776.

The British surrendered in 1781.

The Treaty of Paris was signed in 1783.

But I say to you, love your enemies
and pray for those who persecute you.
Matthew 5:44

★ Assignments for Lesson 18 ★

American Voices — Read the excerpts from "The Crisis" by Thomas Paine (pages 47-48).

English — Thomas Paine was an expert in the style of writing known as persuasive argument. Persuasive writing includes appealing to emotion, building a case by stating certain facts, presenting one's own side as just and right, and casting one's opponent as ignorant or evil.

Bible — Work on memorizing the assigned portion of Leviticus 25:10.

Project — Work on your project.

Student Review — Optional: Answer the questions for Lesson 18.

Construction Began on the Virginia Capitol Building in 1785

Lesson 19

Society and Government After the Revolution

Any war causes hardships for the people affected by it, whether the people are civilians or enlisted in the fighting forces. This is especially true for those who live where the fighting takes place.

Many Americans suffered greatly during the war that secured their independence. The British were merciless about destroying property in the cities and towns they occupied. Farms were ruined both from fighting and from troop movements. Thousands of families suffered hardships when husbands and sons left for the war, and many of those loved ones did not return.

The Revolutionary War was in some ways a civil war that created deep divisions in American communities and families. Many Americans found it difficult to decide whether to remain loyal to England or to become patriots. Most colonial government office-holders and Anglican clergy, some businessmen, and many small farmers remained loyal to England. During and after the war, about 100,000 British loyalists left the United States to live in Canada, Britain, or the West Indies. They took with them a great deal of money and individual talent that could have helped the new nation.

American government and society remained relatively stable through the war and in the years immediately following. This was true because, by the time of the Revolution, America had a strong tradition of self-government and local responsibility. People were used to governing themselves; so when the colonies became an independent nation, Americans largely continued the same forms of local and state governments they had known.

The individual states wrote new constitutions during the 1780s, since their previous governing documents had been written when they were colonies of England. Many of these new state constitutions were experiments in expanded rights for the people. They included bills of rights and broader voting rights. Before the Revolution, the vote was generally given to free white males who owned a certain amount of property. After the Revolution, property qualifications were lowered. Slaves and women, however, were still not allowed to vote.

The war caused serious economic disruption throughout the new nation. Because of the need to supply the Army and the interruption to the American economy caused by the war, prices for food and other items rose significantly. Some businessmen took undue advantage of the situation and made large profits when they sold supplies to the Continental Army. Some poor farmers and shopkeepers resented the hardships they faced while people in the upper class were faring much better. However, the war also brought about some positive changes in the American economy. New industries developed, especially those associated with war. The loss of trade with England spurred the development of new trading relationships with other countries.

The single most important factor in determining wealth and status in America was the ownership of land. The more land a person owned, the greater was his wealth and social status. Large landowners continued to exert considerable influence after the Revolution. However, America offered people a chance at upward mobility. Indentured servants, for instance, who were lowest on the social ladder except for slaves, became landowners after fulfilling their indenture requirements.

Although American society was strongly influenced by English society, it was not an exact reproduction of it. English royalty and nobility, an influential factor in the homeland, did not migrate to America. Landowners in England who could afford to migrate to the colonies became some of the wealthiest and most influential families in America. The Byrd, Randolph, Rolfe, and Mason families, for instance, were some of the earliest settlers in Virginia; and even today descendants of these families are leading figures in Virginia.

Tradesmen with needed skills were much in demand in the colonies. On the other hand, the colonies had fewer household servants than were found in England. Opportunities for owning land and building wealth were so much greater in the colonies than in England that relatively few people in America were willing to spend much time as other people's servants. This possibility for personal advancement was an important dynamic in American society and in the American economy

One major difference between English and American societies was the greater number of slaves in the colonies. Plantation owners in the southern colonies wanted a large supply of cheap labor, and slavery provided this for them. In 1750 slaves outnumbered whites in South Carolina 39,000 to 25,000. Southern whites often lived in great fear of slave uprisings, and colonial legislatures (later state governments) passed slave codes that restricted the movements and activities of slaves. African American slaves had an active and rich culture of their own, but it was largely ignored by whites. Despite all the high-sounding talk of personal freedom, government by the consent of the governed, and new opportunities in America, slaves were one group that did not enjoy opportunities for personal advancement.

Settlement of the West

The Revolution encouraged more rapid settlement of the lands west of the Appalachian Mountains, especially in the areas that would become Ohio, Tennessee, and Kentucky. Traders from the English colonies of Pennsylvania and Virginia entered Ohio sometime after 1730. The first English settler in what would become Tennessee arrived in 1769, and thousands followed over the next several years. Nashville (first called Nashborough) was settled during the war, in 1779-80. Daniel Boone oversaw the carving out of the Wilderness Road through the Cumberland Gap in 1775, and through it Boone led thousands of settlers into Kentucky.

African American slaves maintained and developed their own cultural traditions. The origin of this painting is uncertain, though it likely dates from the late 1700s.

Lesson 19 - Society and Government After the Revolution

The State of Franklin

The settlements just west of the Appalachian crest in the region controlled by North Carolina (the area that later became the eastern part of Tennessee) felt some insecurity about their status during the 1780s. North Carolina found it difficult to govern and protect the area, but it had not ceded the land to Congress. Land speculators were interested in developing the area, but figuring out who actually controlled land rights was difficult.

In 1784 a government formed in the area under the name of the State of Franklin. Neither Congress nor North Carolina recognized the new government, which proved to be ineffective and largely powerless. The State of Franklin fizzled out and disbanded in 1788. The building above, considered to be the "capitol" of the State of Franklin, survived until 1897, when it was disassembled and taken to Nashville for the Centennial celebration of the State of Tennessee.

The western region witnessed many conflicting land claims by the French, the English who controlled Canada, Native American tribes, and American settlers. The Northwest Ordinance passed by Congress in 1787 helped bring order to the area.

Articles of Confederation

The Continental Congress began as a meeting of representatives from the independent colonies to discuss what actions they might take against British policies. When fighting broke out, Congress began functioning as a central government even though it had little power. Americans were highly suspicious of a strong central government. This mistrust, after all, was why they were breaking away from Britain. While the Continental Congress was relatively weak, it did manage to hold the new nation together.

Work began on a governing document for the new nation soon after the Declaration of Independence was adopted. However, writing the Articles of Confederation for the new states took more than a year; and the process of having the Articles ratified by all thirteen states took even longer. One major point of contention was the handling of western lands. States such as Virginia, New York, and Connecticut, which had claims to trans-Appalachian lands, wanted to keep them so that they could get revenue from the sale of those lands. States with fixed borders, such as Maryland, Delaware, and New Jersey, wanted the territories to be given to the central government so that all the states could profit from land sales. States that had western land claims finally agreed to cede their lands to the national government, and the Articles of Confederation went into effect after Maryland ratified them in early 1781.

The Articles of Confederation provided the foundation for much of the phrasing and many of the provisions of the Constitution that came later. However, the Articles were different in significant ways. Each state was declared to be sovereign. Each state had one vote in Congress regardless of population. The Articles made no provision for either a national executive or a national judicial system. Congress could declare war but had no power to tax. Its revenues came from requests made to the states, and the states could ignore the requests if they wished. The colonies had been independent entities for their entire existence, and the new state governments were reluctant to cede significant powers to a national government.

This first attempt at national self-government by the United States under the Articles of Confederation was not a resounding success, as we will see in the next unit. However, it was an important step toward creating the system of government we now enjoy in the United States.

American artist Charles Willson Peale finished this self-portrait around 1785. In the portrait, he is painting a portrait of his wife Rachel. Their daughter Angelica stands behind him.

The rich and the poor have a common bond,
The Lord is the maker of them all.
Proverbs 22:2

★ Assignments for Lesson 19 ★

American Voices — Read the Articles of Confederation (pages 49-54).

Bible — Many people believe that the United States is God's new chosen people. Certainly God has richly blessed America, and we can see His guiding hand in our history. However, no one has ever received a revelation from God stating that He has made a covenant with the United States the way He did with Israel or the way He did for all believers through Christ. God made a covenant with Abraham and his descendants, the twelve tribes of Israel (Genesis 15:1-6 and 35:9-12). God offered a new covenant to everyone who puts their faith in Jesus (Hebrews 9:6-12). A better understanding of God's relationship with the United States is the realization that God has blessed and guided our country and that Christians have a stewardship from God to use well the blessings He has given us. We have a responsibility to take advantage of our freedom to live for Him and to communicate His word.

Work on memorizing the assigned portion of Leviticus 25:10.

Project — Work on your project.

Student Review — Optional: Answer the questions for Lesson 19.

PROCLAMATION.

IT being the indispensable duty of all Nations, not only to offer up their supplications to ALMIGHTY GOD, the giver of all good, for his gracious assistance in a time of distress, but also in a solemn and public manner to give him praise for his goodness in general, and especially for great and signal interpositions of his providence in their behalf: Therefore the United States in Congress assembled, taking into their consideration the many instances of divine goodness to these States, in the course of the important conflict in which they have been so long en-

From the Text of a Proclamation by the Continental Congress (1782)

Lesson 20 - Bible Study

God Is Sovereign

In 1776 representatives of thirteen British colonies in America declared that the colonies were now a separate nation, the United States of America. They declared their independence from Britain "with a firm reliance on the protection of Divine Providence" and on the basis of "self-evident truths" about man and government. After a protracted and costly war, Great Britain recognized the status of the United States as an independent nation. People usually give credit for the creation of the new nation to the courageous and intelligent leadership provided by the men who are often called the Founding Fathers. From the perspective of the Bible, however, the real credit for the establishment of the new nation and government belongs to God.

God is the ultimate and sovereign Power who guides history. Paul said that God "made from one man every nation of mankind to live on all the face of the earth, having determined their appointed times and the boundaries of their habitation" (Acts 17:26). Boundaries of habitation have changed as people have migrated to or invaded other countries. The appointed times for nations and kingdoms have come and gone as rulers and governments have risen and fallen throughout history. The Bible says that all of this is ultimately the work of God.

When Mary glorified the Lord on her visit to Elizabeth, she sang,

He has brought down rulers from their thrones,
And has exalted those who were humble.
He has filled the hungry with good things;
And sent away the rich empty-handed.
                                    Luke 1:52-53

Human history might record that one king or country defeated another, but faith sees what happened as the work of God. History books say that a military leader invaded another country to control it or to exact revenge for a wrong done to him. From God's perspective, however, such events took place to fulfill His divine purpose.

Bible Examples

Many times in the Old Testament, the writers of Scripture provide God's point of view regarding the military and political events being described. Here are a few examples:

When Rehoboam rejected the advice of his older counselors, the Northern Kingdom of Israel rebelled against him and against the dynasty of David's house. On the surface, it appeared to be a problem caused by the generation gap; but the inspired writer of Chronicles says that, "The king did not listen to the people, for it was a turn of events from God that the Lord might establish His word" (2 Chronicles 10:15).

Later, Shishak of Egypt attacked Israel "because they (Rehoboam and the nation of Judah) had been unfaithful to the Lord" (2 Chronicles 12:2). Shishak himself was probably not aware of this divine impetus behind his actions. No doubt he saw his actions as motivated by a desire for conquest and control. The perspective of faith, however, revealed what God was doing through Shishak.

Medieval Illustration of Nebuchadnezzar's Dream

After the Babylonians conquered Judah, God raised up the Persian leader Cyrus to punish the Babylonians. In Isaiah 44:28-45:1, the Lord called Cyrus His shepherd and His anointed. This passage gives God's perspective on what might otherwise be seen as merely political-military maneuvering.

King Nebuchadnezzar had a dream about a statue that was assembled from parts made of different materials. With God's help, Daniel interpreted the dream as a prediction of the rise and fall of successive empires in the Mediterranean and Middle Eastern world. Daniel said of God:

It is He who changes the times and the epochs;
He removes kings and establishes kings;
He gives wisdom to wise men
And knowledge to men of understanding.
Daniel 2:21

The rise and fall of kingdoms that were predicted through Nebuchadnezzar's dreams were the work of God, whether or not the people involved in those events recognized it as such.

Government Is from God

The Bible teaches that government itself is a work of God. Paul wrote that, "Every person is to be in subjection to the governing authorities. For there is no authority except from God, and those which exist are established by God" (Romans 13:1). God established governmental authority among men for our well-being. Sometimes leaders come to power who work against God, but even they are within His sovereign will.

Paul wrote Romans while he was under the political authority of the Roman emperor. Today, although someone might seize power in a country and rule as dictator, most governments in the world are formed by popular vote. Nevertheless, governmental authority is still from God. If God can create monarchies, He can create republics and

Jacob Duché was a professor and minister in Philadelphia. He served as the first chaplain of the Continental Congress from 1774 to 1776, and opened the first meeting of Congress with prayer, as depicted in this 19th-century illustration. As the war turned against the colonists in 1777, however, Duché wrote a letter to George Washington encouraging him to end the war. Duché hoped that Washington could obtain a negotiated peace with the British and that "millions will bless the hero that left the field of war, to decide this most important contest with the weapons of wisdom and humanity." Washington turned over the letter to Congress. The State of Pennsylvania charged Duché with treason, and he fled to England. He returned to Pennsylvania in 1792 and died there in 1798.

democracies. In His sovereignty, God guides, uses, and works through the actions and decisions of people to accomplish His will.

Seeing God's Hand in Current Events

We can see most clearly how the hand of God has worked in human events when inspired prophets or the inspired writers of Scripture tell us God's meaning for certain events, as in the Old Testament passages cited above. When it comes to post-Biblical and contemporary events, God's meaning is less clear because we do not have inspired interpreters explaining God's meaning to us. God's hand has been cited as being behind such events as floods and hurricanes, the defeat of Nazi Germany, the fall of Communism in Europe, and the election (or defeat) of certain political candidates.

We should interpret these and other events humbly and with the recognition that our fallible minds might be in error. At the same time we should resist the temptation in today's world to attribute these events only to weather patterns, military strategy, and political or economic forces. We must interpret both history and current events by the precedents and principles in Scripture and by believing that God is still in charge.

God is indeed in charge. We must realize that God either is in control of the world or He is not. He is in control even though some things happen which we do not like or understand. If everything that happened in the world had to meet with our approval and be within our understanding, we would be sovereign instead of God.

The psalmist said:

The Lord nullifies the counsel of the nations;
He frustrates the plans of the peoples.
The counsel of the Lord stands forever,
The plans of His heart
from generation to generation.
Psalm 33:10-11

As we study American history, we need to remember that God causes the rise and fall of nations and that "My times are in Your hand" (Psalm 31:15a). We should remember Biblical principles such as, "Righteousness exalts a nation, but sin is a disgrace to any people" (Proverbs 14:34). As we continue our study of American history, we will examine other Biblical principles that will help us see American history through eyes of faith.

Oh, the depth of the riches both of the wisdom and knowledge of God!
How unsearchable are His judgments and unfathomable His ways!
Romans 11:33

★ Assignments for Lesson 20 ★

Bible — Recite or write the assigned portion of Leviticus 25:10 from memory.

Project — Complete your project for the unit.

Student Review — Optional: Answer the questions for Lesson 20 and take the quiz for Unit 4.

First Page of the U.S. Constitution

5 The Constitution

The United States Constitution is a remarkable document that has served our nation well for over two hundred years with relatively few changes. Understanding the thinking of the framers helps us to see their vision for our country. We need to be familiar with the specific provisions of the Constitution so that we can understand the workings of our Federal system and guard against any erosion of our rights and freedoms. Living under the Constitution involves being able to interpret it correctly. Following the Bible as our spiritual constitution involves interpreting it correctly as well.

Lesson 21 - From Confederation to the Constitution
Lesson 22 - Basic Principles and the U.S. Congress
Lesson 23 - The Presidency, the Federal Judiciary, and Other Matters
Lesson 24 - Amendments to the Constitution
Lesson 25 - Bible Study: The Bible as Spiritual Constitution

Memory Work Memorize Philippians 2:14-15 by the end of this unit.

Books Used The Bible
American Voices

Project (choose one)

1) Write 300 to 500 words on one of the following topics:

- Write an essay on what you believe to be the main strengths of the U.S. Constitution and what you see as the main threats today to the original meaning of the Constitution.

- Write an essay on the importance of the Bill of Rights and how protecting the rights listed there is essential to maintaining freedom in the United States. See Lesson 24.

2) Create a painting that illustrates one of the amendments to the Constitution in practice today. See Lesson 24.

3) Create a collection of photos that represent each amendment in the Bill of Rights. Compose your photos intentionally and artistically. Your finished project should be in the form of a slideshow on an electronic device, prints of the photographs displayed on a poster, or photos in book form. Include at least one photo for each amendment (ten or more). See Lesson 24.

Opening of the Northwest Ordinance (1787)

Lesson 21

From Confederation to the Constitution

The United States had won the war, but the question remained whether they could win the peace. Several major problems confronted the new nation.

Issues Facing the New Nation

Congress had raised money to finance the war in four ways: issuing bonds (by which individuals loaned money to the government with the promise of later receiving their investment back plus interest), making requests to the states for money (which the states did not always fulfill), arranging loans from foreign countries and banks, and printing paper money. The Continental dollars printed by Congress were not worth much because the government did not have much gold to back them. This led to the expression that described something of little value as being "not worth a Continental." Because of the expenses associated with fighting the war, the new American government carried a large debt. Dealing with this debt became one of the first major issues that the young nation had to address.

A second cause for concern were the economic crises within individual states. These fiscal problems arose from a shortage of hard money and from price inflation caused by uncertainties, profiteering, and a scarcity of goods. Prices increased on many items that citizens wanted and needed. The crisis in Massachusetts resulted in a literal showdown. In 1786 struggling farmers in western Massachusetts, led by Daniel Shays, rebelled against what they felt was unfair treatment by creditors to whom they owed money. They marched on the state capital and demanded relief from the state legislature. Shays' Rebellion was dispersed by the state militia, but it was a signal that people were struggling financially and wanted help. Many feared that similar unrest could arise in other states as well.

The threat of Indian attacks on the frontier was a third issue, especially for many westerners. Settlers wanted protection against such attacks, but with no standing army Congress could not provide such protection on a reliable basis. The individual states were also inconsistent in the protection they provided. Americans believed that the issue of frontier security was real because the colonies had seen occasional violent uprisings on the frontier.

In 1763 a group called the Paxton Boys in Pennsylvania had attacked an Indian settlement and then had marched on the colonial capital demanding more protection from the Indians. Pennsylvania colonial leaders persuaded the Paxton Boys to disband. Then in 1771, a similar group in western North Carolina called the Regulators fought with colonial troops over the issue of security from Indian attacks. The uprising was quelled when Regulator leaders were captured and executed.

Fourth, the young nation faced difficulties in foreign relations. Without a strong central government, the United States could not respond quickly or decisively to a problem with another country. For instance, settlers west of the Appalachians wanted to be able to sell their goods and farm products in the markets of New Orleans. However, Congress could not guarantee that Spain, which controlled New Orleans and the west bank of the Mississippi River, would allow them to do so.

This led to frustration in the West and to an uneasy relationship with Spain. Some Americans wanted to fight Spain, while others wanted to build a more friendly alliance with Spain that would enable trade. America's trading relationships with other countries were also shaky as the new country competed with much wealthier and more experienced British, French, and Dutch traders on the world market.

The states of Ohio, Indiana, Illinois, Michigan, and Wisconsin were formed out of the Northwest Territory. A portion was also attached to Minnesota.

The national government was not strong enough to deal with these issues effectively, so they remained sources of unresolved frustration for several years.

The Northwest Ordinance

The most significant accomplishment of the government during the period between the end of the war and the ratification of the Constitution was the enactment of the Northwest Ordinance in 1787. The Northwest Territory was part of the land that the United States received in the Treaty of Paris that ended the Revolutionary War. The region was bounded by Pennsylvania and the Ohio River on the east, the Great Lakes on the north, the Ohio River on the South, and the Mississippi River on the West. The ordinance dealt with how the region was to be governed, how it was to be divided and organized into territories, and how the territories could become states. The law set precedents for how the country handled other territorial acquisitions in the future.

The ordinance said that when the population of a territory reached five thousand free males, a two-house legislature could be organized. When the number of people reached sixty thousand residents, a territory could apply for statehood and become part of the Union on an equal footing with the original thirteen states. This meant that the new lands would not be permanent territories, something the colonies had endured under English rule. The ordinance provided for religious freedom and for many legal rights for individuals. It required that Indian tribes be treated fairly. The law encouraged the creation of public schools because, as the law put it, "religion, morality, and knowledge [were] necessary to good government and the happiness of mankind." This implied that Congress expected religion and morality to be taught in the public schools. Slavery was outlawed in the Northwest Territory, but runaway slaves who were found there had to be returned to their owners. Five states—the maximum number of states that could be formed according to

Lesson 21 - From Confederation to the Constitution

the Ordinance—were eventually created from the Northwest Territory.

A law passed by Congress in 1785 provided for the territory to be divided into townships of 36 square miles each. A one-square-mile area (640 acres) was called a section. Four sections in each township were reserved for land grants to be given to Revolutionary War soldiers. Money from the sale of land in one other section in each township was dedicated to establishing schools in that township. The remaining land was sold at a minimum of one dollar per acre, with the minimum purchase being 640 acres or one entire section. This arrangement favored those who had enough money to invest in large land speculations. Those who bought land from the government could make a profit by selling smaller parcels to individual settlers at a higher price per acre. The Northwest Ordinance encouraged settlement in the region and provided much needed revenue to the national government.

A Call to Change the Articles of Confederation

During the 1780s, several state legislatures proposed making changes to the Articles of Confederation. A similar proposal came from a meeting of representatives of five states in Annapolis, Maryland, in 1786, which had been organized to discuss problems dealing with sea trade and other questions regarding interstate commerce. The Annapolis Convention went on record favoring revisions to the Articles. Shays' Rebellion took place in Massachusetts about the same time, which caused a number of people to fear the long-term consequences of continuing under the current system.

Later in 1786, Congress agreed that revisions were needed and called for a special convention to deal with the matter. Some state and national leaders simply wanted revisions to the Articles, but others saw the need and the opportunity for a completely new approach to governing the country.

This contemporary woodcut depicts Daniel Shays and Job Shattuck, who were recognized as leaders of the unrest in Massachusetts known as Shays' Rebellion.

The Constitutional Convention

The Constitutional Convention got underway in Philadelphia in May of 1787. Fifty-five delegates from twelve states met over the course of the summer (leaders in the state of Rhode Island were suspicious of the convention's purpose and refused to participate). Most of the delegates were well-educated, financially successful men in their thirties and forties. They were generally younger than those who had led the fight for independence that had begun over a decade earlier.

George Washington was selected to be chairman of the convention, but he took only a small role in the deliberations. The leading figure in the convention was young James Madison of Virginia. Just over five feet tall, Madison came with strong ideas about what direction the convention should take. Thomas Jefferson was serving as ambassador to France and John Adams was the country's envoy to Great Britain, so neither participated in the proceedings.

A majority of the delegates quickly decided to go beyond a mere revision of the Articles of Confederation and to create a new governing document. They also decided to keep their meetings secret, lest rumors get out and cause unrest. This meant that they met during the hot Philadelphia summer with the windows tightly closed!

The delegates wanted to create a national government that was strong enough to act decisively for the nation as a whole but that also recognized the rights of the states and of individuals. They wanted a government that would be effective but whose powers were limited or held in check by balancing the authority of the legislative, executive, and judicial branches of the government. Maintaining these delicate balances was a challenging task.

The Great Compromise

The biggest single issue that the Convention faced concerned how representation would be determined in the national legislature. The Virginia Plan, drafted by James Madison and presented by Edmund Randolph, both of Virginia, proposed that both houses be chosen by population. The smaller, less populous states objected to this plan, fearing that they would have little voice in the new government.

They had been used to having equal power with the larger states under the Articles of Confederation, which gave each state one vote.

In the agreement which has come to be known as the Great Compromise, the delegates to the convention called for the House of Representatives to be chosen by population, with each state having at least one Representative and each member representing about 30,000 people, while the Senate was to consist of two members from each state who were to be chosen by the state legislature. In this way both the large and the small states got something out of the arrangement.

Selecting the President

Another compromise involved the selection of the chief executive or President. The Virginia Plan proposed that he be appointed by Congress; but some delegates objected to this, fearing that he would simply be a puppet of the legislative branch. Others suggested that he be elected by direct popular vote, but this brought out fears of giving too much power to the people.

The compromise that was reached called for the creation of what came to be called the electoral college, in which a small group of electors in each state would vote for candidates for President. Electors

Since the delegates to the Convention agreed to work in secret, no record was kept of the proceedings except shorthand notes by James Madison, who transcribed his notes in the evenings. Except for scattered comments by some of the delegates in letters and other writings, Madison's notes are our only record of what happened in the Convention. To promote unity in the new nation and to protect the reputations of the participants, Madison prevented the publication of his notes until the death of the last delegate. This turned out to be Madison himself in 1836. The portrait at left by Charles Willson Peale shows Madison at age 32, four years before the Constitutional Convention.

Scene at the Signing of the Constitution of the United States, *Howard Chandler Christy (American, 1940)*

were to be chosen as the individual state legislatures saw fit. In many states at first, electors were chosen by the state legislatures instead of by popular vote. Most delegates to the Constitutional Convention believed that the electoral college would not usually give a majority to any one candidate. The Constitution provided for the House of Representatives to decide among the five leading candidates, with each state having one vote.

The Slavery Compromises

Even at this early stage in the nation's history, slavery was a delicate issue. Northern states had outlawed slavery by the end of the Revolution, while southern states continued and defended the practice. The division over slavery led to another series of compromises. The first involved whether and how slaves were to be counted as population. Northern states wanted slaves to be counted as population when Congress imposed on the states direct Federal taxes that were based on state population. This would mean that southern states would carry a relatively greater share of the tax burden than if slaves were not counted as part of the population. Southern states did not like this idea, but they did want the slaves counted when representation in the House of Representatives was determined. The compromise that was reached called for three-fifths of the slaves to be counted as population both for taxation and for representation. Since slaves were not allowed to vote, this meant that the votes of southern whites had relatively greater weight in selecting members of the House than did the votes of northerners.

Another issue concerned the importation of slaves. Some delegates wanted to forbid importing slaves altogether, while the South feared that such a ban would harm their economy. As a compromise, the delegates agreed to continue the slave trade until 1808, when it could then be abolished. To appease the South, the words slaves and slavery were not used in the Constitution.

Ratifying the Constitution

Of the fifty-five delegates who participated in the convention, thirty-nine signed the finished document. A few refused to sign because they believed it gave too much power to the central government or because they saw the lack of a bill of rights as a threat to individual freedom.

The Constitution was submitted for approval not to the state legislatures but to state conventions, which were to be chosen specifically for the purpose of voting on the Constitution. This was done for two reasons. First, convention delegates feared that state legislators might oppose the Constitution if they saw it as a threat to their own power. Second, the delegates wanted the new government to be a product of the people and not the state legislatures.

These slave quarters on Fort George Island, Florida, were built before the Civil War. This photograph was taken around 1900.

The Constitution said that it would go into effect when nine states ratified it, not all thirteen. Convention delegates did not want the new government to be held hostage by one or two states as the Articles of Confederation had been.

Opinion on the proposed Constitution divided into two groups. Those who came to be called Federalists supported the Constitution and believed that it would make the nation stronger and the national government more effective. The group that came to be known as Antifederalists feared the power of the central government and the loss of individual freedoms. The Federalists were more organized and did a better job of influencing voters and state convention delegates. Alexander Hamilton, James Madison, and John Jay wrote a series of anonymous newspaper articles favoring ratification, all signed Publius (which means the Public Man), that were published in New York and reprinted in other states. These articles were later collected and published in book form as *The Federalist* or *The Federalist Papers*. Antifederalists were not as well-organized in their opposition to the proposed Constitution, although a few well-known figures such as Patrick Henry opposed ratification. Federalists assured doubters that a bill of rights would be enacted quickly once the Constitution was ratified and the new national government was formed. Federalists also pointed out that state constitutions already contained such listings of individual rights.

Delaware was the first state to ratify the Constitution. The ninth and deciding state, New Hampshire, approved it in June of 1788. The key states of Virginia and New York, whose support was seen as crucial for the new government to work, ratified in late June and late July, respectively. North Carolina did not approve the Constitution until late in 1789 after the Bill of Rights had been proposed and was being voted on by the states. Rhode Island did not ratify the Constitution until 1790. The Constitution was not defeated in any state, although

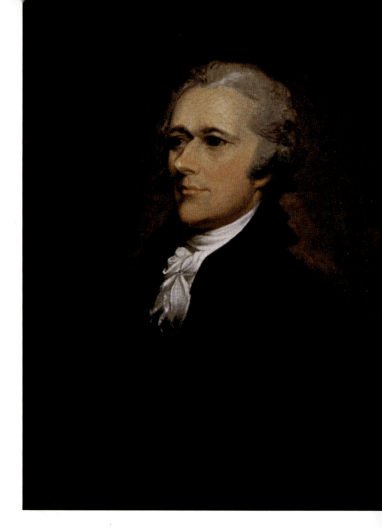

Based on examination of the writing styles of the Federalist Papers, Alexander Hamilton is thought to have written the majority of them. This 1806 portrait of Hamilton is by John Trumbull.

the vote was extremely close in some states (187 to 168 in Massachusetts, which attached a strong recommendation for a bill of rights, and 30 to 27 in New York).

The new nation now had a new government, crafted by some of the brightest men of the day. The Federal system created by the Constitution addressed current concerns and, it was hoped, would enable the new nation to meet the unknown demands of the future. The framers of the Constitution left some issues unresolved in the document, trusting (or hoping) that the new national government would find a way to deal with them. The success of the new government was not assured, but at least something had been done to address the problems that faced the country.

Lesson 21 - From Confederation to the Constitution

*Without consultation, plans are frustrated,
But with many counselors they succeed.
Proverbs 15:22*

★ Assignments for Lesson 21 ★

American Voices Read "The Federalist Number 10" by James Madison (pages 72-76). This is probably the best known of the Federalist series and deals with the question of the dangers of factions or political parties that might arise under the proposed Constitution.

Memorize the Preamble to the Constitution (page 57).

Bible Psalm 119, besides being the longest psalm, is a celebration of God's Word. As you read the psalm this week, answer the following questions. Read verses 1-48 today and answer these questions:

- How can a person keep his way blameless (verse 1)?
- How can a young person keep his way pure (verse 9)?
- Why has the psalmist treasured God's Word in his heart (verse 11)?
- How does the psalmist feel about studying and learning the Word (verses 14, 24, 47)?
- Where does the psalmist find the answers that he gives to others (verse 42)?

Start memorizing Philippians 2:14-15.

Project Choose your project for this unit and start working on it.

Student Review Optional: Answer the questions for Lesson 21.

U.S. Capitol, Home of the House and Senate

Lesson 22

Basic Principles and the U.S. Congress

This lesson and the two following are devoted to reading and gaining a greater understanding of a remarkable document: the Constitution of the United States of America. We will consider the original document as well as the amendments that have been added in later years. Each section will instruct you which part of the Constitution to read before you read the discussion in that section.

Ideas Behind the Constitution

Several overall principles were evident in the Constitution that was submitted to the states in September of 1787 and eventually ratified. First, the document was a careful series of balances and compromises that shared power among the three branches of the national government and that shared power between the national government and state governments. The delegates tried to address the needs and fears of the states and the needs and concerns for an effective central government. This balance of power between the states and the national government came to be called federalism.

Second, the framers expected the new government to be driven by Congress. The powers of the legislative branch were enumerated first, and Congress was given significant ability to limit the power of the other two branches. The delegates were fearful of a strong executive and saw careful legislative deliberation as the key factor in protecting effective government and individual liberty.

Third, the framers feared democracy. Only one house of Congress was to be selected by popular vote. Senators were to be chosen by state legislatures, a process which was one step removed from the people. The delegates expected Senators to be educated, refined leaders from the various states. The President was not to be chosen by popular vote either. Many delegates did not trust the judgment of the populace in general. They feared that the uneducated masses would act in ignorance and could be swayed by emotionally powerful but unwise arguments. The right to vote was governed by the individual states; but no state allowed all adult males to vote, let alone women and slaves. Each state had property ownership requirements of some kind for men to be able to vote, although states gradually eliminated these requirements over the next few years.

Nevertheless, in the Preamble, the Constitution is presented as the work of the people, not the states. The document was intended to create a more perfect union than the one which had existed under the Articles of Confederation.

Lesson 22 - Basic Principles and the U.S. Congress

Limited Government

The framers of the Constitution tried to create a government with limited powers. They feared rulers with unlimited authority because they had suffered under such rule before the Revolution. To them, government was to have only a limited role in people's lives. They expected government to protect the people and to encourage the fullest exercise of the people's rights and abilities, but not to run their lives. The framers wanted a government of laws, not of men. In other words, the paramount legal authority was to be a clearly stated and legitimately ratified legal document, not simply the whim of whoever had power at a given time.

This goal of limited government is reflected in three aspects of the Constitution. First, the Federal government was to exercise only delegated or enumerated powers. The Federal government was not to do whatever the leaders of government wanted to do at any given time. Instead, the Federal government was only supposed to carry out the powers listed or enumerated in the Constitution (to raise and support an army, to coin money, to regulate commerce with foreign countries and among the states, to establish post offices, and so forth). The 10th Amendment says that all powers not specifically given to the national government by the Constitution, and all powers not specifically denied to the states by the Constitution, are reserved to the states and to the people. The principle of limited government was generally followed until the New Deal in the 1930s, when Federal programs multiplied rapidly to meet needs during the Great Depression.

A second aspect of the Constitution that limits the power of the Federal government is the separation of powers. The French philosopher Baron de Montesquieu stated in 1748 that the functions of government can and should be divided into three branches: executive, legislative, and judicial. His writings influenced James Madison and other American political leaders. The framers created a national government that is made up of these three branches. Such a decision was not automatic. The Articles of Confederation, for instance, did not have either an executive or a judicial branch. Some examples will illustrate this separation. Congress passes the budget for the Federal government and has the power to declare war; the President does not have these powers. Congress does not declare whether someone is guilty or innocent of breaking Federal law; Federal courts have this responsibility. The Federal judiciary does not formulate treaties with other nations (a responsibility of the executive branch), nor does it have the power to coin money (something Congress is to do). The separation of powers is intended to prevent the President, members of Congress, and Federal judges from assuming powers that they have not been given and thereby creating a power struggle within the government.

Montesquieu (French artist, c. 1728)

Legal Terms in Article I

Writ of Habeas Corpus. *This phrase is Latin for "You have the body." A writ of habeas corpus is a legal document that orders government officials to tell a judge why a person is being held in jail (that is, why the government has custody of the suspect's body). A person is not to be arrested without a good reason and without his knowing that reason. Kings had often arrested their political enemies for no reason other than to silence the opposition.*

Bill of Attainder. *This is a law that takes away rights when someone is convicted of treason. A conviction for betraying one's country does not mean that the traitor loses all rights.*

Ex post facto law. *This is a Latin phrase meaning "from after the fact." Congress cannot pass a law that makes illegal some action that has already taken place.*

Letters of marque and reprisal. *These government decrees give permission to an individual to seize a vessel of another country as revenge or because of suspicion of wrongdoing. The letter of marque at right was issued to a Frenchman in 1809 by the government of Genoa, then controlled by France.*

Third, the Constitution creates a system of checks and balances that limits even the powers delegated to the branches of the Federal government. The various branches of government balance and keep in check the other branches of government. For instance, Congress declares war; but the President is the commander of the military. Congress passes laws, but the President can veto them—but then Congress can override the veto. The Supreme Court decides whether a law is in keeping with the Constitution and is therefore legitimate, but the members of the Court are appointed by the President and must be approved by the Senate. Federal judges are appointed for life, but they can be impeached and removed from office by Congress. The purpose of these checks and balances is to keep one person or one branch of government from assuming dictatorial powers. Occasionally it might seem that these checks and balances prevent the Federal government from doing anything, and that is precisely what the checks and balances are supposed to do: to keep the government from taking unwise or unwarranted action.

Article I: Congress

Read Article I of the Constitution (*American Voices*, pages 57-60).

The legislative branch of the Federal government, Congress, is given first priority. Ours is a government of the people and their duly elected representatives, not of a single leader or of a small group of leaders. Congress is made up of two bodies, the Senate and the House of Representatives. The Constitution gives the qualifications for those wanting to serve in each body. The House was intended to reflect the will of the people more closely, while the Senate was intended to be the more careful, deliberative, and prestigious chamber. Each body decides how it will be organized and how it will conduct its business. Each body is to keep an official journal of its proceedings. The combined journals of the House and Senate are called the *Congressional Record*.

The House of Representatives. All House seats are up for election every two years (Federal elections take place in even-numbered years). This was intended

Lesson 22 - Basic Principles and the U.S. Congress

to let voters change Representatives soon if desired. In actual practice, the vast majority of incumbent Congressmen are re-elected when they choose to run. Relatively little change takes place as a result of most House elections because state legislatures, which draw the congressional districts, try to protect congressional seats for one or the other of the two main political parties, Republicans or Democrats. Congress numbers itself by these House elections. Representatives and Senators elected in 1788-89 made up the First Congress, those elected in 1790-91 were the Second Congress, the election of 1986 gave us the 100th Congress, and so forth.

The Constitution calls for a census to be taken every ten years. A Federal census first took place in 1790 and has been carried out every ten years since. The original purpose of the census was to determine the number of Representatives each state would have in the House. The Constitution set out the number of Representatives from each state for the first Congress. Each state was to have at least one Congressman or Representative, and the total number of Representatives was not to exceed one for every thirty thousand people. The House continued to increase its membership until 1912, when it had 435 members. In 1929 the House decided always to have 435 members and to apportion those seats among the states according to population. Now House members represent an average of about 687,000 people each. If this rule had not changed, the House would now have about 10,000 members!

The House is given two specific responsibilities. All bills that propose the raising of revenue are to originate in the House. Also, the House is to initiate the process of impeachment against Federal officials. Impeachment means accusation. The House may bring impeachment charges (accusations) against the President and other Federal officers, while the Senate holds the impeachment trial to determine guilt or innocence. The Senate has conducted two impeachment trials against Presidents and several more against Federal judges.

The Senate. The Senate is considered the more prestigious house of Congress, since it has fewer members and its members serve longer terms. Each state elects two Senators. Senators were originally chosen by state legislatures as a safeguard against democracy. This was changed by the 17th Amendment, ratified in 1913, which provided for the popular election of Senators. This change was an attempt to put more power into the hands of the people.

The Senate is divided into three classes. By this provision, one third of the Senate is chosen every two years. Electing only one-third of the body every two years enables significant continuity of membership. When a Senate seat becomes vacant, in most states the governor appoints someone to fill the seat until the next Federal election. In that election, someone is chosen to serve out the remainder of the term until the time that the election is held for the full six-year term.

The Vice President is the presiding officer, or President, of the Senate. This is the only duty in the Constitution for the Vice President besides assuming the presidency if it becomes vacant. In practical terms, the Vice President rarely presides over the Senate except when his vote is needed to break a tie or in other exceptional circumstances.

The United States Congress met in this building in Philadelphia from 1790-1800. After Congress moved to Washington, D.C., the building was used at times as a Federal courthouse.

A View of the Capitol of Washington
William Russell Birch (American, c. 1800)

The Senate has the responsibility of ratifying treaties that the President makes with other countries and also of approving the nominations made by the President to fill many Federal positions, including Cabinet posts and Federal judgeships. The Senate serves as the jury in an impeachment trial, determining the accused person's guilt or innocence.

How a Bill Becomes Law

Any member of the House or Senate may introduce a bill for consideration in his or her chamber. Thousands of bills are proposed in each session of Congress. Each house of Congress has formed several committees of its members that specialize in specific areas, such as the environment, defense, immigration, and so forth. When a bill is introduced in either house, it is assigned to a committee based on the subject of the bill. A committee chairman has significant power in deciding which bills receive consideration. The vast majority of bills that are introduced are assigned to a committee and never heard from again.

The committee discusses a bill and holds hearings in which people give testimony on it. If the committee recommends its passage, it then goes to the floor of that chamber. The House Speaker and the Senate Majority Leader (each chosen by the political party holding the majority in that house of Congress) determine which bills get considered by the full chambers. If a bill passes one house, it goes to the other house where it follows the same procedure (assigned to a committee, voted on by the committee, if approved there considered and voted on by the full chamber). A bill only needs a simple majority of members voting to pass. If a bill passes both houses in exactly the same form, it then goes to the President. If a bill has been changed by amendments in either house, a conference committee is created consisting of members of both houses to craft a single version. The conference bill is then considered by both houses and voted on again.

If the President signs the bill, it becomes law. The President may also choose to veto it and send it back to Congress. If both houses pass it again

Margaret Chase Smith of Maine was the first woman elected to serve in both the U.S. House (1940-1949) and the U.S. Senate (1949-1973).

Lesson 22 - Basic Principles and the U.S. Congress

The Constitution in Practice

The Constitution called for Federal revenue raised within the United States to come from taxes that Congress placed on the states. It was up to the states to determine how they would pay those direct Federal taxes. The Federal income tax, which now accounts for about half of all Federal revenue, did not begin until after the passage of the 16th Amendment in 1913.

The census now provides much information about the character of the American people: age, income, ethnic makeup, kinds of housing, employment, rural and urban living patterns, and much other data. With the increase in Federal programs in recent years, Congress also uses the census to help determine how Federal money will be distributed to the states.

States originally set their own election days, and these days varied greatly. Election days in the various states ranged from the fall of one year into the spring of the next. Congress began its session in December. Now, all Federal elections are held on the first Tuesday that follows a Monday in November (thus, election day can vary between November 2 and 8). Congress then convenes on January 3 following. A 2008 polling place in San Jose, California, is shown at right.

When a House seat becomes empty during a term, the governor of that state calls a special election to fill it. This is usually done fairly quickly, often within sixty days of the seat becoming vacant. The seat is then contested again at the next regular election.

A Representative or Senator may not be arrested while on the floor of Congress or while going to or from Congress. They may say anything they want to, do anything they want to, and drive as fast as they want to going or returning. This provision encourages freedom of debate and prevents, for instance, the President arresting members of Congress to keep them from voting against his wishes on certain legislation.

by a two-thirds majority, it becomes law over the President's veto. If both houses do not pass it with a two-thirds majority, the bill dies. If the President does not want to sign it but does not veto it either, the bill becomes law anyway after ten days, provided that Congress is still in session. This is called a pocket veto, which indicates the President's disapproval but also shows that he knows the bill will become law without his signature.

The Powers of Congress

Section 8 of Article I enumerates the powers that Congress has the authority to carry out. A major function of Congress has become the passage of the annual budget for the Federal government. Because of the size and number of Federal programs, this budget reflects commitments that the Federal government has made to fund certain projects. Most of the funding is for departments, agencies, and other offices overseen by the President in the executive branch. The last clause of Section 8, the "necessary and proper" clause, has been called the elastic clause because it has been stretched to be the basis for Congress passing laws on all kinds of subjects not specifically enumerated in the Constitution.

Sections 9 and 10 of Article I list limitations on the powers of the Federal and state governments.

The United States Congress has seen noble leaders and laughable buffoons, people of character and people who were scoundrels. It has seen many devoted public servants and not a few who were primarily interested in furthering their personal ambitions. All this is true in no small part because the members of Congress represent us, the American people. We send them there, and for the most part we re-elect them. Despite all of its failings, Congress has helped the U.S. become the most powerful and respected nation in the world. What the Founding Fathers created in the Constitution has been a model for many other countries around the world.

The righteous is concerned for the rights of the poor, the wicked does not understand such concern.
Proverbs 29:7

★ Assignments for Lesson 22 ★

Bible Read Psalm 119:49-88. How valuable is the Word to the psalmist (verse 72)?

Work on memorizing Philippians 2:14-15.

Project Work on your project.

Student Review Optional: Answer the questions for Lesson 22.

Former Federal Post Office and Courthouse, Hilo, Hawaii

Lesson 23

The Presidency, the Federal Judiciary, and Other Matters

The leaders of the founding generation had a fear of too much power resting in the hands of one person. They had experienced the problems of being subject to a king, and the philosophers of the Enlightenment warned against authority being exercised by one person or a few. Following the Revolution, the United States tried for several years to have only one branch of the Federal government—a Congress—but it did not work well. What would be the role, the responsibilities, and the risks of a single person at the head of the central government? The framers knew that having no executive would not work, but how could they craft an office that would give that person enough power to do what needed to be done yet not so much power that individual rights and liberties would be threatened?

The office they devised has changed over the years as the needs of the nation have changed and as different men have held the office and shaped it according to their individual understanding of it and their vision for it. Presidents have had to carry responsibilities that the founders could not have imagined, and they have made decisions that have affected the lives of millions of people around the world. The President of the United States has become the leader of the free world, a champion of great causes, and a person in a unique situation to make a tremendous difference in the country and the world.

Electing the President

Read Articles II, III, IV, VI, and VII of the Constitution (*American Voices*, pages 60-64).

The President and Vice President are elected to serve for a term of four years. The 22nd Amendment limits a person to being elected to the presidency no more than twice. Federal elections which involve choosing a President attract much more interest than those which do not. Congressional elections that occur midway during a President's term are called mid-term elections.

Officially, the people do not elect the President. Voters actually choose electors who then vote for President. Each state has a number of electors equal to the number of its Congressmen plus its two Senators. Originally, each elector cast two votes. When the votes were counted, the person with the most votes became President and the person with the second highest total became Vice President. If no one had a majority, the House voted on the top five candidates with each state having one vote.

Unit 5 - The Constitution

Duties of the President

The nation's chief executive is the commander of all of the country's military forces. He also oversees the operation of the executive branch of government, which now involves millions of workers in the Federal bureaucracy. The President conducts relations with other countries, negotiates treaties (to be confirmed by the Senate), and receives official representatives of other countries. He nominates persons to serve in thousands of positions in the executive branch and to hold dozens of judgeships in the Federal judiciary system. The Senate must confirm the appointments of the persons whom the President nominates.

The President is also required to inform Congress from time to time on the state of the union. This is the basis for the President's annual State of the Union message, which is given each year in January. The speech has mostly become self-praise for the President's administration and his recommendations for new legislation. The President has the responsibility to see that the Constitution is obeyed and that all Federal laws are enforced.

It has become customary for a President to propose legislation that he would like to see enacted by Congress (such proposals have to be drawn up as bills and introduced in the House or Senate by members of those bodies). The President claims to have a national mandate for his ideas because of his being elected by a national vote, whereas members of Congress are only elected from states or congressional districts within states. Political party allegiances have become important in determining what proposals become law. When the President and the majority in both houses of Congress are of the same party and agree on priorities, legislation reflecting those priorities is more easily passed. When the President is of a different political party from the majority in one or both chambers of Congress, political stalemate often occurs.

About thirty people have served in all three branches of the Federal government, as an elected or appointed executive official, as a member of Congress, and as a Federal judge. One of these was Lewis B. Schwellenbach (1894-1948). He was a U.S. Senator from Washington state (1935-1940), a Federal judge in Washington (1940-1945), and Secretary of Labor (1945-1948).

This process was changed after the 1800 election. The 12th Amendment called for electors to vote separately for President and for Vice President. If no candidate has a majority, the House selects from the top three candidates, again with each state having one vote. Only rarely has the election been decided by the House or has any serious problem arisen about the decision of the electoral college.

Voters now select 538 presidential electors, one for each of the 435 Representatives and 100 Senators plus three for the District of Columbia (provided for by the 23rd Amendment).

Lesson 23 - The Presidency, the Federal Judiciary, and Other Matters

Section 4 of Article II spells out the basis for impeachment and removal of the President and other Federal officials. Impeachment is to be for treason, bribery, or other high crimes and misdemeanors. Much debate has centered on what the phrase "high crimes and misdemeanors" means. The general understanding that has developed about this phrase is that it refers to wrongdoing which threatens the stability of the government and the nation, as treason and bribery would do.

The Federal Court System

The Constitution created the Supreme Court; and Congress created the Federal district courts, courts of appeal, and other specialized courts, such as those hearing cases having to do with issues of trade and navigation. Federal courts hear cases involving Federal laws and other matters outlined in Section 2 of Article III. Cases arising under state laws are heard in state courts.

Congress allowed for verdicts rendered in Federal district courts to be appealed to Federal circuit courts of appeal. An appeals court does not retry the case. Instead, it reviews whether the procedure used in the trial met constitutional standards of a fair trial or whether the law under which the person was convicted violates the Constitution. A few cases that are heard in appeals courts are reviewed again by the U.S. Supreme Court.

President Ronald Reagan's first nominee to the Supreme Court was Sandra Day O'Connor. She became the first female Justice appointed to the Court.

The Supreme Court of the United States did not have its own separate building until 1935. It met in this room of the U.S. Capitol, now known as the Old Supreme Court Chamber, from 1819 to 1860.

The Constitution does not specifically give any court the power of judicial review, by which a court declares a law to be constitutional or unconstitutional. This power was discussed to some degree in the Constitutional Convention and in the ratification process. The actual practice and power of judicial review by the Supreme Court was firmly established later by Chief Justice John Marshall. We will discuss this more in Lesson 32.

Article III also defines treason as making war against the United States or adhering to and giving aid and comfort to an enemy of the United States. Actual court decisions have further defined treason as taking definite action against the United States, not just talking about it or criticizing the

Republic or Democracy?

The terms democracy and republic technically describe different forms of government. By definition, a democracy is a government by the people, especially the rule of the majority. In a pure democracy everyone votes on every issue. In an elective democracy, the people choose representatives who serve in government. The Canton of Glarus in Switzerland maintains the tradition of an open-air meeting (pictured at right) where all citizens can participate in the debate and vote on local decisions.

A republic is a government whose chief of state is not a monarch. Power in a republic is in the hands of those who are entitled to vote. This is not necessarily all the people.

In the colonial and early national period, many leading Americans feared democracy as being too dangerous. They believed that uneducated people would not make good political choices. They also harbored a fear of the majority becoming tyrannical and abusing the rights of the minority.

The United States began as a republic, but over time it became more of a democracy as more people were given the right to vote.

U.S. An attainder (conviction) of treason shall not work "corruption of blood." This phrase refers to punishment of a traitor's family. Relatives are not to be punished for treason committed by a member of their family.

Other Matters (Articles IV and VI)

Full Faith and Credit. The states are to recognize as legitimate the laws and records of other states. While important, this rule is not absolute. States can make their own laws for what constitutes a legal marriage or for licensing professional practices that might be different from laws passed by other states.

All Privileges and Immunities. A state must grant to people from out of state the same legal procedures and protections that residents of that state enjoy, such as the freedom to travel and to own property in that state.

Extradition. A person suspected of a crime in one state who flees to another state must be returned to the state where the crime was committed if that state's governor demands it. However, the state where the fugitive is found can put him on trial first if he is charged with a crime there also.

The Guarantee of a Republican Form of Government. The Federal government is charged with insuring that state governments are republican in form (elected representatives, limited powers, separate branches of government, and so forth). This is a protection against someone setting himself up as dictator or monarch of a state. The Federal government is also to protect states against invasion and domestic violence.

No Religious Test. All government officials at every level are bound by oath to defend the Constitution. However, no religious test can be required of those who serve in positions of public trust. This means that no government worker can be forced to agree to any religious belief or doctrine.

If a ruler pays attention to falsehood,
All his ministers become wicked.
Proverbs 29:12

★ Assignments for Lesson 23 ★

Bible Read Psalm 119:89-136 and answer these questions:

- How much does the psalmist say that he meditates on the Word (verse 97)?
- How does the psalmist describe the guidance that he receives from the Word (verse 105)?

Work on memorizing Philippians 2:14-15.

Project Work on your project.

Student Review Optional: Answer the questions for Lesson 23.

The Bill of Rights as Proposed in Congress, 1789

Lesson 24

Amendments to the Constitution

The framers of the Constitution knew that their document would have to be changed or amended from time to time. They wanted changes to be possible, but not on the basis of shallow whims. The method used in the Articles of Confederation was cumbersome and impractical. Read Article V of the Constitution (*American Voices*, pages 63-64), which sets forth the methods for amending it.

When two-thirds of both houses of Congress approve an amendment, it goes to the states for their consideration. Three-fourths of the states must ratify an amendment for it to be added to the Constitution. In all but one case, amendments have been considered by state legislatures. Special state conventions were called for consideration of the 21st Amendment. The other way for proposing amendments that is outlined in Article V, the calling of a national convention by two-thirds of the state legislatures, has never been used. Politicians have been uneasy about how such a convention might work and what it might do once it actually met.

The Constitution has been amended twenty-seven times. Only about six other amendments have been proposed by Congress which were not ratified by the sufficient number of states.

The Bill of Rights: Amendments I-X

Read Amendments I-X to the Constitution (*American Voices*, pages 65-66).

When the proposed Constitution was submitted to the states, one reason that some opponents did not favor it was because it did not include a list or bill of rights that would be guaranteed to individuals and to the states. Supporters of the Constitution believed that such a lack was not a crucial issue because they envisioned a limited national government that would not be a threat to individual liberty. Besides, they said, most state constitutions already had lists of rights guaranteed to the people. However, to appease opponents of the Constitution, Federalists promised to draft a bill of rights soon after the Constitution was adopted and the new government was formed. This promise was kept.

State conventions made about 350 suggestions for amendments, although many of these were duplications. James Madison, who was a member of the House in the first Congress, distilled these ideas down to twelve amendments that were passed by Congress and sent to the states. Ten were ratified by the states and are known as the Bill of Rights. One was never ratified, and another was finally ratified in 1992 as the 27th Amendment.

Lesson 24 - Amendments to the Constitution

The Bill of Rights limits the power and intrusiveness of the Federal government. At first these provisions were understood to apply only to actions of the central government. However, Supreme Court decisions have applied the provisions of the Bill of Rights to the actions of state governments.

1st Amendment. The First Amendment covers several important topics. First, it prohibits Congress from giving legal favor to one religious group. At the same time, it guarantees the free exercise of religion. The precise meaning of these phrases has been the subject of many Supreme Court decisions, and the Court has tried to walk a fine line between a government giving what appears to be official endorsement of anything of a religious nature and allowing the free expression of religious belief even by government bodies.

Second, the amendment guarantees the right of freedom of speech and of the press. This clause was intended to insure that political debate by speakers and in publications would be free and not censored by the government. Freedom of speech has been extended by Supreme Court decisions to include ideas that some find morally offensive (although some regulation by local government has been permitted). The First Amendment freedom of speech has also been used to guarantee freedom of expression, including artistic expression and actions such as burning the U.S. flag as a political protest.

Third, the amendment protects the right of American citizens to assemble peaceably and to tell the government what they believe are wrongs that need to be addressed.

2nd Amendment. The American people have the right to own and use guns. This amendment recognizes that when the government controls all weapons, the country is not free. An important element of national security at the time the amendment was passed was the local militia, which was made up of volunteers who rendered military service when called upon to do so. The central government did not maintain a large standing army.

Today, many concerns have been expressed about this right because of the number of crimes committed with firearms. Gun ownership has become regulated by requiring background checks of gun purchasers, requiring gun owners to register their weapons with local authorities, and banning certain classes of people from owning guns (such as convicted criminals and illegal aliens).

3rd Amendment. This provision addressed an issue that had arisen during the colonial period. American colonists had been required to house British soldiers when military commanders ordered them to do so. This was a great irritation to many Americans. The structure of today's military and the housing provided on military bases makes this problem unlikely to occur again.

4th Amendment. American citizens are protected against unreasonable searches and seizures of their persons and property. To be legal, a search must be reasonable and must be supported by a search warrant that is issued by a proper authority and that describes the place to be searched and what is being sought. A search without a warrant can be made of a person if he or she is being pursued or arrested for a crime. Evidence that is found in violation of this protection may not be used in court.

5th, 6th, 7th and 8th Amendments. These amendments preserve the rights of those who have been accused of committing a crime. In our system of justice, a person is presumed to be innocent until proven guilty. These rights protect a person from being a victim of mistakes or improper actions by

the legal authorities. The rights granted in these amendments include: not having to stand trial again for the same crime if he has once been found innocent of it, not being forced to testify against oneself in a trial, the guarantee of due process of law (being treated the way law enforcement commonly treats all people), the right to a speedy and public trial, and not having to pay excessive fines or bail or to endure cruel and unusual punishment.

9th Amendment. This is a blanket statement which says that the enumeration of certain rights in the Constitution does not mean that other rights not listed are not held by the people. No document can list all possible rights. The generally understood rights of the people are reserved to the people even if they are not specifically mentioned in the Constitution.

10th Amendment. Rights that are not specifically given to the Federal government nor specifically denied to the states are reserved to the states or to the people. This embodies the principle of limited government.

This 1870 print celebrated the adoption of the fifteenth amendment. The central image depicts a May 19 parade in Baltimore, Maryland, that involved some 20,000 people. At top center are three African American leaders: Martin Robison Delany was the first commissioned officer in the U.S. Army who was black; Frederick Douglass; and Hiram Rhodes Revels, the first African American in the U.S. Senate. Other images portray African Americans involved in everyday business, family, and religious activities.

Lesson 24 - Amendments to the Constitution

Other Amendments

Read Amendments XI-XXVII to the Constitution (*American Voices*, pages 66-71). We will discuss some of these amendments in more detail later in this curriculum.

11th Amendment (1798). A limitation on the kind of cases that are to be heard in Federal courts, amending the provisions in Article III, Section 2.

12th Amendment (1804). Changes the way that electors vote for President, so that they now vote separately for President and Vice President.

13th-15th Amendments (1865, 1868, and 1870). After the 12th Amendment was ratified in 1801, no additional amendments were passed for sixty years, until the three that resulted from the Civil War. These are called the Civil War Amendments. The 13th Amendment officially outlawed slavery. The 14th Amendment defined citizenship and the rights of citizens in order to protect blacks and former slaves. It also dealt with other matters that arose as a result of state secession and the Confederacy's rebellion against the Federal government. The 15th Amendment guaranteed the right to vote to all citizens regardless of "race, color, or previous condition of servitude."

16th Amendment (1913). Permitted direct Federal income taxes on individuals.

17th Amendment (1913). Provided for the election of U.S. Senators by direct popular vote.

18th (1919) and 21st Amendments (1933). The 18th Amendment created Prohibition, which outlawed the manufacture, sale, and transport of intoxicating liquors. This amendment, passed in 1919, was repealed by the 21st Amendment in 1933.

19th Amendment (1920). Guaranteed to women the right to vote.

20th Amendment (1933). This amendment moved up the day for the inauguration of the President and Vice President from March 4 to January 20. It also changed the day Congress convenes, moving it up almost a year from the first Monday in December to January 3.

Those who favored prohibition and those who opposed it both made arguments to support their views.

22nd Amendment (1951). This change limits a President to two elected terms in office. The two-term tradition began with George Washington. When this amendment was proposed by Congress and ratified by the states, many Democrats considered it a backhanded Republican slap at the late Democratic President Franklin Roosevelt, who was elected four times.

23rd Amendment (1961). Before the passage of this amendment, residents of the District of Columbia were not able to vote in presidential elections. The amendment granted three electoral votes to the District, but residents still do not have representation in the House or Senate. Congress oversees the government of the District.

24th Amendment (1964). This amendment outlawed the poll tax. A poll tax was collected in many states from those wishing to vote in elections. It was usually promoted as a way to raise revenue, but one effect of it was to keep poor people from voting. If someone had to choose between paying to vote and feeding his family, he would probably not vote. It was commonly used in the South after the Civil War to keep blacks from voting.

25th Amendment (1967). Provides for presidential succession. This was passed after the death of John F. Kennedy, when there was no Vice President for over a year. It also gives the procedure to be followed if the President is disabled.

26th Amendment (1971). Gave the right to vote to those eighteen and older. This was passed during the Vietnam War era, when the standard voting age was 21 (although a few states had lower voting ages). Many young men between 18 and 21 were being drafted into the Army but were not able to vote for the people who were creating the policies they were being called to defend.

27th Amendment (1992). This was one of the original twelve amendments submitted to the states by the first Congress. The provision says that a Congress cannot change its own salaries. A congressional election must take place before a pay change passed by Congress takes effect.

> *But let justice roll down like waters*
> *and righteousness like an ever-flowing stream.*
> *Amos 5:24*

★ Assignments for Lesson 24 ★

Bible Read Psalm 119:137-176 and answer these questions:

- What synonyms does the psalmist use for the Word?
- How do you feel about Bible study?
- When do you usually study the Bible?
- What can you do to grow in your Bible study and in your application of what you read in the Bible?
- What problems and divisions have you seen because people have not interpreted the Bible correctly?

Work on memorizing Philippians 2:14-15.

Project Work on your project.

Student Review Optional: Answer the questions for Lesson 24.

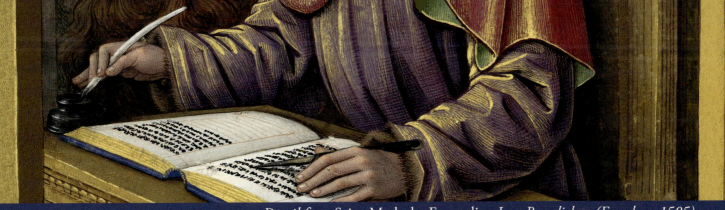

Detail from Saint Mark the Evangelist, *Jean Bourdichon (French, c. 1505)*

Lesson 25 - Bible Study

The Bible as Spiritual Constitution

We all need an ultimate authority on which to base our lives. If we merely live on the basis of what is popular at a given time, we will eventually learn that such a standard does not produce what is good. We will also find that such a standard changes over time. What once was considered to be right will later be seen as wrong. On the other hand, if we live on the basis of what seems right to us individually, that standard will be unreliable and subject to our own whims. It will be difficult to impose this standard on others because they will want to follow what seems right to them.

If we want to live well, we need more than human opinions. Since God created us and knows what is best for us, the standards that He has revealed to us are the authority that we need to follow. Our study in this unit on the Constitution as the ultimate law and authority for the United States leads us to consider the Bible as the spiritual "constitution" for Christians and to consider how we should study it, understand it, and follow it.

The Supreme Law

The Constitution describes itself as the "supreme law of the land" (Article VI). This means that the Constitution, the Federal laws enacted under it, and the treaties concluded by its authority are the final word for every American in matters pertaining to the law. The supreme law for Christians is the Bible, the Word of God. What the Bible says is the ultimate authority for those who want to live within the will of God (2 Timothy 3:16-17).

The writers of the Constitution did not claim to be inspired or incapable of making mistakes. They knew that their work in framing the Constitution involved a series of pragmatic political compromises that were not ultimate truth but that provided the basis for creating a "more perfect union," as the Preamble says. The framers even included a procedure by which the supreme law of the land could be changed as needed. By contrast, the Word of God does claim to be final, inspired, and infallible (2 Peter 1:20-21). It is not subject to change or amendment. In fact, the Bible specifically forbids adding to or subtracting from the revelation of God's will (Deuteronomy 4:2, Revelation 22:18-19).

Succeeding generations of Americans (especially succeeding Justices on the U.S. Supreme Court) have given different interpretations to the words of the Constitution. For instance, in 1896 the Supreme Court said that maintaining separate but equal public facilities for people of different races was an

Unit 5 - The Constitution

President Lincoln Reading the Bible to His Son (c. 1865)

appropriate policy that was within constitutional authority. In 1954 however, a later Court said that separate facilities based on race were inherently unequal and thus violated the Constitution. In another example, the 1st Amendment guarantee of freedom of speech was originally understood to refer to political speech. In more recent times, freedom of speech has come to be seen as including freedom of artistic expression and the freedom to engage in actions that are a form of political speech.

Moreover, the 5th Amendment says that private property can only be taken for public use if just compensation is paid to the property owner. This was long understood to mean that the government could purchase land from a private owner to build something like a railroad or a park for public use. In 2005, however, the Supreme Court ruled that "public use" included the "public good," and so the owners of private property could be forced to sell their land to private developers if the developers could use it to generate more revenue for the government.

By contrast, the proper meaning of Scripture has been given once for all time (Psalm 119:89). Scripture does not change from time to time and from culture to culture to mean different things, and the Bible does not support ideas that conflict with each other.

A Matter of Interpretation

In its simplest form, the process of interpretation involves two steps: determining what a text says, and then determining what a text means. We can know fairly easily what the Constitution says. Determining what the Constitution means involves interpreting it by using certain understood principles. For instance, some people believe that the Constitution should only be understood to mean what the framers meant when they wrote it. Others say that the wording of the Constitution can be taken to mean different things as times and the needs of people change. In like manner, we can know fairly easily what the Bible says. Determining what the Bible means involves applying certain principles that help us to interpret the text in the most accurate and consistent way.

It is important to understand one basic fact: everyone interprets the Bible in one way or another. Some people say, "I don't interpret the Bible; I just read it and do what it says." However, they are not being honest with themselves. When they read a verse and think, "I need to do that," and then when they read another verse and think, "God doesn't expect me to do that," they are interpreting Scripture. When a person reads "Love your neighbor as yourself" and feels compelled to obey it, but then reads about how animal sacrifices were to be made in the tabernacle and temple and doesn't feel compelled to do it, that person is engaged in interpreting Scripture. When people read about Christians in the first century sharing in the Lord's Supper and want to do that, but then read about first-century Christians selling their possessions and giving the proceeds to others and don't want to do that, they are interpreting Scripture. Everyone interprets Scripture. Our goal should be

Lesson 25 - Bible Study: The Bible as Spiritual Constitution

to interpret Scripture as consistently, truthfully, and fairly as possible in order to determine God's will and to put it into practice.

Principles of Interpretation

We will not try to list all relevant principles of interpreting Scripture, but we do want to mention three basic ones. The first and most important one is this: We should read and understand the Bible the way it was written. The Bible was written by books, by inspired authors who believed in God, in certain literary forms. This means, among other things, that a verse has meaning and authority only as it is correctly understood in the context of the book in which it is found. To take a verse or a phrase out of its context to prove a point is called prooftexting, which involves having a practice or belief already established, then finding a verse that you think supports that practice or belief. God used certain literary forms to communicate His revelation: history, law code, poetry, wisdom literature, prophecy, gospel, letter, and apocalyptic. The Bible is literally true. This means, among other things, that the Psalms are literally poetry and that Revelation is literally an apocalyptic writing, which uses symbols and images to make its point.

A second key principle of interpretation is that the meaning of a text is primarily what the writer meant (in the case of the Bible, the writer's meaning is God's inspired meaning). The application of this principle is that a text should be studied in its literary context (what is said and how it is said) and in its historical context (who said it, to whom, and in what circumstances). A passage in one of Paul's letters, for instance, should be understood to apply first to the original recipients in their real-life setting, and secondarily to all believers in all ages and in all cultures. A parable of Jesus should be understood for what it meant to His listeners in the first century and should not be made to say something that He never intended.

Third, Scripture is the best interpreter of Scripture. A passage of Scripture always agrees with and casts the best light on other passages of the Bible. This principle is especially helpful with passages that are hard to understand. Other passages can often illuminate or explain a more difficult passage. One result of this truth is that we should not rely too heavily on what another person says to grasp the meaning of Scripture. Our final authority on the meaning of Scripture should not be what a preacher, pope, cult leader, author, or any other person of authority says. If such a person is right, he is right because what he says lines up with Scripture, not because of his position. Such persons might be able to teach us a great deal, but they should not be our final authority. The Word is our final authority. It is also inadequate to think that the meaning of Scripture is "what the Bible said to me this morning." What you heard from Scripture this morning might be true, and it might be helpful. What you hear in the morning will be more reliable as you spend more and more time studying God's Word faithfully and letting it sink deeply into your heart. However, just because you think something, even if it is as a result of studying the Bible, does not mean that your thought is correct.

Mrs. Ella Watson Reading the Bible to Her Household in Washington, D.C. (1942)

Points to Remember

Some truths are even more basic than the principles of interpretation listed above. We will close with a review of these realities. First, the primary truth is God. He has revealed Himself in His Creation and He has worked in history. He has communicated His will in Scripture and in the living Word, Jesus. God is ultimate; our limited and fallible understanding of His Word is not ultimate. Our purpose in studying the Bible is not simply to know the Bible, but to know God.

Second, God's most important act is Jesus. He is God's central message (John 1:1, 14). Everything in the Old Testament leads up to Him (Luke 24:44). Everything in the New Testament is because of Him. Any interpretation of Scripture that minimizes or omits Jesus has missed God's most important point (Hebrews 1:1-4).

Third, the power of Scripture comes not from our using a certain approach or literary analysis. The power of Scripture is the Holy Spirit, who makes the Scripture living and active (Hebrews 4:12).

Fourth, the mind of man is not the ultimate standard for understanding Scripture. God has given us minds, and we need to use reason in studying the Bible. But God is not subject to our reason. God is reasonable, but He is above reason. He created reason. Some people have used their powers of reasoning to conclude that God does not exist or that the world is the result of evolution. Reason is fallible because man is fallible. Reason is a tool; it is not lord.

Fifth, as we study and interpret Scripture, we need to remember that Scripture interprets us (Hebrews 4:13). It is through Scripture that we learn about our value, our sin, our hope, and our Savior. Scripture teaches, convicts, comforts, and encourages. Let us not arrogantly acquire or display our knowledge of the Bible. Instead, let us humble ourselves before the revelation of God's will in Scripture to see how we can become more of what He wants us to be.

[T]he Scripture cannot be broken . . .
John 10:35

★ Assignments for Lesson 25 ★

Bible — Recite or write Philippians 2:14-15 from memory.

Project — Complete your project for the unit.

Student Review — Optional: Answer the questions for Lesson 25, take the quiz for Unit 5, and take the first history exam, English exam, and Bible exam.

The Washington Family, *Edward Savage (American, 1796)*

6 The New Nation

The Administration of George Washington set important precedents that our country still follows today. Political divisions developed during John Adams' tenure in office that set the pattern for our two-party political system. The Federal government under both Presidents faced and resolved serious issues. The new nation also established the pattern of religious freedom and a broadly accepted civil religion.

Lesson 26 - The First President
Lesson 27 - Conflicts Foreign and Domestic
Lesson 28 - The Man from Massachusetts
Lesson 29 - The End of a Revolutionary Century
Lesson 30 - Bible Study: Religion in the New Nation

Memory Work Memorize Proverbs 29:2-4 by the end of this unit.

Books Used
The Bible
American Voices
Narrative of the Life of David Crockett

Project (choose one)

1) Write 300 to 500 words on one of the following topics:

- Write about the strengths of George Washington that contributed to the successful founding of the new government.

- Write about the diversity in the early days of the United States and how that diversity has been a blessing in helping the U.S. become what it is today.

2) Take a field trip to the oldest church in your town. Ask for a tour and learn the history of the church. See Lesson 30.

3) Write and illustrate a children's book about the life of George Washington or John and Abigail Adams. Your book should be a minimum of fifteen pages. You might need to do research outside the information found in this unit. See Lessons 26 and 28.

Literature

Narrative of the Life of David Crockett

David Crockett was born in Tennessee in 1786. He lived in several places in the state and served as a local official, state representative, and U.S. Congressman. Crockett was known to attend legislative sessions in his frontier buckskin garments.

He became the ideal of the frontiersman and was the subject of many books, articles, and at least one play. Eastern writers developed a mythical Davy Crockett that popularized and idealized frontier life. Crockett wrote his autobiography (assisted by Thomas Chilton) in 1834 to set the record straight about his life but also to capitalize on his growing popularity. Crockett was defeated in his 1835 run for Congress. He moved to Texas, where he hoped to rejuvenate his political fortunes; but he was killed at the Alamo on March 6, 1836.

The Crockett myth reached new heights after his death. A *Crockett Almanac* was published from 1835 to 1856. The almanacs provided the usual farming and astronomical information but also told stories and legends about the famous frontiersman, some of which might even have had basis in fact. The power of the Crockett myth is shown by the emergence in the 1950s of a Davy Crockett craze, which produced a movie, a song, and a wealth of tie-in products such as coonskin caps and children's lunch boxes.

Crockett's autobiography is entertaining and is (at least somewhat) an authentic account of life on the frontier in the early 1800s, with perhaps a few embellishments and adjustments of the facts.

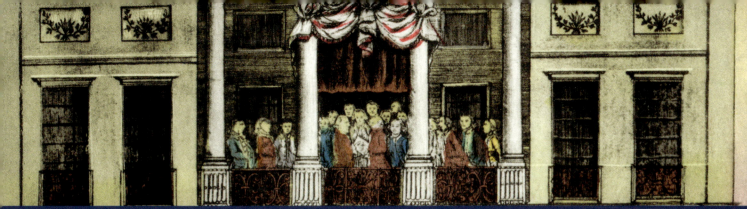

Washington's Inauguration at Federal Hall, New York, Amos Doolittle (1790)

Lesson 26

The First President

When electors cast their ballots for President in early 1789, it was no contest. Every elector cast one of his two votes for George Washington, the widely-respected planter from Virginia, successful leader of the Continental Army, and chairman of the Constitutional Convention. John Adams of Massachusetts received the second highest number of electoral votes and became Vice President. The electoral vote reflected the thinking of most Americans at the time. Washington and Adams were the two most admired and respected men in the country, and they were called upon to lead the nation under the new Constitution.

The nation had faced uncertainties under the Articles of Confederation, but no one could guarantee that the Constitution would be a significant improvement. A common fear was that the difficulties which confronted the nation would continue or even increase, and then a strong individual would gather supporters and seize control of the national government in the name of public safety and security. Some people feared that George Washington would assume the powers of a monarch (and a few people even desired this), but Washington made sure that no such tendencies toward a dominating central government developed during his tenure.

The First Administration

On April 30, 1789, Washington took the oath of office in New York City, the first capital of the new nation. As he finished the oath prescribed in the Constitution, Washington voluntarily added the words "so help me God." Every President since then has added the same words. The new President leaned over and kissed the Bible on which he had placed his hand while taking the oath. Following the ceremonies, he attended a religious service held in honor of the event.

The first Congress created the executive departments of State, War, and Treasury. Washington named Thomas Jefferson as Secretary of State, Henry Knox as Secretary of War, and Alexander Hamilton as Secretary of the Treasury. The heads of the executive departments were appointed simply to oversee the work of the executive branch, but the men also quickly became a cabinet of advisors to the President. This advisory function by the heads of executive departments has continued to today.

Congress also created the position of Attorney General, and Washington chose Edmund Randolph to fill it (it was only in 1870, with the creation of the Justice Department, that the Attorney General's role came to involve heading that department). The President named John Jay as the first Chief Justice of the Supreme Court.

Setting Precedents

In general, the President and Congress moved slowly in the new government. Much of what they did set precedents for all later administrations. Washington's tenure as President involved developing workable procedures through practical experience in many areas of governing. For instance, Congress devoted considerable discussion to how the President should be addressed. Many high-sounding titles were suggested, but Washington put the debate to rest by declaring that he wanted to be called "Mr. President." That practice has continued to this day.

In another matter, the Constitution calls for the President to make treaties with other countries "with the advice and consent of the Senate." When the Administration had concluded its first treaty, Washington met with the Senate, read the treaty to them paragraph by paragraph, and asked the Senators for their input. The responses of the Senators were so varied and often so conflicting that Washington left in frustration. The procedure that developed later was for the President simply to submit a proposed treaty to the Senate for it to debate and vote on.

Hamilton's Economic Policies

One major issue that confronted the Washington Administration was the need to create an economic policy for the national government. In this the new government did take significant steps. Treasury Secretary Alexander Hamilton made a series of proposals to Congress that were intended to give the new government the financial strength and stability it needed.

Assumption of Debt. Hamilton proposed that the national government take responsibility for the debts incurred under the Articles of Confederation by the Continental Congress and by individual states on behalf of the Confederation government. Under the plan the Federal government would issue new bonds for the face value of older certificates. Hamilton hoped that this plan would show that the new government would be responsible for paying its debts. He also hoped that creditors (mostly wealthy Americans) would see in the policy a reason to encourage the success of the new government, since the government would need to succeed for creditors to be able to collect on their bonds. Revenue from the issuance of new bonds could be used as capital for government expenditures.

Some in Congress objected to the plan because it favored the wealthy, who held most of the outstanding domestic debt. Even stronger opposition arose over the assumption of state debts, most of which were owed by northern states. Hamilton got the backing of Thomas Jefferson and Virginia Congressman James Madison for the assumption proposal by

Portrait of John Jay
Gilbert Stuart (American, 1794)

Lesson 26 - The First President

Hamilton promising his support for locating the national capital district on the Potomac River, which separates Virginia and Maryland. The deal worked, and the debt assumption proposal passed Congress.

A National Bank. The second part of Hamilton's plan called for the creation of a national bank. This bank would receive deposits of Federal revenue, print paper money, provide a stable source of credit for businesses, and make short-term loans to the national government.

Eighty percent of the money for the bank was to come from private investors, a proposal which concerned some who feared that those few individuals could dictate the nation's financial policies. Greater opposition arose, however, from Thomas Jefferson and others who believed that the bank was unconstitutional. Jefferson said that the Constitution did not permit Congress to create a national bank. Hamilton argued that the "necessary and proper" clause at the end of Article I, Section 8 permitted Congress to take whatever steps were necessary to accomplish the goals of the Constitution.

The opposition voiced by Jefferson and others essentially provided no alternative for fulfilling the need for a sound financial footing for the country. Faced with the realities of the frail national economy, Congress agreed with Hamilton; and in 1791 it chartered the Bank of the United States for a period of twenty years.

Assistance for American Manufacturers. Third, Hamilton urged government assistance for American manufacturing. Specifically, he proposed enacting tariffs or import taxes on imported goods to make them more expensive than the same items made in the United States. He hoped that this would improve the domestic market for American-made products. Some of the proposed tariffs were enacted.

Frontier Issues

Hamilton also proposed imposing taxes on the production of certain items to raise revenue for

Washington Reviewing the Western Army, at Fort Cumberland, Maryland, *Attributed to Frederick Kemmelmeyer (German, c. 1795)*

the Federal government. One of these was a tax on whiskey. This angered many frontier farmers because whiskey production was one of their main sources of income. They believed that a tax would hurt their revenue. In 1794 some western Pennsylvania farmers refused to pay the tax, terrorized Federal revenue agents, and disrupted the mails and court proceedings. When they did not disperse, President Washington ordered a large military force to move against the Whiskey Rebellion. Most of those involved in the rebellion then dispersed and went home. A few men were arrested. One died in prison, while two sentenced to death for treason were pardoned by the President. The Federal government had effectively made the point, however, that its laws were to be respected.

During Washington's tenure in office, thousands of settlers poured across the Appalachian Mountains to establish new homes in the West. Their movement was hindered, however, by resistance from Indian tribes. In an attempt to facilitate western settlement, several treaties were signed with Native American tribes that gave the United States access to certain parcels of land in which Americans were interested.

Overall, however, the treatment of Native Americans by whites was inconsistent. A few people, such as Thomas Jefferson, hoped that the Indians might be assimilated into American society. Many Americans, however, wanted to eliminate the Indian threat by staging military attacks against them. General "Mad Anthony" Wayne led a force that defeated warriors from eight Indian tribes at the Battle of Fallen Timbers in Ohio in 1794. Following their loss, the Indians gave up their claims to most of Ohio. Indian opposition also continued in the South, but a 1795 treaty with the Creeks ended the worst fighting in that region.

> *The mind of man plans his way, but the Lord directs his steps.*
> *Proverbs 16:9*

★ Assignments for Lesson 26 ★

American Voices — Read George Washington's First Inaugural Address (pages 77-79) and George Washington's Thanksgiving Proclamation (page 80).

Begin reading "The Legend of Rip Van Winkle" by Washington Irving (pages 111-116). You will finish reading the story tomorrow. The story is set just before and just after the American Revolution. This is an example of the kind of literature known as a short story. A short story is fiction but is not as long as a novel. It has fewer main characters and usually only one main plot line. Short stories by one author or on one theme are often published as a collection. "The Legend of Rip Van Winkle" is also an example of a kind of writing known as local color, which draws on the characteristics of a particular locality (geography, culture, customs, language, etc.) to give the story its particular flavor.

Literature — Begin reading *Narrative of the Life of David Crockett*. Plan to finish it by the end of Unit 7.

Bible — Work on memorizing Proverbs 29:2-4.

Project — Work on your project.

Student Review — Optional: Answer the questions for Lesson 26.

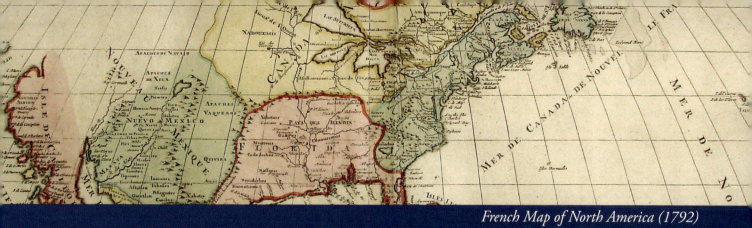

French Map of North America (1792)

Lesson 27

Conflicts Foreign and Domestic

During the Administration of George Washington, the United States was a new nation struggling to establish itself. Our nation was not the world superpower that it is today. European nations were far more powerful militarily and economically. Western civilization was in a time of upheaval and change. As a result, several tense issues involving other countries developed in the first years of the new government; and the United States was drawn into these issues. Many of these matters were the result of developments in France.

The French Revolution of 1789, in which the monarchy was overthrown and a republic declared, was welcomed by many in the United States as a continuation of the fight for greater political liberty that had begun in America. It was widely believed that French revolutionaries had been inspired and encouraged by what America had done in 1776. Thomas Jefferson, who had served as the American minister to France after the Revolutionary War, was a particularly outspoken supporter of the French revolutionary movement. The Washington Administration extended diplomatic recognition to the new French government. However, the Reign of Terror that soon developed in France, in which many opponents and perceived opponents of the revolution were executed by those who had gained power, concerned many Americans because it appeared merely to be tyranny under another name.

The kings of other European nations felt threatened by the developments in France, and French revolutionary leaders spoke threateningly about their desire to extend the revolution into other countries. The revolutionary government of France went to war against the monarchical governments in England, Holland, and Spain in 1793. This raised questions about what the role of the United States should be in those conflicts. Some Americans wanted to support France against other monarchies because France had been America's ally during the Revolutionary War against the hated British monarchy. Others in America, however, wanted to support England because of American economic ties to that country and because of fears of French excesses in their revolution. Washington issued a statement of neutrality, which was later confirmed by Congress. The declaration of neutrality stated that the U.S. would treat both sides equally and fairly. This position of neutrality kept the United States from becoming embroiled in a foreign war and likely being weakened by doing so.

When the French ambassador to the United States, Edmond-Charles Genet, arrived in America in 1793, he went about the country outfitting ships to do battle against France's European enemies

141

and trying to instigate attacks on Spanish-held territories in America. This was highly inappropriate behavior for an ambassador in a neutral country. Washington and his Cabinet insisted that Genet be recalled by France. However, the government in France underwent one of its several changes during the period of its Revolution; and Genet faced arrest and possible execution if he went home. As a result, Washington did not order Genet to leave the country. Genet resigned as ambassador. He married the daughter of New York governor George Clinton in 1794 and eventually became an American citizen.

Britain, meanwhile, did not see neutrality in quite the same way that Washington did. The British government decided to make America pay for any contact it had with France. British ships stopped and seized American trading vessels bound for France. Britain also practiced the policy of impressment, in which sailors on American ships who were suspected of being British nationals trying to avoid service in the British navy were taken prisoner and pressed into service on British ships. Some American citizens were seized by this practice, which understandably outraged many in the United States.

President Washington sent Chief Justice John Jay to negotiate a treaty with Great Britain regarding this and several other outstanding matters. A treaty was signed, but Jay was not able to resolve the major issues satisfactorily and the treaty was widely opposed in the United States. The Jay Treaty passed the Senate by one vote and President Washington signed it only reluctantly. Jay was strongly criticized by many Americans for the way in which the treaty seemed to give in to the British position on many questions. The position of the Administration, however, was that the treaty averted another war with Great Britain, a war which the U.S. quite possibly would have lost.

One clear foreign policy success of the Washington Administration was the Pinckney Treaty with Spain, negotiated by Thomas Pinckney in 1795. The treaty ended Spanish claims in the South (outside of Florida) and guaranteed American access to New Orleans. This pleased the growing western population that wanted to be able to conduct travel and trade on the Mississippi River.

Political Parties

The debate over Hamilton's economic program highlighted two different political and social philosophies that were current in the new country. Hamilton and other Federalists wanted to see a strong central government that encouraged the development of industry. Hamilton trusted the

George Washington, *Gilbert Stuart (American, 1797)*

Lesson 27 - Conflicts Foreign and Domestic

educated and wealthy elite to provide the best leadership in government, and he did not trust the common people. On the other hand, Thomas Jefferson, James Madison, and others who came to be called Republicans did not trust centralized power. They believed that the individual citizen, especially the farmer, was the backbone of a successful economy and society. Both sides had valid points and valid concerns about their opponents' position. Problems arose when each side refused to work with the other to achieve the common good and when a desire for power and loyalty to particular leaders became more important than commitment to what was objectively best for the country.

These differences led to the formation of political parties (or factions, as they were called). The problem with parties, as Washington and others saw it, was that they called for people to be loyal to a group, whether or not the group had the correct position on particular issues or the best candidates seeking election. Opponents of political parties wanted voters simply to support the best individual who had the best ideas. The political conflict between the two factions increased during Washington's second term. Washington did not consider himself to be a member of any political party, but he is often listed as a Federalist because of his support for Hamilton and his recognition of the need for a strong national government.

Washington's Farewell

After one term as President, Washington earnestly wanted to retire to Mount Vernon, just as he had done following his service in the Revolutionary War. However, he agreed to serve a second term when he became convinced that no one else would be able to hold the country together. In 1792 Washington was again chosen President by a unanimous vote of the electoral college, and Adams was re-elected Vice President.

In 1796 Washington decided that two terms were enough. As he prepared to retire from public

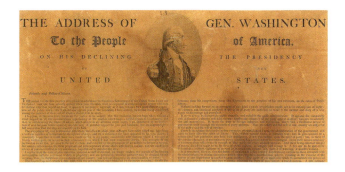

"The Address of Gen. Washington to the People of America, on His Declining the Presidency of the United States" (1796)

life, he wrote a farewell address that was published in many newspapers (he never gave the address in oral form). In the address, which included many passages written by Alexander Hamilton, Washington gave wise fatherly advice to the new nation and warned against the danger of factions and of permanent alliances with foreign nations. Washington retired to Mount Vernon, where he died in 1799. In his will he freed the slaves who worked on his plantation.

Washington's Legacy

When Washington died, Congress selected Henry "Light Horse Harry" Lee, a Congressman from Virginia and a long-time associate of Washington, to deliver a eulogy. The first portion quoted below has endured as an apt description of how the country as a whole felt about the first President. In the eulogy, Lee said:

> First in war, first in peace and first in the hearts of his countrymen, he was second to none in the humble and endearing scenes of private life. Pious, just, humane, temperate and sincere—uniform, dignified, and commanding—his example was as edifying to all around him as were the effects of that example lasting. . . . Such was the man for whom our nation mourns.

Opinions about George Washington have varied widely. In the years following his death, Washington was exalted to almost god-like status in the minds of many Americans. Later generations of historians, however, questioned the value of the role that Washington played. They saw him as just another white, male slaveowner who was interested in helping the ruling class maintain its power.

It is understandable that someone who filled such important positions in the Revolution and in the new government would generate strong opinions among others. From our vantage point in history, it is obvious that Washington legitimately deserves much credit for helping to make the new government work and for keeping the new country unified. He was a man of principle who believed deeply in the cause of American independence and who wanted the new nation to be built on faith, justice, and integrity. Washington was a wise and just man who freely confessed his dependence on God and who received deep loyalty from those who served under his leadership. It is right for us to admire Washington and to think of him as the "Father of Our Country."

The exercise of justice is joy for the righteous,
But is terror to the workers of iniquity.
Proverbs 21:15

★ Assignments for Lesson 27 ★

American Voices — Read George Washington's Farewell Address (pages 81-90).

Finish reading "The Legend of Rip Van Winkle" by Washington Irving (pages 117-120).

Literature — Continue reading *Narrative of the Life of David Crockett*.

Bible — Read 2 Timothy 3:10-12. List three ways in which a Christian who is a public official might be tempted to compromise his faith.

Work on memorizing Proverbs 29:2-4.

Project — Work on your project.

Student Review — Optional: Answer the questions for Lesson 27.

Detail from Action Between U.S. Frigate *Constellation* and French Frigate *Insurgente*, 9 February 1799
Real Admiral John W. Schmidt (American, c. 1965)

Lesson 28

The Man from Massachusetts

George Washington was largely above criticism. Little of a negative nature about him was said by politicians or printed in newspapers during his first term, and only a few more attacks appeared during his second term. Plenty, however, was going on behind the scenes as men were positioning themselves to take power when Washington retired. The young nation had no shortage of political maneuverers. It didn't take long for the two factions, the Federalists and the Republicans, to start attacking each other.

Washington's retirement led to a heated contest for the presidency in 1796. Federalists wanted to maintain their power, but Republicans saw the chance to bring a new direction to the national government. Alexander Hamilton was the leading figure in the Federalist Party; but he had been born in the West Indies, not in America, and thus was ineligible to be President. In addition, Hamilton had managed to make enough enemies even within his own party that not all Federalists respected him.

A meeting (called a caucus) of Federalist members of Congress proposed Vice President John Adams of Massachusetts as their choice for a presidential candidate. Thomas Pinckney of South Carolina received the nod as the vice presidential nominee. Republican Congressmen nominated Thomas Jefferson of Virginia for President, and they placed Aaron Burr of New York in the second spot. Thus both parties showed that they recognized the importance of having geographical balance in the national ticket.

This first contested presidential election witnessed plenty of vicious attacks on the candidates by party representatives in the press. Adams was criticized as being overweight and a secret monarchist, while Jefferson was decried as an atheist and a radical French sympathizer. Thomas Paine, now living in Paris, chimed in with a stinging attack on George Washington.

After the voting for electors was concluded in the states, no clear winner had emerged. Hamilton tried to engineer a last-minute deal to cut Adams out of the election in favor of Pinckney. Hamilton probably thought that he could control Pinckney but could not control Adams. However, Hamilton's plan offended several Federalist electors from New England, who refused to cast any vote for Pinckney. As a result of all the dealings that took place, Federalist John Adams was chosen as President but Republican Thomas Jefferson received the second highest number of electoral votes and became Vice President. This meant that the two leaders of the executive branch came from different political parties. This arrangement could have helped to heal the quickly-widening breach between the two parties, but leaders in both parties were more interested in widening the split for their own political advantage. Adams as President and Jefferson as Vice President only served to increase the tension between the two rival groups.

Adams was a brilliant and able leader with a long record of public service. He served a key role in the Continental Congress and had been a representative of the new nation in both France and Great Britain. Adams was a man of sincere religious faith and strong principles, which he was unwilling to compromise for mere political advantage. This cost him dearly in terms of popular and political support.

Relations with France

The key issues that arose during Adams' Administration involved foreign troubles which in turn led to domestic turmoil. Great Britain had harassed American shipping for some time, but U.S. merchants continued to do business with Britain. Since France was at war with Great Britain, French vessels also frequently intercepted American ships to hinder Anglo-American trade. In 1797 Adams sent representatives to Paris to work out a treaty with France that would end French interference with American trade. After they arrived, the American envoys were approached by three representatives of the French foreign minister, who made three demands. They wanted a bribe to be paid to French leaders (not an entirely unheard-of practice in that day), a large loan made to the French government, and an apology issued by the American government for anti-French sentiments that Adams had expressed in a speech, all for just the promise that the French government would begin to negotiate. The Americans refused (their answer was reportedly "No, no, not a sixpence") and returned home.

President Adams reported on the incident to Congress. He did not name the three French representatives but merely called them X, Y, and Z. Congress and many Americans were outraged. "Millions for defense but not one cent for tribute"

This 1798 British political cartoon portrays the French as stealing the jewelry from a woman representing the United States.

became the American response to the XYZ Affair. Despite this insult, and although French-American conflict was already taking place to some degree on the high seas, Adams refused to seek a declaration of war. However, Adams strengthened the tiny American Navy and called for a 10,000 man army to be formed under the leadership of George Washington. Washington insisted on Alexander Hamilton as his second in command, which meant that Hamilton would actually lead the army in the field should military action ever be called for. Tensions eased between the two countries, however, and the army was never organized.

France finally agreed to negotiate. Talks between France and the United States led to an agreement called the Convention of 1800, which defused the entire situation. Adams could have given in to popular pressure for war, but the result might well have been disastrous for the young and poorly-prepared country. His decision to avoid going to war with France was widely unpopular at the time, but it has since been recognized as the wiser course. His decision probably played a part in costing him re-election in 1800, but it also probably saved the nation.

The Alien and Sedition Acts

Conflict with France led to conflict at home. In response to fears of foreign power and influence,

Lesson 28 - The Man from Massachusetts

in 1798 the Federalist-led Congress passed (and the Federalist Adams signed) a series of laws that restricted the rights of immigrants and the right to criticize the government. The Naturalization Act increased the time an immigrant had to live in the United States before applying for citizenship from five to fourteen years. The Alien Act and the Alien Enemy Act gave the President the right to imprison or deport foreign nationals whom he suspected of being dangerous to the security of the country. The stated purpose for these measures was to limit the potential influence of foreign nationals; but they also conveniently worked against the Republican Party, since most immigrants became Republicans.

The Sedition Act outlawed conspiracy against the United States government. The law also made it a crime to "write, print, utter, or publish" any "false, scandalous, and malicious writings" against the U.S. government, Congress, or the President. This was a clear attempt to stop Republican criticism of the Adams Administration. Many newspapers in that day were published for the express purpose of promoting one party or the other, not for providing an objective account of the news. Adams and the Federalists were frequently targets for abuse in Republican papers; and Republicans were targets in Federalist papers.

In response to the Alien and Sedition Acts, the legislatures of Virginia and Kentucky passed resolutions (written for them by James Madison and Thomas Jefferson) which respectfully stated their loyalty to the United States government but called the Alien and Sedition Acts unconstitutional and urged the other states to work for their repeal. The resolutions spoke of the right of states to refuse to submit to acts of Congress that they deem unconstitutional.

This was the first expression of the idea that states had the right to ignore or nullify Federal laws. These Republican responses to the actions of

John and Abigail Adams were often separated during their 54 years of marriage because of John's public service. They kept in touch with over 1,000 thoughtful and loving letters to each other. These portraits from 1800 are by Gilbert Stuart.

the Federalist-controlled national government also served as the opening shots on behalf of Jefferson's 1800 presidential campaign against Adams.

Ten persons were convicted under the Sedition Act. All were Republicans and became in a sense martyrs for the Republicans. The Alien and Sedition Acts were understandable given the tense and often vicious tenor of the times, but they were unwise moves which helped bring about the end of the Federalist Party.

*Let no unwholesome word proceed from your mouth,
but only such a word as is good for edification
according to the need of the moment,
so that it will give grace to those who hear.
Ephesians 4:29*

★ Assignments for Lesson 28 ★

American Voices — Read the Virginia and Kentucky Resolutions (pages 91-93).

Literature — Continue reading *Narrative of the Life of David Crockett*.

Bible — Work on memorizing Proverbs 29:2-4.

Project — Work on your project.

Student Review — Optional: Answer the questions for Lesson 28.

Peacefield Was Home to Four Generations of Adamses from 1788 to 1927

Lesson 29

The End of a Revolutionary Century

John Adams was one of the least politically-motivated Presidents we have ever had, but he became deeply embroiled in the vicious political divisions that were emerging in the young nation. In 1800 the country saw what it has never seen again: the Vice President was a candidate for the presidency opposing the President himself. The hatred with which Republicans and Federalists spoke of each other in newspapers, speeches, and personal correspondence had only increased during Adams' time in office.

The Federalists nominated Charles C. Pinckney (brother of Thomas Pinckney) to be Adams' running mate. The Republicans again put forward Jefferson and Burr. Adams was deeply hurt that Thomas Jefferson opposed Adams' presidency so strongly. Adams and Jefferson had served together in the Continental Congress and had become close friends when Adams was the American ambassador to Britain and Jefferson was the minister to France. Jefferson denied having any direct role with the President's critics, but in fact the Vice President had been giving financial support to a newspaper editor who was one of Adams' most bitter opponents. Federalists minced no words in condemning Jefferson, but Adams did not take part in the mud-slinging.

Another blow aimed at Adams came from his fellow Federalist, Alexander Hamilton. In October, near the end of the bitter campaign, a letter written by Hamilton was published in a New York newspaper. It described Adams' "defects of character," his "ungovernable temper," and his "eccentric tendencies." Although Hamilton did not question Adams' integrity, he all but questioned the President's sanity and clearly expressed his doubts as to Adams' fitness for office. The letter tore the Federalist Party apart. While the letter hurt Adams, it damaged Hamilton's political career as well.

Adams lost the election. (How the election was decided is another tale of politics that we will take up in a later lesson.) One result of these sharp political differences was that Adams and Jefferson became personal enemies. On the day of Jefferson's inauguration in 1801, Adams left town at 4:00 a.m. and did not attend the ceremony. They never saw each other again, and it was not until many years later that they renewed their friendship through correspondence.

Judiciary Act of 1801

The Federalists not only lost the presidency in the election of 1800, but they also lost their majority in Congress. The drumbeat of Republican criticism had its effect on the minds of many voters. The Federalists did not do a good job of staying in touch

The White House

John Adams was the first President to live in the White House. The City of Washington had dirt streets and only a few buildings on its swampy landscape when Adams moved into the still-unfinished Executive Mansion in 1800. The 1807 drawing at right by architect Benjamin Henry Latrobe shows the proposed addition of porticos to the White House.

The President moved in while Abigail was still preparing to come. John wrote to Abigail, "I pray Heaven to bestow the best of blessings on this House, and all that shall hereafter inhabit it. May none but honest and wise men ever rule under this roof." President Franklin Roosevelt had this prayer carved into a mantelpiece which still stands in the State Dining Room in the White House.

Later in 1800, Adams addressed the first joint session of Congress in the still-unfinished Capitol building. On that occasion he said:

> *"It would be unbecoming the representatives of this nation to assemble for the first time in this solemn temple without looking up to the Supreme Ruler of the universe, and imploring his blessing. May this territory be the residence of virtue and happiness! In this city may that piety and virtue, that wisdom and magnanimity, that constancy and self-government, which adorned the great character whose name it bears, be forever held in veneration! Here, and throughout our country, may simple manners, pure morals, and true religion flourish forever!"*

with average Americans, who increasingly identified with the Jeffersonian Party. The Federalist Party continued to exist for several years, but no other Federalist was ever elected President and Federalists never again had a majority in Congress.

Despite the loss, however, the Federalists still had one more chance to exert political power. Republicans had won a majority in Congress in the 1800 election, but they would not take office until December of 1801. In early 1801, the lame-duck Federalist Congress passed the Judiciary Act to try to ensure that at least the judiciary would be controlled by Federalists. The law created several new judgeships and other positions such as marshals and justices of the peace. Outgoing President Adams filled all of the positions with Federalists. He also nominated Federalist John Marshall to be Chief Justice of the Supreme Court, a nomination the Senate quickly confirmed. We will see in a later lesson how far-reaching the Marshall appointment was.

John Adams made some mistakes politically, and even some of his own Administration worked against him; but when he left office, the country had a growing economy, a much stronger Navy, and was at peace. In retirement he continued to write extensively, including many letters. He died in 1826 at the age of 90.

America in the 1790s

In 1790 the states and territories of the new country contained 3.9 million people. The nation's land area extended from the Atlantic Coast to the Mississippi River and from the Great Lakes to the Gulf of Mexico, an area of roughly one thousand miles by one thousand miles. Eighty percent of

Lesson 29 - The End of a Revolutionary Century

households were farm homes. Few cities in the country had more than 5,000 people. About one-fifth of the population was African American, almost all of them slaves in the South. Half of the population in 1790 was under sixteen years of age.

New England was made up of small farms, busy seaports, and emerging manufacturing towns. The South was mostly agricultural, with many large plantations that were increasingly dependent on slave labor. Tobacco was the main cash crop, but production of cotton was growing. The Middle Atlantic states had the largest cities, the most balanced economy, and the greatest diversity of ethnic and religious backgrounds of the people.

The most vibrant part of the nation was the West, the region between the Appalachians and the Mississippi. Some 150,000 Native Americans lived in the region, compared to a total of 125,000 whites and blacks who lived there. Kentucky had about 150 settlers in 1776; by 1790, the white population had increased to around 75,000. In the last quarter of the eighteenth century, about 300,000 people migrated west through the Cumberland Gap, a pass in the Appalachian Mountains that is near the spot where Tennessee, Kentucky, and Virginia come together. Many of those who settled the mountain areas and the West were of Scots-Irish descent.

This rapid settlement of the region was encouraged by the policy of paying Revolutionary War veterans in the form of western land grants. Many veterans settled there, while others sold their land to speculators who in turn sold the land again to pioneer settlers. Vermont was admitted to the Union as the fourteenth state in 1791; but the next three states came from the area west of the original thirteen: Kentucky (1792), Tennessee (1796), and Ohio (1803).

It was hard work to travel west, create a settlement, and develop the forest-covered land. Many settlers lived off of corn and livestock. The typical house was built of logs with a dirt floor and had only one or two rooms. A stone fireplace provided heat and a place to cook. Settlers enjoyed community events such as cabin or barn raisings, corn shucking contests, harvest festivals, and dances.

The average American wife gave birth eight times. Internal population growth plus immigration caused the United States population to increase rapidly. By 1800 the United States population had grown to 5.3 million, an increase of about thirty-six percent from ten years earlier.

In 1800 the new nation was about to enter a new century. The national government had faced several difficult issues in its first years, but the country was growing stronger and was richly blessed in many ways. The nineteenth century would bring profound changes, great accomplishments, and bitter sorrows to America.

Philadelphia, illustrated here in 1797, was the second most populous city in the United States, after New York City.

What Else Was Happening?

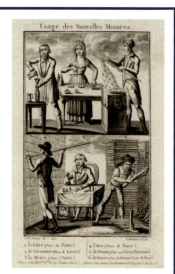

1784   Benjamin Franklin invents bifocal glasses.

1791   French scientists begin to develop the metric system of measurement. A meter is defined as one ten-millionth of the distance from the equator to the North Pole. A liter is the cube of one tenth of a meter; a gram is the weight of distilled water in a container one one-hundredth of a meter cubed. The French woodcut at right from 1800 explains the new system.

1793   A yellow fever epidemic in Philadelphia takes about 5,000 lives. The Federal government flees the city for a time. Philadelphia improves its health care and sanitation facilities as a result of the plague.

1795   The use of lime juice to prevent scurvy is ordered for sailors in the British navy. This produces the slang word limey to refer to the British.

1796   Edward Jenner infects a boy with cowpox to prove that doing so immunizes a person from the more dangerous disease of smallpox. This leads to the widespread practice of vaccination.

1799   A French officer under Napoleon in Egypt discovers the Rosetta Stone, which enables modern researchers to understand Egyptian hieroglyphic writing.

Once God has spoken; twice I have heard this:
That power belongs to God; and loving kindness is Yours, O Lord,
For You recompense a man according to his work.
Psalm 62:11-12

★ Assignments for Lesson 29 ★

American Voices — Read "A Man Worth Knowing" by David McCullough (pages 401-406).

Literature — Continue reading *Narrative of the Life of David Crockett*.

Bible — Read Philippians 2:14-16. Even when society is "crooked and perverse," Christians are called to remain faithful to God. List three challenges of being a Christian in a non-Christian society.

Work on memorizing Proverbs 29:2-4.

Project — Work on your project.

Student Review — Optional: Answer the questions for Lesson 29.

Mt. Zion Methodist Church, Somers, New York, Built in 1794

Lesson 30 - Bible Study

Religion in the New Nation

Most Americans alive today have never lived through a political revolution in which the government where they are living is changed by force. Sometimes American missionaries and businessmen and their families have lived in countries that experienced such upheaval. In those situations, Christians and churches often have been caught in the crossfire and the unstable conditions.

The American Revolution created a religious revolution as well as a political revolution. The religious changes wrought by America's new political freedom from England continue to have an impact on the nation today.

Influences on American Religion

The practice of faith in the new United States did not occur in a vacuum. Let us review the influences on the spiritual thinking and practice of Americans.

The Protestant Reformation. Led by Martin Luther and others, the Protestant Reformation brought new ideas about the identity of the church, the relationship between the church and government, and the nature of an individual's walk with God. A person no longer had to be a member of one particular church in order to see himself as a Christian. The Reformation challenged the long-standing, intertwined relationship between church and state. Luther understood the basis of a person's relationship with God to be one's own faith, not meritorious deeds, membership in a specific church, or citizenship in a particular country. These ideas found wide acceptance in America.

The English Experience. English religious practice contributed to the American idea of tolerating diversity in religion, even though official toleration of religious diversity was slow in coming to Britain. Henry VIII declared his independence from the Roman Catholic Church, but he maintained a state church and claimed to be the head of it. Many Anglican political and religious leaders did not want to accept other groups, but some in Britain were not satisfied with Anglicanism and took religious reform even further.

For a time, non-Anglicans (such as John Bunyan, author of *Pilgrim's Progress*) were sometimes persecuted in Britain, but the overall trend in England was toward toleration of varying religious beliefs. Key factors in this trend were the two revolutions that Britain experienced in the 1600s in which religion played an important part: the Puritan Revolution (Puritan Reformers vs. royalist Anglicans) and the Glorious Revolution (Protestants vs. Catholics).

The first Roman Catholic Diocese in the United States was established at Baltimore, Maryland, in 1789 with John Carroll as the first bishop. Carroll was instrumental in the founding of Georgetown, the oldest Catholic university in the U.S.; classes began in 1792. Georgetown, shown above, is now located in Washington, D.C.

Having had enough of this religious warfare, Parliament in 1689 passed the Toleration Act. Although the Church of England was still the established church, the Toleration Act allowed Protestant sects to exist without threat of persecution or loss of rights. Catholics, however, were still denied recognition for a time. Diversity in religious practice was accepted more easily in America than it had been in Great Britain.

The American Colonial Experience. The colonies contributed the idea of religion being the reason for establishing a community or colony. Some American colonies, such as Plymouth, Massachusetts Bay, and Maryland, were begun in order to provide religious independence from the established ecclesiastical authority in England. German pietists came to America to practice their faith in new communities without interference from the government. The Quakers, though they did not live in their own communities, took religious independence a step further by claiming direct, individual inspiration from God.

Despite problems with established churches in Britain and Europe, several American colonies and early states had established churches. However, the American experience tended toward diversity instead of uniformity in religious practice. Over time, the American colonies became home to Anglicanism, Deism, the seeds of Unitarianism, Pietism, and active denominationalism (such as Methodists, Baptists, and Presbyterians).

Still, not all colonial settlers came for religious purposes. A fair number merely wanted to find economic success, and their presence added a secular tone to life in the colonies.

Results of the American Revolution

Religiously Active. As a result of the American Revolution, the United States was no longer part of a country with an established religion. America moved from the British policy of having a state church while tolerating other groups to a position of freedom of religious practice. Religion was vitally important in the new nation. The Bible was the most widely read book in the colonies. Several states continued to have an established church. The last of these arrangements, the Congregational Church in Massachusetts, did not end until 1833. Many state constitutions required office holders to believe in God and the Bible. The prevailing attitudes and practices in the United States upheld faith in God. We have seen in documents and speeches that have been assigned for previous lessons how the patriots and framers believed in God and called upon Him for guidance and for His blessings on their efforts.

Individual Religious Freedom. The growing attitude in the United States was that religion was a matter of individual conscience. The founding generation of the country knew the problems and wars that had occurred in history because of the practice of having state religions. America was founded on freedom, and in the minds of many people this had to include the right to believe and practice as one wished, according to a person's individual choice. Virginia passed a Declaration of Rights in 1776 that included the guarantee of religious freedom, and ten years later the state enacted a Statute of Religious Freedom authored by Thomas Jefferson.

American Religious Groups. Religious denominations that had their roots in England were reorganized after the American Revolution with distinctly American identities. The Methodist Church in America was organized in 1784. The Anglican Church in America was in disarray for a time, since many of its clergy left the country and since many American Anglicans no longer wanted to be part of the Church of England. What had been the Anglican Church in America was reorganized as the Episcopal Church in 1789. Other denominations also set up their organizational structures in the new nation, but none did so with the purpose of being the state church or believing that membership in their group was required in order to be a citizen.

A Nation of Believers

Almost all of the citizens of the new nation believed in God. A large number of them were religiously active and regularly attended church services. Almost all of our early leaders believed in God and in God's providential working in the world. John Adams wrote to his wife Abigail that the yearly remembrance of the day that brought America's independence "ought to be commemorated as the day of deliverance, by solemn acts of devotion to God Almighty." Years later, when the economy showed an improvement during Washington's term in office, the President warned against giving credit to the government for blessings that are "due only to the goodness of Providence." John Jay, who was a contributor to *The Federalist Papers*, the first Chief Justice of the Supreme Court, and also governor of New York, was an active and dedicated Episcopalian. His faith was evident in the high moral dignity that he maintained throughout his life. After retiring from public service, Jay became president of the American Bible Society in 1821.

The desire by many in government to avoid a state religion did not mean that they wanted or expected no presence of religion in national life. The House of Representatives passed the First Amendment, which guaranteed freedom of religious expression and prohibited any law respecting an establishment of religion, on September 24, 1789. The next day, the same body passed a resolution calling for a national day of prayer and thanksgiving. Apparently the House saw no conflict in these two actions. During the Administration of Thomas Jefferson, a church began meeting in the House chamber of the U.S. Capitol building—and President Jefferson approved and attended.

Trinity Church was built in Holderness, New Hampshire, in 1797. It was a private church owned by the Livermore family, who were Episcopalians. Founder Samuel Livermore was the Chief Justice of New Hampshire and a delegate to the state convention that ratified the Constitution. He went on to serve as a U.S. Congressman and Senator from New Hampshire.

Fifteen Jewish families moved to Newport, Rhode Island, in 1658. The Touro Synagogue, pictured above, was built there in 1759. After George Washington's visit to Newport in 1790, he wrote a letter to the Jewish congregation that included this wish: "May the children of the stock of Abraham who dwell in this land continue to merit and enjoy the good will of the other inhabitants—while every one shall sit in safety under his own vine and fig tree and there shall be none to make him afraid."

This practice was begun partly because the new city did not have many structures, but these meetings continued until after the Civil War. Church services were held in other public buildings at various times as well. These facts show how the leaders of the new nation accepted and expressed faith within the functions of government but avoided establishing one sect or denomination as the official state church.

The Founding Fathers possessed and expressed a great deal of religious faith; and while many such expressions were explicitly Christian, it should be noted that these expressions often did not express faith in Christ as Savior and Lord as conservative Christians believe today. Rationalistic religion, based on man's reason and not on the revelation of God in Scripture, had gained a degree of acceptance during the years before the Revolution. Some of those involved in the Continental Congress, the Constitutional Convention, and the first administrations under the Constitution, were influenced by this thinking. Some did not believe in Jesus as the unique Son of God and only Savior. Benjamin Franklin, for instance, believed in an afterlife; but he believed that a life in this world that was acceptable to God consisted primarily of doing good deeds, not one that was based on faith in Christ. Thomas Jefferson "edited" the Bible by literally clipping out its accounts of the miracles of Jesus, which he believed to be pious but irrational myths. Instead, Jefferson placed value on Christ's moral teachings. Many of the Founding Fathers were members of churches, but the prevailing theology in some of those churches was more liberal than what evangelicals find comfortable today.

The turmoil of war and the reorganization of American denominations took their toll. Historians generally agree that church membership in America declined from the start of the Revolutionary War until the end of the 1700s. This reversed the trend of growing churches that had begun during the Great Awakening of the 1740s. Religious activity was especially lacking on the frontier. This situation changed during the Second Great Awakening, which we discuss in a later lesson.

Civil Religion

The Declaration of Independence (1776) referred to "Nature's God" and expressed a "firm reliance on the protection of Divine Providence." The Articles of Confederation (1777) spoke of "the Great Governor of the World." The Northwest Ordinance (1787) said that religion was necessary to good government and the happiness of mankind. However, the Constitution (1787) makes no mention of God and only refers to religion in its prohibition of any religious test and in the First Amendment.

How does a nation as a whole and its government practice religion when there is a widespread belief in God but (1) a wide diversity of religious beliefs

Lesson 30 - Bible Study: Religion in the New Nation

and practices and (2) the absence of a state church? What has come to be practiced in the United States has been called civil religion, which blends love of country, belief in God, and trust in God's guidance of the United States into a belief system which people from diverse Christian backgrounds—and even those from other religious backgrounds—can accept. American civil religion is demonstrated in many ways. It is the faith system that led to the phrase "In God We Trust" being adopted as our national motto. It is the acceptable level of religion that Presidents invoke when they end a speech by saying, "God bless the United States of America." Civil religion is what helps make a Memorial Day ceremony in a cemetery both a patriotic and a spiritual event. But civil religion is not the same as belief in Jesus as the Way, the Truth, and the Life.

Thomas Paine is a good example of one who held to this civil religion. Paine freely invoked the name of God in his writings about the American Revolution, but in some of his other writings he bitterly denounced the Christian faith as superstitious and harmful. Perhaps Paine was reacting to the problems he saw with established churches in Europe when he made these comments, but his words were clearly anti-Christian.

Civil religion attempts to walk the fine line between official government endorsement of a particular religion (which few people want) and the complete abandonment of all recognition of faith in the public forum (which also goes against what the majority of Americans want). Civil religion allows for the United States Senate to have a chaplain, but today's practice of civil religion forbids the saying of officially-sanctioned prayers at any public school function. Civil religion accepts Federally-backed loans being made to students attending Christian colleges, but it denies any form of direct public assistance to Christian schools. Civil religion does not call for giving financial support to churches from tax revenues, but it does endorse tax exemptions to churches. Civil religion attempts to balance freedom of religion with freedom from religion. It attempts to recognize eternal truth in a society that has diverse perspectives on the truth.

Perhaps 10% or more of the Africans brought to America as slaves were Muslims. One of these was Abdul Rahman, a captured African prince from Fouta Djallon who was sold as a slave in Mississippi in 1788. He was a slave for forty years. He married a fellow slave, and Rahman and his wife later became Christians.

Due to the influence of President John Quincy Adams, Rahman's master freed him in 1828. Rahman raised funds to purchase his wife's freedom, but not enough to free their nine children. Rahman and his wife went to the American colony of Liberia, where Rahman died in 1829.

American Religion

The religious life of the American nation that came about after and partly as a result of the American Revolution can be summarized as follows:

- It is largely Christian, although it does not reflect one particular expression of Christianity. There is a variety of form and an independence of thought among churches and individual believers.

- Several distinctly American religious expressions and movements have developed from time to time. Although America was settled largely by Europeans, European churches and belief systems have not dominated American religious life.

- A religious purpose of our founding is part of our identity as Americans, although this was not the only motivation for the founding of our country.

- America has seen rises and declines in religious activity from time to time.

- Civil religion has allowed official recognition of religious belief without having an established religion.

- Civil religion is helpful in some ways, but it is not a complete expression of the Christian faith or of any other particular kind of religion. It is something like the least common denominator of religious belief and expression.

My thanks to a friend, Bob Keyes, for the use of a paper he wrote that helped me in writing this lesson.

*Blessed is the nation whose God is the Lord,
The people whom He has chosen for His own inheritance.
Psalm 33:12*

★ Assignments for Lesson 30 ★

American Voices — Read the Virginia Statute for Religious Freedom (pages 55-56).

Literature — Continue reading *Narrative of the Life of David Crockett*.

Bible — Recite or write Proverbs 29:2-4 from memory.

Project — Complete your project for the unit.

Student Review — Optional: Answer the questions for Lesson 30 and take the quiz for Unit 6.

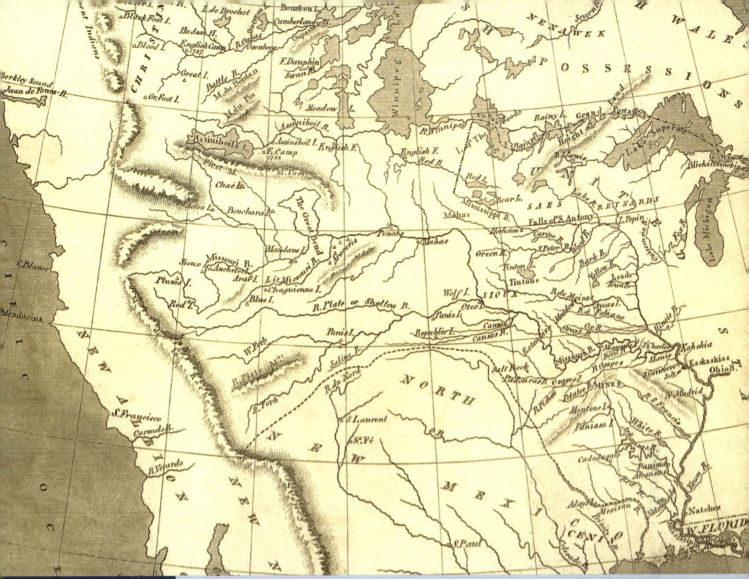

1804 Map of Louisiana

7 An Expanding Nation

Thomas Jefferson's election to the presidency in 1800 ushered in a peaceful revolution that exalted the worth of the individual American. Jefferson's vision of a nation that stretched across the continent was furthered with the Louisiana Purchase. The Supreme Court established its power of judicial review, which has come to play a dominant role in shaping the character of American life. Continued conflict with Great Britain led to the War of 1812. The evangelistic camp meetings of the Second Great Awakening began practices in American religion that still influence us today.

Lesson 31 - Expanding Democracy
Lesson 32 - The Expanding Power of the Supreme Court
Lesson 33 - The War of 1812
Lesson 34 - The Era of Good Feelings?
Lesson 35 - Bible Study: The Second Great Awakening

Memory Work Memorize Isaiah 55:1-3 by the end of this unit.

Books Used The Bible
American Voices
Narrative of the Life of David Crockett

Project (choose one)

1) Write 300 to 500 words on one of the following topics:

- Compare the religious experience in the Massachusetts Bay colony and that on the frontier during the Second Great Awakening.

- Write a letter to a friend in which you discuss your views on a significant national issue.

2) Interview the pastor or minister of your family's church regarding his history with the church he works with and any previous churches he worked with. Ask him about any education or training he received directly related to his work. Compose at least ten questions ahead of time. You can conduct your interview by phone or in person. Be respectful of your interviewee's time and keep the interview within an hour. If possible, make an audio recording of the interview. See Lesson 35.

3) Make a board game of the Lewis and Clark expedition to play with your family. Make the board a map of the United States. Make the game educational, including facts about the Louisiana Purchase, Thomas Jefferson, and the actual expedition. You might need to do research outside the information found in this unit. See Lesson 31.

Monticello, Home of Thomas Jefferson

Lesson 31

Expanding Democracy

On the morning of March 4, 1801, President-elect Thomas Jefferson, dressed in simple clothes, left the Washington boarding house in which he was staying and walked the two blocks to the unfinished Capitol. He gave his inauguration speech in the Senate chamber in his typical low voice that was barely audible, received the oath of office from new Chief Justice John Marshall, and then returned to the boarding house for the evening. Only later would he move into the Executive Mansion, the residence we know as the White House.

Such was the quiet beginning to what Jefferson called the Revolution of 1800. Gone were the days of Federalist pomp and ceremony. Although he was the son of a wealthy landowner and was himself part of Virginia's landowning aristocracy, Jefferson believed in the agrarian ideal that exalted the common man as the strength of the nation. While the first twelve years under the Constitution were given to building up the power of the central government, Jefferson dedicated himself to limiting its power in favor of the rights of the states.

The Administration of Thomas Jefferson did bring a significant change of tone and emphasis to the Federal government. However, Jefferson found, as most other Presidents have also discovered, that the realities of the presidency and the world challenged the theories of government that he brought into office. Despite Jefferson's fears of a strong national government, under his leadership the national government took bold steps that affected the country from that time forward.

The Election of 1800

When the U.S. began, the right to vote was held by free white males who owned some amount of property (how much property was determined by each state as it established voting requirements). During the late 1700s and early 1800s, the property requirements were gradually repealed. This allowed more people to participate in the political process. The election of 1800, in which Jefferson championed the cause of the average American, was a major step in the process of allowing and encouraging broader participation in elections.

Despite furthering this high ideal, the election of 1800 was bitter and vicious. The Federalists had been in office long enough to alienate a good many people with their tax on whiskey, the perceived weaknesses of the Jay Treaty with Great Britain, and the Alien and Sedition Acts. The Republicans, meanwhile, were more than happy to lead the denunciation of these unpopular actions.

In those days, candidates did not campaign themselves. That kind of blatant ambition was considered inappropriate for someone wanting to serve the public. Instead, party spokesmen made speeches and party newspapers honored their own candidates and vilified the opposition. The language used by both sides in describing the opposition in this election was neither kind nor temperate. The Republicans had not held the presidency, so they could easily criticize what the Federalists had done. Adams was characterized by the Republicans as pompous and arrogant. They circulated scandalous rumors about his tenure in foreign service. Meanwhile, Jefferson was portrayed by Federalists as an atheist, and rumors ran wild about his private life also.

Electoral Troubles

The tensions related to the election did not end when state electors cast their votes in the late fall of 1800. The Constitution called for each elector to cast two votes. The candidate receiving the most votes became President, and the one with the second-highest total became Vice President. Jefferson received more electoral votes than Adams and thus clearly defeated the Federalist incumbent; but loyal Republican electors each cast one vote for Jefferson and one vote for Jefferson's vice presidential candidate, Aaron Burr. This created a tie between Jefferson and Burr, the two men who were supposedly running-mates. This threw the election into the House of Representatives.

Thomas Jefferson, *Rembrandt Peale (American, 1800)*

Barbary Pirates

Beginning in the 1500s, the Islamic nations along the northern coast of Africa, called the Barbary States, had interfered with shipping in the Mediterranean and Atlantic Oceans. They worked the waters the way robbers preyed on road travelers. Barbary pirates, as they were called, stopped ships from other nations, kidnapped sailors, and demanded tribute (in other words, protection and ransom money). The United States paid out two million dollars in bribes before 1801.

President Jefferson, however, decided to end the practice. He sent four naval squadrons to the area to attack the pirates, a move which caused the bandits to settle for peace. The first conflict with the Barbary pirates was resolved in practical terms by 1805, though a brief second confrontation occurred in 1815. The painting at right depicts an event in 1804 when Americans deliberately burned the USS Philadelphia *to prevent its use by the pirates.*

Burning of the Frigate Philadelphia *in the Harbor of Tripoli*, Edward Moran (American, 1897)

Republicans won a majority in Congress in the 1800 election, but they would not take office until December of 1801. Thus the House of Representatives that would decide the presidential election was still controlled by Federalists, many of whom salivated at the chance to do in Thomas Jefferson. Some Federalists were willing to make Aaron Burr President, and the stubborn and prideful Burr refused to remove himself from consideration. Alexander Hamilton, who disliked Jefferson, distrusted Burr even more. Hamilton influenced House Federalists on Jefferson's behalf, and the House chose Jefferson as the new President.

The election of 1800 introduced the extreme partisanship that has become standard in America. It also demonstrated serious sectional differences in the nation. Adams carried the New England states while Jefferson won in the middle and southern states. Jefferson's victory was a shift in power away from the Northeast and into the South and West. In spite of the heated political contest, Jefferson tried to sound a conciliatory tone in his inaugural address.

(During Jefferson's first term as President, Congress passed and the states ratified the 12th Amendment, which provided for electors voting separately for President and Vice President.)

Republicans in Power

Once in office, Jefferson did not replace Federalist office holders on a broad scale. However, the Republicans in Congress worked to undo some of what the Federalists had done. The Judiciary Act of 1801 was repealed and replaced by one that created a smaller number of judgeships, which Republicans now filled. Congress also repealed the whiskey tax that had brought on the Whiskey Rebellion.

Jefferson insisted on a more cost-conscious government, which included cutting back on the size of the Army and Navy. Most of the revenue for the Federal government came from import tariffs and western land sales, and these provided enough revenue to lower the public debt during Jefferson's tenure as chief executive.

During Jefferson's second term, the importation of slaves was outlawed on the earliest date allowed in the Constitution, January 1, 1808. Slaves were still bought and sold within the United States, and the number of slaves increased as slaves had children. In addition, the smuggling of slaves into the country continued on a small scale until the time of the Civil War. However, the ending of slave importation was the first step toward changing the nature and power of slavery in the United States.

Jefferson presented his annual messages to Congress in written form, not in person. Jefferson was a poor public speaker; he also wanted to downplay the regal aspects of the presidency. His private secretary, Meriwether Lewis, and others read the messages aloud. The practice of presenting State of the Union messages to Congress in person did not resume until the presidency of Woodrow Wilson in the twentieth century.

Expanding American Territory

Just as the Jefferson presidency expanded participation by average Americans in the political process, it also expanded the territory that the nation controlled. When Jefferson took office, the country extended to the Mississippi River. Many Americans, including Thomas Jefferson, dreamed of a nation that stretched to the Pacific. Spain controlled Mexico and the area that would become the American Southwest; but the land just beyond the Mississippi, including the large area of the northern plains, was claimed by France. Jefferson had his eye on this region for many years.

Americans did not know for sure what was in the northern part of the Louisiana Territory. Rumors had reached the East Coast about volcanoes and great woolly mammoths there. Some still wondered if a northwest passage to the Pacific might be discovered, something for which the earliest explorers to the continent had searched.

Jefferson, an amateur scientist and naturalist, longed to know what could be found in Louisiana. For some time he considered sending his personal secretary, fellow Virginian and Army veteran Meriwether Lewis, on an exploratory trip into the region; but Jefferson realized that such a move might provoke a confrontation with France.

The Louisiana Purchase

Jefferson's interests soon combined with international political realities to create an exciting opportunity for the inquisitive President and the young nation. For a number of years, Spain had controlled Louisiana and the city of New Orleans. When Napoleon came to power and developed visions of a world empire, he forced Spain to return control of the region to France. Jefferson feared that American trade through New Orleans might become difficult if not impossible with the city controlled by France, since the relationship between the two former allies had been strained for some time.

The new American ambassador to France, Robert Livingston, contacted the French government to see if Napoleon would be interested in selling New Orleans to the United States for as much as $10 million. Meanwhile, Napoleon was needing

The 1904 World's Fair in St. Louis commemorated the 100th anniversary of the Louisiana Purchase. The opening was delayed a year to create a bigger event. This postcard from the event shows the approximate boundaries of the Louisiana Purchase.

Lewis & Clark at Three Forks
Edgar Samuel Paxson (American, c. 1911)

money for his war with England and had apparently given up hope of building an empire in the western hemisphere after France failed in its attempt to control the Caribbean island of Santo Domingo. The French representative in the negotiations asked Livingston if the United States would be interested in buying all of Louisiana. Livingston immediately accepted the proposal.

In 1803 the United States agreed to buy the Louisiana Territory for $15 million. By this one move, the Jefferson Administration approximately doubled the land area controlled by the United States and opened the possibility for expanding the nation to the Pacific.

Americans knew the Louisiana Territory was big, but they didn't know how big it really was. The boundaries of the territory were not clear. The region extended up the entire western side of the Mississippi River and then along the Canadian border to what is now western Montana. It also included at least some of what is now Texas as well as Pikes Peak in present-day Colorado. The American representatives in Paris asked the French how much land was actually included in the deal. The French minister replied that he did not know, but he continued, "You have made a noble bargain for yourselves, and I suppose you will make the most of it."

As exciting as it was, the Louisiana Purchase created a constitutional problem for Jefferson. Because he was a strict constructionist, the President was troubled by the fact that the Constitution nowhere gave the Federal government the power to purchase territory. Jefferson resolved the dilemma by making the purchase in the form of a treaty, which he did have the power to do with the approval of the Senate. Some Senators questioned the need for the vast wilderness, but most shared Jefferson's vision of the great possibilities for wealth and expansion; and the Senate ratified the treaty.

Lewis and Clark

Now Jefferson could legitimately send Lewis on an expedition to explore and map the region. As leader of the expedition, Lewis chose a friend he had known in the Army, William Clark (younger brother of Revolutionary War hero George Rogers Clark), to be co-leader. The Corps of Discovery, numbering about fifty men, left St. Louis in 1804 and traveled up the Missouri River. Lewis took notes, mapped the landscape, and drew pictures of flora and fauna. He discovered the prairie dog and other species of animals. When the group met Indian tribes, Lewis gave a set speech explaining that the land was now owned by a new white father in Washington. Lewis had a cannon fired and gave the tribal leaders some gifts. For much of the trip the corps was assisted by a young Shoshone woman, Sacajawea, and her French trader husband, Toussaint Charbonneau, both of whom helped translate for the Americans when they met various Indian tribes.

The Lewis and Clark expedition traveled across the Continental Divide in the Rocky Mountains and beyond the borders of the Louisiana Territory into the Columbia River Gorge, which led them to the Pacific Ocean. On the return trip, the corps split into two groups for part of the journey. They arrived back in St. Louis in 1806 after being gone for over two years. Lewis' reports to Jefferson were made public, and interest in trading, trapping, and settling in the region increased greatly. The lower tip of the territory became the state of Louisiana, which joined the Union in 1812.

Opposition in New England

The Louisiana Purchase opened another chapter of seemingly limitless possibilities for the young nation. It was not, however, welcomed by everyone. A few die-hard Federalists in Massachusetts feared that New England would lose its significance in national affairs as the country expanded west. The group, called the Essex Junto, discussed the possibility of the New England states seceding from the Union to form an independent country. The junto approached Vice President Aaron Burr to get his support. Burr, who became politically alienated from Jefferson during the President's first term, assumed that he would not be renominated for the national ticket. Burr ran for governor of New York in 1804, from which position he thought he could influence New York to join the secessionist movement. During the 1804 campaign, Alexander Hamilton sharply criticized Burr; and Burr challenged Hamilton to a duel. Hamilton, whose son had died in a duel the previous year while refusing to shoot, went to his duel against Burr with the same resolve. Burr shot and mortally wounded Hamilton on July 11, 1804.

Burr lost the governor's election, but he wasn't finished with his schemes. A few years later, Burr became involved in a mysterious plan to set up a separate nation in part of the Louisiana Territory. He was captured as he floated down the Ohio River on a large flatboat and was charged with treason. His jury trial in 1807 was conducted before Chief Justice John Marshall. Burr was acquitted on the grounds that he had not committed an overt act of treason. He left the country for a few years, returned to New York in 1812 to practice law, and died in 1836 at the age of eighty.

During Jefferson's first term, taxes were repealed, the national debt was lowered, Louisiana was acquired, the common man was honored, and national confidence was rising. In 1804 Jefferson easily defeated Federalist Charles Pinckney in the presidential race, carrying all the states except two. His new Vice President was another New York politician, George Clinton.

Portrait of Aaron Burr
John Vanderlyn (American, 1802)

Lesson 31 - Expanding Democracy

During Jefferson's Administration, the United States observed a bicentennial: 1807 marked the 200th anniversary of Jamestown, the first permanent English settlement in North America. "Hail Columbia" was one of the songs used at that celebration. Joseph Hopkinson (pictured at right) wrote the lyrics. The tune, attributed to Philip Phile and known as "The President's March," was composed around the time of George Washington's inauguration. "Hail Columbia" remained popular during the 19th century.

See what the land is like, and whether the people who live in it are strong or weak, whether they are few or many.
Numbers 13:18

★ Assignments for Lesson 31 ★

American Voices — Read Thomas Jefferson's First Inaugural Address (pages 95-97).

Read "I Love Thy Kingdom, Lord," by Timothy Dwight (page 94).

Literature — Continue reading *Narrative of the Life of David Crockett*. Plan to finish it by the end of this unit.

Bible — Start memorizing Isaiah 55:1-3.

Project — Choose your project for this unit and start working on it.

Student Review — Optional: Answer the questions for Lesson 31.

IT IS EMPHATICALLY THE PROVINCE AND DUTY OF THE JUDICIAL DEPARTMENT TO SAY WHAT THE LAW IS.

Quote from John Marshall in the U.S. Supreme Court Building

Lesson 32

The Expanding Power of the Supreme Court

John Marshall was a native of Virginia. He received little formal schooling as a child. Marshall fought in the Continental Army during the Revolutionary War, then studied law and was admitted to the Virginia bar in 1780. He became active in state politics and was elected to the Virginia assembly.

Marshall was a nationalist who supported the ratification of the Constitution and the Federalist Party. This put him in opposition to his cousin and fellow Virginian Thomas Jefferson. President John Adams named Marshall as Secretary of State in 1800 and then nominated him to be Chief Justice in 1801. Adams no doubt enjoyed the irony of nominating a Federalist from Virginia to the post after Jefferson had won the 1800 election.

Marshall was the fourth man to serve as Chief Justice. Until his tenure, the Court was not seen as a major factor in the Federal government. The Court met in the basement of the Capitol building because the Court had been overlooked in the planning of government offices. However, Marshall led the Court into a new era of activism by helping to shape the nature of the country's laws and by defining the federal relationship between the states and the central government. Marshall took the issues involved in individual cases and applied them as general principles to express how he thought the American system of government should work.

Marbury v. Madison (1803)

The most important case that the Marshall Court reviewed stemmed from the political turmoil which was brewing at the very time that Marshall came onto the Court. The Judiciary Act of 1801 reduced the size of the Supreme Court from six justices to five and created a number of new judicial positions. During his last weeks in office, outgoing President John Adams signed the commissions for the men he was appointing to fill these posts. (The story that Adams stayed up late on his last night in office signing commissions was Republican propaganda.)

However, the Secretary of State under Thomas Jefferson, James Madison, refused to deliver many of these commissions; and the new Republican-controlled Congress soon repealed the 1801 law. Federalists claimed that these actions were unconstitutional, since the positions had already been created and the men waiting to fill them were expecting their commissions and salaries.

One of the men appointed under the Judiciary Act of 1801 to be a justice of the peace for the District of Columbia was William Marbury. In keeping with the provisions of the law, Marbury brought a lawsuit before the Supreme Court that attempted to force Madison to deliver his commission. This legal standoff gave Chief Justice John Marshall an opportunity to establish the power of the Supreme Court to practice judicial review; that is, for the Court to review whether a law is within the proper limits of the Constitution. The *Marbury v. Madison* decision had three main parts.

First, Marshall said that the commission issued to Marbury under the Judiciary Act was rightfully his and he deserved to receive it. With this opinion Marshall was sympathetic to the Federalists' pleas.

Second, however, Marshall ruled that the clause of the Act that gave the Supreme Court power to issue writs of mandamus for the commissions (i.e., that gave the Court original jurisdiction in disputes over the Act) was unconstitutional, since it gave the Supreme Court an original jurisdiction which was not specified in the Constitution. Thus Marshall declared the Judiciary Act of 1801 unconstitutional, which meant that the unfilled judgeships no longer existed. In this part of his decision, the Chief Justice said what the Republicans wanted to hear.

Third, to defend his decision, Marshall claimed that the Supreme Court had the power of judicial review. The Court, Marshall said, was bound by the Constitution and by the oath taken by its justices to consider the Constitution when appeals were brought to it concerning Federal law. The Court's right of judicial review had been discussed a few times before this decision, but not decisively. "It is, emphatically, the province and duty of the judicial department to say what the law is," declared Marshall. The opinion by the Chief Justice firmly stated the priority of the Constitution over individual laws. Congress (and state governments) could not ignore the Constitution when passing laws.

Marshall's opinion walked a fine line between Congress, the President, and the Court. The Chief Justice took a strict constructionist view when he said that the Judiciary Act of 1801 added something that the Constitution did not specifically allow. However, he took an activist view in declaring the Court's power of judicial review.

Other Marshall Decisions

Under Marshall's leadership, the Court established several other precedents concerning American constitutional law.

Martin v. Hunter's Lessee (1816) overruled a decision of a state supreme court that went against rights that are outlined in the Constitution.

Fletcher v. Peck (1819) struck down a state law because it violated the constitutional sanctity of contracts.

McCulloch v. Maryland (1819) struck down a Maryland law because it hindered the implied powers of Congress under the Constitution. Maryland enacted a tax on the branch of the Bank of the United States that existed in the state. Marshall's opinion struck down the tax as unconstitutional. First, he said the Bank was a legitimate pursuit of the general power that Congress took from the Constitution to

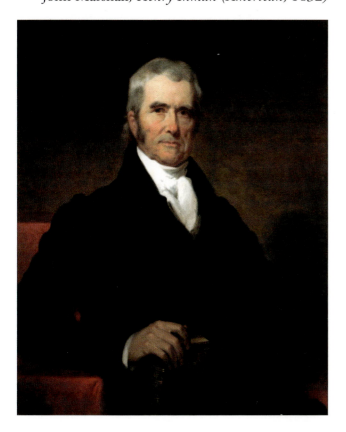

John Marshall, *Henry Inman (American, 1832)*

do whatever was "necessary and proper" to fulfill its duties. Marshall thus accepted Hamilton's loose interpretation of the Constitution. Second, Marshall declared the tax to be unconstitutional because "the power to tax involves the power to destroy," and the Federal government could not be at the mercy of state governments. In Marshall's view, the Federal government was a creation of the people, not the states. States had some areas of sovereignty, but the Federal government had areas of sovereignty granted by the Constitution which the states could not violate.

Dartmouth College v. Woodward (1819) struck down a New Hampshire law that sought to place the private Dartmouth College under state control. The law was unconstitutional, said the Court, because the college had been founded by a corporate charter, which the Court said was a contract that could not be pushed aside by state law. During his four-hour argument before the Court on behalf of the college, Dartmouth graduate Daniel Webster spoke with emotion about his love for the school and how he feared it would be ruined by the state's action. "It is, sir, as I have said, a small college. And yet there are those who love it." Soon tears welled up in Webster's eyes. It was a strong emotional appeal, but it actually had little to do with the merits of the case.

Marshall's Legacy

Marshall served as Chief Justice until his death in 1835. He helped make the judicial branch a strong factor in national government, one that the other two branches could not ignore. He participated in over one thousand decisions and wrote about five hundred opinions. After *Marbury v. Madison*, the Supreme Court did not declare another congressional law to be unconstitutional until 1853, when it struck down the 1820 Missouri Compromise.

Over the years, the Court's power of judicial review has become its chief function. In a typical court case, a defendant is on trial before the law. In a case before the Supreme Court, the law itself is on trial and the justices determine whether the law is guilty of violating the Constitution, which is the supreme law of the land. Judicial review has been used in many kinds of cases. It has upheld and it has struck down both good laws and bad laws. The aggravating problem with judicial review comes when justices inject their own views and philosophies into their decisions and interpret laws on the basis of current social and political thinking instead of simply on the content and original intent of the Constitution.

The Liberty Bell was originally cast in London in 1752 and transported to Philadelphia. It soon cracked and was melted and recast by John Pass and John Stow. Stories about the bell abound, including that it cracked when rung at the funeral of John Marshall in 1835. Apparently the prominent crack occurred in 1846, when it was rung to celebrate George Washington's birthday. It has not been rung since.

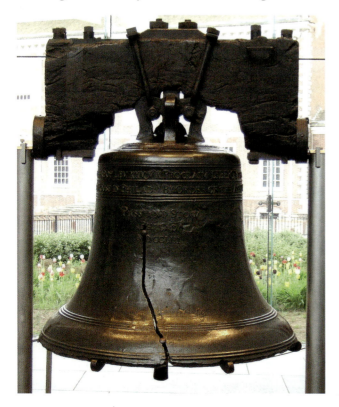

Lesson 32 - The Expanding Power of the Supreme Court

What Else Was Happening?

1804   *Napoleon Bonaparte crowns himself emperor.*

1804   *Beethoven premiers his Third Symphony. He had originally dedicated it to Napoleon out of admiration for the military leader, but then the composer changed the dedication when Napoleon took the role of emperor. That year German artist W. J. Mähler painted the image of Beethoven shown at right.*

1805   *Napoleon achieves his greatest military victory at Austerlitz, defeating the armies of Austria and Russia.*

1807   *Gas street lights are introduced in London.*

1807   *Robert Fulton invents the steamboat.*

1808   *Richard Trevithick makes a public demonstration of his steam locomotive named* Catch Me Who Can.

Vindicate the weak and fatherless;
Do justice to the afflicted and destitute.
Psalm 82:3

★ Assignments for Lesson 32 ★

American Voices   Read the excerpts from the *Marbury v. Madison* decision (pages 98-100).

Literature   Continue reading *Narrative of the Life of David Crockett*.

Bible   In the Bible study lesson for this unit, we will discuss the Second Great Awakening and the desire by many believers in America to return to the simple teachings of the Bible to find their standard of faith and practice. The idea of restoring God's plan is a common one in Scripture. Second Kings 18:1-6 describes the reform led by King Hezekiah to do away with what practices in the temple?

Work on memorizing Isaiah 55:1-3.

Project   Work on your project.

Student Review   Optional: Answer the questions for Lesson 32.

Detail from U.S. Capitol After Burning by the British, *George Munger (American, 1814)*

Lesson 33

The War of 1812

It was in many ways a war that didn't make sense. Just before war was officially declared, one of the chief causes of conflict between the two countries was removed. One side was already involved in fighting another war, and the other side was woefully unprepared. The war was unpopular with people in both countries. During the war, one country's tiny navy repeatedly defeated ships of the other side, and those defeated ships were part of the navy that supposedly ruled the seas. The best-remembered battle of the war took place after the peace treaty had already been signed.

In the early 1800s, the United States was still a youngster in the family of nations. American leaders believed that the country had to flex its muscles to make other nations notice and respect it. A difficulty arose, however, when the youngster became involved in a conflict that was taking place between two older and more experienced fighters.

Interference from Britain

The goal of American foreign policy, from the time of Washington on, was to remain neutral toward the conflict between Britain and France while maintaining as much flexibility as possible in dealing with both of the two warring nations. It was a complicated situation. Jefferson saw friendship with France as a possible help in controlling Britain's power in the western hemisphere; but he also was concerned about the consequences of being an ally of Napoleon, who was obviously thirsting for power.

Britain and France set up blockades around each other's ports, but American ships were usually able to penetrate the blockades (which came to be called paper blockades, meaning that they were blockades on paper but not effective in reality). Thus, the U.S. was able to carry on commerce with both nations. However, Britain ruled the waves in a high-handed manner. It set up patrols outside of American ports which often stopped American ships soon after they left harbor. The British seized vessels on the high seas that they suspected of carrying cargo to the enemy (namely France) or of harboring runaway British sailors. British captains sometimes didn't listen to the protestations of sailors who didn't want to be pressed into service in the British navy, and as a result the British kidnapped more than one American sailor. France sometimes interfered with American shipping also.

In the ultimate insult, in 1807 the British ship *Leopard* fired on and then its officers boarded the American ship *Chesapeake* (a warship, not a trading vessel). About twenty Americans were killed and wounded, and four others were taken as prisoners by the British. America was outraged. Congress was not in session, or it would likely have declared war. Jefferson resisted calls to react with military force, but he demanded an apology and ordered British ships out of American waters. Britain apologized for the *Chesapeake* incident but insisted that it had the right to search American ships and take any deserters that were found.

The Embargo Act

Jefferson's response to the standoff was to call for a boycott of British goods and to seek an embargo from Congress that would not allow any American goods to leave port. In this way he hoped to exert what he called peaceful coercion on England. The Embargo Act passed Congress in late 1807. The law forbade American ships from leaving port without putting up a sizable bond.

The restrictions on trade did eventually hurt England, but not for several years. The French welcomed the move because they thought it would hurt British preparedness for war. The real victim of the Embargo Act was the U.S. itself. American ships rotted in port and the shipping industry suffered greatly. In the meantime, one positive result was the increased development of American industry, which helped the U.S. become less dependent on foreign goods. However, this was a long-term change while the short-term effect was painful for the young nation.

Jefferson was severely criticized for the Embargo Act, especially in New England; but in 1808 the Sage of Monticello was nearly finished dealing with the pressures of the presidency. He was ready to retire to Monticello after his two terms, following Washington's precedent. Jefferson used his influence to help his Secretary of State, James Madison, be elected President that year. In early 1809, Congress repealed the Embargo Act; and Jefferson reluctantly signed the bill into law on March 1, 1809, three days before he left office. The conflict on the high seas, however, was still not resolved. American trade was hurt further by new laws passed under President Madison.

Western Concerns

Conflict on the high seas was not the only irritation that the U.S. felt from Great Britain. The United States was also concerned about Indian attacks on American settlers in the Northwest Territory. Many Americans believed that the attacks were encouraged by the British in Canada. In addition, Native Americans in the Southwest (the area that would become Tennessee, Alabama, and Mississippi) tried to oppose American settlement in that region. The Spanish presence in Florida was too weak to give much help to the Indians, but this Spanish weakness allowed the British to stir up further trouble in Florida. The Native Americans along the American frontier probably were secretly encouraged by the British, but the Indians had their own concerns over increasing numbers of American settlers in the West and the increasing pressures they felt to turn over to the whites more and more of what they saw as their land.

This 1808 British cartoon shows Jefferson defending his embargo policy to a group of disgruntled men who are making complaints such as, "My warehouses are full," "My family is starving," and "It was not the case in George Washington's time."

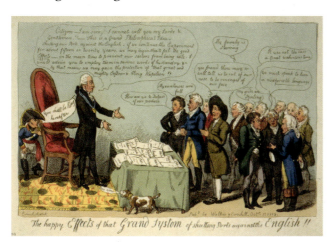

The influential Shawnee leader Tecumseh tried to unite the western tribes, north and south, against the American aggressors. Tecumseh led an attack on American forces commanded by General William Henry Harrison at the Battle of Tippecanoe, in what is now Indiana, in November of 1811. The Indians were defeated, and on the battlefield the Americans found British-made rifles left by the Native American warriors.

In addition to these security issues, western farmers had faced hard economic times for several years; and they blamed Britain's interference with America's Atlantic trade for their difficulties. The solution that many western Americans and their representatives in Congress envisioned was to take on and defeat the British troublemakers, and perhaps even take over Canada to give more land to the expanding United States. The leading proponents of war with Great Britain were the young Congressmen called "War Hawks," who included Henry Clay of Kentucky, Felix Grundy of Tennessee, and John C. Calhoun from South Carolina.

The Decision to Fight

On June 1, 1812, in a move unknown in Britain, President Madison asked Congress for a declaration of war against Great Britain. He listed American grievances against Britain that stretched back for years. Two weeks later, in a move unknown in America, the British government decided to ease its interference with American shipping and appeared ready to negotiate on other matters of concern. However, the years of British interference with American sea trade, the frustration over Indian attacks in the West, and the desire by many Americans for more land added up to a decision to fight.

Congress voted to declare war on June 18, 1812; but the declaration was far from unanimous. The vote in the Senate was 19 to 13, while in the House it was 74 to 49. New England and Mid-Atlantic representatives generally voted against the war, while southern and western members of Congress generally supported it. New Englanders were strongly against the war. Flags there flew at half-mast and Federalist newspapers labeled it "Mr. Madison's War." Nevertheless, in the presidential election of 1812, the incumbent James Madison defeated DeWitt Clinton of New York, who had been nominated by Federalists and disgruntled Republicans. Clinton, however, carried all but two New England and Mid-Atlantic states.

The Early War

The war started out badly for the U.S. The American Army numbered only about 7,000 troops, and its officers were mostly older men. American land assaults against Canada in 1812 failed, in part because state militiamen who accompanied the regular Army refused to cross the border and fight

The USS Chesapeake *was one of the first six ships built for the U.S. Navy. In an encounter with the British HMS* Shannon *in 1813, the mortally wounded commander of* Chesapeake *told his men, "Don't give up the ship." The* Chesapeake *did lose the fierce battle, and the captured ship served in the Royal Navy until 1820.*

Combat Between the English Frigate *Shannon* and the American frigate *Chesapeake*
Christoffer Wilhelm Eckersberg (Danish, 1836)

in Canada. Meanwhile, British troops took Detroit and gained almost complete control of the Great Lakes. American ground forces struggled during the entire war.

The American Navy consisted of sixteen ships, while Britain had almost one hundred vessels just in American waters. American naval strategy consisted of one-on-one encounters with British ships, most of which were successful. American privateers also proved effective against British vessels. In September 1813, a small American fleet defeated the British naval force on Lake Erie. American commander Oliver Perry's flagship was lost, but he was rowed to another vessel and eventually forced the British to surrender. His message to General William Henry Harrison was, "We have met the enemy and they are ours." A few weeks later, Harrison defeated the British at the Battle of the Thames in Canada near Detroit. Tecumseh, fighting with the British, was killed in this encounter.

British Victories and Defeats

The French dictator Napoleon abdicated in April of 1814, and the British war against France finally ended. This left Britain free to concentrate on its war with the Americans. British strategy, however, had only mixed success. A British assault, which was aimed south from Canada toward New York City along Lake Champlain, failed because the American naval squadron stationed on the lake defeated its British counterpart.

The second British attack centered on the Chesapeake Bay. British forces moved up the Potomac and attacked Washington, D.C., in August of 1814. The British burned many of the buildings in the nation's capital, including the Capitol and the White House. President Madison, along with his wife Dolley, was forced to flee the city. Mrs. Madison had the Gilbert Stuart portrait of George Washington removed from the White House and placed in her care. British troops ate the meal that had been set for the First Family in the White House dining room.

A View of the Bombardment of Fort McHenry

They arrogantly toasted "Little Jemmy" Madison before they literally toasted the Executive Mansion.

The British then moved on Baltimore, but their fierce bombardment of Fort McHenry failed to dislodge the Americans. Following this failed attack on Fort McHenry, the British fleet withdrew from the American mainland.

The Southern Front

The war also spread to the South, where American forces achieved their greatest victories under Andrew Jackson of Tennessee. When the governor of Tennessee called for volunteers to serve in the state militia in the fight against Britain, eager Tennesseans oversubscribed the number requested by several thousand. This led to Tennessee's nickname, "The Volunteer State."

Early in the war, when Jackson and his troops were in Natchez, Mississippi, he was ordered to halt and send his militia home. Jackson, however, refused to disband his troops in the wilds of Mississippi. Instead, he led them back to Tennessee himself along the Natchez Trace, walking so that sick soldiers could use his horse. His firm commitment to his men reminded them of the strength of a hickory tree; thus Jackson earned the nickname "Old Hickory."

Jackson later led his Tennessee militia against the Creek Indians in Alabama and defeated them decisively at the Battle of Horseshoe Bend in March

The Star Spangled Banner Flag

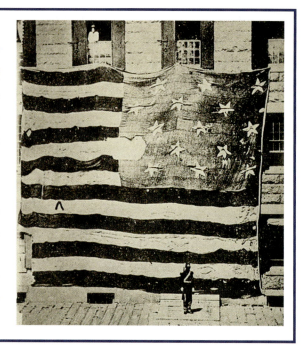

The flag that flew over Ft. McHenry has been a treasured symbol of America since the War of 1812. The original size was 30 feet by 42 feet, but over the years, pieces of the flag were cut off as souvenirs. The photo at right shows the flag in 1873 at the Boston Navy Yard. Since 1907 the flag has been held at the Smithsonian Institution in Washington, D.C.

The flag has fifteen stars and fifteen stripes because for a short time both a star and a stripe were added each time a state was admitted to the union (the flag was actually outdated in terms of the states that were in the Union in 1814). The flag policy was changed to add only a new star for each new state and to maintain the thirteen stripes.

of 1814. This was in retaliation for an Indian attack on Fort Mims near Mobile. Jackson then moved against and defeated the British position in Pensacola, invading Spanish Florida without authorization from President Madison.

The Natchez Trace developed out of forest trails made by animals and the Native Americans who hunted them. European Americans began to use it as the most direct path from Natchez, Mississippi, to Nashville, Tennessee. Inns served travelers along the Trace. Explorer Meriwether Lewis died at one of these inns in 1809, just a few years after his journey across the continent.

Finally, in late 1814 Jackson moved his forces west to New Orleans to counter what he understood was going to be a major British invasion attempt there. British caution in setting up their position near New Orleans allowed Jackson's men to build breastworks of earth and cotton bales. When the Redcoats finally attacked on January 8, 1815, they were mowed down by the American frontier riflemen. Over two thousand British troops were killed or wounded; among the dead was the British commander, General Sir Edward Packenham. The Americans lost only eight dead and thirteen wounded. As a result of this overwhelming victory, Andrew Jackson became a national hero.

The Treaty of Ghent

Officially, however, the war was already over before the Battle of New Orleans took place. British and American representatives had begun negotiations in April 1814. As the war dragged on, many people in both countries became tired of it. Since neither side was apparently capable of a decisive blow, a treaty of peace was signed in Ghent, Belgium, on December 24, 1814, ending the eighteen-month conflict. The two

Lesson 33 - The War of 1812

sides agreed to stop fighting, return prisoners, and restore previously existing borders. The war settled nothing about American rights at sea or British involvement in Indian attacks on the frontier. These and other issues had to be worked out later.

Opposition in New England

As had been the case with the Louisiana Purchase, New England Federalists expressed opposition to the actions of the Federal government. In late 1814, representatives from the five New England states met in Hartford, Connecticut, to discuss their opposition to the war. They drafted resolutions for constitutional amendments that

The Battle of New Orleans at Chalmette, 1815
Jean Hyacinthe de Laclotte (French, 1815)

would limit the war-making powers of Congress, forbid a second term for a President, and forbid successive Presidents from being from the same state (Republicans Jefferson and Madison were both from Virginia). A few New England extremists wanted to secede from the Union and negotiate a separate peace with Great Britain, while others suggested that states which disapproved of a war could in effect nullify a war declaration by Congress and refuse to go along. Representatives from the Hartford Convention arrived in Washington, D.C., carrying their demands about the same time that news of Jackson's victory and the signing of the Treaty of Ghent reached the city, so no one was really interested in hearing what the Hartford delegates had to say.

Samuel Wilson, a businessman in Troy, New York, was a supplier to the Army during the War of 1812. Crates that he shipped to the military were stamped with "U.S." According to legend, soldiers combined the supplier's name with the abbreviation on the crates and said, "Here's another shipment from Uncle Sam." Cartoonists later developed the image of Uncle Sam as a tall man in a stars-and-stripes suit who represents the United States.

Results of the War

The War of 1812 was largely indecisive in military terms, although Jackson's victory at New Orleans probably strengthened the American position in later negotiations with Great Britain and insured congressional ratification of the Treaty of Ghent. The major gain for the U.S. was an increase in national pride and self-confidence. The war has sometimes been called the second war for independence, as the young nation once again held the mighty British lion at bay.

More importantly, however, it established the United States as a strong and independent nation. Americans believed that they had won the war, and they turned their attention to increased westward expansion and to developing an economy and a system of internal improvements that would tie the growing nation together and capitalize on her bountiful opportunities.

*Depart from evil and do good;
Seek peace and pursue it.
Psalm 34:14*

★ Assignments for Lesson 33 ★

American Voices — Read the excerpts from the letters between John Adams and Thomas Jefferson (pages 103-106).

Read "The Star-Spangled Banner" by Francis Scott Key (page 107).

Literature — Continue reading *Narrative of the Life of David Crockett*.

Bible — Matthew 21:12-13 describes a time in the ministry of Jesus when He confronted corruption in the practices in the temple. What did He say that the buyers and sellers had made the temple?

Work on memorizing Isaiah 55:1-3.

Project — Work on your project.

Student Review — Optional: Answer the questions for Lesson 33.

Detail from The Great Horseshoe Fall, Niagara, *Alvan Fisher (American, 1820)*

Lesson 34

The Era of Good Feelings?

In the twenty-four years from 1801 to 1825, America had but three Presidents. All three were Republicans, all were from Virginia, and each served eight years. After Thomas Jefferson came James Madison. Then, just as Jefferson had used his influence to encourage the election of Madison, Madison's influence helped bring about the election of his friend and Secretary of State, James Monroe. Monroe faced only token opposition from the dying Federalist Party in 1816 and none in 1820 (one 1820 elector voted for John Quincy Adams just so George Washington would remain the only unanimous choice). During this period, almost all political leaders came to describe themselves as Republicans. After Monroe took office in 1817, he made a goodwill tour of New England, where one newspaper described the times as the "Era of Good Feelings."

The nation was growing and changing internally. During colonial days, the America that was controlled by people of European descent extended inland only a relatively few miles from the Atlantic coast. After the Revolutionary War, the country grew to include the vast lands between the Appalachians and the Mississippi River. Then in 1803, the Louisiana Purchase almost doubled the area that belonged to the young nation. Thus, a mere twenty years after the end of the war for independence, the United States had grown from thirteen states along the Atlantic coast to an expanding nation that stretched two-thirds of the way across the continent. The millions of acres west of the Appalachians were sparsely populated, but people were moving onto them by the tens of thousands. While these settlers developed the abundant resources of the West, an industrial revolution changed the economy of the eastern cities and the nation as a whole.

Monroe, who was President from 1817 to 1825, was the last veteran of the Revolutionary War to serve as chief executive. Fifteen years younger than Thomas Jefferson, Madison represented the generation that followed the founding fathers. Whereas James Madison was a contemporary of Jefferson, Monroe studied law under Jefferson. Monroe's presidency was a transition from the uncertain period of the republic's beginning to the time when America's existence was an established and accepted fact.

Some Things Were Not So Good

The newspaper headline from Monroe's New England visit made a positive statement, but beneath the surface serious problems existed. Despite George Washington's warnings, partisan politics had come to influence policies, positions, and candidates. The Republicans had internal divisions that eventually

179

Thomas Gallaudet

During President Monroe's New England tour, he spoke at the dedication of the country's first permanent school for the deaf, founded in Hartford, Connecticut in 1817. Thomas Gallaudet, a dedicated disciple of Christ, had taken a special interest in the deaf because of his concern for a deaf child in his hometown of Hartford. Gallaudet traveled to France to learn about methods used there for teaching the hearing-impaired, including a way of communicating letters and words by standardized hand motions. A form of this system has come to be known as American Sign Language, or ASL. Gallaudet founded the school in Hartford to help the deaf be able to know the Lord and to function in society. President Monroe usually dressed in an old-fashioned way, with knee breeches and a tri-corner hat like those worn at the time of the Revolution. The children at the school made up a sign to indicate Monroe that alluded to his hat, and this sign is still used in ASL to refer to the President.

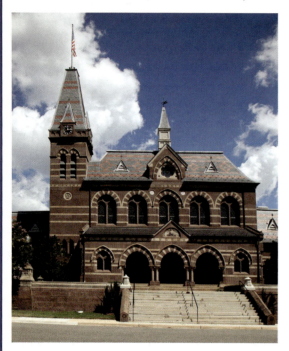

Thomas Gallaudet married Sophia Fowler, one of the students in his school. Edward Gallaudet, one of their sons, was the first president of a Federally-chartered college for the deaf. It was founded in 1857 in Washington, D.C., and was later named Gallaudet University in honor of Thomas. Besides their academic studies, students at the university participate in several intercollegiate sports. The practice of a football team calling its plays in a huddle began with the Gallaudet team, when they perceived that opposing teams were reading their signs to try to determine the play they were going to run.

Chapel Hall at Gallaudet University (Built in 1870)

led to the formation of separate parties. The U.S. economy faced difficulties in the years after the War of 1812. Foreign relations were generally positive, but the country still had some serious outstanding matters to be resolved. Almost one-fifth of the people who lived in the land of the free were held in bondage as slaves. The issue of slavery began to create a serious national debate during this period, a debate that continued to a greater or lesser extent until the Civil War.

Moreover, the country had borrowed heavily during the War of 1812, and the national government's budget was in poor shape. The first Bank of the United States had closed in 1811 because the Republicans then in power believed it to be unconstitutional. As a result, the number of state banks had increased; but many of them were risky ventures with little hard money to back up their loans. In addition, American agriculture and the developing American manufacturing sector were still not ready to meet growing internal demands and to renew avenues of international trade after the war.

The Republican Recovery Plan

Following the war, the Republican Congress developed a three-point plan to encourage economic growth. First, a tariff was enacted in 1816 to protect American industries from cheaper foreign competition. The tariff made foreign goods more expensive than American-made ones. Manufacturers supported the tariff; but New England shipping businesses opposed it, fearing that it would hurt them. Southern planters also opposed the tariff because they were afraid they might lose overseas markets for their agricultural products if countries could not sell their products in the United States. These sectional and economic differences have appeared many times in debates over American economic policy.

Second, also in 1816, Congress created the Second Bank of the United States. Questions about whether the Bank was constitutional took a back seat to the desire of westerners to have a sound national currency and a stable source for loans. Unfortunately, the bank was not able to help much. State banks had created an unstable situation, especially in the West. A few years later, the Bank of the United States demanded payment of loans it had made to these state-chartered banks, many of which were not able to pay and had to close. This led to many businesses closing also. Many people who owned property were not able to make their mortgage payments, and they lost what they owned. This economic downturn was called the Panic of 1819, and it lasted until 1823. Many in the West blamed the Bank of the United States for causing the problems, even though state banking systems had already put the national economy in deep trouble.

Third, the Republican Congress developed an aggressive program of improving transportation through the building of roads, canals, and (later) railroads. The western region needed reliable

---

In December 1811 and January 1812, a series of powerful earthquakes centered at New Madrid, Missouri, shook the Mississippi Valley. One quake was estimated to have equaled 8.8 on the Richter scale, one of the most powerful ever to have occurred anywhere in the world. The shock waves from the quakes awakened President Madison in the White House and caused church bells to ring in Charleston, South Carolina. The earthquakes caused a huge split in the land of northwest Tennessee, and the Mississippi River ran backwards for a time to fill it. The body of water created in this crevice by the quakes is now called Reelfoot Lake. People on the first steamboats that went down the Mississippi River saw the destruction that had been caused by the earthquakes. The loss of human life was relatively small since the region was sparsely populated at the time.

transportation to encourage settlement and to transport farm products to market. Only a handful of roads crossed the Appalachian Mountains, and these roads were mostly paths cleared through the forest. River transportation was relatively more reliable; but varying river depths, debris, floods, and droughts caused plenty of problems for water transportation. Meanwhile, travel in the East was slow enough. The one hundred mile trip between Philadelphia and New York took two days; going from Boston to New York took three. City streets were dirt; roads in the countryside were often muddy ruts.

President Madison questioned the constitutionality of the Federal government funding transportation projects, but President Monroe believed that such projects were "necessary and proper" for the good of the country. The Federally-funded National or Cumberland Road left Cumberland, Maryland, headed west to Wheeling, Virginia on the Ohio River, and eventually was completed to Vandalia, Illinois. Many state governments took on road and canal projects of their own. Roads were called turnpikes because travelers paid tolls which allowed a pike (or stake) to turn and let them pass. County roads were sometimes built using the labor of county residents. Men were often required to work a certain number of days per year on the roads or pay a tax if they did not. Over 3,000 miles of canals were built across the country by 1837.

Developments in Water Transportation

The best known canal project in the country was the Erie Canal in New York State. Conceived by Governor DeWitt Clinton, the 350-mile waterway was begun in 1817 and completed in 1825. The 40-foot wide engineering marvel connected Buffalo on Lake Erie to Albany on the Hudson River, which then flowed south to the port of New York City. The canal cut travel time between Buffalo and New York from twenty days to six, and the cost of transporting freight on canal flatboats and barges also dropped dramatically. The Erie Canal made a handsome profit and tied the Great Lakes region more firmly to New York City and the East Coast.

Another boon to water transportation was the development of the steamboat. Robert Fulton piloted the first steamboat, the *Clermont*, up the Hudson River in 1807. By 1829 over 200 steamboats were in use in the West. Steam-powered boats were too large for canals, but they made river transportation much easier. Before the advent of steam, flatboats were the most common way that people and goods

---

In 1918 New York State completed a modernized canal that incorporated much of the old Erie Canal. This canal continues to carry vessels between Albany and Buffalo. Most of this traffic is recreational, though a small number of cargo ships continue to use the canal since the cost of transportation by ship is cheaper than by train or truck.

Lesson 34 - The Era of Good Feelings?

Two Former Presidents

Thomas Jefferson and John Adams had been close friends for many years in the early days of the nation. They had worked together in founding the country and had spent time together overseas when Adams was the American representative in England and Jefferson served in the same post in France. However, the political turmoil at the end of Adams' term caused them to become enemies. They never saw each other again after 1801. After several years, friends urged them to renew their relationship. Adams wrote to Jefferson in 1812, and they exchanged a remarkable series of letters over the next fourteen years, discussing many aspects of politics and culture. Adams and Jefferson died within a few hours of each other on July 4, 1826, the fiftieth anniversary of the Declaration of Independence, while Adams' son, John Quincy Adams, was President.

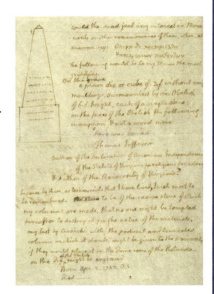

Near the end of his life, Thomas Jefferson left written instructions (shown at right) for the design of his gravestone. He wrote his own epitaph: "Here was buried Thomas Jefferson, Author of the Declaration of American Independence, Of the Statute of Virginia for Religious Freedom & Father of the University of Virginia." According to his instructions, the fact that he was President of the United States is not mentioned on his grave marker.

traveled on the rivers. A flatboat from Nashville or Louisville, for example, could be floated to New Orleans with a load of cotton. When the cotton was taken to market, the crew broke up the flatboat and sold it for lumber, then walked home along the Natchez Trace through Mississippi. Steamboats enabled faster traffic that could move upstream as well as downstream. A flatboat trip from Nashville to New Orleans took four months; on a steamboat, it took about twenty days.

Amazing Changes

Despite the obstacles, Americans continued to move west. The same pulls of cheap land, greater freedom, and the chance for a new start that had brought the first settlers from England tugged at Americans living on the eastern seaboard. The American population almost doubled between 1800 and 1820, from 5.3 million to 9.6 million. Many veterans of the War of 1812 sought out new homes in the West. A new influx of immigrants from Europe was beginning, and many of them moved to the West also. In 1800, 1804, and 1820, Congress reduced the requirements for a minimum land purchase in the Northwest Territory. By 1820 a person only had to purchase eighty acres at $1.25 per acre, and he had four years to pay. This made the rich land of the West accessible to more people. Following Louisiana's admission to the Union in 1812 as the eighteenth state, the next four states created were Indiana (1816), Mississippi (1817), Illinois (1818), and Alabama (1819).

Before the United States was forty years old, it had created a government that was unlike any other in the world; fought two major wars; and dealt with continuing unrest on its borders north, south, and west. It wrestled with trying issues both foreign and domestic. The pace of growth and technological change was dizzying, and the optimism of the American people was seemingly boundless. In the first quarter of the nineteenth century, America was a changing and growing nation.

*For what does it profit a man to gain the whole world,
and forfeit his soul?
Mark 8:36*

★ Assignments for Lesson 34 ★

American Voices   Read "Thanatopsis" and "To a Waterfowl" by William Cullen Bryant (pages 108-110).

Literature   Continue reading *Narrative of the Life of David Crockett*.

Bible   In Revelation 2:1-7, what did the Lord say that He had against the church in Ephesus? What did He command them to do?

Work on memorizing Isaiah 55:1-3.

Project   Work on your project.

Student Review   Optional: Answer the questions for Lesson 34.

Camp Meeting of the Methodists (c. 1819)

Lesson 35 - Bible Study

The Second Great Awakening

Thousands of people thronged the dusty roads near Lexington, Kentucky, in the August heat of 1801. They traveled by foot, horseback, and wagon. Whole families made the trek that for many people required several days. They were all going to a large field near the small village of Cane Ridge. What happened there for six days redefined American religious experience and kindled an outpouring of new and dramatic religious expression. It changed America in the first half of the 1800s and continues to have an impact today.

A Challenging Religious Climate

The period of religious revival in the early 1800s was the result of several factors, most important of which, of course, was the working of God. The period after the American Revolution had seen a general decrease in religious activity in America. The break with England left relationships with British-based denominations uncertain. Americans were consumed with creating a new nation and building their personal wealth. Popular ideas of the times included Enlightenment rationalism and theological Deism, neither of which encouraged religious fervency. Frontier life was often rough and tumble and sometimes bordered on lawlessness. Churches were not a major part of frontier life as settlement began. People moved west to get land and to get rich, not to find God. The influence of the world was strong.

Following the example of John Wesley in England, Francis Asbury and other dedicated Methodist circuit-riding preachers in America rode on horseback from settlement to settlement to preach to small gatherings that became Methodist congregations. This was taking the message to the people instead of waiting for the people to come to a building. However, evangelists on the frontier often despaired at the low level of spiritual interest they found there.

Meanwhile, within religious circles, new ideas were developing. Some ministers questioned the creeds and practices of the traditional religious denominations, and some even wondered why denominations were needed at all. Preachers also questioned the typical requirement that a person receive formal training and ordination in order to preach the Word of God. It seemed to them that being able to preach ought to be based on a changed life, not on having formal educational attainments or being part of a particular religious group.

The first ripples of spiritual re-awakening occurred in several scattered locations. Timothy Dwight led a renewal at Yale in the late 1790s. Individual preachers in New England, North Carolina, and Virginia, and a few in the West, began preaching for conviction and conversion. The turning point and the high water mark of this Second Great Awakening came with the Cane Ridge Camp Meeting in August of 1801.

Cane Ridge

Lexington, Kentucky, the largest city in the West at the time, had a population of about two thousand. Estimates vary as to the number of people who attended the Cane Ridge meeting, but almost assuredly the number was at least ten thousand. For six days, preaching and singing took place day and night. Often evangelists preached in different areas of the encampment at the same time. Presbyterian, Baptist, and Methodist preachers participated and worked together. They urged all of the people to repent, accept Christ as their Savior, and start living for Christ.

The fervent sermons meeting the spiritual hunger of the people led to many confessions of faith. The spiritual atmosphere at Cane Ridge also led to remarkable and unusual physical manifestations that came to be known as exercises. These included the falling exercise (people being overcome and falling to the ground, sometimes lying motionless for an hour or more), the jerks, the dancing exercise, the barking exercise, and the laughing and singing exercises.

When the people headed home from Cane Ridge, a fire had been lit that changed the frontier and changed American religious expression. Hundreds of camp meetings took place in western Pennsylvania, Ohio, Kentucky, and Tennessee. They were called camp meetings because people camped for several days while attending the activities. The practice of holding revivals or gospel meetings today comes in large part from these camp meetings. The emphasis in these meetings was on the need for personal conviction, but they also served as social gatherings for the scattered residents of the frontier. Revivals continued to serve this social function for communities well into the twentieth century.

Changes in American Churches

Camp meetings changed the role of religion on the American frontier. Churches grew in size and number and in their influence in many communities. Believers eventually became involved with such social causes as the temperance movement (which opposed the abuse of alcohol), prison reform, and the abolitionist movement. People were genuinely changed, and life in many frontier families and communities became more stable. The Second Great Awakening also affected the teaching and practices of American churches. The appeals for every person to make a decision for Christ by his or her own free will challenged the widely accepted Calvinistic belief that only a relatively few people were elected for salvation and that nothing a person did could affect his or her predestined fate.

One stream of thought flowing through America at the time was the Scottish Common Sense Philosophy. This view held that all people had a basic

The Cane Ridge Meeting House in southern Kentucky was built in 1791. Barton Stone became the minister there in 1796.

sense of right and wrong which could be guided by means of reason and plain teaching to lead them to do the right things in their spiritual, personal, social, and political lives. Any individual, according to this idea, was capable of hearing and understanding the truth of Scripture if it was explained in a rational way. This view held that people were capable of doing what was right. This idea also conflicted with Calvinism, which taught that people were born sinners, suffered from hereditary total depravity, and were incapable of making right decisions without the prompting of God's Spirit.

Changes in Church Organization

This period of revival also changed the practices of many churches. This change is sometimes called the democratization of religion. People began to think that ministers should be plain folk and not separated from church members by education or lifestyle. Many congregations of believers did not want to be part of a denomination and so declared themselves to be independent and autonomous. Baptists especially emphasized preachers living as the people did and congregations being independent from any denominational structure.

During this period many ministers broke with their denominations in a desire simply to be Christians according to the New Testament. James O'Kelley left the Methodist Church and formed a group called Republican Methodists. Elias Smith left the Baptist denomination to practice what he called primitive Christianity. Barton Stone, the minister at the Cane Ridge Presbyterian Church and a participant in the Cane Ridge camp meeting, left the Presbyterian Church with other ministers. They first formed a separate presbytery, but then they dissolved that body and sought to live and work simply as New Testament Christians. Thomas and Alexander Campbell, father and son, arrived in the U.S. from Scotland a few years after Cane Ridge. Living in western Pennsylvania, they also abandoned the Presbyterian system and advocated primitive

This engraving from around 1885 honors "pioneers in the great religious reformation of the nineteenth century." Clockwise from left are Walter Scott (an associate of the Campbells), Thomas Campbell, Barton Stone, and Alexander Campbell.

New Testament Christianity, in an attempt to "speak where the Bible speaks and be silent where the Bible is silent," as Thomas Campbell put it.

New Religious Groups

The Second Great Awakening gave rise to new religious groups in America. Denominational leaders of the Presbyterian Church opposed the emotional outbursts of Cane Ridge and other frontier camp meetings. The Church hierarchy also insisted on significant formal training for its ministers, even though this meant that rapidly growing churches on the frontier were without ministers for a long time. In reaction to this stance by the Presbyterian Church, a group of Presbyterians met in Dickson, Tennessee, near Nashville, in 1810 to form the

Cumberland Presbyterian Church. Cumberland Presbyterians welcomed the fervent spiritual activity that was taking place on the frontier and did not require as much formal training for ministers.

The groups led by Barton Stone and Alexander Campbell saw themselves as movements dedicated to the restoration of New Testament Christianity. The two groups established fellowship in 1832. They were variously known as the Disciples, Christian Churches, and Churches of Christ. For a time, the Restoration Movement was the fastest growing religious group in America.

Other religious movements developed in the United States later in the first half of the 1800s. We will discuss those groups as well as individual religious leaders in subsequent lessons.

Optimism in America

One factor that influenced the Second Great Awakening and later religious movements was the profound optimism in America at the time. The United States had won its independence from Great Britain in a fight for freedom and personal rights. The country was expanding in terms of population and territory, and it seemed as though the possibilities for America were limitless. The old ways of European monarchies had been thrown off, and in the same way many people wanted to put aside the old religious structures of creeds, institutions, and denominations. This boundless optimism led many Americans to believe that the millennium was possible and even imminent in their new and growing nation.

Thus says the Lord, "Stand by the ways and see and ask for the ancient paths, where the good way is, and walk in it; and you will find rest for your souls."
Jeremiah 6:16a

★ Assignments for Lesson 35 ★

American Voices — Read the Last Will and Testament of the Springfield Presbytery (pages 101-102).

Literature — Finish reading *Narrative of the Life of David Crockett*. Literary analysis available in *Student Review*.

Bible — Recite or write Isaiah 55:1-3 from memory.

Project — Complete your project for the unit.

Student Review — Optional: Answer the questions for Lesson 35 and for *Narrative of the Life of David Crockett* and take the quiz for Unit 7.

Home of Pierre Menard, First Lieutenant Governor of Illinois, in Ellis Grove, Illinois

8 Growing Pains

Westward expansion raised the ominous question of the spread of slavery. The slavery debate was quieted for a time by the Missouri Compromise of 1820, but the issue was not resolved in a satisfactory way. The Monroe Doctrine was a major foreign policy statement by the nation and was an attempt to make the U.S. a significant player in the western hemisphere. The differences between John Quincy Adams and Andrew Jackson highlighted the deep political divisions that existed in the country. The first half of the nineteenth century was a remarkably active time for new religious movements.

Lesson 36 - The Missouri Compromise
Lesson 37 - The Monroe Doctrine
Lesson 38 - John Quincy Adams
Lesson 39 - Andrew Jackson Before the Presidency
Lesson 40 - Bible Study: Nineteenth Century Religious Movements

Memory Work   Memorize Proverbs 14:32-35 by the end of this unit.

Books Used   The Bible
American Voices
Narrative of the Life of Frederick Douglass

Project (choose one)

1) Write 300 to 500 words on one of the following topics:

- Write a report on the contributions of the Adams family to America, especially John and Abigail Adams, John Quincy Adams, Charles Francis Adams Sr., Charles Francis Adams Jr., and Henry Adams. See Lesson 38.

- Respond to the tenets of transcendentalism. Include at least three different quotations from Scripture in your response. See Lesson 40.

2) Memorize Proverbs 14:24-35. If you choose this project, you should recite or write the verses from memory at the end of the week.

3) Make a large jigsaw puzzle of the United States with entire states as the pieces. Make the states to scale. Make slave state puzzle pieces of one color, non-slave states another color, and states that entered the union after the Civil War a third color. You will need to do research outside the information found in this unit. See Lesson 36.

Literature

Narrative of the Life of Frederick Douglass

Frederick Douglass was born into slavery in 1817 in Maryland. He managed to escape in 1838 and went to Massachusetts. His impromptu speech to an antislavery meeting in 1841 revealed him to be an eloquent and passionate spokesman for abolition. Douglass worked in the Underground Railroad that smuggled slaves to freedom, edited an abolitionist newspaper, and became the best-known black spokesman for abolition in the country. Friends eventually gathered enough money to purchase his freedom legally.

Critics of abolition voiced doubts that Douglass had ever been a slave. They said that he was an imposter put forth by the abolition movement. To counter their charges, Douglass published this narrative of his life in 1845. He revised it several times over the years until the final edition appeared in 1882 as *The Life and Times of Frederick Douglass*.

Douglass was a determined and self-motivated man. He respected the Christian faith, but he did not respect everyone he knew who claimed to be Christians. In Douglass' narrative, you will feel his anger at slavery and at the injustices he and others suffered. Be sure to read the Appendix at the end of the book.

Douglass held several government positions during and after the Civil War. He died in 1895.

Missouri River in Central Missouri

Lesson 36

The Missouri Compromise

"This momentous question, like a fire-bell in the night, awakened me and filled me with terror," wrote former President Thomas Jefferson from Monticello. The issue to which he referred was not the report of a foreign attack, nor the problems of an economic downturn, nor was it destruction caused by a natural disaster. Instead, it involved the admission of a new state into the Union, something that had happened several times previously. The state was one created from the Louisiana Territory, which Jefferson had brought into the country. What appeared to be a simple action, however, was not simple at all because it brought to the surface the ominous question of slavery.

Background to the Compromise

The issue of slavery had hung over the nation since colonial times. All of the colonies practiced slavery. Only a relatively few people during the colonial period questioned whether slavery should exist. Slaveholders such as Patrick Henry and Thomas Jefferson agonized over the institution, but they accepted it as a necessary evil.

Opposition to slavery grew in the North following the Revolution. The seven northernmost states abolished slavery between 1777 and 1804, while the other six maintained it. When settlement extended into unorganized territories of the South, including what became Alabama, Mississippi, and Louisiana, southerners took their slaves with them to work the cotton and sugar fields. This ensured the region's continued dependence on slavery.

People in different sections of the country had different ideas about how and whether slavery should be allowed in the territories and in states formed from those territories. Many people in non-slave states generally opposed extending slavery into the territories and had little interest in defending slavery, while slave state leaders defended the expansion of slavery as a right and a necessity. Since the Constitution did not mention slavery, most people believed that the Federal government had no authority to act on slavery where it already existed. It was seen as entirely a state issue. However, opponents of slavery believed that Congress did have the right and the duty to determine how slavery would be handled in the territories and in new states formed from those territories.

As new states were admitted into the Union, Congress developed the practice of maintaining a numerical balance between slave and free states. This practice demonstrates that many people realized the potentially explosive nature of the issue. The numerical balance of the states meant that slave state and free state representation was equal in the U.S. Senate. However, the population in the North and Midwest was growing faster than in the South, so slave state Representatives were beginning to be outnumbered in the House of Representatives. Southerners wanted to keep a balance in the Senate to help defend the rights of slave owners. Slavery's defenders did not want to fall into a minority in the U.S. Senate also and face the possibility that antislavery forces might try to move against slavery on a national level.

The Missouri Proposal

The territory of Alabama, where slavery was practiced, applied for admission as a state in 1819. Its admission would give the Union eleven free and eleven slave states. Missouri territory also applied for admission to the Union in 1819. Slavery existed there as well, so everyone knew that the state would accept slavery. Upsetting the slave-free balance of states was not unusual for short periods of time when a state was ready for admission. However, two factors made the question of Missouri's admission especially momentous. First, Missouri's request for admission heightened the question of what to do about slavery in the Louisiana Territory. Louisiana had already been formed from the territory as a slave state, and Missouri would be the second. In addition, Congressman James Tallmadge of New York proposed an amendment to the bill for Missouri's admission that would prohibit the further introduction of slaves into the state and that would require emancipation of slaves born in Missouri when they reached the age of twenty-five. In other words, the Tallmadge Amendment would require the gradual abolition of slavery in Missouri as a condition for its admission.

The two sides in the slavery debate either desired or feared the extension of slavery throughout the Louisiana Territory and in states that might be formed from it. Allowing slavery to exist without restriction in the Territory would give slaveholding interests at least the hope of maintaining a balance in the Senate. Forbidding slavery would mean that slave interests would have an ever-diminishing voice in national policy.

Statue of Henry Clay in the Kentucky State Capitol

Compromise in Congress

Late in 1819, while the Missouri application for statehood was still before Congress, Maine applied for admission as a free state. Under the leadership of Henry Clay, Congress worked out a compromise. First, Missouri and Maine were both to be admitted, which would maintain the slave-free balance in the Senate. Second, the Missouri Territory was divided. Slavery was banned north of Missouri's southern border, the 36°30' latitude line, except in Missouri itself. Congress enacted legislation to accomplish these ends in March of 1820. The Tallmadge Amendment was not adopted. Most people expected little settlement north of Missouri, and the region

Lesson 36 - The Missouri Compromise

west of Louisiana and the Arkansas Territory did not even belong to the United States at the time. Congress hoped that the Missouri Compromise would settle, at least for a while, the difficult question of the spread of slavery.

However, Congress needed a second Missouri Compromise truly to settle the issue. Maine was admitted to the Union, but Missouri was only authorized to write a state constitution. Missouri lawmakers included a provision in their constitution forbidding "free Negroes and mulattoes" (people of white and African American parentage) from entering the state. Since some African Americans were citizens in other states, this provision violated Article IV, Section 2 of the U.S. Constitution. This section grants the citizens of each state all the privileges and immunities of citizens in all the states. It was unconstitutional for Missouri to forbid citizens of other states from coming there.

Missouri's action re-kindled the issue. Since part of Missouri's state constitution was unconstitutional, was Missouri a state or was it still only a territory? The uncertainty continued into 1821. When Congress met to count the electoral votes from the 1820 presidential election, three votes from Missouri were presented. The outcome of the election was not in question, since President James Monroe received all of the electoral votes except one and Vice President Daniel D. Tompkins received all but a handful; but the controversy over Missouri's right to participate in the election caused a huge uproar. Congress adopted the compromise proposed by Clay. They took two counts of the electoral votes. One included Missouri's votes and the other did not. Congress then simply declared Monroe and Tompkins to be the winners.

As the debate over Missouri statehood continued, opponents of slavery and defenders of slavery used strong language in expressing their respective positions and in issuing warnings about what might happen if the other position were to be adopted. Some raised the possibility of disunion. Once again,

The southern border of Missouri, the 36°30' latitude line, is the same line that divides Virginia from North Carolina and Tennessee from Kentucky. The "bootheel" in southeastern Missouri was included within the state's borders, even though it lies south of that latitude line. Apparently a wealthy and influential landowner who lived in the area persuaded the Missouri territorial government to request that his area be included in the state when it made its application for statehood to Congress. The bootheel, which has much in common with Arkansas and other southern states, is still largely agricultural, as seen above.

Henry Clay brought about a compromise. He proposed that Missouri be admitted, but only with the understanding that it could not deny admission to the state to anyone who was or who might become a citizen in any state. The legislation passed Congress with this language. Missouri accepted it even while it defiantly denied that Congress had the power to bind it in this way. Missouri became a state on August 10, 1821. The entire process from application to admission took over two and a half years.

Thomas Jefferson was concerned about the Missouri Compromise because it introduced slavery as an issue of national policy. The country would no longer be able to keep slavery largely in the background as it had done thus far in its political life. In addition, the debate highlighted the sharp differences between sections of the country over how to deal with slavery. Jefferson feared that one day issues involving slavery might bring about the rupture of the Union. Forty years later, events proved that Jefferson was right.

What Else Was Happening?

1812   Napoleon invades Russia with an army of 450,000 men. When he returns to France after an unsuccessful campaign and a brutal Russian winter, his army numbers 50,000.

1815   Napoleon is finally defeated at the Battle of Waterloo by English forces led by the Duke of Wellington and is exiled to the remote Atlantic island of St. Helena. Napoleon dies in 1821.

1819   Scottish author Sir Walter Scott publishes Ivanhoe and creates the literary genre of historical fiction.

1821   The Roman Catholic Church removes the works of Copernicus from the list of prohibited books.

1821   Simón Bolívar leads the South American nation of Colombia to independence from Spain.

1822   The first of several potato crop failures in Ireland leads to serious famine.

1822   New York City seminary professor Clement Clarke Moore writes the poem, "A Visit from St. Nicholas," for his children. Better known by its opening line, "'Twas the night before Christmas," it has seen numerous editions. This 1912 illustration is by Jessie Wilcox Smith.

*Beyond all these things put on love,
which is the perfect bond of unity.
Colossians 3:14*

★ Assignments for Lesson 36 ★

Literature   Begin reading *Narrative of the Life of Frederick Douglass*. Plan to finish it by the end of this unit.

Bible   The Bible study lesson this week looks at religious activity in America in the first half of the 1800s. One feature of this activity was the rise of several movements or groups that claimed to have a deeper insight into truth than what traditional Christianity offered. Read 1 John 2:23. List three things outside of Christ that people mistake for true spiritual fulfillment.

Start memorizing Proverbs 14:32-35.

Project   Choose your project for this unit and start working on it.

Student Review   Optional: Answer the questions for Lesson 36.

Detail from The Monroe Doctrine, *Allyn Cox (American, 1974)*

Lesson 37

The Monroe Doctrine

Every nation has a foreign policy, which is the way in which it deals with other nations. In the early years of the republic, United States foreign policy tended to be cautious and to maintain neutrality because early American administrations wanted to have good relations with other countries. The country was not militarily strong and thus could provide little assistance to another nation that was at war. In addition, the U.S. did not have overseas territories to protect, and it had little interest in conquering or controlling other lands.

America's main foreign policy interest was in building trade relations with other countries. The American people and government were much more interested in issues having to do with matters inside the United States. As we have noted, the U.S. had long-standing conflicts with Great Britain and France; but primarily the country simply wanted the ability to trade with other nations and the freedom not to become entangled in problems that other countries were having.

Relations with Britain

In the years following the War of 1812, the British government decided that British interests would be better served by being a friend of the United States instead of an adversary. As a result, the U.S. concluded several agreements with Great Britain that reflected improved relations with the former enemy. Warships were removed from the Great Lakes, U.S. fishing rights off Newfoundland and Labrador were reaffirmed, and the U.S.-Canada border was established at the 49th parallel of latitude.

The two countries also agreed to joint occupation of the Oregon Territory, which extended from the 42nd parallel (now the northern border of California) north to the 54°40' line (which now marks the southern border of Alaska). With this shared responsibility over Oregon, the United States extended a measure of territorial control all the way to the Pacific Ocean. Great Britain refused, however, to allow American ships into the British-controlled West Indies, which prevented the United States from taking advantage of that trading market. Britain was still by far the stronger of the two countries, so they were able to make agreements that confirmed this superiority.

Spain and Florida

Another area of foreign policy activity involved Florida, which was controlled by Spain. Florida had been troublesome for the United States for several years. The British had used its outposts in Florida to attack the United States during the War of 1812 and to encourage Indian raids on the U.S. Meanwhile, Spain was losing power and was not able to govern Florida effectively. In 1817 the American government authorized Andrew Jackson to lead an expedition into Florida against the Seminoles to stop their raids. Jackson took over a Spanish outpost and hanged two Seminole leaders. After a court-martial, he executed two British subjects who had helped to stir up the Indians. The forces commanded by Jackson controlled western Florida by mid-1818.

Jackson's actions angered Spain, but Spain was too weak to retaliate. Both countries knew that the U.S. could take Florida whenever it wanted to. To settle the dispute peacefully, the United States and Spain signed a treaty in 1819 that gave the U.S. all of Florida, in return for which the U.S. took responsibility for $5 million in claims by individual Americans against Spain. The treaty also settled the western border of the Louisiana Territory. In the settlement, the United States gave up its claims to part of Texas along the Gulf Coast. The border of the Louisiana Territory was established as being along the Sabine, Red, and Arkansas Rivers, and then heading west to the Pacific coast along the 42nd parallel.

James Monroe, *Samuel Morse (American, 1819)*

The agreement to remove warships from the Great Lakes initiated the pattern that helped the United States and Canada develop the longest non-militarized border between two countries in the world (i.e., a border that is not defended by troops from the nations sharing the border). Ambassador Bridge, which is privately owned and managed, connects Detroit, Michigan, with Windsor, Ontario, Canada.

European Colonization

The United States was also facing more difficult issues involving international relations. With Spain's growing weakness, many of that country's colonies in the western hemisphere followed the example of the United States and declared their independence. Spain refused to recognize these revolutions and threatened to crush them, although it was powerless to do so. A meeting of European nations, which included Austria, Prussia, Russia, and France, discussed intervening against popular revolutions such as those taking place in South America. In Europe, French forces moved into Spain in 1823 to stop anti-government rebels and to reinforce the authority of the Spanish king. The U.S. feared that European countries might move armed forces into the western hemisphere to try to suppress revolutions in the former Spanish colonies. Meanwhile, another threat to American power appeared on a different front. Russia, which owned Alaska, established outposts in California and laid claim to part of the Oregon Territory.

The Monroe Administration did not fear for the security of the United States itself, but it wanted to keep as many options open as it could in dealing with the rest of the western hemisphere. The United States wanted to be able to trade with other countries in the hemisphere, and actions by European countries might limit that (as Great Britain had done in the West Indies). In addition, the U.S. wanted to maintain the possibility of acquiring other territories in the hemisphere, such as Cuba and parts of Mexico.

Great Britain offered to join with the U.S. in opposing the encroachment of other European powers in the region, but Britain had its own reasons for making the offer. Britain did not want to see Russia or Spain become more powerful. Britain also wanted the U.S. specifically to agree that it would not pursue the acquisition of any more territory held by Spain. The Monroe Administration declined Britain's offer because it wanted to chart its own course in the western hemisphere and not be dependent on Great Britain.

Announcement of the Monroe Doctrine

In President Monroe's annual address to Congress on December 2, 1823, he declared the American government's position with regard to the involvement of European powers in the affairs of countries in the western hemisphere. The statement of policy was essentially developed by Secretary of State John Quincy Adams.

Monroe said, first, that European nations should not consider any areas of the western hemisphere as subject to future colonization. Any attempt to do so would be seen as a threat to the United States. Second, Monroe promised that the United States would not interfere with any existing European colonies in the hemisphere and would not become involved in European wars. The statement of these principles came to be called the Monroe Doctrine.

The policy was actually more than the United States was able to deliver at the time. Adams said that he did not want the U.S. "to come in as a cockboat in the wake of the British man-of-war," but most countries recognized that the British navy would in fact be the real peace-keeper in the region. European governments showed little respect for the Monroe Doctrine, but it was the first significant statement of American foreign policy since Washington's declaration of neutrality regarding the Franco-British war following the French Revolution. It was also the first time that the American government expressed its willingness to become involved in foreign conflicts that might develop.

During most of the nineteenth century, the United States was not an active participant on the world stage. The U.S. fought a war with Mexico in the 1840s, but it was not until the end of the 1800s that we became significantly involved in foreign relations. The twentieth century saw the U.S. involved in many parts of the globe diplomatically and militarily. International affairs have been a

Map of the Western Hemisphere (1818)

major, ongoing part of American life since World War II.

The Communist takeover of Cuba in 1960 challenged the Monroe Doctrine. Technically the Cuban revolution was a domestic one, since Fidel Castro was Cuban. However, Castro's Communist government had close ties to the Soviet Union, and this made Cuba something of a Soviet colony. The Cuban Missile Crisis of 1962 was also a direct challenge to the Monroe Doctrine, but the United States was able to get Soviet-made missiles aimed at the U.S. out of Cuba.

The Monroe Doctrine has been a foundational aspect of American foreign policy since it was announced. It has influenced how European nations have related to the western hemisphere, and it has also guided U.S. policies toward other countries.

Behold, the nations are like a drop from a bucket,
And are regarded as a speck of dust on the scales.
Isaiah 40:15a

★ Assignments for Lesson 37 ★

American Voices — Read the excerpts from the Monroe Doctrine (pages 121-122).

Literature — Continue reading *Narrative of the Life of Frederick Douglass*.

Bible — The Transcendental movement of the early 1800s made man the standard for their thinking instead of God. Read 2 Corinthians 10:12. List three dangers of making man the standard and authority for life.

Work on memorizing Proverbs 14:32-35.

Project — Work on your project.

Student Review — Optional: Answer the questions for Lesson 37.

Check Written by Senator John Quincy Adams

Lesson 38

John Quincy Adams

Few public servants have been as brilliant and talented as John Quincy Adams. The son of the second President, John Quincy was involved in American and international affairs from the time he was a boy. He accompanied his father to France during the Revolutionary War and later served as his father's personal secretary. After graduating from Harvard (as his father had done), John Quincy practiced law and then was appointed American ambassador to the Netherlands at the age of 26. Later, he became the minister to Russia. In between those appointments, the younger Adams was a U.S. Senator from Massachusetts.

Recognizing Adams' experience and knowledge, President James Monroe named John Quincy Adams to be his Secretary of State in 1817. Adams was a key figure in the Monroe Administration and, as we have seen, was the principal architect of the policy that has come to be known as the Monroe Doctrine.

The 1824 Election

Several factors pointed toward Adams as the logical successor to Monroe in the White House in 1824. First, Adams himself wanted the position, although he would never be so overt as to declare his intentions publicly. Second, he was the politically active son of John Adams; and many people, John Quincy among them, saw him as carrying on the family legacy of leadership in America. Third, Adams held the position of Secretary of State. That office had come to be seen as the main stepping stone to the presidency. Thomas Jefferson had been George Washington's Secretary of State, James Madison had been Thomas Jefferson's Secretary of State, and James Monroe had been James Madison's Secretary of State. The Republican Party was the only national political organization, so John Quincy appeared to have the inside track.

However, matters were not quite that cut and dried. The Republican Party was divided among several factions, and several men were hungry to obtain more power. A caucus of congressional Republicans nominated Treasury Secretary William Crawford of Georgia for President, even though Crawford had recently suffered a serious stroke. Apparently congressional leaders hoped to put a figurehead in the White House while they would actually run the country.

For sixteen years, the Republican congressional caucus had determined the party's presidential candidate; but the process was seen by many as an undemocratic practice. As the Era of Good Feelings gave way to intense factional and regional differences, state legislatures began offering favorite son candidates as presidential hopefuls.

This was actually closer to what the framers of the Constitution anticipated, with the voters, then the electoral college, and sometimes the U.S. House of Representatives choosing the President from a number of candidates.

The Tennessee legislature nominated Battle of New Orleans hero Andrew Jackson in 1822 for the 1824 election and chose him as U.S. Senator to give his candidacy a national platform. The New England states backed Secretary of State John Quincy Adams. Three states nominated Speaker of the House Henry Clay. John C. Calhoun of South Carolina was also a candidate early on, but he dropped out and offered himself as a candidate for Vice President. Calhoun was eventually elected to that post.

In the balloting that fall, Jackson received the most popular votes and the most electoral votes; but he only received a plurality, not a majority, of electoral votes. Adams placed second, Crawford was third, while Clay finished fourth. The election went to the House of Representatives, where each state had one vote in considering the top three candidates.

Clay was no longer a candidate, but as Speaker of the House he had considerable influence. He still desperately wanted to be President. Speaker Clay did not care for Adams, but he disliked (and feared) Jackson even more. Clay threw his support to Adams, who was chosen by the House on February 9, 1825, less than a month before the inauguration date.

Jackson believed that the presidency, which he thought was rightfully his, had been taken away from him. To increase his bitterness, President Adams soon appointed Clay as his Secretary of State. In Jackson's mind, this was a double blow. First, the election had been stolen from him; and now in what he called a "corrupt bargain," his chief rival was in the driver's seat to become President after Adams. Jackson felt as though he was now two steps away from the office that was rightfully his. The evidence is not completely clear on whether a bargain was actually made between Adams and Clay, but the two men did have one or more private meetings while the House was considering how it would vote. At the very least, it was an unwise move by Adams. Jackson, who had been in Washington as the House made its decision, went home to Nashville furious. He was determined to run again in 1828 and to win.

The first chart below shows the breakdown of votes in the 1824 presidential election. The numbers in each state indicated the number of electoral votes each candidate won in that state. The second chart shows the vote by state in the House of Representatives.

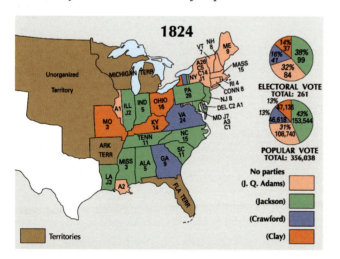

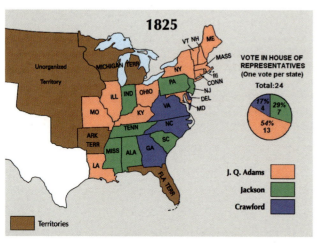

The Adams Presidency

John Quincy Adams was brilliant and talented, but he lacked the ability to understand the common man or to communicate his ideas in a way that helped people accept them. In his first annual address to Congress, Adams said:

Lesson 38 - John Quincy Adams

While foreign nations less blessed with that freedom which is power than ourselves are advancing with gigantic strides in the career of public improvement, were we to slumber in indolence or fold up our arms and proclaim to the world that we are palsied by the will of our constituents, would it not be to cast away the bounties of Providence and doom ourselves to perpetual inferiority?

It sounded to many that Adams was telling Congress to do what they (or he) thought best and not to pay any attention if the people who elected them did not agree with what they wanted to do.

Adams was a strong nationalist who envisioned a country unified by an active central government. Secretary of State Clay advocated what he called an "American System" of Federally-funded internal improvements such as roads, canals, and the clearing of rivers and harbors. Some steps were taken in this area, but Adams failed to present much legislation to Congress and was reluctant to try to persuade members of Congress. His administration also had few significant accomplishments in foreign relations. Adams' leadership was hampered by his own failings, by the appearance of a secret bargain with Clay, and by the congressional election of 1826 when a pro-Jackson coalition gained control. The schedule of import tariffs that was passed in 1828 was the only significant legislation of Adams' tenure, and it only served to provide a stage for intense partisan and sectional conflict.

The Tariff of 1828

Congress had passed a tariff bill in 1824 that included import duties on raw materials such as wool and farm products. Western farming interests supported the measure because it provided protection for their business, but eastern manufacturers complained that it made the raw materials they needed too expensive. In 1828 congressional leaders who supported John Calhoun and Andrew Jackson

William Henry Harrison had his photograph taken during his brief tenure as President in 1841. Since that photograph is now lost, John Quincy Adams is the U.S. President with the oldest surviving photograph. This is one of several taken in 1843 while he was serving in the U.S. House of Representatives. According to his diary, Adams thought the photos were "hideous" because they were "too true to the original."

proposed a tariff bill that set extremely high rates, including duties on raw materials that were even higher than those on manufactured goods.

These Calhoun and Jackson men hoped to kill the tariff by some reverse psychology. Calhoun hoped that New England manufacturing interests, along with representatives from the South and West, would oppose the measure. Jackson supporters hoped that they could play both sides of the street by either supporting or opposing the tariff depending on the political winds of their respective regions. However, their plan backfired. The bill was amended to exempt certain raw materials from tariffs altogether, and New England Congressmen voted for the bill because of the assistance it gave on raw materials and the protection it offered to manufactured goods from their districts. The bill was passed and became law, much to Calhoun's chagrin.

Calhoun had once been an ardent nationalist in favor of high tariffs; now he opposed the tariff he had helped to create. He became a strong proponent of states' rights. Calhoun and others called the new tariff schedule the Tariff of Abominations. Calhoun anonymously published the *South Carolina Exposition and Protest* in 1828, which set forth the idea that a state had the right to nullify a law passed by Congress if the state believed it to be unconstitutional. This philosophy took the idea of states' rights a step further than the Kentucky and Virginia Resolutions had gone regarding the Alien and Sedition Acts in 1798 and 1799.

Adams Continues to Serve

The issues of the day, the increasing popularity of Andrew Jackson, and John Quincy Adams' own failures combined to cause Adams' defeat in the 1828 presidential contest. Like his father, John Quincy Adams was an able public servant; but, also like his father, his greatest service was not in his presidency. The voters of America rejected John Quincy Adams in 1828, but the people of his home state of Massachusetts still admired him. Adams was elected to the House of Representatives in 1830 and was re-elected until his death in 1848. He is the only President to serve in the House after leaving the White House. The journal he kept during this time is a rich source of his reflections on the people and events he witnessed in Washington. While in the House, Adams strongly opposed the expansion of slavery and promoted the Smithsonian Institution.

Augustus Köllner was a German immigrant to the United States who distinguished himself as an artist and engraver. His illustration of Washington, D.C., below shows the city soon after the death of John Quincy Adams. The buildings in the foreground are stables. The U.S. Capitol is on the right. In the distance on the left are the Smithsonian Castle and the Washington Monument, both of which were under construction in 1850.

Lesson 38 - John Quincy Adams

The Adams Family

John Quincy Adams' son and grandsons were public figures in their own right. Charles Francis Adams Sr. (1807-1886) served in the Massachusetts state legislature and was a vocal opponent of slavery and the slaveowning powers of the South. He was the 1848 vice presidential candidate for the Free Soil Party. Adams was elected to Congress as a Republican in 1858 and served there until 1861, when President Lincoln appointed him to be ambassador to Great Britain. His influence in Britain helped to discourage the British government from giving assistance and perhaps even diplomatic recognition to the Confederacy. Charles and his wife Abigail are pictured above at Peacefield, the Adams home in Quincy, Massachusetts (c. 1883).

Charles Francis Adams Jr. (1835-1915) was a Civil War soldier and later a writer and journalist. He helped to expose the corruption of the Tweed political machine in New York and the frauds committed by railroad companies. He served on the Massachusetts Board of Railroad Commissioners and later as chairman of the Union Pacific Railroad. Charles Francis never ran for public office even though he was often urged to do so. His brother Henry Adams (1838-1918) was his father's personal secretary in Congress and in Great Britain. He served for a time as editor of the scholarly journal the North American Review *and wrote the influential autobiography* The Education of Henry Adams. *Sadly, Henry's religious faith was an empty shell of what his great-grandfather's faith had been.*

So we Your people and the sheep of Your pasture will give thanks to You forever; to all generations we will tell of Your praise.
Psalm 79:13

★ Assignments for Lesson 38 ★

Literature — Continue reading *Narrative of the Life of Frederick Douglass*.

Bible — Many religious leaders have tried to predict when the Lord would return. Read Matthew 24:36. List three ways we can prepare for the return of Christ even though we do not know when it will take place.

Work on memorizing Proverbs 14:32-35.

Project — Work on your project.

Student Review — Optional: Answer the questions for Lesson 38.

Detail from Lithograph of Andrew Jackson in 1814, Breuker & Kessler (c. 1840)

Lesson 39

Andrew Jackson Before the Presidency

Andrew Jackson is a key player in the story of American history in the period between 1815 and 1845. Jackson had enormous popularity because of his victorious leadership of American troops in the Battle of New Orleans in 1815. His prominence reflected the increasing importance of the West (that is, the region west of the Appalachian Mountains) in American life and economics. Jackson was a hero of the common man when the common man was gaining an increased voice in American life and politics. He embodied and endorsed their suspicion of those who had privilege and power. Although Jackson generally believed in states' rights and a limited Federal government, he was an ardent nationalist and an activist executive.

Jackson's Early Life

Andrew Jackson was born in the Waxhaw community of South Carolina, just across the border from Charlotte, North Carolina, in 1767. His parents were poor Scots-Irish immigrants who had come to America two years earlier. Jackson's father died a few weeks before Andrew was born.

His mother had hopes that Andrew would become a Presbyterian minister, but Jackson was too hot-headed for that career path. The boy received some schooling; and the story is told that when the Declaration of Independence arrived in Waxhaw in 1776, nine-year-old Andrew Jackson was chosen to read it to the community.

During the Revolutionary War, Jackson's sixteen-year-old brother died from heat exhaustion after a battle. Jackson and his next oldest brother then enlisted in the Continental Army. Andrew was thirteen and served as a messenger and in other non-combat roles. The British army came through and ravaged the Waxhaw area and took the two Jackson boys prisoner. A British officer ordered Andrew to clean his boots. Jackson refused and cited his rights as a prisoner of war. When the officer struck at Jackson with his sword, Jackson defended himself by raising his arm. The sword left scars on Jackson's arm and face, and the incident left a burning hatred for the British in his heart.

Smallpox broke out in the POW camp and infected the two Jackson boys. Their mother successfully appealed for their release, but as they walked the forty-five miles home barefooted, Jackson's brother died. Andrew almost died also. After he recovered, his mother went to be a nurse for soldiers in Charleston, South Carolina, where relatives lived; but she died soon after arriving. This left Andrew orphaned and with no immediate family.

Lesson 39 - Andrew Jackson Before the Presidency

Andrew lived with his extended family and developed a reputation for wild living. He moved to Charleston, received a small inheritance from his grandfather, and lost it gambling. Moving back to Waxhaw, he taught school for a couple of years. When he was 17, Andrew decided to take up law. He moved to North Carolina to study law with a judge, and there he again developed the reputation of a troublemaker.

Move to Nashville

A fellow law student was appointed judge in the Western District of North Carolina (the territory which eventually became Tennessee), and in 1788 he named the twenty-one-year-old Jackson as public prosecutor. This gave Jackson a new start in a new and growing area. Jackson eventually moved to Nashville to further develop his law practice. He stayed in a boarding house run by the widow of John Donelson, one of the founders of Nashville. There he met the Donelsons' daughter, Rachel Donelson Robards.

Rachel was a young girl when her family helped establish Nashville. A few years later they moved to Kentucky, where Rachel met and married Lewis Robards. After Rachel's father, John Donelson, died, Rachel's mother returned to Nashville. Robards was abusive and insanely jealous, so Rachel left him and returned to Nashville as well. Later Robards moved to Nashville and the couple reconciled, but then Andrew Jackson entered the picture. Rachel caught Andrew's eye, and he was infatuated by the attractive Rachel. Robards' jealousy surfaced again, and the married couple's relationship deteriorated. Robards was unfaithful to Rachel, and then he moved back to Kentucky.

In 1790 word reached Rachel that Robards was coming to Nashville once again. She wanted to leave town, so she went to Natchez, Mississippi, to stay with her brother. Andrew Jackson accompanied her. They received word that Robards had obtained a divorce; and in the summer of 1791, Rachel and Andrew were married in Natchez. They returned to Nashville as husband and wife and were accepted into Nashville society.

Then disaster struck. The Jacksons learned in 1793 that Robards had in fact never gotten a divorce. He had only obtained an act from the Virginia legislature (Kentucky was then still part of Virginia) that enabled him to pursue a divorce. Robards now filed for divorce from Rachel on the grounds of adultery. The divorce was finalized, and Andrew and Rachel went through another wedding ceremony in January of 1794. This mistake haunted Jackson for the rest of his life, and his political opponents rarely failed to abuse him for it.

Nevertheless, Jackson was becoming prominent in Nashville. He was a delegate to the state constitutional convention in 1796 that drew up the founding document for Tennessee's admission as a state. The rising political star was elected as a Congressman and then as a U.S. Senator from Tennessee. He did not like the slow, contemplative role of a Senator and soon resigned. He was elected a superior court judge and also major general of the Tennessee state militia, even though he had no military experience.

The Daughters of the American Revolution sponsored the construction of a replica of the original Fort Nashborough in 1930. The name of the settlement had been changed to Nashville after the American Revolution to sound French rather than English.

Andrew Jackson thus established himself as a man to be reckoned with. Then he became involved in land speculation, got heavily into debt, and lost a great deal of money. From this experience, Jackson came to hate debt, paper money, and banks. He slowly rebuilt his fortune, purchased a beautiful 420-acre plantation east of Nashville called the Hermitage, and entered into various business ventures, including horse racing. Jackson had a strong temper, which got him into numerous duels. He killed one man in a duel and was wounded twice in duels himself.

But Jackson also had a tender side. During the War of 1812, in an encounter with Indians that led up to the Battle of Horseshoe Bend, Jackson learned of an Indian child whose parents had been killed. The boy's plight appealed to Jackson because he too had been orphaned as a child and had lost all of his family. Jackson ordered the infant taken to the Hermitage, and the Jacksons reared him there. The boy, Lyncoya, died in 1828 at the age of 16. Andrew and Rachel had no children of their own but reared several children of relatives. They adopted Rachel's nephew, who became Andrew Jackson Jr.

A National Figure

Jackson's victory in the Battle of New Orleans in 1815 made him a national hero and also gave him revenge against the British. A few years later, Jackson thought that he had authority from President Monroe to take whatever steps were necessary to deal with the threat of the Seminole Indians. Jackson's invasion of the Florida territory was denounced by several politicians, including Henry Clay, who was a rival for the political favor of westerners. Jackson and Clay became enemies from that time on.

General Jackson began expressing his views on national politics in letters and conversations with friends. He believed that many people in the national government were corrupt and were using their positions for personal gain at the expense of the nation's welfare. For instance, the Panic of 1819 convinced Jackson that the Bank of the United States was hurting people and that the Federal government had a serious problem with corruption. Political leaders in Tennessee and throughout the nation agreed with Jackson and saw his candidacy as their opportunity to gain power in Washington.

The Election of 1828

As the presidential election of 1828 approached, the politic turmoil of the nation had left the Era of Good Feelings far behind. Vice President Calhoun strongly opposed President Adams. Adams himself was in political trouble even as he was nominated for re-election. Andrew Jackson eagerly sought another opportunity to make his case to the American people after being robbed of the presidency (in his opinion) four years earlier.

Andrew Jackson Jr.
Ralph Eleaser Whiteside Earl (American, c. 1820)

Lesson 39 - Andrew Jackson Before the Presidency

Portrait of Rachel Donelson Jackson
Ralph Eleaser Whiteside Earl (American, c. 1831)

America again had two major national political parties. The supporters of John Quincy Adams and Henry Clay called themselves National Republicans. Those who backed Andrew Jackson called themselves Democratic Republicans or Democrats. The party name is especially significant. When the country was founded, democracy was something many people feared. Now, however, since democracy was spoken of favorably by increasing numbers, calling oneself a Democrat was not so risky.

The Tennessee legislature again nominated Andrew Jackson for President in 1825. Jackson resigned from the Senate to pursue his candidacy. The supporters of Old Hickory, led by New York Senator Martin Van Buren, developed the first truly national political operation. This included lining up influential newspapers for their side. Jackson supporters generated a significant amount of publicity about their hero and about the alleged failings of John Quincy Adams. Democrats hosted political barbecues and gave ringing speeches about their man, although it was still considered inappropriate for the candidate himself to campaign.

The rival political operations engaged in a great deal of mudslinging during the 1828 campaign. Adams supporters pointed out Jackson's tendency to take high-handed actions as a military leader. They also put the worst possible light on the disputed marriage of Andrew and Rachel. No attacks hurt and infuriated Jackson more than those concerning his beloved Rachel. The Jackson forces countered with reminders of the corrupt bargain four years earlier, and they made sleazy and unsupported charges about what Adams had done while minister to Russia. Adams was portrayed as a friend of the Tariff of Abominations and of the Bank of the United States, while Jackson was presented as a friend of the common man and a champion of integrity.

Jackson was helped in the election by the trend toward easing voter requirements and by his popularity among recent immigrants who had become citizens. Three times as many people voted in the 1828 election as had participated four years earlier. Jackson received 56 percent of the popular vote and won a better than two-to-one landslide in the electoral college (178 for Jackson to 83 for Adams). John C. Calhoun was re-elected as Vice President.

Rachel Jackson's Death

The Jacksons prepared to leave their beloved Hermitage for Washington, but sorrow unexpectedly replaced joy. Rachel Jackson had not been well for some time. She was happy for Andrew that he had been elected President, but she dreaded moving to Washington. Rachel had been shielded from the attacks on her during the campaign, but in December of 1828 she heard some of the slurs that had been circulated about her and Andrew during the campaign. She collapsed under the strain.

Rachel died December 22 and was buried at the Hermitage on Christmas Eve. Jackson's greatest victory was now dimmed by the loss of his beloved wife. He blamed his political opponents for her death and never expressed any forgiveness toward them until he joined the Presbyterian Church late in his life. We will continue Jackson's story in the next unit.

> *Nevertheless, each individual among you also is to love his own wife even as himself, and the wife must see to it that she respects her husband.*
> *Ephesians 5:33*

★ Assignments for Lesson 39 ★

Literature — Continue reading *Narrative of the Life of Frederick Douglass*.

Bible — Many people in the first half of the 1800s were carried away by unorthodox religious teachings that led them away from following Christ. Read Hebrews 13:9. List three reasons why people are attracted to heretical beliefs.

Work on memorizing Proverbs 14:32-35.

Project — Work on your project.

Student Review — Optional: Answer the questions for Lesson 39.

Interior of United First Parish Church, Quincy, Massachusetts

Lesson 40 - Bible Study

Nineteenth Century Religious Movements

In the first half of the 1800s, the United States bustled with intense political activity, a growing population, expansion across the continent, industrial development, and literary production. It was a time of great optimism and patriotism. Historian George Bancroft published his *History of the United States* in 1834. It went through many later editions. Bancroft identified God as the mover and motivation behind everything that had happened in America beginning with the founding of the colonies. He was also a strong supporter of Jacksonian democracy. One observer noted that every page "voted for Jackson."

This period was also an active time in the religious sphere. The impact of the Second Great Awakening continued for many years, and most Christian denominations and movements grew during this period. In addition, however, several leaders and movements arose that espoused unusual doctrines, some of which were as much or more based on American thinking as they were on the Bible. Influencing much of the religious thought of the day was the optimistic but false belief that America was the closest thing to heaven on earth and that it might usher in a millennium of Christ reigning on earth.

Unitarian/Universalism

Americans turned away from Calvinist Puritanism in three specific ways. The first involved a movement toward Unitarianism and Universalism. Most Puritan congregations in New England became Congregationalist churches with a much less severe theology. In the early 1800s, Unitarian beliefs came to dominate Congregationalist churches. Unitarians believe God is one Person, as opposed to being three Persons as traditional Christian doctrine holds (hence the "uni" in the name). They believe Jesus was a good man with a life worthy of being emulated but not the sole Savior and unique Son of God. Unitarians denied Calvinist teachings on hereditary depravity and the salvation of only the elect. For them the central importance of religion was in providing an individual spiritual experience, which meant that they downplayed universal truth. Leading Unitarian minister William Ellery

In 1639 members of the church in Boston established a branch in nearby Quincy, Massachusetts (see photo above). John and Abigail Adams and John Quincy and Louisa Adams attended there. All four are interred in a crypt on the lower level of the current building, built in 1828. The congregation is now a member of the Unitarian Universalist Association.

Channing said, "I am surer that my rational nature is from God than that any book is an expression of his will." Although Unitarians denied traditional Christian teachings, they developed their own denominational structure as a Church.

While Unitarianism flourished among the wealthy, Universalism developed among working people. This doctrine held that God was too merciful to condemn anyone to hell and thus salvation was universal. Unitarianism and Universalism eventually merged in the twentieth century.

Christian Evangelicalism

A second reaction to Calvinism arose among more orthodox Christian believers. This movement was typified by evangelist Charles G. Finney. After a conversion experience in 1821, Finney became the leading evangelist of his day. Through his study of the Bible, Finney became convinced that all people were capable of making a decision about putting their faith in Christ. This was a denial of the major Calvinist tenets of hereditary total depravity and limited atonement. Finney's presentation of the gospel drew thousands of eager responses.

Transcendentalism

The third reaction to Puritanism was in the philosophy of transcendentalism. This was a movement away from the emphasis on reason that had characterized the Enlightenment and Deism. Transcendentalists believed that they had realized a higher order of truth that transcended the mere human senses. Those who adhered to this thinking emphasized intuition instead of reason, encouraged self-examination, gloried in the possibilities of the individual and of human nature in general, and praised the beauties of nature. To them the divine nature (which they called the Over-Soul) permeated everything and everybody. Transcendentalism also rejected Calvinist and Puritan theology, but it went further to reject the traditions and teachings of organized religion in general. Transcendentalists believed in what they called God, but to them the deity was a nebulous Over-Soul in which everyone and everything took part. What transcendentalists really worshiped was man: his abilities, his intuition, and his possibilities.

The Transcendental Club was founded in Boston in 1836. *The Dial* was a quarterly journal of transcendental thought edited by Margaret Fuller and published from 1840 to 1844. The leading figure in the transcendental movement was Ralph Waldo Emerson (1803-1882).

A descendant of eight generations of ministers, Emerson became a minister himself but left that work when he disagreed with church doctrine. He is best known for his essays and poems. "Nature" (1836) set forth many basic transcendentalist principles. "The American Scholar," an address given in 1837, said that Americans drank from the same well of inspiration as Europeans and should not be afraid to exercise their own abilities. "We have listened too

Ralph Waldo Emerson
Samuel W. Rowse (American, 1878)

long to the courtly muses of Europe. . . . We will walk on our own feet; we will work with our own hands; we will speak our own minds."

Emerson's best-known disciple, Henry David Thoreau (1817-1862), tried as best he could to live out the transcendentalist philosophy. Thoreau graduated from Harvard and worked for a time in the family pencil-making business. Then he left the beaten path and followed a different drummer. For over two years (1845-1847, with a trip to Maine in the midst of the period) he lived in a shack he had built by Walden Pond outside of Boston. He published his observations on the experience in 1854 as *Walden, or Life in the Woods*. "The mass of men lead lives of quiet desperation. . . . I went to the woods because I wished to live deliberately, to front only the essential facts of life, and to see if I could not learn what it had to teach, and not, when I came to die, discover that I had not lived."

Thoreau refused to pay a poll-tax as a protest against the Mexican War and was jailed briefly. His thoughts on the issue were presented in the speech (later the essay) "Civil Disobedience." He believed that going along unquestioningly with government policies with which one disagreed enabled evil and lessened the individual. The essay was said to be formative in the thinking that led to the non-violent protests of Mohandas Gandhi, Martin Luther King Jr., and those opposing the Vietnam War in the 1960s.

Thoreau wrote other works and left thirty-nine books of unpublished journals at his death. His writings sold poorly during his lifetime and were not widely read. It was only in the twentieth century that his thinking came to be appreciated by large numbers of people.

Mormonism

Western New York State saw so many religious leaders and movements emerge in the early 1800s that it came to be called the Burned-Over District. Charles G. Finney was one such leader, and Joseph Smith was another; but Smith was far from orthodox. Smith claimed that in 1820 he saw a vision of God and Christ, who told him that all existing religious systems were in error. Three years later, according to Smith, the angel Moroni led him to buried gold plates on which were written the Book of Mormon. Smith translated the plates, which he said were written in an ancient language, by sitting on one side of a curtain and dictating to a scribe on the other side. Smith claimed that Jews came to America and that Christ appeared to them. Much of the Book of Mormon sounds a great deal like the King James Bible, and Smith's claims about the language on the plates have been discredited by scholars.

Smith came to be regarded by some of his followers as a prophet, and he started drawing thousands of adherents to himself in 1830. He stressed human goodness, a close-knit community of believers, and the need for his followers to be different from the world. Smith also claimed the right to have several wives. Mormons (also called Latter-Day Saints) believe that God is married. They also believe that

This 1843 portrait of Joseph Smith was drawn by Bathsheba Smith, wife of one of his cousins.

if two Mormons marry in one of their temples, they have a celestial marriage. Their teaching holds that after the husband dies, he becomes a god. Mormons believe that they can be baptized for their dead and unsaved relatives, through a misinterpretation of 1 Corinthians 15:29. This is why they have developed such an interest in genealogical studies, as part of an effort to track down all of their ancestors.

As Smith's influence grew, the Mormons were persecuted because of their unusual beliefs. They left New York State and eventually settled in Nauvoo, Illinois, in 1839. Five years later, a split in the group over polygamy, along with a rising anti-Mormon sentiment on the part of many who lived near them, led to Smith and his brother being arrested.

The Church of Jesus Christ of Latter-day Saints (LDS) is now headquartered in Salt Lake City, Utah. The LDS Church has built over 100 temples around the world. The Salt Lake Temple is pictured below.

A mob attacked the jail and shot both Joseph and Hyrum Smith.

Smith's successor as leader of the Mormons was the strong-minded Brigham Young. Young, who eventually had 56 children by 16 of his 27 wives, promised to leave Nauvoo. He led his flock away from settled places to the Great Salt Lake in Utah. They arrived in 1847 and found a desolate landscape. By hard work they transformed the area into a flourishing and economically successful community. Utah became a territory in 1849. Mormons have a wide influence in the western United States and maintain an active missionary program in America and around the world.

Millerites

William Miller, a Baptist preacher, became convinced that the second coming of Christ was imminent. He gathered a large following in preparation for it, calculating the date to be 1843. When it did not happen then, he recalculated the advent of Christ and determined that it would occur in 1844. Many members sold their possessions in anticipation of the event; but the second date passed also, and many of his followers left, returning to their previous churches or abandoning religion altogether. Miller regrouped in 1845 and began the Adventist Church. The Adventists wondered why their prediction had not come true. They decided that they had been wrong and that they needed to meet on and observe the seventh day of the week as the Sabbath. The largest group that developed from the Millerites are the Seventh Day Adventists, but other Adventist churches also exist.

Utopian Communities

As a manifestation of the optimistic outlook in America at the time, over one hundred communal or utopian experiments were set up in the 1800s. Most of these had some religious basis. Almost all of

Lesson 40 - Bible Study: Nineteenth Century Religious Movements

This illustration from around 1830 shows the Shaker mode of worship at their community in Lebanon, New York.

them did not last long. The term utopia comes from the novel *Utopia* by Sir Thomas More published in 1516. The book describes a fictitious island civilization where everything runs smoothly. The word utopia means no place.

Ann Lee Stanley came to New York State from England in 1774. She claimed to be the female incarnation of God. The strange rituals and dances that she and her followers performed led to their being called Shakers. By 1830 about twenty groups of Shakers had been established in New York, Ohio, and Kentucky. Shakers held property in common, developed fine woodworking and other production skills, and practiced celibacy in preparation for the perfection that they believed awaited them. Shaker communities grew by means of converts and the adoption of children, but their numbers dwindled after 1860.

George Rapp established the community of Harmony in southwest Indiana in the early 1800s. When it foundered, Scottish industrialist Robert Owen purchased the town in 1825, renamed it New Harmony, and tried to create the perfect industrial community without a basis of religious belief. The experiment fell into discord and dissolved in 1827.

John Humphrey Noyes formed a small group of Perfectionists at his home in Vermont in 1836. Ten years later he declared the doctrine of complex marriage, which meant that every man in the community was married to every woman in the community. He was run out of Vermont in 1848 and set up the Oneida community in New York. The inventor of a quality steel trap joined the community in the mid-1850s, and the production and marketing of steel traps supported the community financially. The community continued until 1879, when Noyes fled to Canada to avoid prosecution for adultery. In 1881 the remaining members changed the nature of the group to that of a business which produced (and still produces) stainless steel flatware.

Transcendentalists formed the Brook Farm commune in 1841. It attracted many of those who believed in the transcendental philosophy. Nathaniel Hawthorne joined the group but quickly became disillusioned and left after only a few months. On the other hand, some participants were positive about the experience. The central building burned down in 1846, and the project was abandoned the following year.

The Rapp-Owen Granary at New Harmony, Indiana

Robert Owen persevered in his attempts to organize what he saw as the ideal society. His Association of All Classes of All Nations published the illustration at left in 1838. He called on landowners, capitalists, clergymen, and government officials to support the creation of planned communities such as this.

Utopian communities have never worked because heaven cannot be created on earth by human effort. We are too sinful and too selfish to create the perfect society. Christ's purpose was not to create a commune but rather a holy people who live in the world while being distinct from the world. The developing conflict over slavery showed just how far America was from Utopia.

. . . fixing our eyes on Jesus, the author and perfecter of faith, who for the joy set before Him, endured the cross, despising the shame, and has sat down at the right hand of the throne of God.
Hebrews 12:2

★ Assignments for Lesson 40 ★

Literature — Finish reading *Narrative of the Life of Frederick Douglass*. Literary analysis available in *Student Review*.

Bible — Read Colossians 2:8 and 1 Timothy 6:20-21. List three empty philosophies and false concepts of knowledge that compete with Christianity in the marketplace of ideas today.

Read Acts 4:32. List three ways in which the early church was successful in the life of its fellowship and three reasons why modern utopian communities have not been successful.

Recite or write Proverbs 14:32-35 from memory.

Project — Complete your project for the unit.

Student Review — Optional: Answer the questions for Lesson 40 and for *Narrative of the Life of Frederick Douglass* and take the quiz for Unit 8.

Westward the Course of Empire Takes Its Way, *Emanuel Leutze (German-American, 1861)*

9 Democrats and Whigs

Andrew Jackson's activist presidency redefined the role of the nation's chief executive. South Carolina's objections to Federal tariff laws raised the issue of state sovereignty that eventually came to a head with the Civil War. The policy of Indian removal from eastern lands was a tragic page in American history. The second two-party system (Whigs and Democrats, which replaced Federalists and Republicans) continued the pattern of politics that we still have. Many in America believed that it was the destiny of the nation to expand across the continent.

Lesson 41 - Jackson's Issues
Lesson 42 - Van Buren and the Whigs
Lesson 43 - Moving Westward
Lesson 44 - Polk, Texas, and Mexico
Lesson 45 - Bible Study: Protest

Memory Work Memorize Acts 5:29-32 by the end of this unit.

Books Used
The Bible
American Voices
Uncle Tom's Cabin

Project (choose one)

1) Write 300 to 500 words on one of the following topics:

- Alexis de Tocqueville wrote in the 1830s, "There is no country in the world where the Christian religion retains a greater influence over the souls of men than in America." How is this still true and how is it not? If things have changed, what has changed and why do you think as you do?

- Write a speech to be given in Tennessee explaining and justifying the United States' acquisition of Texas, or write a five-minute speech to be given in Massachusetts opposing the annexation of Texas. See Lessons 43 and 44.

2) Read a biography of one of the Presidents discussed in this unit: Andrew Jackson, Martin Van Buren, William Henry Harrison, John Tyler, or James K. Polk.

3) Design a book cover for one of the famous works written by one of the American authors discussed in Lesson 42 in the medium of your choice (e.g., paint, colored pencil, pencil, ink, or pastels).

Literature

Uncle Tom's Cabin

When President Abraham Lincoln met Harriet Beecher Stowe during the Civil War, he is reported to have said, "So you're the little woman who wrote the book that made this great war." Stowe's tale was published in magazine serialization in 1851 and in book form the following year. She based her story on what she learned about slavery while living in Cincinnati, a haven for runaway slaves from Kentucky and states further south. The book has some stereotypes and melodramatic scenes, but overall it effectively portrays how slaves were subject to both brutality and callous indifference.

Stowe's novel sold 300,000 copies in its first year, equivalent to three million copies today based on population comparisons. The book had a dramatic effect in both the North and the South. In the North, it crystallized opposition to slavery as people began realizing what they had allowed to be done in their country. On the other hand, Stowe's novel heightened the defense of slavery in the South as southerners insisted that the novel's portrayals of slave conditions were not realistic. Several replies were written by southerners, some in novel form; but none were as widely read as Stowe's book.

Stowe wrote other novels, but none had the impact of *Uncle Tom's Cabin*. You have three weeks to read it.

Detail from "President's Levee, or all Creation going to the White House," Robert Cruikshank (British, 1841)

Lesson 41

Jackson's Issues

The election of Andrew Jackson as President signaled a new day in American politics. Jackson was the first President from the West. In fact, he was the first President who was not from Virginia or Massachusetts. All six previous Presidents over the first forty years under the Constitution had come from those two states (Washington, Jefferson, Madison, and Monroe from Virginia; the two Adamses from Massachusetts). Jackson and his supporters believed that this change wrested power from the Eastern Establishment and returned it to the people. Long-time political leaders, by contrast, worried that the nation was degenerating into unstable rule by frontier ruffians.

Jackson's inauguration cemented both perspectives in the minds of those who held them. Thousands of everyday Americans attended his inauguration. When the festivities moved to the White House, the furniture was trampled by the crowds that pressed in to get a glimpse of their hero, Old Hickory. Only when someone thought to take the refreshments onto the lawn did the crowd leave the White House. Jackson's opponents bemoaned what they saw as the triumph of King Mob.

During his eight years in office, President Jackson dealt with several major issues that confronted the nation and the national government.

A New Federal Government

It was Jackson's belief that appointed government positions should not be held by the same people for a long time. He said that new appointees should fill the jobs for a period of time, and then they should be rotated out and replaced with others. This appeared to be a rationalization for the spoils system, the making of political appointments on the basis of party loyalty. The term comes from the phrase, "To the victor goes the spoils," which describes how the winning army usually captures booty from a conquered army or people. Jackson did not practice wholesale replacement of government workers, but he did appoint friends to government jobs.

Besides his formal Cabinet, which was made up of the heads of the executive departments, Jackson also had an informal group of advisors with whom he discussed policy and politics. This group included some who held official positions plus Washington newspaper editors and other political associates. Since it was not the official cabinet, Jackson's critics dubbed it the kitchen cabinet, which suggested that the group met informally instead of as an official body.

The Nullification Controversy

Vice President John Calhoun believed that a state could go its own way and nullify a Federal law, a claim which President Jackson fiercely rejected. Jackson believed in a limited role for the national government, but he was a strong unionist. Calhoun, South Carolina Senator Robert Hayne, and others believed that the South's economic troubles were a direct result of Federal tariffs. Hayne and Daniel Webster held a debate on the issue in the Senate in 1830 during consideration of a bill regarding the sale of western lands.

Later that year, the controversy erupted in a confrontation between Jackson and Calhoun at a dinner in Washington. When the President was asked to offer a toast, he toasted "The Federal Union" and added "It must be preserved." Calhoun, who was also present, jumped in and replied, "The Union—next to our liberty, most dear!" The significance of each man's toast as a challenge to the other was not lost on anyone present, least of all Jackson and Calhoun themselves. The rift between the two men became wider, and in 1832 Calhoun resigned as Vice President to run for a Senate seat from South Carolina.

In 1832 Congress passed another tariff that placed high duties on cloth and iron. In November of that year, a South Carolina convention declared the tariffs of 1828 and 1832 to be nullified in the state. The convention said that the laws would not be enforced in the state and threatened to secede from the Union if the Federal government used any force against the state.

Jackson declared that South Carolina's Ordinance of Nullification was treason and threatened to hang anyone who interfered with the carrying out of Federal law. Senator Henry Clay forged a compromise tariff that called for the gradual reduction of rates until 1842. The new law was more acceptable to the South, although many in New England and the Middle Atlantic states opposed it. The bill was passed in March of 1833. The same day, Congress passed the Force Act, which authorized the President to use force in the collection of tariffs. South Carolina backed down and rescinded its ordinance of nullification, but to save face it then

John Calhoun was the second and last man to serve as Vice President under two Presidents. George Clinton was Vice President during Thomas Jefferson's second term and in James Madison's first term until Clinton died in office on April 20, 1812. Calhoun was the only Vice President to resign until Spiro Agnew did so in 1973.

John Calhoun and his wife Floride lived in this home, called Fort Hill. After their death, it passed to their daughter Ann, wife of Thomas Green Clemson. The Clemsons left the estate to the State of South Carolina for the establishment of a college, with the requirement that the home be maintained as an historical museum. That college is now Clemson University, and the home is open as the John C. Calhoun Mansion and Library.

Lesson 41 - Jackson's Issues

declared the nullification of the Force Act! South Carolina never enforced its stance, and this resolved the issue by allowing both sides to claim victory. Tariffs were lowered, but the Union was preserved and the authority of the Federal government was affirmed.

The Bank War

President Jackson opposed the Bank of the United States for four reasons. First, as a strict constructionist, he believed the Constitution did not authorize Congress to establish a bank outside of the District of Columbia. Second, Jackson believed that the Bank had not provided a sound and uniform currency. Third, he believed the Bank got involved in politics by making loans to certain Congressmen and by putting family and friends of Congressmen on the Bank payroll. Fourth, Jackson was leery of all paper money; and the Bank was the biggest issuer of such notes.

Historians generally agree that the Bank did help establish a more stable economy than the country had known without it. Its paper notes were sound. The Bank's policies limited the influence of state banks, many of which were not strong. However, the charge of political involvement was generally true.

The Second Bank of the United States had been chartered in 1816 for a period of twenty years. Its director, Nicholas Biddle, and Senator Henry Clay wanted to renew the charter several years before it expired. In 1832 Clay pushed the renewal bill through Congress; and Jackson vetoed it in July of that year. Since Clay was the presidential candidate of the National Republican Party in the 1832 election, the Bank was a major issue in the presidential campaign.

Jackson's veto was not overridden by Congress, and the incumbent President decisively defeated Clay in the 1832 election. Clay had hoped that a Jackson

"Andrew Jackson Slays a Monster Bank" (1833)

veto would not play well with the voters, but the veto message appealed to the common man's resentment against the power of a few. Jackson interpreted his election victory as a mandate to continue his attacks against the Bank. In 1833 he authorized the Treasury Secretary to withdraw Federal funds from the Bank and place them in selected state-chartered banks around the country. By the end of that year twenty-three of these so-called "pet banks" had received deposits of Federal funds.

Clay introduced and led to passage a resolution in the Senate censuring the President for his actions. The censure resolution said that the President had assumed power "not conferred by the Constitution and laws, but in derogation of both." Jackson replied by saying that the Senate had accused him of an impeachable offense without giving him the opportunity to reply. Three years later, after a long battle led by Thomas Hart Benton of Missouri, a one-time Jackson enemy, the Senate expunged the censure resolution from its record.

Unfortunately, Jackson's bank veto and his removal of Federal funds from the Bank probably contributed to a national economic downturn that occurred during his second term. The Bank's director, in an effort to build back the Bank's resources, called in many loans, which led to a crisis for state banks and other debtors. The downturn was then followed by a period of inflation. Jackson issued an executive order in 1836 that required most payments for public lands to be made in silver or gold instead of paper notes. This reduced the number of land sales made, led to the hoarding of hard money by the public, and weakened confidence in state banks. All of these factors contributed to a serious depression, called a panic, in 1837.

Indian Removal

Relations between European-Americans and Native Americans had often been difficult since European settlers came to this land. Through treaties, warfare, and sometimes trickery and deceit, white Americans had taken over much of the land that Native Americans considered theirs.

Before he became President, Jackson helped negotiate a treaty with the Chickasaw tribe that gave to the United States clear title to the western third of Tennessee and a small portion of western Kentucky. He told the Indian representatives that this was best for them and warned them of dire consequences if they did not sign. Jackson's reputation as a successful Indian fighter probably helped influence the Chickasaw to sign the treaty.

The American government developed the policy of purchasing land claimed by Native American tribes east of the Mississippi and allowing them to move to unorganized territory west of the Mississippi (mostly in what would become Oklahoma, but also in parts of Arkansas and Kansas). Advocates of this policy had varying motives. Most simply wanted the land and wanted to get the Indians out of the way. A few people encouraged the Indians to accept these treaties as a way to protect their people and culture from white encroachment.

Jackson strongly favored the Indian removal policy. He believed that whites and Native Americans could not coexist. Several tribes were affected by the removal policy, including the Chickasaw and Choctaw in Mississippi, the Creek in Alabama, the Seminoles in Florida, and the Sauk and Fox tribes in the upper Midwest. The western land promised to these tribes was given to them, as the treaties put it, "in perpetuity."

The best-known removal effort involved the Cherokee of eastern Tennessee, northern Georgia, and western North Carolina. A good number of the Cherokee had come to believe in Jesus. The Cherokee had also taken on many of the white man's ways. They adopted a constitution based largely on

Sequoyah

One Cherokee, Sequoyah (sometimes spelled Sequoia), did what no other individual has ever done. He single-handedly developed a written language for his people. When Sequoyah was serving under Andrew Jackson in the Creek Wars in Alabama, he noticed that white soldiers received letters from home and could read written orders from superior officers. Sequoyah believed that these "talking leaves" could help his people. For twelve years he worked on developing a syllabary (SILL-ah-barry) that used written symbols for syllables in the Cherokee language. Some Cherokee were suspicious that Sequoyah was engaged in witchcraft. His wife once burned all of his work, and on another occasion a group of Cherokee burned down his cabin. Finally a group of Cherokee tribal leaders watched a demonstration in which Sequoyah communicated in writing to his daughter, and they were convinced that what he had created was good. The New Testament was translated into the syllabary in 1825. Sequoyah never learned English.

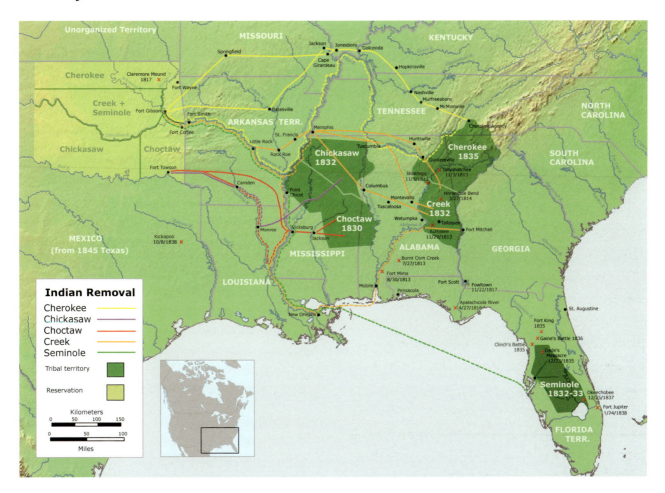

This map shows the several "Indian Removals" of the 1830s orchestrated by the government of the United States.

the United States Constitution, and they published a newspaper, *The Phoenix*. Some Cherokee even owned slaves.

The desire by whites for Cherokee land was intensified with the discovery of gold on tribal lands in Georgia in 1829. The Cherokee Constitution of 1827 said that they were not subject to any other nation, but Georgia passed a law in 1828 claiming jurisdiction over Cherokee land. The Supreme Court, led by Chief Justice John Marshall, said that the Court did not have jurisdiction in the dispute between Georgia and the Cherokee since the Cherokee were, as he put it, a "domestic dependent nation" and not a foreign state. However, Marshall said that the Cherokee had an unquestioned right to their land until they wanted to sell it.

An 1830 Georgia law required whites to register and to pledge allegiance to Georgia before taking up residence on Cherokee land. Two white missionaries refused to obey the law. The case was taken to the U. S. Supreme Court, which ruled the law unconstitutional and said that Georgia had no jurisdiction on Cherokee land. President Jackson is supposed to have said in response, "Marshall has made his decision, now let him enforce it" (i.e., let Marshall protect the Cherokee from white encroachments).

The Federal law which called for the removal of the Cherokee was passed in 1830 during the Jackson Administration. Negotiations between the U.S. government and Cherokee leaders on how this was to be carried out lasted for years. Most Cherokee opposed the move. Under pressure from the government, some Cherokee leaders signed an agreement with the U.S. government in 1835, which turned over their eastern lands to

Elizabeth Brown Stephens was a Cherokee who traveled the Trail of Tears as a teenager. This photograph was taken in 1903.

the U.S. in exchange for money, land in the West, and transportation expenses. Finally, in 1838 President Martin Van Buren ordered U.S. troops led by Winfield Scott to move the Cherokee out. About 12,000 were forced out of their homes. Whites reportedly moved into the Cherokees' houses as the Cherokee were leaving them.

The Cherokee were made to wait during hot weather in open-air detention camps near Chattanooga, Tennessee, without adequate food, clothing, or shelter. They were then forced to walk all the way to Oklahoma during the harsh winter. About 4,000 Cherokee died as a result of this treatment. Some white ministers traveled with the Cherokee, offering help and support as best they could. Chief John Ross, one of the Cherokee leaders, opposed the treaty but went west with his people.

A small number of Cherokee escaped into the mountains of North Carolina and never moved west. They came to be called the Eastern Band of the Cherokee. After the Cherokee moved to Oklahoma, the leaders who had signed the agreement were killed by their own people. The Cherokee called this removal "The Place Where They Cried." Today we know it as "The Trail of Tears."

Changes in Politics

The 1832 election saw significant changes in American politics that affect us even today. In 1831 the first national political convention was held in Baltimore. It was organized by the Anti-Mason Party, a group that opposed the Masonic movement (we will have more to say about the Masonic controversy later). The Anti-Masons were the country's first third party, they held the first national political convention, and they wrote the first party platform. The convention nominated William Wirt, who had been Attorney General under Monroe and Adams, as its presidential candidate. Ironically, Wirt himself was a Mason.

Conventions caught on as a way to show that a political party reflected the will of the people. More people felt that democracy was a good thing. The National Republicans held a convention in December of 1831 and nominated Henry Clay as their candidate for President. Democrats held their convention in 1832 and nominated Andrew Jackson and Martin Van Buren as their national ticket.

Jackson defeated Clay 219-49 in the 1832 electoral college voting. With Jackson's victory, the National Republicans crumbled and a new party emerged. In England many years earlier, the Whig Party had been organized to oppose the high-handed rule of King George III. Now a Whig Party was organized in the United States to oppose what people saw as the high-handed tactics of King Andrew I. The Whigs drew together a few die-hard Federalists, Republicans from the North, and a fair number of Jackson's opponents in the South (since Jackson had managed to create several political enemies even in his home state).

The new political party arrangement heightened intense party loyalties, gave rise to state and local political machines that organized workers and dispensed government jobs and favors, and promoted the idea that people should vote for the party regardless of who its candidates were. Loud, boisterous campaigns developed, which featured bands, speeches, and dinners. Issues and reason gave way to emotional appeals and party loyalties. The country had come a long way from George Washington's warnings about factions.

Jackson's Legacy

Jackson left office in March of 1837, still adored by millions of people. He returned to the Hermitage, where he oversaw the operation of the plantation and the restoration of the mansion which had been severely damaged by fire a few years earlier. The former President wrote letters and welcomed guests, and these activities allowed him to continue to have input in the politics of the nation. Jackson lived most of his life in pain from a bullet lodged near his heart as the result of a duel, and his pain in old age was even more intense. He joined the Presbyterian Church in 1838 and lived as a devout believer until his death in 1845.

Andrew Jackson is one of those prominent leaders who arouse strong emotions both favorable and unfavorable. As a leader of men, Andrew Jackson inspired millions. His firm belief in an indivisible Union helped the country weather the nullification crisis, which has been called a prelude to the Civil

This daguerreotype image of Andrew Jackson was taken a few months before his death.

War. Jackson wanted to give a voice to the average American. He gave new importance to the West and challenged the old Virginia-Massachusetts axis of power. Even though he believed in a limited Federal government, he gave new dynamism to the presidency. He oversaw the paying down of the national debt and conducted an administration that was largely free of corruption.

Jackson's record is not without tarnish, however. His opposition to the Bank of the United States, without offering a workable alternative, probably hurt the nation's economy for several years. The policy of Indian removal was a sad chapter in our nation's history. In addition, many of Jackson's appointments were not good. For instance, the man he appointed as Customs Collector of the Port of New York, Samuel Swartwout, stole over a million dollars while he was in that position.

The Hermitage (2007)

Unit 9 - Democrats and Whigs

Jackson's influence did not end when he left Washington. He appointed five justices to the Supreme Court, including Chief Justice Roger B. Taney, successor to John Marshall. Jackson also had a significant influence over the next two Democratic Presidents, Martin Van Buren and James K. Polk. In many ways Jackson still stands as the symbol for the age in which he lived: a man who loved democracy, displayed unfailing personal courage, and had an unwavering commitment to the greatness of America.

Many streets, cities, and counties are named after Andrew Jackson. Jackson Square in New Orleans was named in his honor in 1815. It features an equestrian statue of the general that was erected in 1856.

He has told you, O man, what is good; and what does the Lord require of you but to do justice, to love kindness, and to walk humbly with your God?
Micah 6:8

★ Assignments for Lesson 41 ★

American Voices — Read the excerpts from Daniel Webster's "Second Reply to Robert Hayne" (pages 123-127).

Read "America" by Samuel Smith (page 133).

Literature — Begin reading *Uncle Tom's Cabin.* Plan to finish it by the end of Unit 11.

Bible — This week we will look at some songs of faith that were written during this period in American history. What attitudes of faith and gratitude does "America" (also known as "My Country 'Tis of Thee") express?

Start memorizing Acts 5:29-32.

Project — Choose your project for this unit and start working on it.

Student Review — Optional: Answer the questions for Lesson 41.

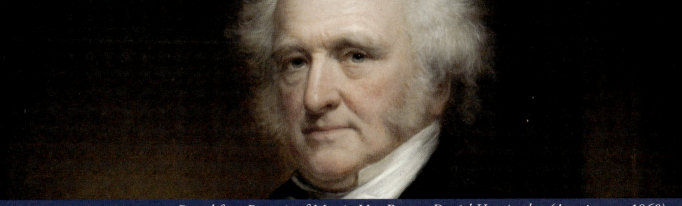

Detail from Portrait of Martin Van Buren, *Daniel Huntingdon (American, c. 1860)*

Lesson 42

Van Buren and the Whigs

Martin Van Buren was a skillful political operator from the town of Kinderhook, New York. One of his nicknames was Old Kinderhook. He also came to be known as the Little Magician for his skill in making political deals. Van Buren was a leading figure in the political machine called the Albany Regency. He had been a U. S. Senator and then was governor of New York for two months before Andrew Jackson chose him to be Secretary of State in his first term. During Jackson's second term, the Red Fox of Kinderhook (still another of Van Buren's nicknames) served as Vice President. Since Jackson wanted Van Buren to follow him into office, Van Buren was the Democratic nominee for President in 1836.

The new Whig Party fielded three regional candidates: Hugh White of Tennessee, Daniel Webster of Massachusetts, and William Henry Harrison of Ohio. The Whigs hoped that each would be more popular than Van Buren in his respective region. If this happened, no candidate would have a majority of electoral votes. The election would then be thrown into the House of Representatives, where the Whigs believed they had a chance of winning. Van Buren and the Democrats foiled the Whigs' strategy, however. Old Kinderhook received a clear majority of popular and electoral votes.

Martin Van Buren was the first President of Dutch descent and the first President to be born after the Declaration of Independence created the new nation. He was the last sitting Vice President to be elected President until George H. W. Bush in 1988. John Adams and Thomas Jefferson are the only other two sitting Vice Presidents who have been elected President. Other Vice Presidents have tried, including Richard Nixon in 1960 and Al Gore in 2000.

The Panic of 1837

Van Buren's tenure, like that of Herbert Hoover many years later, was crippled by a severe economic downturn that took place soon after he entered office. Only two months into his term, a New York bank panic ushered in a depression. The weakness of the overall banking system, due in part to the policies of the Jackson Administration, contributed greatly to the distress. Factories closed, unemployment rose, farmers received low prices for their crops, and thousands of people showed up at bread lines and soup kitchens. Canal and railroad projects were halted. The country as a whole did not recover from the Panic of 1837 until 1843.

The President did his best to help the Federal government through the panic. He persuaded

Unit 9 - Democrats and Whigs

During Martin Van Buren's presidential campaign, the Democratic Party formed OK Clubs around the country. OK stood for the man they supported ("Old Kinderhook"). This abbreviation came to be used to express approval for anything, and OK entered the world vocabulary. This photograph of Van Buren was taken by Matthew Brady (c. 1856).

Congress to issue short-term notes that enabled the government to meet its immediate obligations (while increasing the national debt, however). Van Buren also promoted the idea of an independent treasury to handle Federal revenues and maintain Federal cash flow. The independent treasury was not to be a bank, but it would free the government from depending on shaky state banks. The independent treasury was created in 1840, but the law was repealed during the Administration of President John Tyler.

Tippecanoe and Tyler, Too

The hard economic times in the U.S. meant that Van Buren faced a difficult re-election campaign in 1840. At the same time, the Whigs had several things going for them. Whigs Daniel Webster and Henry Clay were recognized throughout the nation as intelligent, eloquent men. The need for an improved national financial structure, which the Whigs favored, was becoming apparent. Whig leaders believed that 1840 could be their year for success.

However, the nominee for the Whig Party in 1840 was neither of the high profile men, Clay or Webster, but military hero William Henry Harrison. Harrison was called Old Tippecanoe in honor of his victory over an army of Indians led by Tecumseh at the Battle of Tippecanoe Creek in 1811. Harrison later commanded American forces in the victory over

The *Caroline* Affair

During Van Buren's term, an incident on the Canadian border threatened the peace of U.S.-Canadian relations. A small band of Canadian insurgents wanted their country to be free from control by Great Britain. In 1837 they took refuge on an island in the Niagara River. Sympathetic Americans sent supplies to them on the American steamer Caroline. *Canadian government forces captured, burned, and set adrift the* Caroline, *an act which angered Americans. One American was killed on the same night. A Canadian deputy sheriff was arrested and tried for the* Caroline *incident three years later, but he was acquitted. Nothing further ever came of the incident, but it disturbed relations between the two countries for a time.*

The Destruction of the Caroline *Steamboat by Fire, on the Falls of Niagara*, George Tattersall (British, c. 1837)

Lesson 42 - Van Buren and the Whigs

the British at the Battle of the Thames in Canada during the War of 1812. Following his military career, Harrison lived in Cincinnati and served in several state and national offices. He had a positive record of public service and, perhaps of more value to the Whigs, he had no known positions on any national issues. At 67 years of age, Harrison was an able leader, even though some Whigs probably hoped he would be a figurehead and let Whigs in Congress run the country.

To balance the ticket, the Whigs nominated John Tyler from Virginia. Tyler was a slave-owner and a former Democrat who left that party over differences with Andrew Jackson. He was anti-Bank, anti-tariff, pro-nullification, and pro-states' rights. He once said that the word nationalism was not in his vocabulary.

A Democratic journalist wrote that Harrison was unfit for the presidency and not really even interested in it. Give him a barrel of hard cider and a yearly pension, the critic said, and Harrison would be content to sit in his log cabin and study moral philosophy. The Whigs seized on this comment and presented Harrison as a man of the people (sort of a Jacksonian Whig), the log cabin and hard cider man, while they portrayed Van Buren as a slick, upper class political maneuverer. Whigs were proud to offer their ticket of "Tippecanoe and Tyler, Too," while to them "Martin Van Ruin" was nothing but "Van, Van, is a used-up man." The slogans, speeches, and songs made for a colorful campaign.

Harrison won the election, probably helped more by frustrations with the economy under Van Buren than by Whig campaign tactics. Old Tippecanoe received only a slight majority of the popular vote, but he won a landslide 234 to 60 electoral victory over the incumbent Van Buren. With Clay as Majority Leader in the Senate and Webster as Secretary of State, the Whigs looked forward finally to implementing their agenda.

At his inauguration on March 4, 1841, the now 68-year-old Harrison gave a long speech in bad weather without wearing a hat. He developed

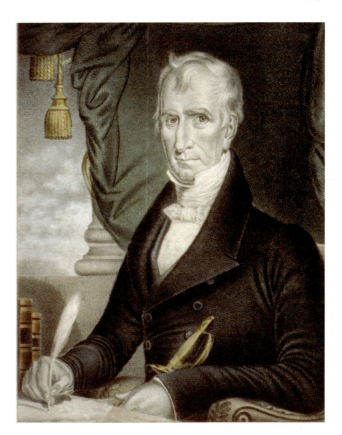

This portrait of President Harrison was published around 1845 by Nathaniel Currier (who later went into partnership with James Merritt Ives).

pneumonia and died a month later. For the first time in the history of the nation, a sitting President had died, and John Tyler was sworn in as the unlikely President. Some didn't recognize him as President at all, but only considered him to be the acting President. Others referred to him as His Accidency.

Tyler was out of step with the national Whig leadership and was a roadblock to the Whig agenda. He vetoed renewal of the Bank of the United States as well as several tariff measures sponsored by Henry Clay. Six months after Tyler took office, five of the six members of his Cabinet resigned. The sixth member, Secretary of State Webster, resigned in 1843. The Whigs cast Tyler out of their party, whereupon Tyler filled his Cabinet with Democrats. After months of inaction, Tyler finally signed a tariff bill when the government was almost broke. Whig members of the House called for an impeachment vote, but the motion failed by a large margin.

The Growth of American Literature

The first half of the nineteenth century saw an explosion of literary output in America that was the real beginning of American literature. This period gave us the first American authors who were successful both in this country and in Great Britain. They found their greatest success in writing about America and the experience of Americans.

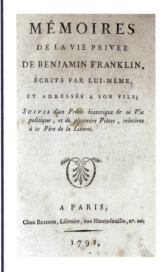

Early American Writing

Earlier American writing included personal journals and essays such as *The Autobiography of Benjamin Franklin*. This work was not published during Franklin's lifetime. The first edition appeared in 1791, not in English, but in a French translation (as seen at left).

Ministers such as Jonathan Edwards and Cotton Mather wrote significant works of theology. The Revolutionary period produced brilliant political writing and oratory from the likes of Patrick Henry, Thomas Jefferson, and Thomas Paine, as well as *The Federalist Papers*. Timothy Dwight ("Columbia") and Joel Barlow ("The Columbiad") wrote long narrative poems that were epic treatments of America, and Philip Freneau wrote more conventional poetry. John Trumbull wrote a prose satire of the Revolution, *M'Fingal*; and Charles Brockden Brown authored an early novel, *Wieland*. Political writing and speeches reflected the best thinking of the day on politics, and those works (or quotations from them) continue to be appreciated.

Most literary efforts by Americans in the early national period have not remained popular and few are widely read today. As an English critic sneered around 1800, "Who reads an American book?" His harsh remark was not entirely misplaced. This appraisal of American writing was soon to change, however, as American literary efforts matured. The first American writers to achieve notoriety in both England and America were Washington Irving and James Fenimore Cooper.

Washington Irving (1783-1859)

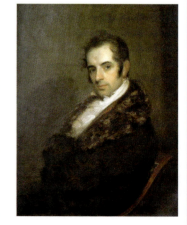

Irving studied law but loved literature. He wrote articles for literary magazines before 1809, when he published *Knickerbocker's History of New York*. The tales of historical fiction in this volume showed true genius and received wide acclaim. The portrait at right by American artist John Wesley Jarvis dates from this time.

Then in 1819 and 1820, Irving published *The Sketch Book* (in two volumes) under the pseudonym Geoffrey Crayon. This work included the stories for which Irving is best known, "The Legend of Rip Van Winkle" and "The Legend of Sleepy Hollow." Irving achieved what no other author had done before: an American, writing about America, receiving critical praise on both sides of the Atlantic. Irving wrote other fiction as well as biographies of Columbus and Washington. He also served as minister to Spain for four years.

James Fenimore Cooper (1789-1851)

Cooper was a country gentleman who once read an English novel and declared that he could write a better book himself. On his wife's dare, he wrote *Precaution*. It was not great, but it opened the door. His next book, *The Spy* (1821), was set during the American Revolution and was more kindly received in both England and the U.S. Cooper wrote many other novels, recollections, and a *History of the United States Navy* (1839). Cooper had served in the Navy for four years. The portrait at right by John Wesley Jarvis shows him in naval uniform (1822).

Cooper is best remembered, however, for the five books in his Leatherstocking series, published from 1823 to 1841, which feature Natty Bumppo as the quintessential American frontier hero. *The Deerslayer*, *The Last of the Mohicans*, *The Pioneers*, *The Pathfinder*, and *The Prairie* follow Bumppo (also called Leatherstocking and Deerslayer in the series) from the 1740s in upstate New York, through the French and Indian War, to the western plains in 1804. Cooper's plots are not always easy to follow and his dialogue is often artificial, but his adventure stories from the American frontier captured the imagination of many readers.

Other Frontier Writing

Fascination with the American frontier encouraged other writing that highlighted western exploration and settlement. Davy Crockett published the story of his life in 1834, and Francis Parkman (pictured at left) recounted his experiences on *The Oregon Trail* in 1847-1849. This was also the period when the tall tale grew in popularity, exemplified by the northern plains legends of Paul Bunyan and his blue ox, Babe. It seemed as though the storytellers of America tried to capture the expanse and adventure of the American West with stories that stretched the limits of the imagination. They also encouraged the ideal of the self-reliant individual toughing it out on the frontier.

Nathaniel Hawthorne (1804-1864)

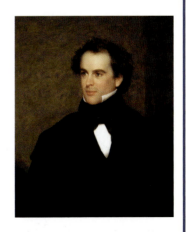

Perhaps the most significant and widely-read author of this period is Nathaniel Hawthorne, who was born in Salem, Massachusetts. He was a descendant of one of the judges involved in the Salem witch trials (Nathaniel added the "w" to his last name to try to separate himself from his family's past). He attended Bowdoin College in Maine, where he met fellow students Henry W. Longfellow and future President Franklin Pierce. Artist Charles Osgood, also from Salem, painted this portrait of Hawthorne about 1840.

Hawthorne wrote unsuccessfully after college except for *Twice-Told Tales* (1837, second series 1842). He took a job at the Salem Customs House (built in 1819, pictured below at left). When the presidency changed hands, he lost his government position. This gave him the opportunity to write seriously, and *The Scarlet Letter* was published in 1850. Hawthorne might have changed the spelling of his name, but he could not escape the reality of his Puritan past. While transcendentalists denied that evil really existed in any ultimate sense, Hawthorne wrestled with the reality of sin and evil in individual lives, in communities, and over generations as in *The House of the Seven Gables* (1851). He had an unusual ability to convey the workings of the human heart.

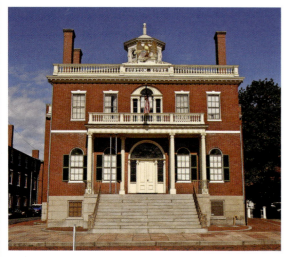

For a few months, Hawthorne joined the Brook Farm commune, a transcendentalist utopian experiment. He left disillusioned (the farm folded soon thereafter), and the novel *The Blithedale Romance* (1852) was based on his experience there. When Franklin Pierce was elected President, Pierce named Hawthorne American consul in Liverpool, England. He produced additional work while living overseas. Hawthorne was loved and respected by the public and by fellow authors. Hawthorne is the best example of the Romantic period of American literature. Moving away from the emphasis on reason, Romantic authors focused on nature, the emotions, the moods of people, and other non-measurable but very real aspects of human life.

Herman Melville (1819-1891)

Herman Melville, a friend of Hawthorne, also wrestled with sin and the struggle of life in his writings, but from a perspective that involved much less faith in God than Hawthorne had. Melville, pictured at right, had only about two years of formal schooling. His work as a seaman gave him the background for most of his writing, including *Moby Dick* (1851), the story of how one man's obsession with a great white whale destroyed himself and those around him. Melville's work was not appreciated in his lifetime. Critics began rediscovering his work in the 1920s.

Edgar Allen Poe (1809-1849)

Poe wrote many poems and many more short stories exploring issues of fear and death. He is usually considered the first horror writer, and his bouts with alcoholism probably intensified his dark outlook. Poe wrote for emotional effect and not so much to address social and individual issues. Poe was an American writer, but his writings really had little to do with America.

As the 1844 election approached, both national parties were in disarray. The issue that would bring the Democrats back into power was westward expansion. With it, however, came another issue that would haunt the country for years to come: slavery.

John Tyler
George Peter Alexander Healy (American, 1859)

Tyler hoped to receive the Democratic nomination for President in 1844, but by then he was a man without a party. He returned to Virginia and was elected to the Confederate Congress in 1861. He died in 1862 before he could take his seat.

Tyler had eight children from his first marriage and seven from his second. John Tyler was born in 1790. His son Lyon was born in 1853. Two of Lyon's sons, Lyon Jr. (b. 1924) and Harrison (b. 1928) lived into the 21st century.

Seeing the people, He felt compassion for them, because they were distressed and dispirited like sheep without a shepherd.
Matthew 9:36

★ Assignments for Lesson 42 ★

American Voices — Read the excerpts from *Democracy in America* by Alexis de Tocqueville (pages 134-136) and the poems by Oliver Wendell Holmes Sr. (pages 129-130).

Literature — Continue reading *Uncle Tom's Cabin*.

Bible — What attributes of God does Holmes praise in "Lord of All Being, Throned Afar"?
Work on memorizing Acts 5:29-32.

Project — Work on your project.

Student Review — Optional: Answer the questions for Lesson 42.

"North Platte," Daniel Jenks (American, 1859)

Lesson 43

Moving Westward

Brown dirt and small, scrubby bushes stretched as far as the eye could see. Famine, disease, and wild animals threatened travelers every day. They might get lost. Native Americans might attack. Despite these dangers, people on this journey saw it not as some kind of punishment but as the embodiment of progress, expansion, and hope.

The scene was the Oregon Trail, one of several trails that brought settlers from the East as America moved west. Daniel Jenks of Rhode Island headed for California in 1859. He kept a diary about his experiences and made drawings of what he saw, such as the ones above and on page 233.

The Reality of Expansion

Much of American history is the story of expansion: geographically, intellectually, and culturally. Never was this more true than during the second quarter of the 1800s. As the United States neared mid-century, a new generation was growing into maturity. They had been born after independence from Britain, and they had benefited from the sacrifice of the founders. The Louisiana Purchase and the War of 1812 had convinced many Americans that their country offered almost boundless opportunities, and they wanted to capitalize on those opportunities.

Westward expansion during this period was unmistakable. By 1860 over half of the population lived west of the Appalachian Mountains. Many were crossing the Mississippi River to settle in the Louisiana Territory. The census figures for this period show the country's rapid growth, which was spurred by healthy lifestyles and a huge increase in immigration.

The Idea of Manifest Destiny

Even after the Louisiana Purchase, many Americans believed that the nation's borders were incomplete. Their eyes were on the land that stretched all the way to the Pacific. John Louis O'Sullivan, editor of the *Democratic Review*, expressed this belief when he wrote in 1845 that, "Our manifest destiny is to overspread the continent allotted by Providence for the free development of our yearly multiplying millions."

With the phrase "manifest destiny," O'Sullivan captured the thinking of many Americans. To them it was obvious—manifest—that God's destiny for the United States was that it extend across the continent. This gave many Americans a moral rationalization for how they treated other peoples as the U.S. expanded.

Oregon and California

Settlers began moving onto the Great Plains that lay within the Louisiana Territory. However, Native Americans used large portions of this land as their buffalo hunting grounds. Conflicts with the tribes of the Great Plains led many pioneers to look for other places to settle. Word of fertile land and a pleasant climate in the Oregon Territory drew people there.

The Oregon Trail started in Independence, Missouri, and followed the Platte River through Nebraska. It then went into Wyoming, Idaho, and what is now eastern Oregon. From that point the trail followed the Columbia River Gorge to the Willamette Valley. Thousands of settlers embarked on the difficult journey through an often barren landscape, sometimes with tragic consequences.

The United States and Great Britain jointly administered the Oregon Territory, which stretched north from California and included much of what is now British Columbia. Joint occupation had little practical impact for many years; but as more and more Americans moved into Oregon, the Americans wanted the region to be governed solely by the U.S. Control of Oregon became an issue in the 1844 presidential election.

Meanwhile, the area of California also became a subject of interest to Americans. Although Mexico owned California, it exerted little control over it. The California coastline attracted shipping companies eager to develop trade with Asia. Great Britain, France, and Russia all expressed interest in taking over the region. Andrew Jackson had approached Mexico about purchasing northern California, but Mexico rejected the offer.

"Cherokee Pass, Rocky Mountains," Daniel Jenks (American, 1859)

Texas

As keen as American interest was in Oregon and California, the first significant issue in this period of western expansion involved another area of Mexico called Texas. Southerners interested in expansion turned their eyes toward this area, which lay immediately west of the southern part of the Louisiana Territory. Texas was sparsely populated, so Americans considered it ripe for the taking.

American involvement with Mexico was related to political unrest within Mexico itself. Mexico attempted to revolt against Spanish rule in 1807, but the effort failed. After many years of continuing unrest, Spain finally withdrew in 1821 and Mexico became independent. Americans wanted to move into Texas to develop it and to establish trade with the Mexicans. American Moses Austin received a

Santa Anna (1794-1876) entered service in the Spanish army in Mexico in 1810. He turned against Spain during the Mexican Revolution of 1821. In addition to leading Mexican troops against the Texians, he fought later against the French and then against the United States in the Mexican War. He lost power in the 1850s.

Joel Poinsett, U.S. ambassador to Mexico in the 1820s, discovered a beautiful flower there. He brought it back to the U.S. and cultivated it. We now call it the poinsettia.

large land grant from the government of Mexico, but he died before he could develop the grant. His son, Stephen, started a colony on the Brazos River and encouraged other Americans to settle there (and, of course, to buy land from him). Many who wanted to get a new start in a new land moved to Texas, including a significant number from Tennessee led by Davy Crockett. Large landowners from the South brought their slaves with them.

Since the limits of the Austin grant were unclear, and since Mexico feared an American takeover of the region, Mexican troops were stationed in the area. Northern politician Lewis Cass expressed the American view of the situation: "We do not want the people of Mexico, either as citizens or subjects. All we want is a portion of territory, with a population that would soon recede or identify itself with ours." Many Americans believed that they deserved whatever they were able to take. The American settlers in Texas approached the Mexican government about Texas becoming a separate nation; but the Mexican dictator, General Antonio López de Santa Anna, refused.

The Lone Star Republic

After a period of increasing tension between the American settlers and the Mexican government, on March 2, 1836, the Texians (as the Texas-Americans called themselves) declared Texas to be an independent nation. The Republic of Texas was

Lesson 43 - Moving Westward

nicknamed the Lone Star Republic for the single star on their flag. The star was a symbol of their willingness to stand alone, but it also was a statement of their desire to become a new star on the American flag. Their declaration of independence from Mexico was prompted by a desire to be annexed by the U.S. and to become a new state.

Santa Anna fought back against the Texian independence movement, beginning with an attack on a group of Texians holding out at an abandoned Catholic mission called the Alamo in the little town of San Antonio. Santa Anna had demanded their surrender on February 23, but the group refused. Twelve days of fighting followed. The Texians inside the mission were prepared to defend their position to the death. According to legend, the commander of the Americans, Colonel William Travis, drew a line in the dirt inside the Alamo and asked who of the 185 men present were willing to give their lives in the cause of freedom. Everyone crossed the line except one French mercenary, who left. Davy Crockett was among the defenders. Jim Bowie, who was ill, had his cot carried across the line.

On March 6, 1836, the Mexicans overwhelmed the Alamo and killed all but one of the men, who convinced the Mexicans that he had been fighting against his will. Also, one Texian woman was released to take a message to Sam Houston, commander in chief of the Texas forces. Before the Alamo's defenders died, the Texians killed about 1,500 Mexicans.

Alamo Village near Bracketville, Texas, was built as a movie set in the 1950s using authentic adobe bricks. It operated as a tourist attraction for nearly fifty years.

Sam Houston (1793-1863) had been a friend of Andrew Jackson and had fought with Old Hickory at the Battle of Horseshoe Bend in Alabama. He had been a Congressman from Tennessee and had served as the governor of Tennessee before resigning to move to Texas. After Texas became a state, he served as U.S. Senator until 1859. He was elected governor of Texas but was forced out of office when he refused to support joining the Confederate States of America.

The battle at the Alamo inspired the Texians to continue the fight. Sam Houston gathered an army of volunteers and defeated the Mexicans at the San Jacinto River in April of 1836. Their battle cry was, "Remember the Alamo!" After the battle, Santa Anna signed a treaty recognizing the independence of Texas, but a new government in Mexico repudiated Santa Anna and the treaty, refusing to accept the independence of Texas.

The battle for Texas moved to the political realm, as Texas formed a government and applied to the United States for annexation. Complicating the issue even more was the debate in America over slavery. Southerners saw Texas as a way to expand the number of slaveholding states. Many northerners opposed the annexation of Texas because it would expand the influence of slavery. The Texas question dominated American politics over the next ten years.

American Poetry

The first American poet to gain widespread popularity was William Cullen Bryant (1794-1878). "Thanatopsis" was published in 1817. Bryant wrote moving poems that often expressed faith in God. Oliver Wendell Holmes was a physician and medical school professor who wrote poetry and novels.

When the USS *Constitution* was scheduled to be scrapped in 1830, Holmes wrote the poem "Old Ironsides," which helped preserve the famous ship.

The leading poet in America before the Civil War was Henry Wadsworth Longfellow (1807-1882). The 1863 photo at left shows Longfellow (on the right) with Massachusetts Senator Charles Sumner. Longfellow was a literary scholar who taught at Bowdoin College and then Harvard. He produced a huge body of work, including the long narrative poems "Evangeline," "The Song of Hiawatha," and "The Courtship of Miles Standish," all published before the Civil War. He also wrote many well-known and beloved shorter poems such as "The Children's Hour," "The Midnight Ride of Paul Revere," and "The Village Blacksmith" (see manuscript on page 237). Longfellow wrote with feeling for his subjects and used classical rhythm and rhyme. His work was widely read during his lifetime and has been ever since. Some modern critics who do not share Longfellow's views and values unfortunately dismiss his writing as simplistic and trite.

Emily Dickinson (1830-1886) wrote about two thousand poems but only a few were published during her lifetime. She lived as a recluse in Amherst, Massachusetts. Her poems are appreciated now for their thoughtfulness and sensitivity. She wrote much about death and solitude.

Walt Whitman (1819-1892) took a different direction with his free verse. Whitman celebrated what he saw as the vast scope and promise of America, though he also had a preoccupation with himself. His most famous work was "Leaves of Grass," first published in 1855 with many subsequent editions.

Poetic Techniques

Poetry is a form of literary expression that is intended to touch the thoughts and emotions of the reader relatively quickly by the use of words, rhyme, and rhythm. Poetry evokes emotion by telling a story, recalling a memory, or describing a scene.

Rhyme. A unit of thought in a poem is called a stanza. In a traditional poem, the last words in succeeding lines rhyme or have the same sound ("Twinkle, twinkle, little star / How I wonder what you are"). Sometimes every other line rhymes, or the rhyming arrangement can be more complicated. The rhyme can be described using letters. Two succeeding lines that rhyme are called a couplet. Rhyme can be described as a-a, b-b, c-c, etc.

> I shot an arrow into the air,
> It fell to earth, I knew not where; (a-a)
> For, so swiftly it flew, the sight
> Could not follow it in its flight. (b-b)

An every-other line rhyme is a-b-c-b, where the second and fourth lines of a stanza rhyme, but the first and third do not. Sometimes words within lines rhyme ("The port is near, the bells I hear, the people all exulting").

Rhythm. A line of poetry can have rhythm that is indicated by its accent pattern or meter. The analysis of a poem's rhythm is called scansion or scanning a poem. The segment of a line that is part of a recognizable pattern is called a foot. Patterns of rhythm have been given names. The first word in the name tells its accent pattern, while the second tells the number of feet in a line.

One common form of rhythm is iambic pentameter (eye-AM-bik pen-TAM-eh-ter) . An iambic foot has two syllables with the second accented. Pentameter means that a line has five iambic feet:

If EV/-er TWO/ were ONE/, then SURE/-ly WE

Iambic trimeter (TRIM-eh-ter) has three iambic feet. Iambic tetrameter has four feet.

There IS/no FRIG/-ate LIKE/ a BOOK (iambic tetrameter)
To TAKE/ us LANDS/ a-WAY (iambic trimeter)

Trochaic tetrameter (Tro-KAY-ik teh-TRAM-eh-ter) has four feet, each of which has an accented then an unaccented syllable. A poet might make small adjustments to any strict form. This line has four feet, but it has an extra syllable in the first foot and lacks a syllable in the last foot:

BY the rude/ BRIDGE that/ ARCHED the /FLOOD

Poets have also used longer and more complicated rhythms. Anapestic tetrameter, for instance, has four feet with the rhythm: unaccented-unaccented-ACCENTED:

'Twas the NIGHT/ be-fore CHRIST/-mas and ALL/ through the HOUSE

A poet might develop a particular meter for a poem:

LIS-ten my/CHILD-ren and/YOU shall/HEAR
Of the MID/night RIDE/ of PAUL/ Re-VERE.

Rhyme and rhythm are not the only use of sound in a poem. Alliteration is the repetition of initial sounds in successive words, often done to create a dramatic impact ("The foe long since in silence slept / Alike the conqueror silent sleeps"). Consonance is the repetition of consonant sounds when vowels differ ("since in silence slept"); assonance is the repetition of stressed vowel sounds with different consonants ("mellow wedding bells"). Onomatopoeia is the use of words that express sounds (crash, thud, slap, etc.).

Much modern poetry is less dependent on rhythm and rhyme. Poetry without regular rhythm and rhyme is called free verse; blank verse is iambic pentameter without rhyme. In these poetic styles the impact of the poem is made by the thoughts expressed and how the words are arranged as opposed to rhythm and rhyme. The use of these styles can be a statement of the modern poet's view of the world as less predictable and patterned than what poets from previous generations saw.

What Else Was Happening?

1827 John James Audubon publishes the first volume of the Birds of America series with life-size drawings.
1828 Noah Webster publishes his first dictionary, containing 12,000 words and 40,000 definitions.
1830 The world population is estimated to be 1 billion.
1834 Charles Babbage publishes research on a "calculating machine," but this first computer is never finished.
1835 Samuel Colt invents the six-shot revolver.
1837 Queen Victoria begins her sixty-four-year reign in Great Britain. She will rule until 1901.
1837 John Deere builds a plow with a steel moldboard which can till tough prairie soil.
1839 Louis Daguerre demonstrates his first photograph on silver-plated copper, called a daguerreotype.
1840 Britain introduces a gummed sticker that pays for delivery of a letter anywhere in the country. This Penny Black postage stamp is shown at right.
1843 The first printed Christmas cards are introduced.
1844 The Young Men's Christian Association (YMCA) is founded in London.
1846 German astronomer Johann Galle discovers the planet Neptune.
1849 French physicist Armand Fizeau calculates the speed of light with remarkable accuracy.
1850 Charles Dickens publishes David Copperfield.

But godliness actually is a means of great gain when accompanied by contentment. For we have brought nothing into the world, so we cannot take anything out of it either. If we have food and covering, with these we shall be content.
1 Timothy 6:6-8

★ Assignments for Lesson 43 ★

American Voices — Read "My Faith Looks Up to Thee" by Ray Palmer (page 128), "The Arrow and the Song" by Henry Wadsworth Longfellow (page 138), and "I Hear America Singing" by Walt Whitman (page 186).

Literature — Continue reading Uncle Tom's Cabin.

Bible — Work on memorizing Acts 5:29-32.

Project — Work on your project.

Student Review — Optional: Answer the questions for Lesson 43.

Battle of Monterrey, Mexico, Lithograph by Sarony & Major (1846)

Lesson 44

Polk, Texas, and Mexico

The political maneuverings regarding Texas, many of them behind the scenes, were complicated. Following the Battle of San Jacinto, the people of Texas drafted a constitution, elected Sam Houston to be their president, and voted to be annexed by the United States. However, President Andrew Jackson was not willing to support the annexation of a slaveholding territory as a possible new state, even though his old friend Sam Houston was its president. The Administration feared that a war with Mexico and domestic conflict within the U.S. would result from annexation. However, Jackson finally did recognize the Republic of Texas on his last day in office in 1837, leaving the problem to Martin Van Buren.

Meanwhile, France and Britain also recognized the Republic of Texas and began trade talks with the new country. Great Britain had abolished slavery throughout its empire in 1833, and Britain hoped to use its influence to encourage the abolition of slavery in Texas. The increased British influence in Texas concerned many Americans, but uncertainty within the American government about what to do led to several years of inaction. American officials did not want to start a war with Mexico, nor did they want to throw the slave state/free state count in the Senate out of balance.

In 1844 the John Tyler Administration made a treaty with the Republic of Texas that would annex Texas to the U.S. as a territory. About the same time, Secretary of State John Calhoun wrote to the British minister in Washington, defending slavery as a help to blacks and telling the British not to push for abolition in areas outside of its own empire. When the Calhoun letter was published, it increased fears among anti-slavery groups in the U.S. that the drive to annex Texas was a thinly-veiled attempt to increase the extent and power of slavery. The publication of the letter aroused such strong opposition by opponents of slavery that any immediate possibility of bringing Texas into the Union was dead. The treaty was defeated in the Senate.

The Election of 1844

Texas and Oregon were major issues in the 1844 presidential contest. The Whig nominee, Henry Clay, opposed annexing Texas, although the Whig platform said nothing about the issue. The leading candidate for the Democratic nomination was former President Martin Van Buren, who also opposed annexation. However, Van Buren's position against annexation cost him support among southern Democrats, and the party convention deadlocked on selecting a nominee. On the eighth ballot, James K. Polk of Tennessee was placed in nomination as an alternative to Van Buren. Polk was selected on the ninth ballot to carry the Democratic banner. Polk was the first dark horse candidate to receive a presidential nomination. The expression "dark horse" comes from horse racing, in which a dark horse that is not in the spotlight manages to win. A dark horse candidate is one who seemingly comes out of nowhere to gain a victory.

When Clay heard the news of Polk's nomination, he sneered, "Who is James K. Polk?" This was typical Clay arrogance, since James K. Polk was far from unknown. Having received his political education from Andrew Jackson, Polk was called Young Hickory. He served fourteen years in the U.S. House of Representatives, and he was Speaker of the House for the last four of those years (a post that Clay himself had once held). Then Polk served one term as governor of Tennessee. A hard-working politician, Polk, who stood a mere 5'7" tall, was also called "Napoleon of the Stump" for his intense speaking style.

The Democratic platform for 1844 called for the "reoccupation of Oregon and the reannexation of Texas." The phrase implied that both areas rightfully belonged to the United States and ought to be acquired free and clear without delay or complication. Polk also called for the acquisition of California, lower tariffs, and the renewal of the Independent Treasury.

Seeing how popular Polk's position on Texas was, and sensing the desire for expansion on the part of many Americans, Clay backpedaled on Texas. He said that he would support the annexation of Texas if it were accomplished without war. This obvious change of his position to gain votes in the South cost Clay support in the North. A third party in New York State, the anti-slavery Liberty Party, pulled enough votes away from Clay to give Polk the state and the election. Polk received only 38,000 more votes than Clay and actually lost his home state of Tennessee to Clay; but Polk had a large electoral majority. At forty-nine, Polk was the youngest President to date.

Oregon Resolved

During the campaign, Polk stated that he wanted the United States to own all of the Oregon Territory. The slogan for this position became "54° 40' or Fight," referring to the latitude line that was the northern border of the territory. Britain, of course, did not want to give up all of Oregon.

In 1846 the two countries agreed to extend the border between Canada and the U.S. on the 49th parallel of latitude to the Pacific Ocean. Thus Great Britain and the United States divided the Oregon Territory between them (Great Britain still controlled Canada also). The result was neither the 54° 40' wanted by the Democrats nor a fight, but

Samuel Morse used his new invention, the telegraph, to relay the news of Polk's nomination from Baltimore to Washington, D.C. The news was so surprising that many in Washington thought that the telegraph message was in error.

Lesson 44 - Polk, Texas, and Mexico

most Americans decided it was better to settle the Oregon question with this compromise than to risk a conflict with Great Britain, especially since the U.S. was already embroiled in a confrontation with Mexico.

"Mr. Polk's War"

After Polk won the 1844 election on an expansionist platform, Congress passed a joint resolution in early 1845 that offered annexation and statehood to Texas if Texans approved. Outgoing President John Tyler signed the measure on March 1, 1845; and Texas joined the Union in December of that year. Mexico did not recognize the annexation of Texas, nor did it recognize the Rio Grande as the southern border of Texas. Mexico said the Nueces River, which lay further north, was the true border. Polk tried to negotiate with Mexico over the purchase of Texas, California, and all of the territory between them; but Mexico was insulted by the Texas annexation and refused to negotiate. Polk sent American troops to the Rio Grande area, Mexican forces attacked them, and the United States declared war on May 13, 1846. Whigs and many in New

When U.S. forces surrounded the Mexican city of Vera Cruz, American General Winfield Scott asked the Mexican General Juan Morales to allow civilians to leave the city. Morales refused. The U.S. bombarded the city for three days, as depicted in this contemporary print, before the Mexicans surrendered.

A one-term Whig Congressman from Illinois, Abraham Lincoln, repeatedly introduced "Spot Resolutions" in Congress (example shown above). Lincoln demanded that Polk identify the spot on American soil where American troops were fired upon as Polk claimed. The area in which the skirmish took place was disputed, since Mexico did not recognize it as belonging to the U.S. Many people believed that Polk's Administration provoked the war to gain unquestioned control of Texas and to gain as much additional territory as possible.

England opposed the war as an expansionist and pro-slavery move. They called it "Mr. Polk's War." Once again talk surfaced in New England about seceding from the Union.

During the war, the U.S. suffered few battle casualties. More soldiers died from disease than from military engagements. The U.S. defeated Mexican forces in Texas, then the American Army invaded Mexico and captured Mexico City in September of 1847. Meanwhile, a group of Americans in Sacramento acted to take California from Mexico and declared the independent Republic of California in June of 1846. A month later, the U.S. Navy Pacific fleet took control of the situation on the Pacific Coast and declared California to be a territory annexed to the United States.

The war ended with the signing of a treaty in February of 1848. The United States got Texas, California, and the New Mexico area in between for $15 million. The U.S. also agreed to take over claims that individual Americans had against the Mexican government to a total of about $3 million. This was essentially what Polk wanted to achieve through negotiations with Mexico, and one wonders if the same outcome could have been accomplished diplomatically and without war; such is history. The treaty gave the U.S. the largest increase in its land area since the Louisiana Purchase, and it brought under U.S. control about as much territory as Jefferson's deal had.

In many ways the Mexican War was a prelude of things to come. The conflict saw the first use of war correspondents reporting back to American newspapers using telegraph lines. In addition, many West Point graduates who fought together against the Mexicans later saw combat in the

In his last annual address to Congress in December 1848, Polk confirmed the discovery of gold in California. This led to a huge migration of gold-seekers into California the following year, which is why they are called Forty-Niners. This illustration shows gold diggers working along the Sacramento River.

Civil War on opposite sides. These military officers included such men as Robert E. Lee, U.S. Grant, Thomas (later known as Stonewall) Jackson, George McClellan, Braxton Bragg, and George Pickett.

General Scott's Grand Entry into the City of Mexico, September 14th, 1847 (Published 1848)

James and Sarah Polk

Andrew Jackson got to see his political protege and fellow Tennessee Democrat enter office before he died in June of 1845. The Polks were regular churchgoers. They opposed hard liquor, dancing, and card-playing. When the President and First Lady appeared at the inaugural ball, the dancing stopped for two hours while the first couple greeted everyone present. When they left, the dancing began again.

Sarah Childress Polk was an intelligent and unusually well-educated woman for her day. She scanned the newspapers for information and editorials that she thought her husband ought to know about. The First Lady often hosted receptions for the public at the White House. She later reported to her husband the comments she heard from the people who came to the receptions.

James K. Polk believed that the government should not take on large spending programs because he thought they would influence voters to elect candidates on the basis of what those candidates offered to do for the voters. In 1846 Congress lowered tariffs and created the Independent Treasury. Thus, along with the acquisition of Oregon, Texas, and California, Polk accomplished all of the major planks of his platform. Also during his term, a treaty was concluded that gave the U.S. the right to build a canal or railroad in Panama.

Polk left office exhausted in March of 1849, and the couple moved to Nashville, Tennessee. James died of cholera three months later, and Sarah lived in Nashville as a widow another forty-two years. She died in 1891. George Peter Alexander Healy painted these portraits of the Polks.

Aftermath of the Mexican War

The Whig Party won a majority in the U.S. House in the 1846 mid-term election, largely because of widespread unhappiness over the war with Mexico. Polk was able to accomplish little in the last half of his term. The Whigs won the presidency in 1848 (Polk never planned to seek a second term and did not run), and Polk felt that he and his party had been rejected by the American people.

This period of expansion enlarged the continental United States to nearly its present size. The small Gadsden Purchase in what would become southern Arizona and New Mexico was concluded in 1853, when it was considered a prime possibility by Southerners for a transcontinental railroad. The war with Mexico gave Americans another burst of pride, although a significant number opposed the conflict. Geographic expansion, however, raised anew the larger question of slavery that would soon tear the nation apart.

The border between the United States and Mexico has continued to be a point of contention, even in the 21st century. This photograph shows the fence between Nogales, Arizona, and Nogales, Mexico in 2009.

*To do righteousness and justice
is desired by the Lord more than sacrifice.
Proverbs 21:3*

★ Assignments for Lesson 44 ★

American Voices — Read the poems by Emily Dickinson (page 176) and "O Holy Night," translated by John Dwight (page 185).

Literature — Continue reading *Uncle Tom's Cabin*.

Bible — Work on memorizing Acts 5:29-32.

Project — Work on your project.

Student Review — Optional: Answer the questions for Lesson 44.

1920 Demonstration in Detroit Against a Proposal to Require All Michigan Children to Attend Public Schools

Lesson 45 - Bible Study

Protest

People who were alive during the 1960s and 1970s have vivid memories of thousands of people protesting the war in Vietnam. Many cities and college campuses saw demonstrations against American military activity in Southeast Asia. Those who are a little older can remember the civil rights demonstrations of the early 1960s, when thousands marched in protest against legal segregation and discrimination against blacks. During that period, protests were a common occurrence.

Many of those protesters went to jail for what they did, just as Henry David Thoreau did for his refusal to pay a poll tax in protest against the Mexican War. Thoreau and the protesters of the 1960s and 1970s did not go to jail for their beliefs. They were put in jail because the way in which they protested violated the law.

Protest is a long-standing tradition in the United States. Our country began with a defiant declaration of our independence from Great Britain. That declaration listed many actions of the king which the Continental Congress protested as being illegal, immoral, or unethical. The First Amendment to the Constitution guarantees the freedom of speech and of the press, and these provisions give people the right to protest the actions of the government. The same amendment also guarantees the right to assemble peaceably and "to petition the government for a redress of grievances." This is nothing if not the right to protest government action. Such protests can be regulated—for example, by having to be peaceful, and perhaps by requiring the local authorities to issue a permit for such an assembly—but they may not be regulated to the point that legitimate free speech and protest are stifled.

Protest is also a strong tradition in the Bible. Many prophets in the Old Testament, and Jesus Himself in the New Testament, protested the way in which the established order was conducted. Christians are told clearly in Romans 13 to obey the civil government. They are never told to rebel against the civil authorities, even if the authorities are wrong. However, many people who throughout history have protested against a power structure are today seen as heroes, and many of those did so in the name of Christ.

Not all protests, however, are good. Several times in the Old Testament, people rose up in protest against the rightful authority because of the protesters' sin, not because of righteousness. Many churches have experienced divisions when one group protested a standing policy or position, insisted on having its way on an issue, and refused to come together with fellow believers who happened to see things differently.

The key to understanding the legitimacy of protest is in the statement made by Peter and the other apostles in Acts 5:29, "We must obey God rather than men." God's standard of right and wrong must be the standard of all who follow Him. If we can obey men while we obey God, so much the better. If by obeying God we violate the laws of men, we are violating a lesser standard by obeying the greater standard. The laws of men should be respected and followed as much as possible. The Declaration of Independence warns against changing governments "for light and transient causes." However, the laws of men can be wrong. When those laws themselves violate God's laws of justice and truth, we must obey God rather than men.

Protesters in the Old Testament

God sent Moses to lodge a protest to Pharaoh against the way that His people were being treated. Through Moses, God told Pharaoh, "Let My people go." The battle of wills between God and Pharaoh eventually led to the exodus.

When David committed the sin of adultery with Bathsheba, God sent the prophet Nathan to protest David's actions to his face. The prophet's words were a stinging indictment of the king's moral failure (2 Samuel 12:1-15). David was the king, but he had done wrong.

During the period of the Divided Kingdom, time and again God sent prophets to protest the faithlessness of kings. Elijah and Amos are two examples of God's messengers who spoke pointed protests against the leaders of government. In 1 Kings 22, many prophets were predicting victory for the kings of Israel and Judah; but Micaiah was the lone voice of truth in predicting defeat for Ahab and Jehoshaphat.

Not every protest in the Old Testament was of God. Many times during the exodus the people faithlessly protested about their conditions, or their lack of food, or some other matter (see, for example, Exodus 14:10-12 and 16:2-3). Sometimes God used a faithless protest to accomplish His will. The elders of Israel wanted Samuel to appoint a king because his sons were not faithful in the work of the tabernacle. The sons of Samuel were doing wrong, but the desire for a king was a rejection of God's leadership. God used the situation, however, to further His will for Israel (1 Samuel 8:1-9).

The same was true when Jeroboam and the northern tribes protested the policies of Rehoboam and his father, Solomon. When Rehoboam rejected the advice of his older counselors and adopted the defiant attitude of his peers, Jeroboam refused to submit to Rehoboam and the northern tribes set up their own kingdom. The rejection of the king that God had put in place was wrong, but God used it for His purposes (1 Kings 12:1-19).

This 13th-century illustration by English artist William de Brailes depicts the Israelites complaining about the lack of water in the wilderness.

Lesson 45 - Bible Study: Protest

Jesus, the Protester

In the Sermon on the Mount, Jesus took aim at the ways in which the rabbis had reinterpreted Scripture: "You have heard that it was said . . . . But I say to you . . . ." In Mark 7, Jesus protested the way that the scribes and Pharisees had elevated their traditions above the word of God. He told parables that condemned the Jewish leaders (for instance, see Matthew 21:33-46). Even though Jesus was faithful in keeping the Law and accepted the tradition of the synagogue, he was not willing to accept the status quo regarding the religious opinions and attitudes of the Pharisees.

In His most pointed protest demonstration, Jesus drove the buyers and sellers from the temple and overturned the tables of the money changers and those selling doves (Matthew 21:12-13). Of course, when He did this He was not destroying other people's property. Everything that He touched actually belonged to Him! He was protesting how other people were abusing what belonged to Him and how they were defiling His Father's house. The apostles continued Jesus' pattern in the early church, and as a result they often came into conflict with the Jewish authorities (see Acts 4 and 5).

Later Protesters

In the early centuries of the church, many Christians resisted the pagan authorities, refused to deny Christ, and were put to death for their faith. After the Roman Catholic Church gained control over most religious practice in Europe, some refused to bow to the pope and suffered as a result. Martin Luther is well-known for his reform efforts, but other believers resisted long before Luther.

In the early 12th century, Peter Waldo and his followers in southern France (called Waldensians) refused to submit to papal authority for their faith and practice. In the century that followed, believers in the French town of Albi (called Albigensians) again resisted the authority of the church. These groups

Christ Driving the Money-Changers from the Temple
Rembrandt (Dutch, 1626)

were harshly suppressed by Catholic authorities. Sometime later, the Catholic Church instituted the Inquisition, which tried and condemned many believers for what the Church hierarchy considered to be heresy but which sometimes was merely opposition to Catholic tradition.

When Martin Luther protested Catholic practices, his defiance ushered in a wave of individuals and groups that sought to take control of their own spiritual lives. Groups such as the Anabaptists, as well as the Puritans and Separatists in England, resisted what they saw as religious error in the predominant religious organizations of their day and time. As we noted in the lesson on the Second Great Awakening, many preachers in nineteenth century America protested the divisions and other traditions of denominationalism and wanted to return to simple New Testament Christianity.

Matters to Bear in Mind

Whenever the faithful encounter injustice, some will choose to resist the injustice in some way. They might offer merely silent protest, or they might take to the streets or the printing press to announce their opposition. In doing so, they take a risk. Sometimes they will be put in jail for breaking a law (a law which protesters might believe is immoral or wrong). Sometimes they will purposefully break a law to call attention to their cause. When the opposition is strong enough, or when the authorities are strong enough, or when the cause is important enough, protesters might even lose their lives. This happened during the civil rights movement in America in the 1960s. Protests increase awareness of a problem, and sometimes those protests lead to change.

Our most important calling is to follow God. The standard for deciding what should be done is God's revealed truth. From time to time throughout history, one person or a small group is convicted of the need to stage a protest in order to bring a church or a society closer to what they believe is God's will. When a protest is staged against what is wrong, God's way can be renewed or rediscovered.

But Peter and John answered and said to them, "Whether it is right in the sight of God to give heed to you rather than to God, you be the judge; for we cannot stop speaking about what we have seen and heard."
Acts 4:19-20

★ Assignments for Lesson 45 ★

American Voices — Read "Civil Disobedience" by Henry David Thoreau (pages 146-158).

Literature — Continue reading *Uncle Tom's Cabin*.

Bible — Recite or write Acts 5:29-32 from memory.

Project — Complete your project for the unit.

Student Review — Optional: Answer the questions for Lesson 45 and take the quiz for Unit 9.

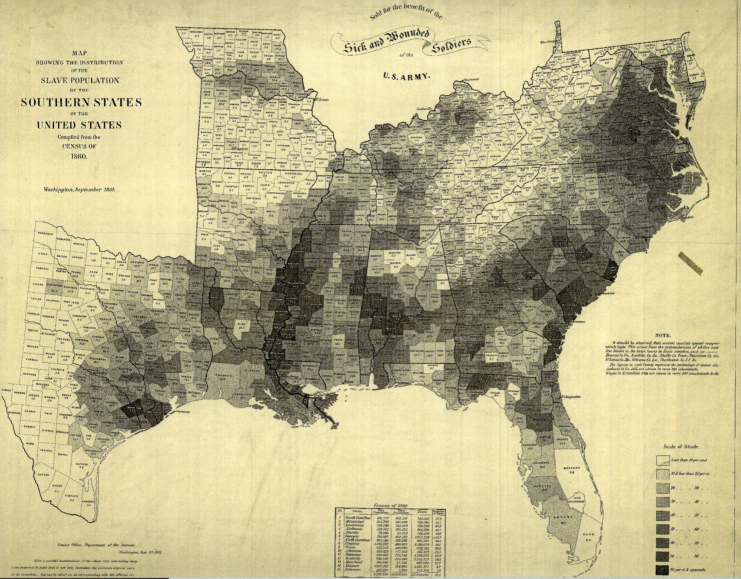

Slaves as a Percentage of the Population of Each County in 1860

10 Challenges and Changes

Slavery was the key issue facing America in the first half of the nineteenth century. In this unit we examine how slavery operated and what it meant to the people involved. We also look at the abolitionist impulse that developed to try to end the practice of slavery. America experienced profound changes in the period, as cities grew, industry developed, and the ethnic makeup of the country changed because of a flood of immigrants. America's material growth and success during this period remind us that God defines real success.

Lesson 46 - Slavery
Lesson 47 - Abolition
Lesson 48 - The Growth of Cities and Industry
Lesson 49 - Immigration and Other Changes
Lesson 50 - Bible Study: God Defines Success

Memory Work Memorize Philippians 4:8 by the end of this unit.

Books Used
The Bible
American Voices
Uncle Tom's Cabin

Project (choose one)

1) Write 300 to 500 words on one of the following topics:
   - Summarize the historical arguments in support of slavery and the arguments opposing slavery. Give your opinion on the issue and on how the issue should have been settled.
   - Write about how being an immigrant in this time period might have affected your fears, beliefs, connections with family, and dreams.
2) Research Gullah cooking traditions and prepare a Gullah-style meal for your family. See Lesson 46.
3) Create a collection of photos of yourself or another person performing tasks that were once done by hand or with simple tools and are now mostly done by machine (i.e., sewing, washing laundry, washing dishes, mowing the lawn, etc.). Take two photos for each task—one of "the old-fashioned way" and one of the modern method. Compose your photos intentionally and artistically. Your finished project should be in the form of a slideshow on an electronic device, prints of the photographs displayed on a poster, or photos in book form. Include at least ten examples (twenty photos). See Lesson 48.

Slave Traders in Gorée, Senegal

Lesson 46

Slavery

Dutch merchants brought twenty black Africans to Jamestown in 1619. By 1860 about 4.5 million blacks lived in the United States, 4 million of them slaves. The story of black slavery in America had a profound influence on the entire country, not just the South, in the period leading up to and including the Civil War. The story does not end there, however. The U.S. has lived with and (often insufficiently) dealt with the effects of slavery ever since.

History of Slavery

Slavery has existed since ancient times. Many countries and cultures have practiced it; and it continues even today, although now it is done in violation of national and international law. The Bible talks about slavery, but the people of God were taught to handle it differently from the way the world did.

The Law of Moses gave humane regulations about how Israelites were to treat their slaves (for example, see Leviticus 25:44-55). The New Testament deals with slavery as a reality of the world. Christians are nowhere told to rise up to abolish it, but the way of Christ did usher in profound changes in how slavery was viewed and handled. Paul told Christian slaves and masters to love and respect one another (as in Colossians 3:22-4:1). The apostle also encouraged slaves who were able to gain their freedom to do so (1 Corinthians 7:21). The gospel carried in it the seeds of love that eventually led to the outlawing of slavery in Western civilization. Leading abolitionists in Great Britain and the United States were motivated by their Christian faith.

Slavery has not been the same in all times and places. In the ancient world it was not based on skin color. Slaves were usually prisoners of war taken from conquered nations. Many were well-educated and served their masters' families as tutors, overseers, or in other responsible positions. They were not free, but neither were they kept in chains.

Slavery was being practiced by tribes in Africa when European traders started making contact with them. Sometimes whites entered the land and captured Africans who were then sold as slaves, but more often European traders made deals with local chieftains who themselves captured other Africans or sold conquered peoples to the Europeans.

Slave ships that carried their human cargo had notoriously horrendous conditions. Africans were packed onto ships in as large numbers as possible with minimal food and medical care. The captain of a slave ship hoped that enough Africans survived the trip to make his effort profitable.

Unit 10 - Challenges and Changes

Slave Life

Farms and plantations in America had different levels of slave work. The lowest rank (and hardest work) was that of field hands. Next came house slaves, and then above that were slaves who became skilled craftsmen. A few were hired out to other landowners for specific jobs.

Colonies and states had laws called slave codes that limited the rights of slaves. Slaves were treated as property, not human beings. Slaves could not legally marry. Harsh punishment of and even the killing of a slave were not considered crimes. Owners could whip slaves, but whipping white workers was illegal. Other severe punishment meted out to slaves included branding and, in some places, dismemberment (cutting off a hand or foot). Runaway slaves who were captured sometimes had to wear headgear similar to a cage over their heads that could not be removed.

Slaves were usually allowed to marry and to have families because most masters knew that they got more work from contented slaves than from angry and unruly ones. Most slave families were kept intact; but sometimes they were split up, with one or more family members being sold because of an owners' greed or as punishment for rebellion. Slaves always knew that the threat of being sold hung over them.

John Newton was the captain of a British slave ship in the early 1700s. His conscience was eventually convicted about his part in this terrible treatment of other human beings. He quit that work, came to faith in Christ, and eventually became a minister. Newton later wrote the hymn, "Amazing Grace," which expresses thanks to God for the grace "that saved a wretch like me." He wrote his own epitaph, shown on his grave above.

It is estimated that between 1700 and 1810 about eight million Africans were transported as slaves, and of that number one million died on the way. Most slaves were carried first to the British West Indies, and then some were brought from there to the American continent.

This British diagram from about 1789 shows how slaves were packed tightly on slave ships for the Atlantic crossing.

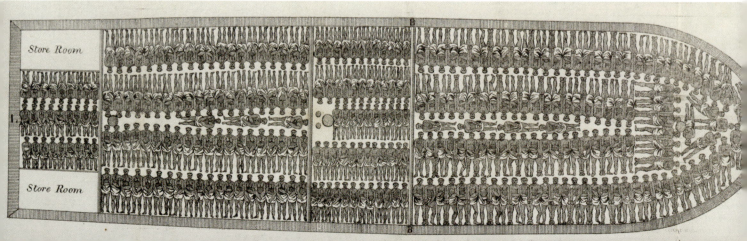

Lesson 46 - Slavery

New Orleans, at the mouth of the Mississippi River, was a major slave-trading market. Slaves had a great fear of being "sold down the river." This illustration is from the 1850s.

Some white planters and their adult sons exploited slave women sexually. The rape of a slave was not considered a crime. For some reason many white women accepted this behavior from the men in their families, but a liaison between a male slave and a white woman was considered much worse. A person with one white parent and one black parent was called a mulatto. A handful of southern mulattos obtained a fair degree of wealth and even owned slaves. They made up what was called a brown aristocracy.

Many slaves adopted the Christian faith which they learned in their new land. Phillis Wheatley, the slave-poet in Boston, was thankful that she was brought to America and learned the truth of Christ instead of being left in the paganism she had previously known. The conversion of some of the slaves was a good thing that God brought about in the midst of a bad situation. Slaves often took spiritual refuge from their plight in their religion. They compared themselves to the Israelites when that nation was enslaved in Egypt, and slaves looked forward to freedom in the Promised Land.

African American Culture

The slaves brought to America were not simply "Africans." They were from particular tribes, each of which had its own identity, language, and culture. As they mixed together under the control of English-speaking owners, they developed a simplified common language known as pidgin English. Pidgin uses such phrases as "This be good-good" for "This is very good," "I go now-now" for "I am going very soon," and simplified verb tenses such as "I be going to town."

Slaves had a rich and active cultural life, including songs, dances, stories, and folk beliefs, that drew on their African and West Indian backgrounds. Whites usually ignored this black culture, but it was nevertheless present and has come to be more appreciated in recent years.

A culture known as Gullah has survived on the coasts and islands of South Carolina and Georgia among the descendants of slaves in that region. They have preserved many aspects of traditional African culture. Their language, folktales, food, and crafts (such as the baskets shown at right) share similarities with those of the people on the west coast of Africa, particularly Sierra Leone.

Life for free blacks was not good either. Even after northern states outlawed slavery, those states still practiced legal and social discrimination against blacks. Free blacks were sometimes accused of being runaway slaves and were captured and taken South. Throughout the country, the races were kept separate and the whites ruled.

Richard Allen (1760-1831) was born as a slave in Pennsylvania. He became a Christian at age 17. After his owner became a Christian also, Allen and his brother were able to purchase their freedom in 1783. Allen preached around the new United States to both blacks and whites. He worked to help former slaves and, because of segregation in churches, helped to establish the African Methodist Episcopal Church.

Lesson 46 - Slavery

The American practice of enslaving blacks not only treated people as beasts; it also made beasts of slave owners, as evidenced by the many incidents of harsh whippings and sexual exploitation of slaves. Southerners became extremely defensive about slavery. Their way of dealing with the issue was not to talk about it, and anyone who did talk about it was portrayed as a troublemaker. Southern leaders erected what some have called an intellectual blockade around their society to limit discussion of the issue. Southerners tended to idealize their society, a view which made them blind to the faults in their society and which prevented change. Northerners, at the same time, were fond of criticizing the South but were blind to the racism and discrimination in their own region.

Uncle Tom's Cabin *continued to influence American perceptions of slavery for decades after the Civil War. Edwin Long, a British artist, painted* Uncle Tom and Little Eva, *shown above, in 1866. Dramatic companies made numerous adaptations of the story for the stage, including the one advertised by the 1881 poster below. Thomas Edison's film company released a fourteen-minute version in 1903, and several other silent film versions were made. These dramatic presentations often portrayed slaves in exaggerated, stereotypical ways, and the main actors were usually white with blackface makeup.*

Economics

The South was not dependent on slave labor until the invention of the cotton gin made large-scale cotton plantations profitable. The development of the textile industry in the northern U.S., as well as growing overseas markets, encouraged more cotton production. Southerners with enough money to do so moved from the Atlantic seaboard into the new areas of Alabama, Mississippi, Louisiana, and Texas, taking their slaves with them and creating an even larger cotton domain.

The importation of slaves was abolished in 1808, but the buying and selling of domestic slaves was big business. The expansion of slavery across the South and the lack of new, imported slaves made the slaves already present even more valuable. Field hands could bring $300-400 in the 1790s; their price rose to $1,500-$2,000 by the 1850s. Not all southerners were slave owners, but the majority of southerners defended slavery and believed that the South's economy depended on the use of slave labor.

Today it is hard for Americans to believe that white Americans, including white Christians, owned slaves and defended slavery. Some whites practiced slavery; many whites looked the other way. Some Americans expressed unhappiness with the practice; a few Americans decided to do something about it. We will learn about the abolitionists in the next lesson.

Opening his mouth, Peter said: "I most certainly understand now that God is not one to show partiality, but in every nation the man who fears Him and does what is right is welcome to Him.
Acts 10:34-36

★ Assignments for Lesson 46 ★

Literature — Continue reading *Uncle Tom's Cabin*. Plan to finish it by the end of Unit 11.

Bible — This week we will consider how God's definition of success contrasts with the world's definition. Read Philippians 3:2-11. List three marks of success as the world defines it and three marks of success as God defines it.

Start memorizing Philippians 4:8.

Project — Choose your project for this unit and start working on it.

Student Review — Optional: Answer the questions for Lesson 46.

Publication of the American Anti-Slavery Society Calling for the End of Slavery in the District of Columbia (1836)

Abolition

All of the thirteen original colonies permitted slavery. Enlightenment thinking as well as Christian conviction led to a movement in the North to abolish slavery when the U.S. gained its independence. Northern states gradually did away with slavery in the early 1800s. During the colonial and early national period, many southerners lamented slavery as a necessary evil. Churches and ministers often criticized the institution of slavery. On the whole, however, few people wanted slavery to end.

People in the South had gotten used to it and had justified it for many years. Politically, slavery was seen as a state-by-state issue, not a national issue. If a state wanted to allow slavery, most people believed that it was the business of that state. If a choice had to be made, most people would rather maintain the Union with some slave states than risk dividing the Union by forcing a national policy decision on the issue.

The American Colonization Society was founded in 1817. Its goal was to finance the purchase of slaves and the cost of their resettlement to Africa. The group acquired land from an African chieftain in 1821 and sent the first freedmen there the next year. Because of its goal of liberty for former slaves, the new nation was called Liberia. Its capital was named Monrovia in honor of James Monroe, who was President at the time. The nation became self-governing in 1847. However, the colonization approach had only limited success. By 1860 only 15,000 former slaves had been resettled to Monrovia, a tiny percentage of the U.S. slave population of about four million. Purchasing the freedom and financing the resettlement of slaves was an expensive task, and the society always had limited funds. Besides, Africa was not home for most of the slaves. The majority had been born in America and wanted to continue living in America, but not as slaves.

In the early 1800s, most newspapers were started for the purpose of promoting a particular viewpoint or political position, not simply for reporting the news. The first newspaper in the country devoted to abolition was *The Manumission Intelligencer*, begun in 1819 by Elihu Embree in Jonesborough, Tennessee (Tennessee was a slave state, but many people in East Tennessee opposed slavery).

Benjamin Lundy founded *The Genius of Universal Emancipation* in Ohio in 1821. It was published for a time in Greeneville, Tennessee, which is not far from Jonesborough. Embree and Lundy were both Quakers. In 1827 Lundy identified about 130 abolitionist groups in the country, over 100 of which were in the South. These newspapers and groups promoted the idea of gradual emancipation of slaves.

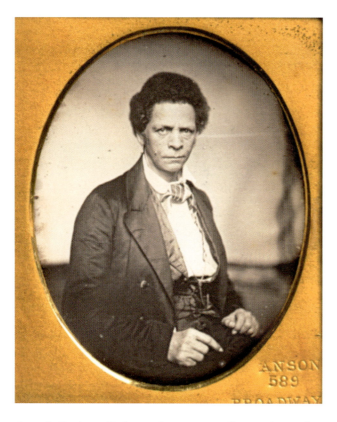

Joseph Jenkins Roberts (1809-1876) was born free in Virginia. He moved to Liberia in 1829. Roberts was the first African American governor of Liberia from 1842-1847, and he was elected as the first president of Liberia after it became an independent country in 1847.

One idea was for slave children born after a certain year to be free at birth. These abolitionists wanted to see slavery end, but they wanted as little disruption to American society as possible.

The Liberator

The tone of the slavery debate changed in 1831. In January of that year, a Massachusetts printer named William Lloyd Garrison published the first issue of *The Liberator*. Garrison had worked on Lundy's paper but became dissatisfied with the gradualist approach.

Garrison's language was strong and uncompromising. He urged the immediate and complete end to slavery because he saw it as a moral wrong. Garrison spoke from his personal Christian convictions about slavery. The circulation of *The Liberator* was small, but its reputation became widespread. Garrison was severely criticized in the South. Pro-slavery writers wondered which was the real threat to American society: those who had a calm respect for the long-accepted institution of slavery, or those whom supporters of slavery saw as incendiary troublemakers like Garrison.

The Case of the *Amistad*

In 1839 about fifty members of the Mende people in West Africa were captured and sent as slaves to Cuba. They were put on the Spanish vessel Amistad *to be taken to their final destination. The slaves took control of the ship, killed two crewmen, and ordered the remaining crew to take the ship to Africa. The* Amistad *was then seized by a U.S. warship and the slaves held as pirates.*

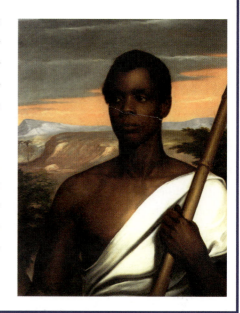

President Martin Van Buren wanted the slaves surrendered to Cuba, but in 1841 the U.S. Supreme Court ruled that the men were free on the basis of international law that prohibited the slave trade. Donations from abolitionists and other sympathizers paid for the men's legal fees and their return passage to Africa. The painting at right depicts Sengbe Pieh (also known as Joseph Cinqué), a leader of the enslaved Mende. American artist Nathaniel Jocelyn painted it in 1840.

Nat Turner

Another event that occurred later in 1831 also heightened the tension over slavery. Whites in the South had lived in fear of a slave revolt for many years. This was especially true in areas where slaves outnumbered whites. Gabriel, a slave in Richmond, Virginia, planned an uprising in 1800; but his plans were discovered. As a result, twenty-five slaves were executed and ten were deported. In 1822 Denmark Vesey, a free black in Charleston, South Carolina, plotted to free slaves and kill whites; but he and some of his co-conspirators were discovered and hanged while others were deported.

In August of 1831, a Virginia slave named Nat Turner claimed to have a religious experience in which he was called to kill whites. He gathered a small group of followers that went out one night killing whites, first on Turner's home plantation and then at nearby plantations. A total of fifty-five whites were murdered by Turner and his band. Then an unknown number of blacks was lynched by whites in reprisal. Turner and others were executed for their actions. Many in the South blamed Garrison for inciting Turner's actions, but no evidence exists that suggests Turner ever read or heard about Garrison

William Lloyd Garrison
Nathaniel Jocelyn (American, 1833)

and his ideas. In addition, Garrison was a pacifist at the time and opposed the use of violence.

The South reacted strongly to the Nat Turner rebellion. In Tennessee, for instance, the right of free black property owners to vote under the state's original 1796 constitution was taken away when the state rewrote its constitution in 1834. Southern writers, politicians, and some churches began defending slavery as a positive good. They said that slavery was mentioned and not condemned in the Bible, that it helped the southern economy, and that it provided a form of social security for black individuals and families.

Defenders of slavery claimed that blacks were not capable of performing any more demanding work, that slavery freed masters and others to pursue higher goals, and that it was better than what they called the wage slavery in northern factories. These defenders of slavery also raised fears of interracial marriage and race wars if any steps were taken to end slavery. Many in the North knew that Turner's actions were not the answer to slavery, but they searched desperately for a workable solution to what was termed the "peculiar institution."

The Discovery of Nat Turner

The Tension Builds

Both sides of the slavery debate began to be more active. In 1832 Garrison helped form the New England Anti-Slavery Society. The next year, brothers Arthur and Lewis Tappan of New York formed first a state and then a national anti-slavery society. They pressed for an immediate end to slavery and full civil equality between blacks and whites. In 1834 Theodore Weld led an extended discussion of slavery at Lane Seminary in Cincinnati, Ohio, a city that was a refuge for many slaves who escaped from the South. Seminary president Lyman Beecher tried to suppress the discussion. Beecher's daughter, Harriet, was married to faculty professor Calvin Ellis Stowe. The Stowes moved to Bowdoin College in Maine in 1850, but strong impressions about slavery had been made on Harriet. Weld became an evangelist against slavery. He published several books on it in the late 1830s and trained men to go out two by two to speak against slavery.

Proslavery forces increased their activities also. In 1835 a mob destroyed an abolitionist mass mailing that was awaiting delivery in the Charleston, South Carolina, post office. President Jackson wanted Congress to pass a law against the distribution of what he called incendiary literature through the mails. Congress did not pass such a law, but the Postmaster General did not require the delivery of abolitionist material by postal workers. Southern newspapers posted rewards for Garrison and the Tappan brothers.

Some in the North also reacted negatively to the abolitionists. Manhattan saw three days of riots in 1834 in which the homes and churches of abolitionists were destroyed. A mob once led Garrison through the streets of Boston with a noose around his neck. He was rescued by police who put him in jail. In 1837 a mob killed antislavery editor Elijah Lovejoy in Alton, Illinois. This made Lovejoy a martyr for abolition and for freedom of the press.

Opponents of abolitionism were motivated by several factors. Some said they wanted to keep blacks in their place. They feared what would happen if the different races lived together in the same society. Others had sympathy for the South and wanted to take a stand for southern interests. Still others saw the abolitionists as inflammatory and dangerous and wanted to silence them.

A few blacks had an impact on American thinking about slavery. Frederick Douglass was an escaped slave who became an eloquent speaker and writer for abolition. He was probably the most influential black person in America at the time. Sojourner Truth felt led by God to carry the

Abolition efforts in other countries also had an impact on thinking in the U.S. Great Britain outlawed slavery throughout its empire in 1833, thanks largely to the untiring efforts of William Wilberforce, who was motivated by his deep faith in Christ. France abolished slavery in 1848. These changes encouraged American abolitionists and increased the pressure on defenders of slavery. The statue of Wilberforce at left stands outside his birthplace in Hull, England. The house is now a museum that tells the story of the slave trade and its abolition.

antislavery message to the American people. She was a tremendously effective public speaker. Harriet Tubman conducted many people to freedom on the Underground Railroad, a loose network of homes and other hiding places that thousands of slaves used to gain freedom in the North and in Canada.

The abolitionist movement suffered division in 1840. Garrison wanted a total reformation of society and embraced several reform ideas, including greater rights for women. He wanted women to be able to participate fully in conventions and meetings. Other abolitionists preferred to concentrate on the slavery issue and feared that involving themselves in other controversial topics would weaken their chances of gaining a hearing from the American public on the main issue of slavery. They did not want to submit to a "petticoat government" of women, as one man put it. The Garrison faction carried the day and women were fully involved in his organization, but they did not advocate any changes in women's

Frederick Douglass, *Unknown Artist (c. 1844)*

rights. The anti-Garrison faction broke away from his organization.

Some Christian denominations divided north and south over the slavery issue. In 1844 the Methodist Episcopal Church, South separated from the national Methodist organization. The next year, the Southern Baptist Convention was formed as Baptists from the South objected to calls for abolition by northern Baptists.

The Impact of Abolitionism

Many abolitionists hated gradualism, but their effect on American thinking was just that: gradual. It took many years and many different events to bring about the shift in American public opinion that moved abolitionism from the fringes to the mainstream. The constant pressure that abolitionists exerted at the risk of their own safety eventually had an impact, even if it was not in the way that anti-slavery forces wanted.

One big source of frustration for abolitionists was the political system. They were not able to affect

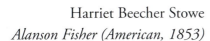

Harriet Beecher Stowe
Alanson Fisher (American, 1853)

Unit 10 - Challenges and Changes

Harriet Tubman, born into slavery in Maryland in 1820, is shown above in 1911. In addition to working with the Underground Railroad, she worked for the Union Army during the Civil War as a cook, nurse, scout, and spy. She continued to work for the good of others until her death in 1913.

politics the way they wanted to. Garrison gave up on the political system. He called the Constitution "a covenant with death and an agreement with hell" for its acceptance of slavery. He once burned a copy of the Constitution at a Fourth of July abolitionist rally. To Garrison it was wrong even to vote because doing so made one a participant in what he saw as an evil system.

Abolitionists were fervent and impatient in their beliefs. In 1855 events of the previous few years led abolitionist Gerrit Smith to say, "The movement to abolish American slavery is a failure." Little did he know that a few years later, slavery would be abolished in the United States, but at a tremendous price.

*There is neither Jew nor Greek,
there is neither slave nor free man,
there is neither male nor female;
for you are all one in Christ Jesus.
Galatians 3:28*

★ Assignments for Lesson 47 ★

American Voices — Read "To the Public" (from the first issue of *The Liberator*) by William Lloyd Garrison (pages 131-132).

Read "Bury Me in a Free Land" by Frances E. W. Harper (page 183).

Literature — Continue reading *Uncle Tom's Cabin*.

Bible — Read Luke 16:19-31. List three ways to avoid being blinded by material success and popularity so that you can see God's definition of success.

Work on memorizing Philippians 4:8.

Project — Work on your project.

Student Review — Optional: Answer the questions for Lesson 47.

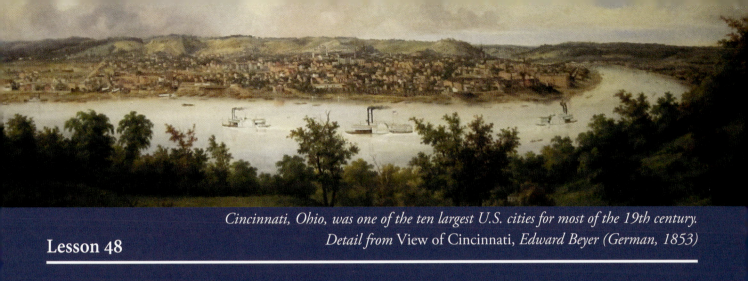

Cincinnati, Ohio, was one of the ten largest U.S. cities for most of the 19th century. Detail from View of Cincinnati, *Edward Beyer (German, 1853)*

Lesson 48

The Growth of Cities and Industry

The second quarter of the 1800s saw tremendous expansion and change in America. In the fifty years from 1780 to 1830, America won a war for independence against Great Britain, produced the Constitution and the Bill of Rights, concluded the Louisiana Purchase, fought another war with Great Britain, announced the Monroe Doctrine, and witnessed the expansion of democracy as evidenced by the election of Andrew Jackson. Manufacturing, technology, agriculture, and transportation underwent huge changes during this period. The U.S. population almost quadrupled, and the nation that started as thirteen colonies along the Atlantic coast grew to twenty-four states, two of them west of the Mississippi River.

Twenty years later, in 1850, the nation had won yet another war and had spread to the Pacific coast. Eleven years after that, however, the nation was at war with itself. The growth that the nation experienced during the second quarter of the nineteenth century did not solve its problems. Instead, it forced the country to face some crucial, long-standing issues.

Florida entered the Union as the 27th state on March 3, 1845; Texas was admitted as the 28th state the following December. Both were slave states. The next two states admitted were Iowa (29th, 1846) and Wisconsin (30th, 1848), both free states. This gave the Union fifteen free states and fifteen slave states.

From East to West, From Country to City

The trend in America was from the individual to the group, from the farm to the city, and from the home to the factory. One change in living patterns involved more people moving west. Laws passed by Congress in 1820 lowered both the minimum amount of Federal land that a settler had to purchase as well as the price per acre of land. This encouraged more people to move west. The Ohio Valley and the Great Lakes region saw a dramatic increase in population during this period.

America also became a more urban country. In 1820 only one in fourteen Americans lived in towns with a population of 2,500 or more. By 1850 one of every six Americans lived in communities of 2,500 or more. During this thirty-year period, while the national population doubled, the urban population increased five times. The four largest cities in 1860 were New York (with over one million people), Philadelphia, Boston, and Baltimore. (By comparison, today over eighty percent of Americans live in metropolitan areas that have 600,000 or more people. These areas include many small towns and suburbs that surround large cities.)

263

From the Farm to the Factory

The U.S. also started changing from a farm-based to a manufacturing-based economy in the early 1800s. However, some of the first major advances in manufacturing were machines that helped farmers: the iron plow, the harvester, and the cotton gin.

The steel-tipped plow invented by John Deere was an improvement over wooden models. Iron could break soil more easily, especially the tough prairie sod west of the Mississippi. Cyrus McCormick patented his reaping machine or harvester in 1841 and sold thousands of them that were produced in his plant in Chicago. Before the reaper was invented, a farmer could harvest about a half-acre per day with a hand scythe. The McCormick reaper enabled two men to harvest about twelve acres per day.

Cotton

In 1793 Yale graduate Eli Whitney was on his way to a teaching position when he stopped to see a friend whose family owned a plantation in Georgia. Whitney heard the family lament the difficulty of separating seeds from the fibers in the cotton boll. He tinkered with an idea until he developed the cotton gin (short for engine). The gin utilized two sets of teeth, one rotated through the other, which separated the seeds from the fibers. Whitney's invention revolutionized cotton production and breathed new life into southern agriculture. With the gin, a plantation worker could process fifty times as much cotton as he or she previously could by hand. Whitney, by the way, never went to his teaching job.

Cotton production increased and spread into the new southern states of Alabama, Mississippi, Louisiana, and Texas. Once the Napoleonic Wars were over in Europe after 1815, the demand for cotton in Europe skyrocketed. The crop provided over half of all American exports in the second quarter of the nineteenth century. The South also supplied raw material for northern textile mills and in turn became a market for the products of northern industry. This increase in cotton production also helped spread and make permanent the southern way of life: plantation-based, controlled by large plantation owners, dependent on and defensive of slavery, with a large gap between wealthy and poor.

Eli Whitney's patent application for the cotton gin is shown below. Whitney also obtained a contract to produce rifles for the U.S. Army. At the time, every rifle was manufactured individually. Whitney developed a way to make rifles with interchangeable parts. A factory produced triggers, stocks, barrels, and other parts that could be made into finished guns on an assembly line. Whitney's invention revolutionized not only gun production but also the entire manufacturing economy.

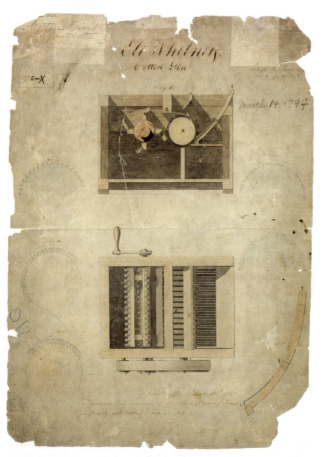

Steam engines also spurred manufacturing growth. The first successful steam engine was invented in 1705. James Watt improved it in 1765. The steamship made transatlantic travel more common. Clipper ships with their tall masts and many sails had their heyday from 1845 until the Civil War; but they did not have much cargo space and were not as popular or useful as steamships. Steamboats revolutionized travel and trade on U.S. rivers, too. This image shows St. Louis along the Mississippi River about 1859.

The American Industrial Revolution

The production of goods in the United States had from colonial times been based in the home, where a man or family, perhaps with one or two hired men, made individual pieces to order. This method of manufacturing changed in the early 1800s.

Mills were built beside rivers to utilize water power. England had developed this means of production some years before. The laws of England forbade anyone from taking plans for mills out of the country. In 1789 Samuel Slater left England with the plans for a water-powered textile machine in his head. The next year, he helped build a mill in Pawtucket, Rhode Island, that produced cotton yarn. By 1815 hundreds of textile (cloth) mills could be found throughout New England. The rivers that powered these mills were near the coast, so their location helped get products to market. The development of textile mills spurred both the garment industry and the production of heavy machinery for the mills.

Lowell, Massachusetts, was at the heart of this major change in the textile industry and in American manufacturing. A spinning and weaving plant was built there in 1822. An important development in manufacturing at this time was the specialization of the workers. Instead of each employee performing all the steps in the process of making an item, different workers did the same repetitive work all day, each as part of the production process.

Factory owners believed that they were helping society by creating a way for people to earn money more reliably than on farms or in small shops. Factory owners carefully oversaw female workers who lived in dormitories after they had left family farms to seek higher living standards. The women in Lowell were provided educational and cultural opportunities, were required to attend church, and had to observe evening curfews and temperance in the use of alcohol. They worked thirteen-hour days and six-day weeks. By 1840 22 mills and factories were in operation in Lowell. This increased dependence on female laborers took place as many men in the East were heading for new lands in the West. Despite the careful oversight provided for female workers in Lowell, the change in living and working arrangements began to pull women away from their homes; and the practice of careful oversight did not continue as factories increased rapidly in many parts of the country.

Lowell, Massachusetts (c. 1850)

Unit 10 - Challenges and Changes

immigrant families, including the children, worked for the same company and developed a pattern of dependency on whatever wages the company owners provided.

In 1844 Charles Goodyear developed a process called vulcanization that improved rubber. That same year, Samuel Morse unveiled his perfected telegraph. Other changes during this period were improvements in canning and refrigeration, stoves, and home construction. Cities began to offer gas lighting and sewer systems and indoor plumbing.

Organizing Labor

Not all factories were as idyllic as the ones in Lowell claimed to be. Industrialists usually had their eyes on the bottom line. They often tried to increase their profits by paying workers as little as possible and by providing facilities that were as primitive as possible. Issues of worker safety were not usually addressed.

In the 1820s and 1830s, skilled craftsmen in eastern cities formed the first unions in America. They used their influence for political power and to push for social reforms such as free public schooling. In the 1840s, unions began to pressure employers to improve work conditions. The ten-hour work day (six days a week) became more common in this decade, though laws were usually written to give employers enough exemptions that the ten-hour limit could easily be evaded. The first national labor organization was the National Typographical Union, formed in 1852.

Railroads

Just as the needs of agriculture prompted the first developments in industry, agriculture also served as an impetus in the development of the American transportation system, since farmers over a wide area wanted better ways to get their crops

In 1846 Elias Howe invented the sewing machine, which Isaac Singer soon improved. The Singer Sewing Machine Company was one of the earliest multinational corporations based in the United States. This 1892 Singer advertisement shows its machines in use around the world. The machine was a boon to women sewing for their families, but ironically it also gave new life to the piece-making (or putting out) industry, which involved women making garments at home for stores to sell.

The period from 1820 to 1840 saw an eight-fold increase in manufacturing, while the urban population only doubled. The manufacturing age permanently changed the fabric of American society. To many Americans, factories were becoming what Charles Dickens had described in England: a source for profits by greedy owners and a source of fear by workers that economic downturns would cost them their jobs.

Working at home began to be replaced by working away from home. Sometimes entire

Lesson 48 - The Growth of Cities and Industry

to market. For centuries, rivers have played a key role in transportation and settlement. However, as America moved west, other forms of transportation were needed since no river connected the East with the region west of the Appalachian Mountains.

The first commercial railway went into operation in England in 1825. The idea quickly caught on in both Great Britain and the United States; and by 1840, the United States had 3,300 miles of railroads in use. In 1860 the U.S. counted over 30,600 miles of track, two-thirds of which were built in the 1850s.

The first trains went only ten miles per hour and were dirty and dangerous, but they had many benefits. Trains could go directly overland to more destinations than boats could reach on water routes. Railroads not only helped agriculture and manufacturing concerns, but they also spawned growth in related industries such as iron making and track construction.

Because of the expense involved in laying track, railroad companies often asked state governments to help with the cost of the railroads. Governments at various times helped the railroad industry by owning rail lines, performing land surveys, selling stock in rail companies, giving land grants to companies, lowering tariffs on iron, and making loans to companies. The huge amounts of money involved in building railroads often led to corruption in the construction process. Rail companies often gave bribes or kickbacks to legislators who promoted their interests. Rail lines charged governments enormous amounts for work that did not cost as much as was charged. Railroad executives sometimes lined their own pockets with government money that had been earmarked for paying company expenses.

Dan Rice (1823-1900) was one of the most famous entertainers of the 19th century. He dressed in outlandish costumes to sing, dance, perform tricks with animals, and offer political commentary.

Community Building in the City

During the colonial and early national periods, most Americans spent the large majority of their time merely surviving. Farming, shop work, and housekeeping, all without modern conveniences, left little free time except for seasonal breaks and Sabbath observances.

With the advent of city life, factory work, and improved farming techniques, people had more leisure time; and they looked for ways to fill it. Almost every community had a lecture hall, where speakers and specialists drew large crowds. Circuses and horse racing were common, as were cockfighting, drinking, and gambling. Boxing matches became popular, often staged between immigrants eager to gain quick money and fame. Boxing had few rules in this period, and matches often lasted as long as the participants did.

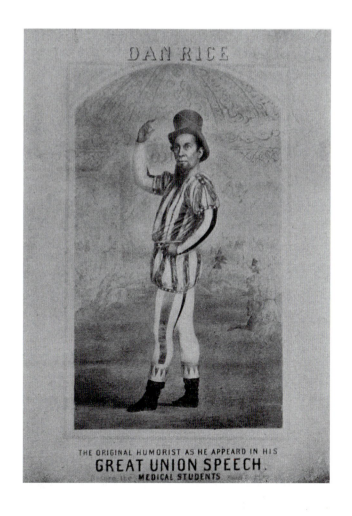

Daniel Emmett wrote the song "Dixie" for a minstrel show. Years later, the song became a kind of national anthem for the Confederacy. Ironically, Emmett was from Ohio and did not like the way his song was used by the South.

Many cities offered theaters where citizens could witness performances of Shakespearean plays, melodramas, and minstrel shows. Minstrel shows were productions by white performers in blackface pretending to be black entertainers. The shows portrayed blacks in a stereotypical way. Perhaps the person most widely associated with minstrel shows was the composer Stephen Foster, who wrote many songs for the shows such as "Old Man River," "My Old Kentucky Home," and "Camptown Races." Theater audiences were mostly men and were often far from quiet and respectful during performances.

*Whatever you do, do your work heartily,
as for the Lord rather than for men,
Colossians 3:23*

★ Assignments for Lesson 48 ★

Literature   Continue reading *Uncle Tom's Cabin*.

Bible   Read John 19:1-11. List three ways in which Jesus is a good example of success in God's eyes as opposed to success in the world's eyes.

Work on memorizing Philippians 4:8.

Project   Work on your project.

Student Review   Optional: Answer the questions for Lesson 48.

Castle Clinton National Monument (Formerly Castle Garden), Manhattan

Lesson 49

Immigration and Other Changes

One change that dramatically affected American cities was the huge influx of immigrants who came to America during this period. Europeans saw America as the land of opportunity just as earlier generations had. The impact of European immigration during this period was enormous. By 1860 the U.S. population stood at approximately 31 million people. Of that number, one person in eight was foreign born.

Most immigrants landed in New York or Boston and had to fend for themselves immediately upon arriving. Many did not know English and became victims of criminals and con men. The Castle Garden immigration processing facility was opened in lower Manhattan in 1855. The new arrivals were given a quick health check and received assistance from labor officials.

The immigrants found themselves in a cultural mix. They felt most comfortable with the language and ways they had known, so many lived together in neighborhoods dominated by one nationality. Native language newspapers were begun to provide necessary information, create a sense of community, and provide a link to the old country. The common term for the part of a city where people of one nationality live is the Italian word for the district in Rome where Jews were required to live: ghetto.

Irish

About 1.6 million Irish came to America in the first half of the 1800s. They left Ireland partly from resentment toward British rule but more as a result of the economic hardships they faced. A series of disastrous potato famines led to about one million deaths in Ireland and a desire by many others to escape their homeland. The British government, meanwhile, did little or nothing to help Ireland during the famines.

Most of the Irish who came to America had no desire to return to farming. Instead, they stayed in the cities and looked for other kinds of work. Many got into construction work, while some were hired by the city government, sometimes as a favor in hopes that they would vote for the ruling party's candidates. Immigrants were often easy prey for political bosses who gave them favors in exchange for their votes. Large numbers of Irish lived in poor, dirty slums that surrounded a local Catholic parish church. The Church was the main connection they had with their homeland.

Some Irish went into factory work. By 1860 half of the workers in the Lowell, Massachusetts, textile factories were Irish. For several reasons, few Irish moved to the South. The South was far from where

269

Boston was one main port of entry for the Irish. Even today the Irish culture is strong in Boston. The Irish are a Celtic people, which is the reason why the NBA team in Boston is called the Celtics. The team's symbol is a shamrock. The city's St. Patrick's Day parade is one of the oldest and biggest in the world.

they entered the United States, the immigrants had little interest in farming, and they found it hard to compete with slave labor. Despite widespread poverty among the Irish, some became financially successful in the United States. The stereotype of the Irish New York policeman comes from the reality of many Irish being hired as policemen in the hope that they and their families would vote for the politicians who got them their jobs.

At the time that many Irish were becoming citizens, states were lowering or dropping property ownership requirements for voting. Many Irish became voters in the 1820s and 1830s. They identified strongly with the Scots-Irish Andrew Jackson because of his appeal to the common man and because he shared their hatred of the British. The large Irish turnout helped give Jackson his victory in 1828.

Germans, Scandinavians, and Chinese

Some 1.2 million Germans came to America during this period. German immigrants who came in colonial times were mostly religious pietists who maintained their farm-based lives (the Pennsylvania "Dutch," for instance, were actually "Deutsch" from Germany). Many in the early nineteenth-century wave, however, were well-educated teachers and professionals. A good many arrived with enough money to buy land and build factories. Ferdinand Schmacher, for instance, started out selling oatmeal in jars and eventually created the Quaker Oats Company. Levi Strauss was a tailor who followed the gold rush to the West and designed rugged pants made of blue denim that were later called blue jeans or Levis.

A fair number of people from the Scandinavian countries also came to the U.S. Many of these settled in the Midwest and took up the farming life they had known back home. Some left the fishing work of the old country to become farmers. Another group that came in significant numbers were the Chinese, who were drawn to the American west coast in the 1850s as mining and railroad work boomed there. They often took hard, low-paying construction jobs and sent some of the money back to their families in China.

Nativist Reaction

Even though white Americans were themselves descended from immigrants, a strong feeling of prejudice arose against the new immigrants. Part of the prejudice was religious. Almost all of the Irish

Chinese Miners in California, 1857

Lesson 49 - Immigration and Other Changes

In the early 1840s, Catholic leaders raised an objection to public school teachers leading students in Protestant hymns and reading from the King James Bible. Anti-immigrant and anti-Catholic groups used this to gain support of their views. Violence erupted in Philadelphia in 1844. St. Augustine Catholic Church was destroyed (as shown above), and several people were killed.

and many of the German newcomers were Roman Catholic, and many Protestant Americans did not like the presence of so many followers of the pope. Americans also feared that the immigrants would be willing to work for lower wages and thus take jobs away from native-born citizens. Another factor was that the immigrants were simply different, with different languages and customs. To many people, what is different is automatically suspicious.

Immigrants were mistreated in many ways. Many businesses posted signs in their windows that read "No Irish Need Apply." Newcomers were subjected to mob attacks, which were sometimes spurred by anti-Catholic speeches or sermons. The American Party was formed in 1854, and its members vowed never to vote for a foreign-born or Catholic candidate. Party members wanted to keep information about their organization secret, so when anyone asked them about it they said, "I know nothing." Because of this, the party became known as the Know-Nothing Party. In 1854 American Party candidates won some state and local offices, carried the Massachusetts legislature, and elected forty Congressmen. However, the anti-immigrant cause became insignificant compared to the national debate over slavery.

Changes in Education

In the early years of the republic, local communities funded schools; but state support was rare. Nevertheless, most American children received some form of education. Children learned to read in the family setting, at church, by tutors, or in local public or private schools. The 1840 census revealed that 91% of whites could read. This was the highest literacy rate the world had seen since the American Revolution.

During this era, Americans of all ages wanted to learn. Societies and institutes were established that offered lectures, special interest classes, and evening classes for working people. The relative lack of support for public education did not mean that people were not interested in learning. It simply meant that most people did not assume that education was a function of the state or Federal government.

The push for state-financed education came from a belief that formal schooling provided a better chance for people economically and would improve the nation by reducing ignorance and crime. In 1837 the Massachusetts State Board of Education appointed Horace Mann as its first secretary of education. Mann actively encouraged such reforms as formal teacher training and a minimum school year length (he proposed six months for the lower

The first state-supported school for training teachers opened in 1839 in Massachusetts. May Hall, shown below, was built in 1889. The institution is now known as Framingham State University.

grades). Mann called public education the great equalizer of men, something the state could do to give children from all families a chance to succeed.

Public schools commonly went through the eighth grade. In 1860 the entire nation only had about 300 high schools. Teachers were generally men who taught as a part-time or temporary job. Through the reforms that took place in the nineteenth century, teachers became better trained and came to be seen as professionals in their field. Eventually women were allowed to become teachers.

The South had fewer public school students than the North, but it had more college students. This was because public grade school education was not a high priority in the South, but wealthy Southerners often sent their children to college. In 1850 half of the nation's white illiterates lived in the South, even though the South had less than half of the nation's population.

Social Reform

Americans saw vast possibilities for their country. To them, America was fulfilling John Winthrop's vision of a city on a hill. They were convinced that their country offered the best hope for humanity of any nation on earth.

Many of these optimistic thinkers wanted to bring about reforms that they felt were long overdue and that would take the United States further along the road toward social and moral perfection. These

"Tree of Temperance" (c. 1855)

"The Fruits of Temperance" (1848)

causes were often promoted by women who now had the time to devote to interests outside of the home. Popular causes included Sabbath-keeping, the outlawing of duels, reform of prisons and institutions for the mentally ill, and the abolition of slavery. Many worked in these causes as a result of their Christian faith. Also during this time, some women and a few men started pressing for more equal rights for women.

The temperance movement took great strides during this period. The consumption of alcoholic beverages in the nation was astounding. One estimate made in 1810 was that Americans drank an average of three gallons of hard liquor per year for every man, woman, and child, not counting beer, wine, and cider. Since women and children were less likely to drink, the actual consumption by men was even higher.

Opponents of alcohol noted the need for Christian people to lead blameless lives. They pointed out the danger of inebriated factory workers and the anguish suffered by families of alcoholics. The

American Society for the Promotion of Temperance was formed in 1826 by a group of Boston ministers. This group helped in the creation of the American Temperance Union in Philadelphia in 1833.

The word temperance technically means moderation of use, but some reformers advocated complete abstinence from alcohol. One temperance group encouraged abstainers to put a T beside their signature to indicate "Total Abstinence." This led to such people being called "teetotalers." The efforts of these groups did help bring about an overall reduction in alcohol consumption in the country.

The United States enjoyed cheap and plentiful land, an abundance of raw materials, and a good climate. The people had little fear of a foreign attack. It was a positive and optimistic time for many living in America (though by no means all; slaves and Native Americans, for example, were major exceptions). The nation was still predominantly agricultural and rural, but significant changes in American life had begun.

> *And they sang the song of Moses, the bond-servant of God, and the song of the Lamb, saying, "Great and marvelous are Your works, O Lord God, the Almighty; Righteous and true are Your ways, King of the nations!"*
> *Revelation 15:3*

★ Assignments for Lesson 49 ★

American Voices — Read the Seneca Falls Declaration (pages 143-145).

Literature — Continue reading *Uncle Tom's Cabin*.

Bible — Read Mark 8:27-37. List three common temptations to sin that a person faces as he or she becomes economically successful. List three ways that immigrants might define success.

Work on memorizing Philippians 4:8.

Project — Work on your project.

Student Review — Optional: Answer the questions for Lesson 49.

View of Pottsville *(Pennsylvania), John Rowson Smith (British, c. 1833)*

Lesson 50 - Bible Study

God Defines Success

The young United States achieved many significant successes: two victorious wars against Great Britain, the acquisition of large new territories, and striking economic growth. Since the late nineteenth century, the U.S. has been a major player in world affairs. Today, political success is often defined as winning elections and maintaining power in government. Politicians like to be popular, so they watch the opinion polls closely and sway with the winds of change in order to achieve political success. Spin doctors present information in the most positive way they can in order to please the most people and to declare their party's policies as successful.

God, on the other hand, is not interested in opinion polls, popularity contests, or human victories. God cares about faithfulness. A life of faithfulness is successful in the eyes of God, regardless of how that person is viewed by other people; whereas a life that is unfaithful to Him, regardless of how much fame, wealth, and power the person has, is unsuccessful.

We know that God defines success this way because of how Scripture portrays kingdoms and rulers in the ancient world. For instance, when Moses lived in Egypt, the pyramids were already standing and Egypt was the dominant world power. However, to the Israelites Egypt was the evil, pagan place of bondage. In God's eyes, the mighty ancient kingdom of Egypt was a failure. Scripture does not even mention the pyramids.

King Saul, *Lidia Kozenitzky (Jewish, 2009)*

274

Lesson 50 - Bible Study: God Defines Success

Later, during the unsettled period of the Judges, Saul looked the part of a king. He was "a choice and handsome man, and there was not a more handsome person than he among the sons of Israel; from his shoulders and up he was taller than any of the people" (1 Samuel 9:2). Saul, however, was a failure as king because he was unfaithful to God's commands (1 Samuel 15:1-26). It is interesting to note that the average height of American Presidents is taller than the height of the average American. People are easily impressed with appearances, but we know from experience that Presidents can be moral failures.

In the Old Testament books of Kings and Chronicles, the factor that determined whether a king of Israel or Judah was a success or a failure was how faithful he was to God. If a king was unfaithful to God, he is presented as a disappointment, regardless of how long he reigned or what great military victories he won. Baasha reigned 24 years as king of Israel (1 Kings 15:33), but he receives only three paragraphs in the inspired narrative because he did evil in the eyes of the Lord. Ahab reigned 22 years in Israel (1 Kings 16:29), but the account of his rule emphasizes his spiritual failures. On the other hand, Josiah took the throne of Judah when he was eight years old, and he only lived to be thirty-nine (2 Kings 22:1); but this boy-king rates almost two entire chapters in the text because he reformed the temple worship and was faithful to God.

The emphasis that the Bible places on Israel might lead us to think that it was a major player in ancient Near Eastern affairs. However, Israel received scant mention in the records of other ancient nations. To other nations, Israel was not important in the political and military maneuverings of the ancient world; but to God, Israel as His chosen people was the key to what He was doing in the world.

Roman Ruins in France

Christ and the Rich Young Ruler, *Heinrich Hofmann (German, 1889)*

History books emphasize the glory that was Rome. The might and extent of the Roman Empire are well-known. In the Book of Revelation, however, Rome is portrayed as the disgusting harlot, the great Babylon that was going to fall at the hands of God because of her enmity against God's people (Revelation 17:9, 18; 18:2-8). Rome was militarily powerful but spiritually void. In God's eyes, Rome was a failure.

The rich young ruler was by all typical assessments a successful person. He was young and wealthy, a leader among his people, and a strict adherent to the Law. Jesus challenged him to change his definition of success to God's definition, and the young man went away sorrowful. The disciples were amazed, and they wondered aloud who can be saved if this successful man could not. Jesus told them that man's accomplishments are ultimately meaningless, but that with God all things are possible (Mark 10:17-27). In other words, God grants success; and His success is defined in spiritual terms.

Success and Failure Today

Accepting God's perspective in the world in which one lives is hard. The Northern Kingdom of Israel, for instance, turned a deaf ear to the criticisms of the prophet Amos because Israel was enjoying great economic success. Those who should have listened to Amos were deafened to God's word by their prosperity. Perhaps that situation should cause us to reflect on our own day.

When historians look back at certain periods in history and at major historical events and

Lesson 50 - Bible Study: God Defines Success

individuals, they usually follow human standards to determine success and failure. The decade of the 1930s in America, for instance, is usually seen as disastrous because of the Great Depression. In God's eyes, however, the period might be a success because many Americans grew in spiritual resilience.

In addition, human success is often short-lived. Andrew Jackson led the Democratic Party to a position of great power, but his Democratic successor was defeated in his bid for re-election. Many people who had become wealthy during the prosperity of the 1820s and 1830s were severely hurt in the Panic of 1837. People who made headlines during their own day are now forgotten in the mists of history.

When the standard one uses to measure success is righteousness instead of popularity, power, or material prosperity, one's evaluation of people and events changes drastically. As we study the continuing rise of the United States in terms of material wealth and world power, let us remember to look for the things that God recognizes as indicative of true success. Looking at history through the eyes of faith requires us to see things from God's point of view (2 Corinthians 5:16).

American Fashions, Fall and Winter, 1849-50, from John R. Shankland of Philadelphia

*But the Lord said to Samuel, "Do not look at his appearance
or at the height of his stature, because I have rejected him;
for God sees not as man sees, for man looks at the outward appearance,
but the Lord looks at the heart."*
1 Samuel 16:7

★ Assignments for Lesson 50 ★

American Voices — Read "The Great Stone Face" by Nathaniel Hawthorne (pages 159-170). This short story contrasts the typical American view of success with a deeper and more spiritual definition of success.

Literature — Continue reading *Uncle Tom's Cabin*.

Bible — After reading "The Great Stone Face," list three ways in which you can "fix your eyes on Jesus" (Hebrews 12:2) and so become like Him (2 Corinthians 3:18).

Recite or write Philippians 4:8 from memory.

Project — Complete your project for the unit.

Student Review — Optional: Answer the questions for Lesson 50, take the quiz for Unit 10, and take the second history exam, English exam, and Bible exam.

Harpers Ferry, West Virginia

11 A Time of Crisis

The intense national debate over slavery reached its peak in the 1850s. The stances that people in different sections of the country took regarding slavery increased the growing divisions in the Union. The Compromise of 1850 was an attempt to deal with some aspects of slavery, but it did not solve the central question. Violence erupted over slavery in Kansas and in John Brown's raid on the military arsenal at Harpers Ferry. In the Bible study for this unit, we see what the New Testament says about how Christians should handle differences among believers.

Lesson 51 - Sectionalism
Lesson 52 - Trouble in the Territories
Lesson 53 - Twilight of the Giants
Lesson 54 - Stumbling Toward War
Lesson 55 - Bible Study: Differences

Memory Work Memorize Psalm 133 by the end of this unit.

Books Used The Bible
American Voices
Uncle Tom's Cabin

Project (choose one)

1) Write 300 to 500 words on one of the following topics:

- Would you have been an abolitionist, a defender of slavery, a compromiser, or would you have held some other position during the 1850s? Would you have been part of a church that endorsed slavery, opposed slavery, or said nothing about slavery? Write an essay on what you think would have been your position. Be honest with yourself.

- Write a letter to someone explaining the way people do things where you live (either in your family or in your community, or both) and how those ways are different from the way others do those things. This can become a humorous piece, but do not be cruel or mean in what you say.

2) Make an audio recording or video of yourself singing or playing at least five spirituals sung by African American slaves during the 1800s.

3) Make an illustrated poster contrasting different, but equally acceptable, ways of living and doing things (such as types of houses, church practices, food, clothing, etc.). Your poster should include at least ten examples. Use the medium of your choice (e.g., collage, photography, drawing, painting, or pastels).

Drayton Hall and Plantation, South Carolina

Lesson 51

Sectionalism

In the United States today, several factors bring our country together. The national media inform the entire country almost immediately about events happening around the nation. As radio and television reporters do this, they use basically the same accent and speech patterns. Just about wherever you go in America, you will likely find the same restaurants and stores. We still have regional speech patterns, and different parts of the country do have their distinctive attributes; but our interconnectedness as a country is much stronger than in the past.

By contrast, a significant aspect of American society before the Civil War was the reality of sectionalism. Even though the United States was one country, the different sections of the country had different social and economic patterns and different ways of looking at life in the U.S. These differences were a major factor in the country growing apart, especially over the issue of slavery.

America was diverse from its very beginning. The New England colonies, for instance, developed a different way of life from that known in the southern colonies. When settlers moved across the Appalachians, the West developed a different way of life from that in the East. As the country expanded to fill the continent, the people, lifestyles, and interests that made up the United States became ever more diverse.

My Way Is Best

Just as people can be ethnocentric about their own country in relation to other countries, Americans can be ethnocentric about their particular region of the country. Different habits and ways of life have developed in different parts of the country. People who live in each area tend to think that their own way of doing things is best and that any other way is strange and not quite as good.

These sectional differences can extend beyond mere manners and habits. People from different regions can become defensive about their own economic interests and way of life if they feel threatened by any proposed changes or by national laws that affect them adversely. It is this defensive sectionalism that developed in the United States and that eventually contributed to the breakup of the Union. The different sections of the country had long held conflicting views, but they were always advocated within the context of the Union. When loyalty to the Union was lost, the differences among the sections proved fatal for the nation.

The negative side of sectionalism appeared several times in American history before the Civil War. The compromises that were part of the formation of the Constitution involved balancing the interests of southern slave states and northern free states. Some New Englanders opposed the War of 1812 and talked of seceding from the Union. Many in the same region were against the Mexican War and again made noises about forming their own confederacy. South Carolina threatened secession during the Nullification Crisis of the early 1830s. Conflicts developed over the preferred route for the first transcontinental railroad. Debates over tariffs and internal improvements often reflected the conflicting interests of the different parts of the nation.

Slaves in the Cotton Fields

Americans before the Civil War were alike in significant ways. A large majority of Americans in all sections of the country lived on farms or in small towns. The country had a general consensus regarding religious beliefs and devotion to the Union. In other important ways, however, differences were emerging among the regions that eventually led to bitter conflict.

The South

The slaveholding states of the South had the most distinct and clearly stratified social system in the country. People were expected to know their place and stay there. In addition, the existence of and defense of slavery made for a life that was clearly different from how Americans in other sections lived.

The majority of southerners were small farmers. In North Carolina, for example, over seventy percent of farmers owned one hundred acres or less. Across the South, slaveowning families accounted for only about one-fourth of the population. In 1860 fewer than 11,000 planters owned fifty or more slaves. However, the plantation owners were the social and economic rulers of society. They made up only four percent of the adult white male population, but they owned over half of all slaves as well as the land that produced most of the cotton and tobacco and almost all of the region's sugar and rice. In Alabama in 1850, slave owners made up thirty percent of the population but accounted for seventy percent of state legislators. Their personal interests influenced what these men saw as best for society.

The southern economy was driven by the plantation-owning interests. The South supplied most of the cotton for the rest of the world. Its biggest market was the British textile industry. Southern plantations also shipped cotton to the North for use in domestic textile mills. As slaves and land became more expensive, wealth was concentrated in even fewer hands.

Slaves Planting Sweet Potatoes in South Carolina (1862)

The planter class fostered the southern aura of magnificent hospitality and a strict code of honor. Men were especially defensive about the honor of their families and womenfolk, and duels were common over the slightest perceived insult. Plantation wives were kept busy managing household affairs and domestic servants.

The southern middle class consisted of plantation overseers, small farmers (many of whom worked alongside any slaves that they owned), and skilled workers and shopkeepers. They lived in small houses, often a two-room cabin on a small farm. Although a minority owned slaves, the majority of the white population supported the institution of slavery. This support might have come partially out of fear of economic competition and social unrest if the slaves were freed. Lower class whites ("poor whites") lived in crude houses in mountainous regions or on land too poor for successful farming. They eked out an existence from season to season and were disdained by the rest of white society.

Black society in the South, both slave and free, was separate from white society. One-third of the population of the South was slaves. In South Carolina, Georgia, and Mississippi, slaves outnumbered whites. In 1860 a half million free blacks lived in the U.S., about evenly divided between North and South. Some became skilled craftsmen, such as blacksmiths, carpenters, or (like Frederick Douglass) shipbuilders.

Southern agriculture was diverse enough to support the region's food requirements. Corn was commonplace, and southern farms produced well over half of the nation's livestock. The downside of the cotton-based southern economy, however, was that it was dependent on outside factors for its continued success. Its cotton was shipped on vessels owned by northerners to mills in the North or in England. The South had few manufacturers, which made it dependent on outside industry. If the cotton markets slumped, the South got into economic trouble. The key word for the South was dependent.

The North, Midwest, and West

A key word to describe the North at the same time was diverse. Most northerners were still small farmers, but an increasing number were city dwellers. Many people worked in factories at low wages and were sometimes called wage slaves. However, workers did have the freedom to move and change jobs, a freedom that slaves did not have. The North had a much larger industrial base than the South. By 1860 northern factories made the U.S. the third largest manufacturing nation behind Great Britain and France.

The North had a larger population than the South because of high birth rates and the influx of immigrants. Immigration also brought an ethnic and cultural diversity to the North that was lacking in the South. Social classes existed in the North, but social and economic standing was less rigid than in the South.

In 1860 about one third of the U.S. population lived in the Midwest between Ohio and Iowa. This growing agricultural area was helped by the development of railroads. Texas, California, and other parts of the West were frontier areas that welcomed those with bold and adventurous spirits.

The illustration at right depicts the Weccacoe Engine Company responding to a fire in Philadelphia. Firefighter James Queen painted it around 1857. He also painted the image below of a factory.

Lesson 51 - Sectionalism

The Impact of Sectionalism

The different economies and outlooks among the regions led to conflicts over national policies. Southern cotton growers, for instance, depended on trade with other countries and wanted low import tariffs to encourage it. Northern industrialists, on the other hand, wanted protection from overseas competition and thus favored high import tariffs. Westerners pushed for internal improvements such as roads, canals, and railroads to connect them to the East Coast; but southerners did not directly benefit from such projects and usually opposed them.

The other main issue that engendered sectional conflict was slavery. The conflict intensified over the question of extending slavery into the territories and into new states of the West. In the 1830s, the antislavery movement reached the U.S. House of Representatives. Several petitions were presented in Congress calling for the abolition of slavery in the District of Columbia. Congress had the power to do this because it had oversight of the District.

Many of the petitions were introduced by Representative John Quincy Adams. In 1836 the House adopted a gag rule, which automatically tabled (i.e., killed) all such petitions. Members of the House, from both the South and the North, simply did not want to consider any Federal laws concerning slavery. Adams fought the rule as a denial of the people's right to petition the government for redress of grievances, and the rule was eventually repealed in 1844.

The Wilmot Proviso

Sectional interests influenced the deliberations of Congress. In 1846 soon after the Mexican War began, President Polk requested $2 million from Congress to conduct negotiations with Mexico. Freshman Democratic Representative David Wilmot from Pennsylvania proposed an amendment to the appropriation request. The proposed amendment

David Wilmot (1814-1868)

would require that slavery never be allowed in any territory that was gained by using the $2 million. His proposal was based on the provision of the Northwest Ordinance which banned slavery in that territory and in the states formed from it.

The Wilmot Proviso created hot debate in Congress. The untouchable topic had been brought up for discussion. The House passed the amendment, but the Senate rejected it. The same idea was introduced and voted on repeatedly, and it was always defeated. A little later, Senator John C. Calhoun of South Carolina proposed resolutions (which were never voted on) which said that the territories were owned by all the states, not the Federal government. All Americans, Calhoun said, had a right to take their possessions into all territories; thus, in his view, Congress had no right to forbid slavery in any territory.

Popular Sovereignty

The two positions by Wilmot and Calhoun outlined the debate over slavery for the next several years. Free-soilers wanted slavery excluded from the territories, while proslavery advocates insisted on the right of settlers to take slaves into whatever territory settlers wished, unimpeded by Congress. The most attractive-sounding middle ground was put forth by Michigan Democratic Senator Lewis Cass. He proposed that territories be organized on the basis of popular sovereignty (antislavery men called it squatter sovereignty). This idea held that the people living in a given territory should decide whether the territory would be slave or free.

This sounded fair and democratic, but Cass did not specify when such a determination was to be made. If the decision was made when an area became a territory, slavery could be banned fairly easily. However, Calhoun believed that this was unconstitutional since Congress did not have the right to ban slavery nor to give that right to territories. If the slave-or-free determination was made when a territory applied for statehood, then both proslavery and antislavery advocates had a fair chance of carrying the day. Many in both camps supported popular sovereignty as the best way for their point of view to be adopted. Popular sovereignty sounded good; but as we will see, the one time it was applied to organizing a territory it led to a disaster.

The debate over slavery tied up Congress for most of the period leading up to 1861. Even more, it caught up the nation in a continuing and increasingly heated discussion over what to do about the South's peculiar institution.

Nathanael said to him, "Can any good thing come out of Nazareth?"
Philip said to him, "Come and see."
John 1:46

★ Assignments for Lesson 51 ★

Literature — Continue reading *Uncle Tom's Cabin*. Plan to finish it by the end of this unit.

Bible — In the Bible study lesson for this unit we will discuss what the Bible says about handling our differences. Read Romans 12:3-13. List three good ways to handle the fact that we have differences, as described in this passage.

Start memorizing Psalm 133.

Project — Choose your project for this unit and start working on it.

Student Review — Optional: Answer the questions for Lesson 51.

San Francisco, California, 1851

Lesson 52

Trouble in the Territories

John Sutter was born in Germany in 1803. He came to the United States in 1834 and eventually settled in the Sacramento Valley of California, which at the time was a province of Mexico. Sutter was given a 49,000 acre land grant and became a Mexican citizen. His colony attracted many settlers, including a good number of Americans.

When a group of Americans declared California to be independent of Mexico in 1846, Sutter sided with the Americans. After California was annexed to the U.S., Sutter began construction of a new sawmill on his property. On January 24, 1848, workers excavating for the mill discovered gold. After President James K. Polk announced the find in his message to Congress in December of 1848, 80,000 people rushed to California in search of gold the following year. Over 50,000 of them came overland, while the rest came by ship, either by sailing around South America or by taking passage to Panama, going overland across the isthmus, and then sailing from Panama on to California.

The population explosion in the California territory raised the possibility of its statehood, which further intensified the question of slavery in the western territories. Wisconsin had become the thirtieth state in May of 1848, giving the Union fifteen slave states and fifteen free. The Mexican War had ended earlier that year, but Congress had taken no action on statehood for California or for any part of the new southwest region because of the impasse over slavery. The House voted for the new territories to be free; but southerners resented this, and some in the South began talking about leaving the Union.

The 1848 Election

The 1848 election saw both major parties dodge the issue of slavery in the territories. The Democrats nominated Lewis Cass of Michigan while the Whigs tapped Mexican War hero Zachary Taylor. The Free Soil Party was composed of antislavery people who were disgruntled with both major parties. In 1848 they nominated Martin Van Buren for President and Charles Francis Adams Sr., the son of John Quincy Adams, for Vice President.

Zachary Taylor had never voted in a presidential election, and his position on the issues was unknown. The Whigs hoped to win the White House purely on Taylor's military reputation, and it worked. A key element in Taylor's victory was the fact that his vice presidential running mate was Millard Fillmore of New York. Fillmore's popularity in his home state, coupled with the impact of the Free Soil Party there, gave the Whigs that state and the election. However, the Democrats controlled Congress.

"Old Rough and Ready" Zachary Taylor was born in Virginia. He was a cousin of James Madison and Robert E. Lee. Taylor spent forty years in the Army. In 1835 his daughter married Jefferson Davis over Taylor's objections, but she died three months into the marriage. Taylor and Davis were reconciled when they were both serving in the Mexican War. At the time of his election as President, Taylor was living in Louisiana and owned a plantation and slaves in Mississippi. This 1848 portrait of Taylor is by American artist Joseph Henry Bush.

Although Taylor was a slave owner, he believed that slavery could not exist in the West. After he became President, Taylor called for California to be admitted to the Union as a free state and indicated his willingness for New Mexico to be admitted under the same terms. The provisional governments that had been formed in both areas were antislavery. The admission of both states as free would upset the slave-free balance of states and set a precedent for future western states to ban slavery.

Taylor's position angered the South. In 1850 a convention was held in Nashville, Tennessee, to discuss a unified southern position against what was termed "northern aggression." Five states were officially represented, while delegates from four other states attended unofficially. The assembly adopted resolutions demanding equal access to the territories for slave owners.

Clay's Final Compromise

Northerners did not want to delay the admission of California any longer, and southerners did not want California admitted under the terms being discussed. Henry Clay, the seventy-three-year-old master of compromise, proposed a series of measures in the Senate designed to break the deadlock:

- California would be admitted as a free state.
- The rest of the area received from Mexico would be organized as the Utah and New Mexico territories, which would decide for themselves whether or not to permit slavery.
- A border dispute between Texas and New Mexico regarding the Rio Grande would be settled in New Mexico's favor, but Texas would receive compensation from the Federal government to settle pre-admission debts.
- The slave trade would be abolished in the District of Columbia, although slavery would continue to be permitted there.
- A new and tougher Fugitive Slave Law would force the return of slaves captured in free states to their southern owners.

The Senate debate over these proposals in early 1850 brought together for the last time some of the most eloquent spokesmen of the day. Henry Clay made an impassioned plea for his proposal as the only means to save the Union. John C. Calhoun prepared a speech warning of the dangers to the Union that the proposals carried and of the determination of

Lesson 52 - Trouble in the Territories

the South to stand by its rights, but he was too ill to deliver it himself. He was carried into the Senate on March 4 to hear it read by a southern colleague. Calhoun died March 31. On March 7, Daniel Webster spoke not as a New Englander or a Whig, he said, but as an American wanting to preserve the Union. He believed that slavery could not exist in the West, so he favored admitting California as a free state. However, to maintain peace he also supported the Fugitive Slave Law. This infuriated Webster's fellow northerners, who believed that he had betrayed his antislavery principles.

The outlook for Clay's compromise was not good. Clay's Omnibus Bill containing all five components encountered tough going in Congress. In addition, President Taylor let it be known that he planned to veto the measure. Then on the hot July 4 of 1850, Taylor, now sixty-six years of age, attended festivities at the base of the unfinished Washington Monument. He went back to the White House, drank cold milk and water, apparently ate some raw food, developed a gastric disorder, and died five days later.

New President Millard Fillmore indicated his willingness to sign the compromise, and Clay broke his bill into separate parts so that his proposals could be passed more easily. Different coalitions within Congress enabled the passage of the separate bills. For instance, antislavery men and advocates of compromise voted for the admission of California; while proslavery men and compromisers voted for the Fugitive Slave Law. Many people in the country breathed a hopeful sigh of relief when all of the measures passed. They wanted to believe that the Compromise of 1850 was the answer to the national dilemma.

The package of legislation had several difficulties, however. (1) By leaving the slavery question open for Utah and New Mexico, the Compromise of 1850 only delayed the conflict there. (2) Since the different aspects of the compromise had been passed by different coalitions, no majority in Congress supported the entire package. (3) More immediately, the Fugitive Slave Law incensed many northerners. The law denied a jury trial for alleged fugitives. It applied to any slave who had ever run away, meaning that former slaves living in the North could be returned after having lived free for many years. In addition, the measure said that any citizen ordered by law enforcement officials to assist in the capture and return of fugitive slaves had to do so. Antislavery northerners saw the law as forcing them to work for something they opposed. The many incidents of non-compliance with the law in the North indicated the resistance that people felt toward it. Few slaves were actually returned to their owners under the law.

Millard Fillmore
George Peter Alexander Healy (American, 1857)

The 1852 Election

The 1852 election revealed that the Whig Party was coming apart. A split had developed between northern Conscience Whigs who opposed slavery and southern Cotton Whigs who supported it. Northern Whigs blocked the nomination of Millard Fillmore and were able to place another Mexican War hero, Winfield Scott, at the top of the ticket.

Divisions were apparent among Democrats as well. Northern Democrats generally wanted to leave the question of slavery to the states and were willing to go along with the expansion of slavery in the territories in the name of popular sovereignty. Southern Democrats, by contrast, were more strident in their support of slavery and wanted to see the right to own slaves protected in the territories and in future states. The Democrats nominated Franklin Pierce of New Hampshire, who had also served in the Mexican War and who supported the Compromise of 1850.

In the election, Pierce carried all but four states. He won a majority in both the North and the South (the last candidate to accomplish this feat until 1912, except during the unusual circumstances of 1868). The loss crushed the Whig Party, which soon passed out of existence. The new President did not have much time to savor his victory, though, as new crises soon confronted the nation.

The Transcontinental Railroad and Popular Sovereignty

The thoughts of many Americans were on the West. California entered the Union as the 31st state in September of 1850. Interest ran high in the development of other western territories as well, such as Oregon, Utah, and New Mexico. In addition, the U.S. was developing a desire for trade with the Far East. China opened four ports to American trading vessels in 1844, and Christian missionaries came to have a burden for the people of China. Commodore Matthew Perry began American contact with Japan in 1853, and trade with that nation got underway in 1858.

These political and economic developments, coming at a time of rapid expansion of railroads, led many Americans to dream of a rail line that ran across the entire continent and brought the nation together. Many politicians and businessmen east of the Mississippi River tried to use their influence to have the line built from their respective areas. One key politician who took a special interest in this issue was Illinois Democratic Senator Stephen Douglas. Douglas was short in stature but long on ambition. He believed in the United States and in himself. Sadly, his drive to become President led him to propose a policy that created an American tragedy.

Gaikokujin Sen No Uchi: Jōkisen (Foreigners' Ship: Steamship)
Utagawa Hiroshige II (Japanese, 1861)

Lesson 52 - Trouble in the Territories

Douglas wanted the transcontinental line to begin in Chicago, and he proposed that the region west of Iowa and Missouri (that is, the area that would become Kansas and Nebraska) be organized as territories that would eventually become states in order to provide government protection for the rail line. However, Douglas wanted these territories to forbid slavery. Southern Senators blocked this proposal because they wanted slavery to be allowed in all territories and also because they were hopeful that the cross-country rail line might be built along a southern route beginning from New Orleans and going to southern California.

Douglas saw that his plans were being derailed by southern opposition, so he compromised. He agreed to let the territories of Nebraska and Kansas decide by popular sovereignty whether they would be slave or free. Since both areas lay north of the 36°30' line that divided slave and free territories in the 1820 Missouri Compromise, Douglas proposed repealing the 1820 measure. Antislavery men felt betrayed by the idea. They said that, by supporting this proposal, the South was going back on an agreement it had made in 1820. Douglas was criticized as wanting to extend slavery. In fact, Douglas opposed slavery. He hoped that the two new states would be organized free, and he believed that they would be since he thought that slavery would not work on the prairie. However, he was not willing to let his personal opposition to slavery get in the way of his political ambition.

Bleeding Kansas

Congress passed the Kansas-Nebraska Act in May of 1854. The law allowed the question of slavery to be settled in the Kansas and Nebraska territories by popular sovereignty. That fall, the Democrats lost big in mid-term congressional elections because of widespread opposition to the Kansas-Nebraska Act. Shortly after the election, various antislavery groups and factions, including the few remaining northern Whigs, came together to form the Republican Party.

The U.S. Army Corps of Engineers surveyed the Great Plains in the 1850s to determine a possible railroad route from the Mississippi River to the Pacific. This illustration of bison around Lake Jessie, North Dakota, is from their report.

The name of the party was an attempt to hearken back to the days of Thomas Jefferson.

Northerners hoped both Kansas and Nebraska would both be organized free, while southerners hoped at least one would permit slavery. It soon became apparent that Nebraska would forbid slavery, so the focus of attention came to be on Kansas. Some of those who settled in Kansas simply wanted to own land in a new territory, but many settlers entered the territory with either a proslavery or antislavery agenda. Both sides of the slavery issue rushed people into the territory in the hope that they could sway the voting that would form the territorial government. When an election was held for a territorial legislature in 1855, proslavery forces stole the election and set up a government in Lecompton which President Pierce recognized. Free-soilers rejected the Lecompton government and formed their own government for the territory in the town of Lawrence. This gave Kansas two competing territorial governments.

The proslavery forces obtained an indictment from a friendly judge against the antislavery government, and a posse set out for Lawrence to do away with the antislavery presence. Proslavery men wreaked destruction on the town, destroying a printing press and other property and causing one death. In response, four days later a free-soiler named John Brown led a group that attacked a proslavery settlement at Pottawatomie Creek and killed five

This sheet music was published around 1856 for the song "Ho! for the Kansas Plains". The illustration shows a Native American and a settler on either side of a confrontation between proslavery and antislavery groups.

men in front of their families. The exchange of violence escalated, and by the end of 1856 over 200 people had been killed and $2 million in property had been destroyed. The territory became known as Bleeding Kansas.

Conflict in Congress

The United States Senate was the setting for another, related conflict in 1856. Republican Massachusetts Senator Charles Sumner addressed the body in mid-May, lamenting what was happening in Kansas even before the Lawrence and Pottawatomie incidents. He blamed the South's desire for additional slave states as the reason for the conflict, and he poured especially hateful words onto South Carolina's Democratic Senator Andrew Butler. Sumner questioned Butler's integrity and character. He said that Butler was committed to the harlot Slavery; and he ridiculed Butler's manner of speech, even though Butler had been affected by a recent stroke and was absent from the Senate at the time.

What Else Was Happening?

1851 The first World Exhibition takes place in the Crystal Palace in London. The opening ceremony is depicted at right.
1851 Louis Napoleon leads a bloodless revolution in France, wiping out democratic gains. He crowns himself Napoleon III.
1851 Taipei radicals begin revolts against the ruling Ch'ing dynasty in China.
1852 The first steam-powered dirigible balloon is flown at a speed of just under seven miles per hour.
1854 Louis Pasteur develops a process to prevent spoilage that comes to be called pasteurization.
1855 German chemist Robert Bunsen mixes air with coal gas to produce a flame for use in laboratory experiments. The device producing this flame comes to be called the Bunsen Burner.
1855 Peru abolishes slavery.
1856 Human bones are found in a cave in Germany's Neander Valley. They come to be seen as evidence of what is called "Neanderthal man."
1858 The first messages are sent along a transatlantic telegraph cable.
1859 The Suez Canal is begun. When it is finished ten years later, ships no longer have to go around Africa to sail between the Atlantic and Indian Oceans.

Lesson 52 - Trouble in the Territories

Butler's nephew, Preston Brooks, was a South Carolina Congressman who took Sumner's insults to heart. Two days after Sumner's speech, Brooks entered the Senate chamber and confronted the Massachusetts Senator at his desk. Brooks began beating Sumner about the head and shoulders with his heavy, gold-headed cane, which broke in the attack. Sumner gripped his desk so firmly that he pulled it out of the floor as he fell. The Senator was incapacitated for over two years. He kept his Senate seat, however; and his empty chair made him a martyr for the antislavery cause. When the House censured Brooks, he resigned; but his South Carolina district re-elected Brooks, and several of his constituents sent him new canes to take with him when he returned to Congress. The whole affair increased the tension between the two sides. Americans were now attacking each other physically over the question of slavery.

Depiction of Brooks' Attack on Sumner

> *Let all bitterness and wrath and anger*
> *and clamor and slander be put away from you,*
> *along with all malice.*
> *Ephesians 4:31*

★ Assignments for Lesson 52 ★

American Voices   Read the excerpts from "Crime Against Kansas" by Charles Sumner (pages 188-192).

Literature   Continue reading *Uncle Tom's Cabin*.

Bible   Read Romans 14:1-23. List three attitudes discussed in this passage that we should have toward other believers who have different opinions from ours.

Work on memorizing Psalm 133.

Project   Work on your project.

Student Review   Optional: Answer the questions for Lesson 52.

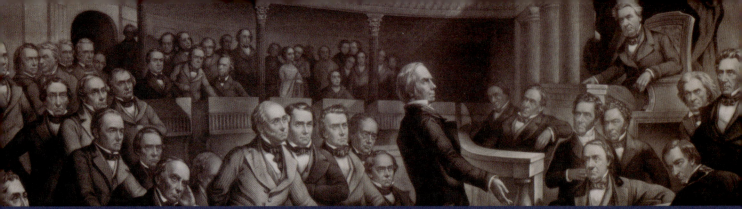

Debate in the U.S. Senate, 1850

Lesson 53

Twilight of the Giants

The debates in the U.S. Senate over the Compromise of 1850 brought together for the last time three political figures who dominated much of the first half of the nineteenth century. Each had significant impact on legislation and on the popular thinking of their times. Each was hugely influential in his own region but often misunderstood or despised outside of his own region. All three wanted to be President, but none was elected to serve as chief executive. This lesson examines the careers of those three men: Henry Clay, Daniel Webster, and John C. Calhoun. They are depicted above in a debate about the Compromise of 1850. Clay is standing and speaking in the center. Daniel Webster is seated to the left of Clay leaning on his hand. Calhoun is beside the Speaker's chair.

Henry Clay (1777-1852)

Henry Clay was the master of political compromise. During his legislative career, Clay crafted several plans that gave at least something to both sides in a political dispute while avoiding a complete division of the country. In doing this, Clay proved himself to be a skilled political negotiator.

Clay was born in Virginia, but in 1797 he moved to the new state of Kentucky as a twenty-year-old lawyer. He saw possibilities for advancement in an area where new leadership would be needed. Clay settled in the growing town of Lexington and was elected to the state legislature in 1803. The Kentucky state legislature chose him to fill out a United States Senate term in 1806, even though he was not yet the constitutionally-required age of thirty (no one seemed to notice, and he was duly sworn in). While in the Senate he gave impassioned speeches that turned heads. In the evenings he developed a reputation as a gambler.

In 1807 he was re-elected to the state house of representatives and was chosen to be speaker of that body. Three years later, Clay was chosen for another brief stint in the U.S. Senate. In 1811 he was elected to the U.S. House of Representatives, and in his first term Clay was chosen as the Speaker of the House. Clay used his position to advance his ideas and his friends, and he became known as a War Hawk who encouraged the U.S. to go to war against Great Britain. Clay was a member of the U.S. commission that went to Europe in 1814 and, with their British counterparts, drafted the peace treaty which ended the War of 1812.

Following his service on the peace commission, in 1815 Clay again assumed his seat in Congress and ardently advocated what he called the American

Lesson 53 - Twilight of the Giants

Quotations from Henry Clay

Government is a trust, and the officers of the government are trustees; and both the trust and the trustees are created for the benefit of the people.

I have heard something said about allegiance to the South. I know no South, no North, no East, no West, to which I owe any allegiance. The Union, sir, is my country.

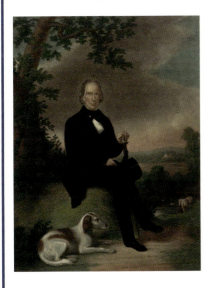

All legislation, all government, all society is founded upon the principle of mutual concession, politeness, comity, courtesy; upon these everything is based. . . . Let him who elevates himself above humanity, above its weaknesses, its infirmities, its wants, its necessities, say, if he pleases, I will never compromise; but let no one who is not above the frailties of our common nature disdain compromises.

The Constitution of the United States was made not merely for the generation that then existed, but for posterity—unlimited, undefined, endless, perpetual posterity.

I had rather be right than be President.

Portrait by J. W. Dodge (American, 1843)

System. This was a program of Federally-funded internal improvements, such as roads and canals, that would facilitate travel and commerce and bring the growing nation closer together. It also involved a protective tariff to help American manufacturers and the re-establishment of a national bank. When the issue of Missouri's admission to the Union as a slave state threatened the fabric of the nation, Clay played a key role in crafting the Missouri Compromise of 1820. Clay retired from Congress in 1821, was re-elected in 1822, and again became Speaker of the House.

In 1824 Clay made his first run for the presidency. He was defeated in the four-way race that resulted in the election of John Quincy Adams. His agreement to support Adams' candidacy apparently resulted in Adams naming him Secretary of State, a "corrupt bargain" in the eyes of Andrew Jackson and Jackson's supporters.

Clay was elected to the U.S. Senate in 1831 and again ran for President the following year against Andrew Jackson. Again, Clay was defeated. In 1833 Senator Clay helped to formulate the lower tariff that ended the nullification crisis. The following year, the Whig Party formed in opposition to Jackson's policies, with Clay as one of its leaders.

Clay resigned from the Senate in 1842, and two years later he was nominated by the Whigs as their presidential candidate. Again, Clay met defeat, this time at the hands of James K. Polk. Clay was elected to the Senate in 1849 and helped to fashion the Compromise of 1850. He resigned from the Senate in late 1851 and died June 29, 1852.

Daniel Webster (1782-1852)

The most gifted orator of his day, an ardent nationalist, and a Federalist who became a Whig, Daniel Webster was born in New Hampshire in 1782. He attended Dartmouth College (which is located in New Hampshire) and then became an attorney in 1807.

Quotations from Daniel Webster

God grants liberty only to those who love it, and are always ready to guard and defend it.

The Bible is a book of faith, and a book of doctrine, and a book of morals, and a book of religion, of especial revelation from God.

America has furnished to the world the character of Washington. And if our American institutions had done nothing else, that alone would have entitled them to the respect of mankind.

Inconsistencies of opinion, arising from changes of circumstances, are often justifiable.

I was born an American; I will live an American; I shall die an American.

Portrait by Francis Alexander (American, 1835)

Webster was elected to the U.S. House of Representatives in 1812 as an outspoken opponent of the war with England that had already been declared. He believed that the war would hurt New England's economic interests, especially its international trade. In 1814 Webster began arguing cases before the U.S. Supreme Court, an activity he continued even while he was a member of Congress. Then in 1816, Webster decided to move to Boston because he believed that such a change would further his political and legal careers. Nevertheless, he retained his seat in Congress from New Hampshire until that session of Congress ended in March of 1817.

Webster quickly developed a positive reputation in Boston; in 1822 he was elected to Congress from Massachusetts. Five years later, the Massachusetts legislature chose him to be a U.S. Senator. He served in the Senate until he became Secretary of State under William Henry Harrison in 1841. He remained in that post until 1843. While Secretary of State, Webster negotiated a treaty with Great Britain that settled the boundary lines with Canada between Maine and New Brunswick and west of Lake Superior. He was re-elected to the Senate in 1843 and served there through the debate on the Compromise of 1850. Soon after Millard Fillmore became President, he chose Webster to be his Secretary of State. Webster held that role until his death in 1852.

During his career, Webster supported what he saw as the most important interests of New England. At first he supported a low tariff to help the Massachusetts shipping industry; but then he switched and supported a high tariff to protect Massachusetts manufacturers. Although he was a Whig, he strongly endorsed Andrew Jackson's nationalist stance in the nullification crisis with South Carolina. In 1850 Webster opposed the expansion of slavery but feared the breakup of the Union even more; thus he supported the Compromise of 1850. As Secretary of State, Webster tried to administer strict enforcement of the Fugitive Slave Law, which cost him support among northern Whigs.

In 1836 Webster was one of three regional Whig candidates for President. He carried only Massachusetts. Webster was considered for the Whig nomination in 1848 and 1852, but he was not selected by the party as its candidate either time.

Lesson 53 - Twilight of the Giants

John C. Calhoun (1782-1850)

John Caldwell Calhoun of South Carolina, a graduate of Yale and trained as an attorney, is widely regarded as one of the most brilliant men ever to serve in Congress. He was a strong defender of slavery and a leading advocate of states' rights in their relationship with the Federal government.

Calhoun was elected to the South Carolina legislature in 1808, then was elected to the U.S. House of Representatives in 1811. In Congress he was an ardent supporter of the War of 1812 with England. He served as Secretary of War under President James Monroe (1817-1825). During this period, Calhoun was a strong nationalist who supported Clay's American System of Federally-funded internal improvements, a national bank, and a strong central government.

In 1824 he briefly sought the presidential nomination but later decided to seek the position of Vice President, which he won in the election that year. After serving under John Quincy Adams, Calhoun was again elected Vice President when Andrew Jackson was elected President in 1828. However, Calhoun came to believe that southern interests were hurt by a strong Federal government; so he developed the theory of a state's right to nullify a Federal law. Calhoun and Jackson had sharp disagreement over this issue, and Calhoun resigned as Vice President before Jackson's first term ended.

Calhoun was elected to the U.S. Senate in 1832 and served in that body for most of the rest of his life. He believed that the right to own slaves should be extended into the territories and that civil war and disunion would result if this right were not protected. He served as John Tyler's Secretary of State in 1844 and 1845, and in that position he helped to bring about the annexation of Texas.

Calhoun died a few days after his last speech was read in the Senate during the debate over the Compromise of 1850.

Quotations from John C. Calhoun

A power has risen up in the government greater than the people themselves, consisting of many and various powerful interests, combined into one mass, and held together by the cohesive power of the vast surplus in the banks.

It is harder to preserve than to obtain liberty.

The object of a Constitution is to restrain the Government, as that of laws is to restrain individuals.

The Government of the absolute majority instead of the Government of the people is but the Government of the strongest interests; and when not efficiently checked, it is the most tyrannical and oppressive that can be devised.

Beware the wrath of a patient adversary.

In looking back, I see nothing to regret and little to correct.

Portrait by George Peter Alexander Healy (American, c. 1845)

*O Lord, who may abide in Your tent? Who may dwell on Your holy hill?
He who walks with integrity, and works righteousness,
and speaks truth in his heart.
Psalm 15:1-2*

★ Assignments for Lesson 53 ★

American Voices — Read the excerpts from the speeches on the Compromise of 1850 by Henry Clay, Daniel Webster, and John C. Calhoun (pages 171-175).

Literature — Continue reading *Uncle Tom's Cabin*.

Bible — Read 1 Corinthians 12:4-27. List three positive attitudes that are taught in this passage about the different gifts or abilities that God gives us.

Work on memorizing Psalm 133.

Project — Work on your project.

Student Review — Optional: Answer the questions for Lesson 53.

U.S. Capitol Dome Under Construction (1857)

Lesson 54

Stumbling Toward War

President Franklin Pierce was an ineffective leader who generally supported the South's position. For instance, he sent diplomats to Ostend, Belgium, in 1854 to discuss the possibility of buying or taking Cuba from Spain. Since Cuba already had slavery, the declaration of American interest in Cuba, called the Ostend Manifesto, was seen by many as an attempt to extend slavery. The Pierce Administration had to give up the idea when it met severe criticism in America and in other countries.

For the 1856 election, the Democrats backed away from Pierce and instead nominated James Buchanan of Pennsylvania. Buchanan was a long-time Congressman and a former diplomat. He had served as Secretary of State under James K. Polk. Buchanan endorsed the Kansas-Nebraska Act and said that Congress should not interfere with slavery in the states or the territories. The American ("Know-Nothing") Party and a remnant of the Whig Party both nominated Millard Fillmore, but all knew he had little chance of winning.

The new Republican Party tried a trick that the Whigs had used by nominating a military hero, John C. Fremont, known as The Pathfinder. Fremont had become well-known by mapping the Oregon Trail in 1842. His work had encouraged further western settlement. Fremont was leading a small band of men in California during the Mexican War when another group set up the Bear Flag Republic in California, a move that Fremont endorsed. The Republican platform of 1856 supported a transcontinental railroad and internal improvements and opposed slavery and the repeal of the Missouri Compromise. This was the first time that a major political party had taken a specific stand against slavery. The Republicans' slogan was, "Free Soil, Free Speech, and Fremont."

The Democrat Buchanan swept the South except for Maryland and carried a handful of northern states to win the election. Fremont carried eleven northern states. Overall, the Republican Party did remarkably well after being in existence for less than two years.

The *Dred Scott* Decision

Two days after Buchanan was inaugurated in March of 1857, the U.S. Supreme Court handed down its decision in the case of *Dred Scott v. Sanford*, a decision which appeared to support the proslavery cause. Dred Scott was a slave owned by an Army surgeon in St. Louis, Missouri. Scott's master had taken him to Illinois and then to the Wisconsin Territory—both free areas—before returning to St. Louis. After his master died in 1843, Scott tried to buy his freedom. In 1846, with help from antislavery supporters, Scott sued in a Missouri state court, claiming that he was actually free since he had lived in free areas. A jury decided in his favor, the Missouri Supreme Court ruled against him on appeal, and the case was finally brought before the U.S. Supreme Court.

Chief Justice Roger B. Taney (pronounced TAW-ney) from Maryland and four other justices from slave states joined together to deny Scott's appeal. Taney said that Scott had no standing before the Court because he was not a citizen. Taney denied that the founders envisioned slaves or their descendants ever being citizens. Further, Taney held that being a citizen of a state did not automatically make a person a citizen of the United States. Moreover, the Court ruled that the Missouri Compromise of 1820 was unconstitutional since it had denied citizens equal rights of property by declaring certain areas of the country as free. The Court affirmed the idea that slavery was a state and not a Federal issue.

The *Dred Scott* decision strengthened the belief of proslavery men that antislavery forces were trying

---

Roger Taney was Chief Justice of the Supreme Court from 1836 until his death in 1864.

The June 27, 1857, edition of Frank Leslie's Illustrated Newspaper *contained this feature article about Dred Scott and his family. Dred and his wife Harriet are shown at the bottom. Their daughters Eliza and Lizzie are in the middle.*

---

to rob them of their constitutional rights. On the other hand, it affirmed to opponents of slavery their belief that the Federal government was controlled by people who wanted to protect and extend slavery. The *Dred Scott* decision said, in effect, that popular sovereignty was illegal because it would deny people their property ownership rights since slaves were considered property. The Court also rendered invalid any attempt by Congress to reach a compromise, since it said slavery was not an issue that the Federal government could address. The *Dred Scott* decision served to harden the positions of both sides.

Lesson 54 - Stumbling Toward War

Further Uncertainties

Later in 1857, President Buchanan, like Pierce before him, endorsed the proslavery government of Kansas. However, Congress ordered another election the next year to be overseen by the Federal government. In that election, the antislavery forces won the day. Kansas was now firmly in the antislavery camp and ceased to be an issue in the slavery debate. However, it did not become a state until January of 1861.

An economic downturn in 1857 was another blow to the stability of the Buchanan presidency. The U.S. economy suffered from slower grain sales to Europe, over-production by American manufacturers, and continued problems in the banking system that was controlled by the states. The failure of a major insurance company precipitated a recession which lasted for two years. However, the sale of cotton to foreign buyers recovered fairly quickly, leading many in the South to believe that cotton's importance in the national and world economy was too great to be trifled with.

Lincoln and Douglas

Illinois was the scene of a contest in 1858 that further dramatized the conflict over slavery. Senator Stephen Douglas was up for re-election, and he hoped that a victory would propel him toward an 1860 run for the presidency. The Republicans nominated as his opponent Springfield attorney and one-time Whig state legislator and Congressman Abraham Lincoln. Lincoln had once worked on a riverboat to New Orleans and had seen the impact of slavery on people's lives. He fiercely opposed slavery and wanted to prevent its spread to the territories. However, he was not an abolitionist. He did not advocate direct action to end slavery where it existed in southern states. In addition, he did not believe

These statues in Jonesboro, Illinois, commemorate the third debate between Abraham Lincoln and Stephen Douglas.

that the two races could peacefully live together as equals. Lincoln had become a Republican in 1856, when he backed Fremont for President. In 1858 he was the most prominent Republican in Illinois and the logical choice to oppose Douglas. He gave his famous "House Divided" speech when he accepted the party's nomination to run against Douglas for the Senate.

Lincoln challenged Douglas to a series of debates around the state, and seven debates were held. The two candidates could not have made a sharper contrast. Douglas was short, stout, cocky, well-dressed, and eloquent. Lincoln was tall (about 6'4"), lanky (about 180 pounds), dressed in well-worn clothes, and used a homespun, humorous speaking style. Lincoln said that he wanted to contain slavery to the states where it currently existed. He believed that it would eventually die out. The Republican candidate portrayed Douglas as promoting slavery. On the other hand, Douglas said he favored popular sovereignty and painted Lincoln as an abolitionist. Lincoln charged that Douglas was indifferent to the moral question of slavery, whereas Lincoln said he believed it was wrong ("If slavery is not wrong then nothing is wrong," he said).

Lincoln challenged the idea of popular sovereignty on the basis of the *Dred Scott* decision. How could the people of a territory, Lincoln asked, legally exclude slavery? Douglas replied that all a territorial legislature had to do was simply refrain from passing laws concerning slavery; slavery could not establish itself, he said. As many in the nation had their eyes on the Illinois Senate race, Douglas' efforts to maintain the middle ground cost him support from both northern and southern Democrats. Douglas was not antislavery enough to satisfy northerners and not proslavery enough to satisfy southerners.

The senatorial election, however, was not directly in the hands of Illinois voters. State legislatures chose U.S. Senators in those days. The Lincoln-Douglas debates were actually intended to influence voters to elect candidates for the Illinois state legislature who represented their respective sides. Lincoln supporters got more total votes, but Democrats won a majority of seats and Douglas was re-elected to the U.S. Senate. However, the Democrats lost control of the U.S. House of Representatives in the 1858 election. A majority of the body was antislavery, but still it did not take any action against slavery.

John Brown's Raid

One more dramatic incident led up to the momentous events of 1860 and 1861. John Brown had killed for the abolitionist cause in Kansas but then had disappeared from public view. On October 16, 1859, Brown led a raid on the military arsenal at Harpers Ferry, Virginia (now in West Virginia). Apparently his purpose was to arm slaves and encourage them to revolt. Brown took a few hostages and remained holed up in the arsenal while a force led by Robert E. Lee and J. E. B. Stuart invaded the arsenal and captured

This photograph from about 1846 shows John Brown holding a flag thought to represent a theoretical organization called the Subterranean Pass Way, Brown's violent addition to the Underground Railroad.

Lesson 54 - Stumbling Toward War

John Brown's Fort

The structure shown below was originally built in 1848 as the fire engine and guard house of the United States Armory and Arsenal at Harpers Ferry. It became a tourist attraction known as John Brown's Fort after the raid.

In 1891 the building was dismantled, taken to Chicago, reassembled for the World's Columbian Exposition, and then disassembled again. After the pieces were abandoned for three years, journalist Kate Field arranged to have them returned to Harpers Ferry.

The building has been moved twice more since then. Pieces have been lost and put in the wrong locations, so it is not an exact replica of the original structure. Now managed by the National Park Service, it sits near its original location. The missing bell from the tower is located in Massachusetts. Union soldiers "liberated" it during the Civil War and sent it to their hometown.

Brown. In all, fourteen people were killed in the incident and seven conspirators were captured. Brown was convicted of treason and was executed on December 2, 1859.

Prominent northern Republicans, including Lincoln, condemned Brown's raid; but William Lloyd Garrison and other antislavery leaders supported him. Brown became a martyr for the abolitionist cause. Ralph Waldo Emerson said that Brown's death would make the gallows as glorious as the cross. Apparently Brown had been financed by northerners; and the whole incident panicked and infuriated many southerners, who saw no difference among Brown, abolitionists, and the Republican Party. Many southerners were already paranoid about the possibility of a slave insurrection, and John Brown's raid only confirmed their fears.

When Congress assembled in December of 1859, the antislavery Republican Party controlled the House. The debate over slavery created a standoff in Congress as the nation awaited the election of 1860.

The Last Moments of John Brown
Thomas Hovenden (American, 1884)

This 1856 map of the United States shows the slave states in blue and free states in red.

> *Whoever sheds man's blood, by man his blood shall be shed,*
> *For in the image of God He made man.*
> Genesis 9:6

★ Assignments for Lesson 54 ★

American Voices Read the "House Divided" speech by Abraham Lincoln (pages 193-197.)

Literature Continue reading *Uncle Tom's Cabin*.

Bible Read 1 Peter 4:7-11. List three ways that Christians are to act toward one another that are taught in this passage.

Work on memorizing Psalm 133.

Project Work on your project.

Student Review Optional: Answer the questions for Lesson 54.

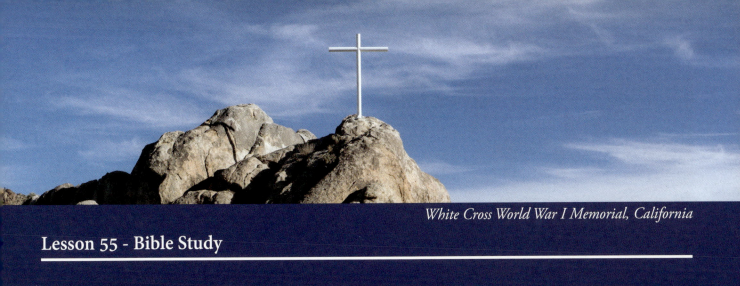

White Cross World War I Memorial, California

Lesson 55 - Bible Study

Differences

People have differences. We differ from each other in terms of our appearance, our family backgrounds, and our ethnic and national backgrounds. We are different because we have different experiences that affect our attitudes and beliefs. Men and women are different from each other because "male and female He created them" (Genesis 1:27), and these gender differences go far beyond mere physical characteristics. We have different personalities. Some are outgoing while others are shy; some are reluctant while others are bold; and the list goes on.

Differences are often the source of conflict. Two nations do not like each other, so they go to war. A husband and a wife do not understand why they are different from each other, so they have marital conflict. Two groups of Christians do not see a matter in the same way, so they divide and question each other's faithfulness to Christ. The Christians in Rome had a problem because they did not value the diversity in their fellowship and instead condemned those whose scruples were different from their own (Romans 14:1-15:13).

However, differences do not have to be a source of conflict. Diversity can be a strength or a weakness depending upon how people see it and use it. Diversity allows a group to do more than it could if all were alike. Diversity also encourages growth as people learn from each other. Paul said that a body is stronger because of the diversity of its members (1 Corinthians 12:12-28).

In the period before the Civil War, the United States struggled with its diversity. As we have noted, people in different sections of the country developed different—and often conflicting—views on issues. Defenders of slavery and opponents of slavery showed little respect for one another. The way that the people of the United States and the state and Federal governments handled their differences eventually led to war. In this lesson we will consider what the Bible says about handling differences.

Oneness in Christ

It is hard to imagine a more radical difference between people than the difference that existed in

Also known as the Mojave Memorial Cross, this memorial was original erected in 1934. After the area became the Mojave National Preserve, administered by the National Park Service, in 1994, someone objected that a cross on Federal land violated the First Amendment. After a lengthy court battle, the land around the cross was made private land in exchange for other land given to the government.

The Hmong are a people group from mountainous regions of Southeast Asia (parts of modern China, Vietnam, Laos, and Thailand). This photo is of a 2012 Hmong New Year Celebration in Chico, California.

the ancient world between Jews and Gentiles. This difference involved their spiritual worldview, their ethnic background, their experiences, and how they viewed the other group. For the most part, Jews and Gentiles did not care for each other and did not understand or respect each other.

The gospel of Christ was first preached to Jews, but then God nudged some Jewish Christians to share the good news with Gentiles (see Acts 10 and 11). This caused no small degree of concern among some believers, but the apostles explained that it was the work of God and that the church should not make distinctions between Christians from different backgrounds (Acts 15).

Paul explained that in Christ people who were different from each other were made into one new kind of person (Ephesians 2:11-22). Christ "broke down the barrier of the dividing wall" (Ephesians 2:14), and thus all believers are fellow-citizens of God's household (Ephesians 2:19). No difference between believers is more important than the oneness that they share. The unity of believers is not a brittle and tenuous compromise that Christians cobble together by their own wits. Instead, it is a gift from God, created by the death of Jesus on the cross. Christians can either cherish and treasure their unity as a stewardship from God, or they can abuse and fracture this precious gift and treat it as worthless.

Some Differences Are Wrong

Not all differences are morally neutral. Some differences that arise among believers involve sin. Jesus recognized that people wrong one another. He gave specific instructions for what to do when someone sins and when someone is sinned against (Matthew 5:21-24, 18:15-20). Paul told the Christians in Galatia to handle gently someone who had become entangled in sin (Galatians 6:1).

Not all differences in belief are merely matters of opinion. Many passages in the New Testament deal with false teachings and with those who cause hindrances and stumbling blocks in the fellowship (see, for instance, Romans 16:17-18, 1 Timothy 1:3-4 and 6:3-5, Philippians 3:18-19, and Colossians 2:8). The Bible does not teach that all belief systems are equally valid. Some ideas are right, and some are wrong. Christians are to oppose false teachings lovingly, but to oppose them just the same. The church in Corinth had been splintered by divisions, partly because of loyalties to various preachers (1 Corinthians 1:10-12). Paul said that the divisions at least served the purpose of making evident who was approved and who was not (1 Corinthians 11:18-19).

Some Differences Are Good

Another problem in Corinth was that people had begun to compare and rank the spiritual gifts God had given them. In 1 Corinthians 12, Paul explained to them how they should see their differences. All of their gifts, he said, are from the same Spirit (verse 4). They should exercise their gifts for the common good (verse 7). God created the different parts of the human body so that it could function fully (verse 18). If the body were all hand or all foot, it could not accomplish what it can with hands and feet and all the other members (verses

15-19). A member of the body should not feel inferior to or superior over other members (verses 21-25). God arranged the body with just the right members for just the right purposes (verse 24-25). All the members of a body rejoice or suffer as one (verse 26).

In Ephesians 4:1-16, Paul says that within the oneness that comes from God, Christ has given many gifts and roles "for the equipping of the saints for the work of service, to the building up of the body of Christ" (verse 12). The differences among us in terms of what we bring to the fellowship by the grace of God are intended to help us keep from being tossed around by false doctrine and to help us grow up in Christ. Every member of the body has a role to play in the spiritual growth of the fellowship (verses 14-16; see also Romans 12:4-8 and 1 Peter 4:10-11 for similar ideas).

Some Differences Are Matters of Opinion

Romans 14:1-15:13 teaches that some differences in belief and practice are merely matters of opinion and should not cause divisions in the body. Some Christians are weak in faith. They should be accepted in the fellowship, but not in a condescending way (14:1). The two specific issues Paul mentions involve eating meat versus eating vegetables only and regarding one day as special versus regarding all days alike (14:2, 5). Each member of the body should be fully convinced in his own mind about such matters and should remember that all of us answer to the Lord and not to each other (14:4, 6). We should not judge our brothers or regard our brothers with contempt (14:10). "The faith which you have, have as your own conviction before God" (14:22).

Instead, we should strive not to cause a brother to stumble by influencing him to do something he believes is wrong (14:13). We do not live for ourselves (14:7). We should not hurt a brother over a minor issue like food (14:15). This is not what the kingdom of God is about (14:17).

Paul's goal in this teaching is for the Christians in Rome to "accept one another, just as Christ also accepted us to the glory of God" (Romans 15:7). It is quite likely that Jewish Christians and Gentile Christians in Rome were having a hard time getting along with each other. Jewish Christians might have had scruples about not eating meat that had been sacrificed to idols, and they might have wanted to keep observing Jewish feast days. Gentile Christians, by contrast, had no such scruples about food and considered all days the same. None of this was as important as the need to glorify God with one voice and with one accord (15:6).

Designed by J&R Lamb, this is one of the Singing Windows at the University Chapel of Tuskegee University in Alabama. The windows illustrate traditional Negro spirituals.

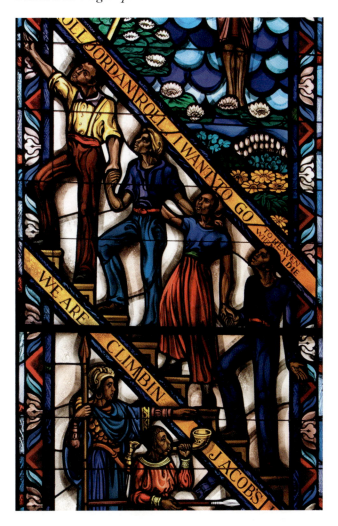

The difficult part in applying this passage today is that it is a matter of opinion what constitutes a matter of opinion. The tendency on the part of many Christians is to see all perspectives and beliefs that are not the same as their own as not just different opinions but as doctrinally wrong positions. This tendency has caused much of the division in the Christian world. We have been quicker to condemn than to accept those who differ from us.

The world has many ways that it divides people, including ethnically, economically, and religiously. Christians who act just as divisive as the world does weaken the church's message to the world. However, when Christians accept their differences as a source of strength, accept each other's personal faith as their own business before God, and cherish their precious unity in Christ, they will have a richer spiritual life and will have a powerful message to a divided world.

> "I do not ask on behalf of these alone, but for those also who believe in Me through their word; that they may all be one; even as You, Father, are in Me and I in You, that they also may be in Us, so that the world may believe that You sent Me."
> John 17:20-21

★ Assignments for Lesson 55 ★

Literature — Finish reading *Uncle Tom's Cabin*. Literary analysis available in *Student Review*.

Write a paragraph on why you think *Uncle Tom's Cabin* was so important in the debate over slavery.

Bible — Recite or write Psalm 133 from memory.

Project — Complete your project for the unit.

Student Review — Optional: Answer the questions for Lesson 55 and for *Uncle Tom's Cabin* and take the quiz for Unit 11.

Bombardment of Fort Sumter, Currier & Ives (1861)

12 The Nation Divides

Leaders in both the North and the South let the confrontation over slavery proceed to the point of war. Many approached the issue as a question of state sovereignty, but the ideal of nationalism led others to think that slavery in any of the states was not something they wanted in the Union. Once shots were fired, it was hard for either side to back down. The physical aspects of war are troubling enough, but the spiritual questions involved make it even more difficult.

Lesson 56 - 1860: Election and Secession
Lesson 57 - 1861: Inauguration and Fort Sumter
Lesson 58 - North and South
Lesson 59 - Early Battles
Lesson 60 - Bible Study: War

Memory Work   Memorize Isaiah 2:2-4 by the end of this unit.

Books Used   The Bible
American Voices
Co. Aytch

Project (choose one)

1) Write 300 to 500 words on one of the following topics:

- Do you believe that the Civil War was inevitable? Explain your answer.

- Write about your beliefs regarding war and a Christian's participation in war. Does Jesus' admonition to turn the other cheek apply to nations or just to individuals? Is it true that if those who do wrong are not opposed or punished, they will likely do wrong again? Explain your answer.

2) Interview a Christian who has served in the armed forces. If possible, also interview a Christian who has been a conscientious objector, or read an interview or article about one. How were their experiences similar, and how were they different? How are their worldviews different? Do either of them have any regrets about their decisions? Compose at least ten questions ahead of time. You can conduct your interview(s) by phone or in person. Be respectful of your interviewee's time and keep the interview within an hour. If possible, make an audio recording of the interview(s).

3) Create a model of a structure that was significant in the Civil War. Locate one or more photos of the structure. Make your model as close to scale as you can and from the material of your choice (e.g., wood, cardboard, clay, STYROFOAM™, LEGO® bricks).

Literature

Co. Aytch

Literature about the Civil War is extensive. You can find novels, journals, books about particular battles, books from the northern perspective, books from the southern perspective, and specialty books focusing on narrow topics such as firearms of the Confederacy.

Sam Watkins was a Confederate soldier from Columbia, Tennessee. He wrote his recollections of the war twenty years later in the local newspaper, and they were collected in book form as *Co. Aytch: A Side Show of the Big Show*. (The title is pronounced "Company H." A company is a unit of about 120 soldiers, and "aytch" is the letter name of the company pronounced with a southern drawl.) Watkins' book has been called the best memoir of a Civil War foot soldier. Watkins died in 1901.

Lincoln Home, Springfield, Illinois

Lesson 56

1860: Election and Secession

The Union was dividing. Already the Methodist and Baptist Churches had divided north and south. The Whig Party had also split north and south before it crumbled and gave way to the Republican Party. People in all parts of the country were losing patience and wanted the issue settled.

But what was the issue? Some said it was slavery, while others said it was states' rights. Many talked about the extension of slavery into the territories, but others concentrated their attention on the states where slavery already existed.

The proposals for resolving the conflict varied as well. Some wanted to abolish slavery, while others wanted its expansion guaranteed. Abolitionists were not satisfied unless the issue was confronted directly, but many southerners did not want to discuss it at all. For some people it was a moral issue; others saw it as an economic one. People differed over what the primary goal of Federal policy should be. Was it (a) to guarantee the right to own slaves, (b) to preserve the Union, or (c) to allow states and territories to determine their own course with regard to slavery? In addition to the sharp differences over issues of substance, the fact that each side stereotyped the other in the worst possible light did nothing to bring about a resolution.

At least part of the struggle was due to the fact that America was changing from an agricultural people concentrated east of the Mississippi River into an increasingly industrialized nation that spanned the continent. The interests of the people were as diverse as the regions they inhabited. While Americans had much in common, the growing differences were straining the bonds of union.

The Democrats

The Democratic National Convention for 1860 was held in April in Charleston, South Carolina, a state where political leaders were not known for their moderation and willingness to compromise.

The Tokugawa shogunate sent the first diplomatic mission from Japan to the United States in 1860. The Japanese officials were photographed with members of the U.S. Navy in Washington, D.C., as seen below.

Harper's Weekly published these illustrations of the 1860 Democratic National Convention in South Carolina. Delegations from different parts of the country occupied their own rooms or buildings. Notice the room full of cots for delegates at left. The committee room of the Massachusetts delegation is shown at right.

The leading candidate for the party's presidential nomination was Senator Stephen Douglas of Illinois. Douglas supporters wanted the party platform simply to make a non-committal promise to abide by Supreme Court decisions regarding slavery without going into more detail. Southern Democrats, however, insisted on a statement guaranteeing the right of slavery in the territories.

When the Douglas platform plank was adopted, many southern delegates walked out of the convention. The assembly was adjourned while attempts were made to reconcile the differing factions. When this did not happen, the convention ended. Northern Democrats reassembled in Baltimore in June and nominated Douglas. Meanwhile, southern Democrats had met in Richmond, Virginia, and nominated the sitting Vice President, John C. Breckenridge of Kentucky. Now the Democratic Party had also divided north and south.

The Republicans

Still not even ten years old, the Republican Party gathered in Chicago smelling a chance for victory in the presidential race. Chicago was Abraham Lincoln's back yard, but the leading contender for the nomination was New York Senator William Seward. However, Seward was known to be strongly antislavery; and many Republicans believed that a win could be theirs if they had a more moderate candidate to face the divided Democrats.

In the eyes of many delegates, Abraham Lincoln was the ideal moderate candidate. He was against slavery personally and against its spread into the territories, but he was not an abolitionist. When Seward failed to win the nomination on the first ballot, support for Lincoln grew; and the tall attorney from Springfield, Illinois, received the nomination on the third ballot. Hannibal Hamlin, a former Democrat from Maine, was nominated for Vice President. The Republican platform condemned John Brown's raid on the Harpers Ferry arsenal, affirmed the right of states to order their own internal institutions, and opposed the extension of slavery into the territories.

Background on Lincoln

Abraham Lincoln had been born in Kentucky in 1809. His family moved to Indiana for a short time and then settled in central Illinois. Lincoln received little formal education but was an eager learner. He operated a store for a while and then became

Lesson 56 - 1860: Election and Secession

an attorney in Springfield. He served in the state militia during the Black Hawk War, a brief conflict with Native Americans; but he saw no action himself. Lincoln married Mary Todd of Lexington, Kentucky, whom he met while she was visiting her sister in Springfield. Lincoln served as a Whig state legislator for four terms and as a U.S. Congressman for one term.

The repeal of the Missouri Compromise in 1850 accelerated his growing political interests. Lincoln hated slavery, but he believed that states had the right to practice it if they wished. He was adamant, however, that slavery be kept out of the territories. Lincoln became a Republican and supported Fremont for President in 1856. Two years later he ran unsuccessfully for the U.S. Senate seat held by Stephen Douglas.

A Crowded Field

In addition to Lincoln and the two Democratic contenders, a fourth candidate entered the election fray when conservative Whigs gathered and renamed themselves the Constitutional Union Party in the hope of offering a compromise candidate to the voters. They nominated John Bell of Tennessee, a former Whig whose opposition to the Democrats dated back to the days of Andrew Jackson. Bell had been the only southern Senator who voted against the Kansas-Nebraska Act. His concern for the Union outweighed any narrow sectional interest.

This 1860 print by Currier & Ives was published a few weeks before the 1860 election. It compares the presidential election to a baseball game, with Abraham Lincoln winning the ball.

Unit 12 - The Nation Divides

During this time, some of the states voted on different days. When Stephen Douglas saw that he had lost, he traveled to the South to try to keep the Union together. Douglas wore himself out in the campaign. Work, ill health, and excessive drinking took its toll. He died in June of 1861 at the age of 48.

The Constitutional Union platform simply voiced support for the Constitution, for the Union, and for the enforcement of the laws.

The Republicans believed that if they could hold on to the states that Fremont had carried in 1856 and pick up two more large northern states, they could win. The election was actually two contests: Lincoln versus Douglas in the North, and Bell versus Breckenridge in the South.

Lincoln swept the North except for New Jersey and received enough electoral votes to win, even though he received only 39 percent of the popular vote nationwide. Some of his margins of victory in the northern states were narrow, and he got no votes at all in nine southern states. Douglas finished second in the popular vote but a distant fourth in the electoral college, receiving only the votes of Missouri and some from New Jersey. Breckenridge carried most of the South and was second in electoral votes, followed by Bell, who carried Tennessee, Kentucky, and Virginia.

The Union is Dissolved

Despite Lincoln's assurances that he would not interfere with slavery where it existed, many in the South did not believe they could trust a Republican administration. On December 20, 1860, a special state convention in Columbia, South Carolina, repealed the state's ratification of the U.S. Constitution and declared that its union with the other states was dissolved. Other southern states followed suit. By February 1, 1861, Mississippi,

James Massalon painted the inauguration of Jefferson Davis (c. 1878) from a photograph taken at the event.

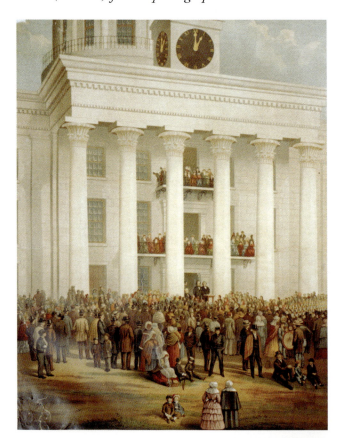

Lesson 56 - 1860: Election and Secession

Florida, Alabama, Georgia, Louisiana, and Texas had also seceded. Representatives of these seven states met in Montgomery, Alabama, in February to form the Confederate States of America. The Constitution they adopted was based largely on the United States Constitution. It specifically protected the practice of slavery. The representatives of the Confederate states elected Jefferson Davis, former U.S. Senator from Mississippi, as president and Georgia Congressman Alexander Hamilton Stephens as vice president. Now the Union itself was divided.

Men, women, and children across the South began wearing secession badges or cockades. They varied in size, shape, and color, though blue was a favorite.

If possible, so far as it depends on you, be at peace with all men.
Romans 12:18

★ Assignments for Lesson 56 ★

American Voices — Read the excerpts from the Constitution of the Confederate States of America and from the "Cornerstone Speech" by Alexander Stephens (pages 204-211).

Literature — Begin reading *Co. Aytch*. Plan to finish it by the end of Unit 13.

Bible — Start memorizing Isaiah 2:2-4.

Project — Choose your project for this unit and start working on it.

Student Review — Optional: Answer the questions for Lesson 56.

Aerial View of Fort Sumter

Lesson 57

1861: Inauguration and Fort Sumter

As southern states left the Union and tensions mounted, the North played a waiting game. President Buchanan said that secession was wrong but that he had no authority to coerce a state to remain in the Union. The South Carolina state government demanded that Union troops leave Fort Sumter in the Charleston harbor, but Buchanan refused to pull them out. When the President sent a supply ship to the fort in January of 1861, South Carolina cannons drove it away; but Buchanan refused to retaliate. Lincoln did not consult with the Buchanan Administration between his election and the March 4 inauguration.

Attempts at Reconciliation

Some efforts at compromise and reconciliation were attempted. Various proposals were introduced in Congress, including one guaranteeing the continuation of slavery where it existed and allowing slavery in territories south of the 36°30' parallel. A peace conference with delegates from twenty-one states met in Washington in February of 1861. Its suggestions were largely ignored by Congress.

Congress did pass a constitutional amendment guaranteeing slavery where it then existed. Following House approval, the Senate passed it at dawn on Lincoln's inauguration day; but events overtook it. Southern states no longer considered themselves part of the Union, and few northern states wanted to make such a promise.

By the time of Lincoln's inauguration, seven of fifteen slave states had declared their secession from the Union. A Confederate government had been formed and Jefferson Davis had been sworn in as its president. The rebel government had seized Federal installations in those seven states, such as post offices, customs houses, arsenals, and forts. The only two positions in those states that were still in Federal hands were Fort Pickens in Pensacola, Florida, and Fort Sumter in Charleston, South Carolina. Fort Pickens remained in Union hands throughout the Civil War.

Fort Pickens, 1861

Lesson 57 - 1861: Inauguration and Fort Sumter

Lincoln's Inauguration

March 4, 1861, dawned a sunny but blustery day in the nation's capital. President James Buchanan called for Abraham Lincoln at the Willard Hotel. As they rode to the Capitol, Buchanan told the incoming chief executive, "If you are as happy, my dear sir, on entering this house as I am on leaving it and returning home, you are the happiest man in the country."

In his inaugural address, Lincoln restated his position that he had no intention of interfering with slavery where it existed. He also said that the Union was permanent and that secession was wrong. He laid before the South the challenge that if war came, it would be their doing and not his. Lincoln pleaded for Americans to be friends and not enemies. He looked forward to the time when "the better angels of our nature" guided the thoughts of the people.

The Inauguration of Abraham Lincoln, March 4, 1861

Conflict at Fort Sumter

As March wore on, Fort Sumter ran low of supplies while Confederate forces laid siege to it. President Lincoln decided to resupply the 69 men at the fort and notified the South Carolina governor of his intentions. No munitions were included in the shipment.

Divided Loyalties

The division of loyalties in southern states led to some interesting responses to secession. As Tennessee was considering whether to secede, Franklin County on the Alabama border threatened to secede from Tennessee and join Alabama if the Volunteer State did not leave the Union. Even today, Franklin County high school sports teams are called the Rebels.

After Tennessee seceded, Scott County, on the Kentucky border, refused to recognize the action and declared itself to be the Independent State of Scott. No action was taken by either the county or the state to defend or attack this pronouncement, and the county remained part of Tennessee. Scott County was later the home of Howard Baker, elected in 1966 as the first Republican U.S. Senator from Tennessee since Reconstruction. The county government did not formally request readmission to the State of Tennessee until 1986.

The Big South Fork of the Cumberland River, pictured at left, begins in Scott County.

Unit 12 - The Nation Divides

4:30 a.m. on April 12, 1861, and shelled the fort for twenty-six hours. Anderson finally surrendered; the only two fatalities in the fort were two men who were killed when the colors were being lowered. War between the states had begun.

Mobilization and Further Secession

The next day, President Lincoln issued a call for 75,000 volunteers to be raised by state militias. On April 19, he declared a blockade of southern ports. His call to arms led four more states to pull out of the Union over the next few weeks: Virginia, Arkansas, North Carolina, and finally Tennessee in early June. In each state, public opinion was divided. The people who lived in the mountainous areas of these states had few slaves and expressed strong Union sentiment. East Tennessee, for instance, supplied thousands of men for the Union Army during the war. A group of counties in western Virginia refused to recognize the state's secession and were eventually admitted to the Union as West Virginia in 1863.

William Waud, an English architect and illustrator, moved to the United States before the Civil War. He worked for Frank Leslie's Illustrated Newspaper *as a war artist. Above is his drawing of slaves mounting a Confederate cannon for the attack on Fort Sumter.*

Confederate president Jefferson Davis and his cabinet decided not to allow this to happen. General P. G. T. Beauregard, commander of the Confederate siege forces, demanded that the fort surrender. The Union commander, Major Robert Anderson, refused. The Confederates opened fire at

Cannon Inside Fort Sumter

Lesson 57 - 1861: Inauguration and Fort Sumter

The secession of eleven slave states left four slaves states still in the Union: Delaware, Maryland, Kentucky, and Missouri. These are known as border states—those that allowed slavery but did not secede. Delaware never seriously considered secession, but the other three witnessed sharp political battles over the issue. If Maryland had seceded, it would have left the District of Columbia surrounded by Confederate states. Lincoln used every means he could to prevent the secession of Maryland, including suspending the writ of habeas corpus and putting pro-Confederate leaders in jail. Kentucky also remained in the Union, but its people were deeply divided. Opinion in the Bluegrass State moved back and forth as Union and Confederate forces controlled various parts of the state. Missouri Unionists disarmed a Confederate militia in May of 1861 and enabled the state to remain in the Union, although rival groups engaged in skirmishes throughout and even after the war.

American artist Winslow Homer was twenty-five years old in 1861 when he was assigned to illustrate the Civil War for Harper's Weekly *magazine. He painted this image of* Officers at Camp Benton, Maryland, 1861 *twenty years later in 1881.*

Northern artist Frederic Edwin Church painted Our Banner in the Sky *as a response to the attack on Fort Sumter.*

Unit 12 - The Nation Divides

Built in 1835, this home in Montgomery, Alabama, was the executive residence for Jefferson Davis and his family during the first few months of the Civil War. It fell into disrepair after the war, but it is now restored and open as the First White House of the Confederacy. It is furnished with period pieces, including many items owned by President and Mrs. Davis.

There are six things which the Lord hates,
Yes, seven which are an abomination to Him . . .
A false witness who utters lies,
And one who spreads strife among brothers.
Proverbs 6:16, 19

★ Assignments for Lesson 57 ★

American Voices	Read Abraham Lincoln's First Inaugural Address (pages 198-203).
Literature	Continue reading *Co. Aytch*.
Bible	Work on memorizing Isaiah 2:2-4.
Project	Work on your project.
Student Review	Optional: Answer the questions for Lesson 57.

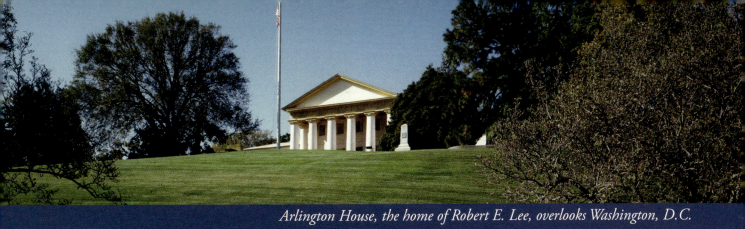

Arlington House, the home of Robert E. Lee, overlooks Washington, D.C.

Lesson 58

North and South

Even a century and a half later, Americans still disagree about the war that began in 1861. It is called by different names: the Civil War and the War Between the States (some diehard southerners refer to it as the War of Northern Aggression or the War for Southern Independence). The two sides used different names for some of the battles. The North referred to battles by nearby bodies of water or other natural features (such as Bull Run Creek and Pittsburgh Landing), while the South used the names of nearby towns (Manassas Junction and Shiloh Church). Opinions differ over whether the root cause of the war was slavery or states' rights. Some Americans are happy to leave the war in the past, while others are still fighting it in their hearts.

Robert E. Lee perhaps best symbolizes the agony of the divided nation. Lee was the son of Revolutionary War hero "Light Horse Harry" Lee, and his wife was a descendant of Martha Custis Washington. Lee graduated second in his class at West Point and served in the U.S. Army with distinction for many years, including during the Mexican War. When fighting erupted, Lee was offered the command of Union forces. He disliked slavery and did not see the good of secession, but he could not bring himself to fight against his home country (meaning Virginia). He resigned his U.S. Army commission, returned to Virginia, and soon accepted the command of the Virginia militia and later of the main Confederate army in the East.

It is no myth that brother fought against brother. Many northern and southern families were divided in their loyalties. First Lady Mary Todd Lincoln had a brother, three half-brothers, and three brothers-in-

Robert E. Lee with His Son William, c. 1845

law who served in the Confederate army. Southern General J. E. B. Stuart fought against his father-in-law. The list of both well-known and obscure families who were thus divided is a long one. About 100,000 southerners joined the Union Army, and many northerners went south to fight with the rebels.

Comparing North and South

Americans of all sections had much in common. The nation was largely Protestant. Most of the free population was descended from British settlers or from western or northern Europeans. They spoke the same language. They shared intangible values such as a commitment to democracy, a pioneer spirit, and faith in and pride in America. At this time in history, however, Americans allowed their differences to outweigh what they had in common. The North and the South were in many ways developing into two different cultures.

At the outbreak of hostilities, the country had 34 states, Kansas having been admitted in January of 1861. Eleven states were in the Confederacy and 23 in the Union. Four of the Union states had slavery. The population of the Union was about twenty-three million compared to about nine million in the South. Of that nine million, about 3.5 million were slaves. The states of Missouri, Kentucky, Maryland, and Delaware had a total of about 500,000 slaves.

Railroad in Georgia

Mary Todd Lincoln

In addition to a greater population (which meant a larger pool of potential fighting men), the North outstripped the South in many other factors. It had much more industry than the South did; it manufactured almost all of the country's firearms and railroad equipment. The North had about 20,000 miles of railroad track compared to 10,000 in the South, most of which had developed in the 1850s. While southern farms were devastated by the war, northern farms continued to produce their crops and even exported some of their production to other countries. The North had a much stronger financial position, with larger banks holding more capital than could be found in the South.

The North could field a larger and better supplied army, although the standing Army at the outbreak of hostilities numbered only about 13,000 men and many of those were at posts in the West. The Union had a superior Navy; in fact, except for a few ships that were captured from the Union, the Confederate Navy was almost non-existent. Still, the North's military advantage was not clear. Its forces were being asked to invade and hold a large area. Union armies had to be supported by long supply and communication lines, which made them extremely vulnerable. The South had several talented military officers, and it had the advantage of fighting a defensive war on its home turf. The southern states left the Union and then said, in effect, "If you want us, you'll have to come and get us." The captive work force of slaves allowed more southern men to serve in the military than if slaves had not been working.

Armies on both sides were largely made up of volunteers, who were usually ill-trained and often ready to go home when their one-year or two-year tour of duty was over. Men were often commissioned as officers because of their social standing, not their military experience. In both North and South, when a military draft was

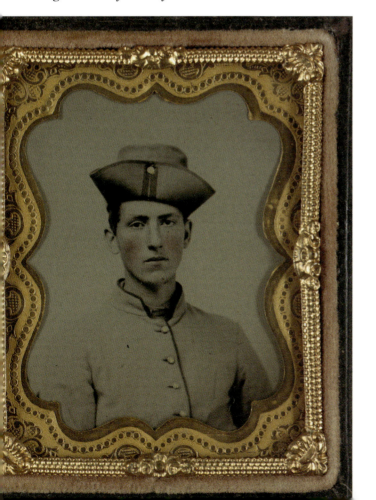

Albert Martin served in the Washington Louisiana Light Artillery Battery.

Corporal Kager Mays, from Kentucky, was a member of the 108th United States Colored Infantry. He died of fever in 1865.

begun it met violent resistance from the populace. A provision in the draft laws allowed for men to avoid service by paying a fee or providing a substitute. This led to the criticism that the conflict was a rich man's war, but a poor man's fight.

The two sides shared one important factor: the war affected everyone. No state, no town, and no family was untouched by the war. Just about every family had a father, son, brother, or uncle who fought. Of fourteen million free males in the country at the time, 2.8 million served in uniform (two million for the Union, the rest for the Confederacy). Just under ten percent of Union forces were African Americans.

An Irrepressible Conflict?

Historians and history buffs have long debated whether the conflict was inevitable. With the advantage of hindsight, it does seem inevitable that the Federal government and the states had to address the issue of slavery directly. The trend of events internationally was toward the abolition of slavery. The British Empire and other countries had abolished slavery a few years earlier without bloodshed.

Meanwhile, the South felt increasingly isolated and defensive. After many years of ignoring the issue, the North eventually became willing to press for some decisive action or legislation. Conflict was already taking place in the United States (such as that in Kansas) with slavery as the leading factor in it. What was needed on both sides was diplomatic skill, a commitment to peace, and a willingness to address the central issues openly and fairly. However, these were sadly lacking as the conflict began.

What is the source of quarrels and conflicts among you?
Is not the source your pleasures that wage war in your members?
James 4:1

★ Assignments for Lesson 58 ★

Literature — Continue reading *Co. Aytch*.

Bible — Work on memorizing Isaiah 2:2-4.

Project — Work on your project.

Student Review — Optional: Answer the questions for Lesson 58.

150th Anniversary Re-enactment of the First Battle of Bull Run (2011)

Lesson 59

Early Battles

Keeping up with all of the military activity of the Civil War and understanding the relative chronology and importance of the battles is challenging. This is especially true if military history is not your favorite part of history. Many books have been written about individual battles or specific armies, but in this curriculum we will not go into much detail on the battles. As you read the story of the conflict, consult the chart on pages 330-331 to keep it all in perspective.

Overall Strategies

The Union utilized a three-pronged military approach against the Confederacy:

1. Defend Washington and attack Richmond, Virginia, which became the Confederate capital later in 1861. Richmond and Washington, D. C., are only about 100 miles apart. The closeness of these two capitals made for dramatic conflict and made control of the two cities an important military objective.

2. Maintain a naval blockade of southern ports. The Union set this up in 1861. Although blockade runners were able to get through, it was generally effective in cutting off southern trade with other countries and in keeping military supplies out of the Confederacy.

3. Divide the Confederacy by its main water routes: the Mississippi, Tennessee, and Cumberland Rivers. All three rivers flow through or next to Tennessee. The first and third aspects of northern strategy are the reasons why Virginia and Tennessee witnessed more battles in the war than any other states.

Union General Winfield Scott proposed the last two aspects of the strategy. It was portrayed in a newspaper cartoon as a large Anaconda snake strangling the Confederacy. As a result, the approach came to be known as the Anaconda strategy. Scott advised against attacking Richmond, but other Union military leaders (as well as Lincoln) favored it, and it became an important part of the North's war effort.

The Confederate strategy was simpler. Rebel leaders wanted to hold the Union to a stalemate that they believed would lead to a favorable turn of events. The South hoped that Britain or France would recognize the Confederacy and enter the war

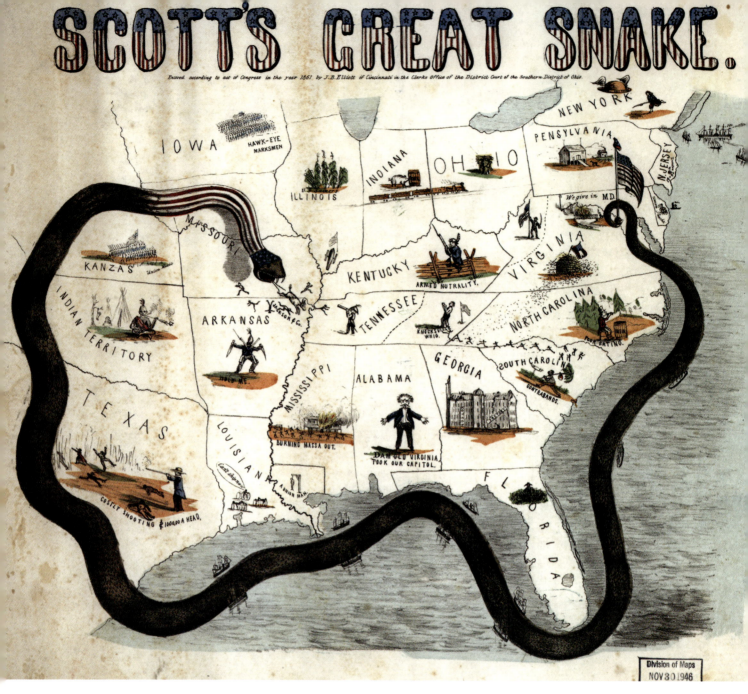

This 1861 illustration of Winfield Scott's strategy was created by J. B. Elliott of Cincinnati.

---

as its ally. Confederates believed that these European countries were so dependent on southern cotton that one or both of them would feel compelled to assist the South. Southerners also hoped that a prolonged war would turn northern public opinion against the conflict and increase pressure in the North for a negotiated peace.

Over the course of the war, heavy fighting occurred in several places across the South. In addition, scores of smaller skirmishes occurred as armies moved across the landscape in pursuit, retreat, or repositioning maneuvers. Every Confederate state, three of the border states (all but Delaware), and five other northern states saw military action. Battles were fought in the eastern theater (generally Virginia) at the same time that other battles were taking place in the western theater (generally Tennessee and along the Mississippi River).

First Battle of Bull Run

The front between North and South stretched hundreds of miles from Virginia across Tennessee and into the area west of the Mississippi. Both

Lesson 59 - Early Battles

sides geared up for war; both sides expected a short conflict resulting in a relatively easy victory; both sides were wrong.

General P. G. T. Beauregard assembled a southern army about 25 miles away from Washington, D.C., at Manassas Junction, Virginia. Lincoln sent Irvin McDowell and 30,000 troops against them in hopes of smashing through all the way to Richmond. Hundreds of civilians rode buggies out from the nation's capital to watch what they expected to be an easy win over the Johnny Rebs. On July 21, 1861, McDowell's army found Beauregard's troops, who had dug in along the small Bull Run creek. McDowell's attack was stopped by Confederate reinforcements. One southern general called his men's attention to Thomas Jackson's unit of Virginians by saying, "Look at Jackson standing there like a stone wall"; and Stonewall Jackson he became.

When the Union attack was stymied, northern soldiers began a disorganized retreat back to Washington. Terrified civilians who had been spectators clogged the roads alongside the

General Stonewall Jackson at the Battle of Bull Run
Henry Alexander Ogden (American, 1900)

This is the reconstructed house of Judith Henry, an eighty-five-year-old widow whose farm became part of the Manassas battlefield. After Confederate sharpshooters took positions in her house, Union artillery fired at the house. Mrs. Henry was mortally wounded by the cannon fire.

discouraged soldiers. The Confederates were jubilant, but they were too disorganized themselves to pursue the Yankees. The battle was a sobering wake-up call to both sides that the war would be longer and costlier than almost anyone had realized.

No other major action took place for the rest of the year, as both sides built up their strength and waited for an opportune time to move. The Union blockade of the southern coast tightened, and Union Admiral David Farragut (who had been born in Tennessee) put New Orleans and the lower Mississippi into Union hands in the spring of 1862.

Early Action in the West

Confederate General Albert Sidney Johnston established a defensive line with some 40,000 troops about 150 miles long across western Kentucky, across the Mississippi River, and into Arkansas. The line was an attempt to protect the western front and especially the three main rivers of the South, which are close together in that region.

In early 1862, General Ulysses S. Grant moved out of Cairo, Illinois, with a flotilla of gunboats. He headed east on the Ohio and then south on the Tennessee River to punch a hole in Johnston's defensive line. Grant first attacked the Confederates' Fort Henry on the Tennessee, and it fell to the Union Army on February 6. Grant then moved his men overland in bitterly cold weather (around 12 degrees at one point) toward the still-unfinished Fort Donelson on the Cumberland River. The Confederate leaders escaped to

Fort Donelson

On March 9, 1862, the Confederate ship Merrimac *(an abandoned Union ship that had been refitted with an iron hull and renamed the* Virginia*) engaged the Union ironclad* Monitor *in Chesapeake Bay. They fought to a draw and both withdrew. The Confederates destroyed the* Merrimac *when they lost control of Norfolk a short time later. The encounter has been called the first modern naval battle. This illustration of the battle is from 1886.*

Lesson 59 - Early Battles

Nashville and left the fort with a lower-ranking officer, who requested terms of surrender from Grant. Grant replied that no terms but "immediate and unconditional surrender" would be accepted. The Confederates bristled. They had no choice but to surrender, however, which they did on February 16.

These twin victories thrilled the North and gave U.S. Grant the nickname of "Unconditional Surrender." They also opened the door for Union forces to advance on Nashville, which they took before the end of the month. Johnston's line was broken, and the Confederate general's forces retreated and regrouped at Corinth, Mississippi.

Suffer hardship with me, as a good soldier of Christ Jesus.
No soldier in active service entangles himself in the affairs of everyday life,
so that he may please the one who enlisted him as a soldier.
2 Timothy 2:3-4

★ Assignments for Lesson 59 ★

Literature — Continue reading *Co. Aytch*.

Bible — Work on memorizing Isaiah 2:2-4.

Project — Work on your project.

Student Review — Optional: Answer the questions for Lesson 59.

Year	Western Theater	Eastern Theater	Political/Social Developments
1860			Nov. 6 – Lincoln elected Dec. 20 – South Carolina secedes
1861		Apr. 12-14 – Confederate shelling and surrender of Fort Sumter Union naval blockade of Southern coast July 21 – First Battle of Bull Run, VA (Confederate victory) Union General McDowell replaced by McClellan	Jan.-Feb. – Mississippi, Florida, Alabama, Georgia, Louisiana, and Texas secede Mar. 4 – Lincoln inaugurated April-June – Virginia, Arkansas, North Carolina, and Tennessee secede Confederate negotiations with Britain and France
1862	Feb. 6, 16 – Ft. Henry and Ft. Donelson in Tennessee fall to Union Apr. 6-7 – Battle of Shiloh, TN (Union victory) May 1 – New Orleans surrenders to Union naval forces led by Farragut May 30 – Corinth, MS, falls to Union Dec. 31-Jan 2, '63 – Battle of Stones River, Murfreesboro, TN (Union victory)	Mar. 9 – Ironclads *Monitor* (Union) and *Merrimac* (Confederate) fight to a draw Mar.-May – Union Peninsular Campaign against Richmond, VA May 31 – Battle of Seven Pines, VA Union General McClellan replaced by Halleck Aug. 30 – Second Battle of Bull Run, VA (Confederate victory) Union General Halleck replaced by McClellan Sept. 17 – Battle of Antietam, MD (Sharpsburg); Confederate forces withdraw to VA; Union General McClellan replaced by Burnside Dec. 13 – Battle of Fredericksburg, VA (Confederate victory) Union General Burnside replaced by Hooker	Feb. 23 – Nashville falls to Union; Andrew Johnson named military governor of Tennessee Apr. 16 – Confederate draft begun – Slavery abolished in D.C. June 19 – Slavery excluded from territories July 11 – Union draft begun Calls in the North for negotiated peace and also for greater war effort Sept. 22 – Lincoln issues Preliminary Emancipation Proclamation

Lesson 59 - Early Battles

Year	Western Theater	Eastern Theater	Political/Social Developments
1863	Grant moves down Mississippi River, takes Jackson, MS; siege of Vicksburg begins May 18 July 4 – Vicksburg falls, Union controls Mississippi River Union takes Chattanooga, TN, presses on to Chickamauga, GA Sept. 19-20 – Confederate victory, Union retreats to Chattanooga Nov. 24 – Union captures Confederate position on Lookout Mountain; Union controls East Tennessee	May 1-5 – Battle of Chancellorsville, VA; Stonewall Jackson mortally wounded; Union General Hooker resigns, replaced by Meade July 1-3 – Battle of Gettysburg, PA (Union victory)	Jan. 1 – Lincoln issues Emancipation Proclamation Nov. 29 – Lincoln's Gettysburg Address
1864	Sherman (Union) and Hood (Confederacy) near Atlanta, GA; Hood evacuates to return to Middle Tenn.; Sherman takes Atlanta Sept. 2 Nov. 15 – Sherman destroys Atlanta Nov. 30 – Battle of Franklin (Union victory) Dec. 15-16 – Battle of Nashville (Union victory); main CSA forces defeated west of Appalachians Dec. 24 – Sherman takes Savannah, GA	Mar. – Grant named Union commander May 5-6 – Battle of the Wilderness, VA June 1-3 – Battle of Cold Harbor, VA	Nov. – Presidential Election, Lincoln/Johnson vs. McClellan/Pendleton
1865	May 10 – Jefferson Davis captured in GA	Feb. 17 – Columbia, SC, falls to Union Apr. 9 – Lee surrenders to Grant at Appomattox Court House, VA Apr. 14 – Ft. Sumter reactivated Apr. 26 – Confederate General Joseph Johnston surrenders at Durham, NC	Mar. 4 – Lincoln's Second Inaugural Congress debates harsh vs. mild reconstruction Apr. 14 – Lincoln assassinated

The Battle of Shiloh, or Pittsburg Landing, 1862

Lesson 60 - Bible Study

War

Since the dawn of human history, few years have passed in which one people has not been fighting against another somewhere in the world. In one of the earliest periods recorded in the Bible, kings in the time of Abraham went to war against each other (Genesis 14). Records of war are common among many ancient peoples. Looking at history from the perspective of faith must include a consideration of the issue of war.

What the Bible Says

On one hand, the Bible speaks against killing and war. One of the Ten Commandments is traditionally translated "Thou shalt not kill" (Exodus 20:13), although more recent translations more accurately render it, "You shall not murder." Isaiah 2:4 looks forward to the day when the nations:

> . . . will hammer their swords into plowshares
> and their spears into pruning hooks.
> Nation will not lift up sword against nation,
> and never again will they learn war.

Jesus told Peter to put his sword away because "all who take up the sword shall perish by the sword" (Matthew 26:52).

On the other hand, God sometimes directed Israel to go into battle. The Lord told Israel to enter Canaan and to destroy the nations that lived there (Joshua 1:5-6, 6:21). One way for the Israelite army to show complete devotion to the Lord was to destroy everything and everybody on the enemy's side. When Saul spared the life of an enemy king, he was disobeying God. Samuel the prophet had to finish the job (1 Samuel 15:9, 32-34). Sometimes

The text of Isaiah 2:4 is found on this wall in a New York City park located near the headquarters of the United Nations. The park is named for Ralph Bunche (1904-1971), the first African American to receive the Nobel Peace Prize. He worked for peace between Israeli and Arab leaders in 1949.

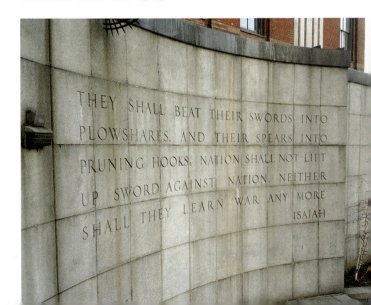

332

the Lord told David to pursue and defeat his enemies (1 Samuel 30:7-8). We can also read the startling passage that praises the one who attacks Babylon and "who seizes and dashes your little ones against the rock" (Psalm 137:9).

Despite this divine call to arms on occasion, in other passages the Lord told the people of Judah not to offer resistance. God said that Judah was going to be conquered by the Babylonians under Nebuchadnezzar and that any resistance to the invaders would be futile disobedience against Him (Jeremiah 27:8). God told Habakkuk that Babylon's destruction of Judah was right and proper (Habakkuk 1:6-12) and that Babylon's subsequent defeat would also be right and proper (Habakkuk 2:4-8).

In the New Testament, Christians are never told to take up arms against their enemies. Instead, Jesus taught His followers to love their enemies, to turn the other cheek when they are attacked, and to pray for those who persecute them (Matthew 5:39-44). Paul counseled obedience to the (pagan) authorities because the government "does not bear the sword for nothing" (Romans 13:4). Revelation describes the fall of Rome, which came at the hands of a conquering army, as a great victory for God over that evil empire (Revelation 18:1-8). It appears, then, that God's preference is for peace, but He sometimes uses war to accomplish His purposes.

Subsequent Perspectives

After the close of the Biblical record, we only have human judgments regarding war and a Christian's participation in war; and these provide a varied testimony. Before Christianity became the state religion of the Roman Empire, it was against the law of Rome for a Christian to be a soldier. To Rome's pagan rulers, Christians were likely to be disloyal to the empire. After Christianity became the

Serving Without Fighting

Desmond T. Doss Sr. was the first conscientious objector to receive the Medal of Honor. Doss was a Seventh Day Adventist who did not believe in killing or using a gun, but he wanted to serve his country. During World War II, Doss rejected a deferment from service as a conscientious objector. He preferred to call himself a conscientious cooperator and volunteered to join the Army. Doss was assigned to serve with the medical corps in the infantry.

Although he was often harassed and ridiculed for his beliefs, Doss was always willing to rescue his wounded fellow soldiers despite the risks he faced. On one occasion, Doss rescued about 75 wounded soldiers on Okinawa, carrying them one-by-one under enemy fire over difficult terrain. His effort took about twelve hours. Doss was awarded the Medal of Honor by President Harry Truman in October of 1945 (see photo at right). Doss died in 2006 at the age of 87.

Two other U.S. Army medics who were conscientious objectors received the Medal of Honor for their service during the Vietnam War. Thomas W. Bennett and Joseph G. LaPointe Jr. were both killed while tending to wounded comrades.

state religion, by contrast, it was illegal for a soldier not to be a professed believer. Rome's Christian leaders believed that Christian soldiers would be the most loyal to what they saw as their holy causes.

Many times in history, kings and other leaders have spoken of "holy wars" (such as the Crusades) or "just wars" (such as the Allied assault on Nazi Germany). This has not been a claim made by just one side in a conflict. In the American Civil War, for instance, both sides claimed that God was on their side.

The harsh reality of war, the various claims made in the name of God during war, and the teachings of Jesus about dealing with conflict raise important questions for Christians today. Does everyone who claims the blessings of God for military undertakings reflect the true thinking of God? Can a Christian serve in the military while claiming allegiance to One who said we should love our enemies and turn the other cheek if attacked?

Toward Some Answers

First, we cannot say with absolute certainty that any of the wars that have been fought since the end of the Biblical record are within God's will. No one

Gettysburg hosted a reunion of Union and Confederate soldiers on the 50th anniversary of the battle there in 1913. More than 50,000 Civil War veterans attended the event. The elderly veterans reenacted Pickett's Charge with the Confederates walking across the fields toward their Union counterparts. Instead of meeting each other with bullets and bayonets, they met with tears and embraces.

Lesson 60 - Bible Study: War

About 1,800 Civil War veterans attended the 75th anniversary of the Battle of Gettysburg in 1938. President Franklin Roosevelt spoke at the dedication of the Eternal Light Peace Memorial.

---

received a divine revelation, for instance, about the Napoleonic Wars, the War of 1812, or the Vietnam War the way that Joshua did about his wars. We can say, however, that wars fought for national pride or for the purpose of aggression and acquisition of land are not in keeping with God's will, except for those which God specifically endorsed in Scripture.

The reality of war is probably best understood as an example of how God patiently endures an element of this sinful world and uses it to accomplish good. God's ultimate will is that we live peaceful and quiet lives because this is the best way for the gospel to be spread (1 Timothy 2:1-4). In our fallen world, however, individuals and nations fight each other. War is never good; but sometimes war counters a greater evil, such as Nazi Germany or international terrorism. Perhaps this is a fair way to apply Paul's words about how the state does not bear the sword for nothing (Romans 13:4). Even this, however, is not a perfect guide. Good and evil are sometimes hard to discern in war. How, for instance, should we view the NATO bombing attack in 1999 on Yugoslavia for their policies against Kosovo? Was that a just war against a greater evil that needed to be stopped, or was it a political move designed to make certain world leaders look impressive?

Second, since the New Testament does not specifically address what a Christian should do about participation in war, it is a matter that is best left to the individual conscience. Many faithful and dedicated Christians have served in the armed forces. Much good can come from such difficult events. For instance, the experiences of many soldiers who served in foreign lands during World War II led to a growth of missionary outreach from America to other countries following the war.

On the other hand, many faithful and dedicated Christians have declared themselves to be conscientious objectors, refusing to fight on the grounds of their religious beliefs. We should not look

Unit 12 - The Nation Divides

with disdain at those who disagree with our own view. That would violate Jesus' clear teaching about love and Paul's clear teaching about acceptance of those within the faith with whom we differ (John 13:34-35, Romans 14:1-4).

Finally, everything does not have to fit within the boundaries of our reasoning ability. War is indeed terrible. Its cost in lives and resources is enormous. Good has come from war, however, as evils greater than the cost of war have been checked. As we seek to live within His kingdom while we live among earthly and sometimes warring kingdoms, we must maintain the eye of faith to believe in and to stand for that which we cannot see (2 Corinthians 4:18, Hebrews 11:1).

The Peace Monument, erected in 1877 in Washington, D.C., honors the U.S. sailors who died during the Civil War. The statue shows Grief weeping on the shoulder of History.

*Blessed are the peacemakers,
for they shall be called sons of God.
Matthew 5:9*

★ Assignments for Lesson 60 ★

Literature — Continue reading *Co. Aytch*.

Bible — Recite or write Isaiah 2:2-4 from memory.

Project — Complete your project for the unit.

Student Review — Optional: Answer the questions for Lesson 60 and take the quiz for Unit 12.

McLean House, Site of Lee's Surrender, Appomattox Courthouse, Virginia

13 The Terrible Conflict

The War Between the States consumed all of America. Early successes by the Confederacy were not enough to counter Union victories in the West and later in the East. Lee's surrender to Grant in April of 1865 brought almost all fighting to an end, but recovering from the effects of the war would take many years. Lincoln's assassination cast a pall on the country and changed the political tone in Washington. As is always the case in times of difficulty, opportunities arose on the front lines for faith to shine.

Lesson 61 - 1862
Lesson 62 - 1863
Lesson 63 - 1864-1865
Lesson 64 - Costs of the Conflict
Lesson 65 - Bible Study: Faith on the Front Lines

Memory Work Memorize Ephesians 6:10-13 by the end of this unit.

Books Used The Bible
American Voices
Co. Aytch

Project (choose one)

1) Write 300 to 500 words on one of the following topics:

  • Write about the importance of leadership. Choose a particular leader you admire and use him or her as an example of the qualities you want to emphasize.

  • Write a letter home as though you were a soldier in the Civil War. Tell about your thoughts, feelings, and experiences.

2) Write and illustrate a book about the Civil War geared for the early elementary level. Think about how to deal with such difficult issues as slavery, war, and violence with a young audience. Conclude your book on a hopeful note. Your book should be a minimum of fifteen pages.

3) Take a field trip to a site related to the Civil War or to the era. Perhaps you can find a house or church built during the 1860s, a museum of artifacts, or a site related to a famous person who was involved in the Civil War. If you are not able to visit a site in person, choose a Civil War battlefield site that interests you and research it. Whether you visit in person or conduct research, make a tri-fold brochure about the site with a description, illustrations or photographs, and details for visiting.

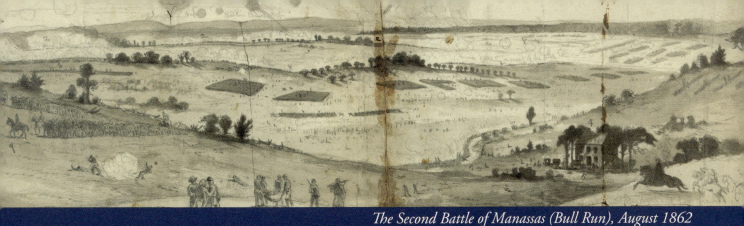

The Second Battle of Manassas (Bull Run), August 1862

Lesson 61

1862

Early 1862, Eastern Theater

The close proximity of the two capitals (Washington and Richmond) made the Virginia landscape between them the scene of intense fighting for almost the entire war. After the Union loss at Bull Run in July of 1861, President Lincoln replaced Irvin McDowell with General George McClellan as the commander of the Union Army of the Potomac. McClellan enjoyed the intense loyalty of his troops, but he was indecisive in battle. He did not want to fight unless he was absolutely sure of victory. McClellan spent the rest of 1861 and the first part of 1862 training his army and looking for a confrontation with the Rebels that would give him a sure thing.

McClellan eventually devised a plan to move his troops by ship from near Washington to the Virginia coast east of Richmond. Since he did not move overland, his supply lines were not subject to interruption by Confederate raiders. The Union forces landed on a peninsula between the James and York Rivers and headed for Richmond. However, Lincoln insisted that part of McClellan's army remain behind to defend Washington. This made McClellan uncertain of victory, so he did not move forcefully against the Confederates. As a result, the engagements during the Peninsular Campaign of March through May were indecisive.

General Robert E. Lee, commander of the Confederate Army of Northern Virginia, sent Thomas "Stonewall" Jackson up the Shenandoah Valley to threaten Washington. This pinned a large Union force in a defensive position near the capital. Jackson then quickly returned south and rejoined Lee, and the Confederates attacked McClellan's troops in the Seven Days' Battle of June 25 to July 1, 1862. The Union forces fought well, but McClellan eventually lost his nerve and retreated. Lincoln replaced McClellan with Henry Halleck as general-in-chief and placed most of the troops under the command of John Pope. The arrogant McClellan despised Lincoln, referring to him as a "well-intentioned baboon." McClellan sometimes lectured the President on military strategy.

Early 1862, Western Theater

While Union forces struggled in the East, they enjoyed greater success in the West. The strategic location of Tennessee, with its proximity to major rivers and railroad centers, made it the scene of frequent heavy fighting. Grant's successes at Fort Henry and Fort Donelson enabled the Union armies to invade Tennessee and begin movements further

339

The Battle of Shiloh took its name from the Shiloh Meeting House, a Methodist church built around 1853. A new church, built in 1949, stands on the original site. This reconstructed log church was built in 2001. Volunteers at the Shiloh National Military Park observed the 150th anniversary of the battle by placing thousands of luminaria to represent the killed and wounded soldiers of both sides.

south. Having gained control of Nashville and the lower sections of the Tennessee and Cumberland Rivers in western Tennessee and Kentucky, the attention of the Union forces turned to the major railroad centers of Corinth, Mississippi, and Chattanooga, Tennessee. If the Union controlled these two cities, it would seriously disrupt Confederate troop and supply movements across the South. Grant moved his army from Fort Donelson overland back to the Tennessee River and headed south toward Corinth.

As Grant's army moved sluggishly along, a Confederate army under Albert Sidney Johnston attacked Grant on April 6 near Shiloh Church in southern Tennessee, a few miles north of Corinth. The fighting was fierce, and Grant's forces appeared to be headed for defeat. However, Union reinforcements commanded by General William Tecumseh Sherman arrived overnight and rallied the Union force to victory. Johnston was mortally wounded and died on the battlefield. The discouraged Confederate forces retreated to Corinth, but the Union army was too weakened to pursue.

The fighting at Shiloh was devastating for both sides. The number of killed and wounded men totaled almost 20,000, more than the American losses in the Revolutionary War, the War of 1812, and the Mexican War combined. That such loss of life could occur in two days of fighting was another sobering reminder to the entire nation that the war was far costlier than anyone had imagined. Grant had blundered by leaving his troops vulnerable to attack on the first day, and he was removed from command by General Halleck.

Union troops eventually regrouped and moved on Corinth, taking the town on May 30. As the Union army approached, Confederate forces in and around Corinth commanded by P. G. T. Beauregard escaped south to Tupelo. Union General Don Carlos Buell, who had been stationed in Nashville and who had been involved at Shiloh, returned to Nashville with the forces under his command. Confederate troops under Braxton Bragg moved east toward Chattanooga to defend that rail center.

The news that New Orleans fell to Union naval forces on May 1 was another blow to the Confederacy. Additional Union forces moved southward down the Mississippi River to sever completely the western part of the Confederacy from the eastern. Memphis,

This 1862 illustration from Harper's Weekly *shows "the starving people of New Orleans fed by the United States military authorities."*

Lincoln visited McClellan after the battle of Antietam. According to legend, the indecisive McClellan once telegraphed Lincoln, "Have captured two cows. Please advise." Lincoln replied, "Milk 'em, George."

Tennessee, fell to the Union on June 6, 1862. At that point, the South maintained control of the river only along the Mississippi state border. Northern forces advanced from both north and south to complete the severing operation.

Late 1862, Eastern Theater

In Virginia the Union tried another assault on Richmond from the north. Confederate forces led by Lee and Jackson engaged the Union armies on August 30 at Bull Run Creek, or Manassas Junction, at almost the same site as the battle that had taken place the previous year. The Confederate armies once again decisively defeated the Union, and the Union armies withdrew to a position outside of Washington. Lincoln gave the command back to George McClellan. McClellan wrote to his wife, "Again I have been called upon to save the country."

Lee resolved to invade the Union. He hoped to gain a decisive victory which might lead to recognition of the Confederacy by a foreign country. Lee invaded Maryland and planned to proceed to Pennsylvania. McClellan attacked Lee's forces on September 17 and seemed headed for victory, but Confederate reinforcements arrived to stem the Union tide. McClellan backed off, which allowed Lee to return to Virginia. Lincoln was furious at McClellan for the general's failure to press for a decisive victory. The President wrote McClellan, "If you don't want to use the Army, I should like to borrow it for a while." He removed McClellan and reassigned him to recruiting duty in New Jersey. McClellan never again commanded troops in action. He was replaced by Ambrose Burnside. The one-day toll at Antietam Creek (Sharpsburg) was the highest of any single day during the war. The Confederates suffered 2,700 killed and 10,000 wounded or missing. Union casualties totaled 12,000, including 2,108 killed.

Burnside led an attack on Lee's well-fortified position at Fredericksburg, Virginia, in cold weather on December 13, 1862. Union forces suffered huge losses and Burnside withdrew. The slaughter on that day prompted Lee to remark, "It is well that war is so terrible—we should grow too fond of it." Lincoln replaced Burnside with "Fighting Joe" Hooker.

Late 1862, Western Theater

A Confederate army under Braxton Bragg moved north from Chattanooga, invaded Kentucky, and headed for Louisville in the early fall of 1862. The force was stopped at Perryville, Kentucky, southwest of Lexington, on October 8 by Union forces under Don Carlos Buell who had come out of Nashville.

Antietam National Cemetery was dedicated in 1867 on the fifth anniversary of the battle. It contains 4,776 graves of Union soldiers who died in Maryland. This photograph shows the cemetery about 1890.

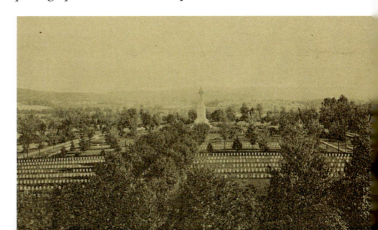

Unit 13 - The Terrible Conflict

Bragg pulled back into Tennessee and returned to Chattanooga, while Buell returned to Nashville.

Lincoln replaced Buell with William Rosecrans, whose army left Nashville and headed southeast for Chattanooga. Bragg moved northwest to meet the advancing Union troops, and the two armies met at the Battle of Stones River, near Murfreesboro, on December 31, 1862. The engagement lasted until January 2, 1863, with the Union side gaining victory. Bragg withdrew to Chattanooga and the Union army continued its advance toward Chattanooga.

Cannon at the Stones River National Battlefield

Prepare plans by consultation,
And make war by wise guidance.
Proverbs 20:18

★ Assignments for Lesson 61 ★

American Voices Read the "Battle Hymn of the Republic" and "Goober Peas" (pages 212-213).

Literature Continue reading *Co. Aytch*. Plan to finish it by the end of this unit.

Bible This week's Bible study looks at how faith was practiced in the midst of the Civil War. In the Bible assignments leading up to Lesson 65, we will consider what the New Testament says about Roman centurions. The centurion has been called the backbone of the Roman Army. His position, as reflected by his title, was that of a commander of one hundred men. With all of the secular influences around him, it was easy for hardened centurions to live a worldly, pagan lifestyle. However, the centurions described in the New Testament showed a remarkable openness to Jesus and the gospel.

Read Luke 7:2-10. List three positive attributes of this centurion.

Start memorizing Ephesians 6:10-13.

Project Choose your project for this unit and start working on it.

Student Review Optional: Answer the questions for Lesson 61.

Detail from The Twentieth Maine, *H. Charles McBarron (American, 20th century)*

Lesson 62

1863

The Emancipation Proclamation

Abraham Lincoln had declared during the 1860 campaign and again in his inaugural address in March of 1861 that he did not believe the President had the authority to do anything about slavery where it then existed. Northern public opinion was divided on the question of emancipation for the slaves. Abolitionists favored immediate freedom, and some of them supported racial integration in society. Others were willing for slavery to exist in the South, but they did not want it to exist in new states or territories. Still others wanted to see slavery ended, but they did not favor social integration.

The issue of what to do about slavery in the midst of war was an even more complicated one. Lincoln said from the first that the war was being fought to preserve the Union and that slavery was a secondary issue; however, the South's captive labor force was one military advantage for them. In addition, runaway slaves (called contraband) showed up in Union army camps, and commanders did not know what to do with them. The slow progress in the war, especially Union defeats in the East, frustrated many northerners who wanted Lincoln to take more decisive action.

In April of 1862, Congress emancipated slaves in Washington, D.C. In June Congress emancipated slaves in U.S. territories. That summer Lincoln decided to move toward complete emancipation. He believed that it would raise sagging Union morale and give the North a moral cause for which to fight. Making the conflict a war about slavery would be more likely to insure that Britain and France would not recognize the South or provide assistance to the Confederacy. However, Lincoln wanted to wait until after a Union victory so that the move would not seem to be made out of desperation.

The battle of Antietam was not a clear-cut Union win, but it was close enough. On September 22, Lincoln issued a preliminary Emancipation Proclamation announcing that all slaves in areas still in rebellion on January 1, 1863, would be "thenceforeward and forever free." Although it was a bold move in many ways, the proclamation was still relatively moderate. States could avoid the impact of the proclamation by ending their rebellion and rejoining the Union by the January 1 deadline, though none did so.

In addition, the proclamation did not apply to southern areas held by Union forces, nor did it apply to northern states where slavery still existed. Maryland and Missouri abolished slavery by state action, but slavery continued in Kentucky and Delaware until

This painting by Henry Louis Stephens shows a man reading about the Emancipation Proclamation in a newspaper.

the war ended. The 13th Amendment that finally abolished slavery throughout the country was not ratified until December of 1865, several months after the conclusion of the conflict.

The Emancipation Proclamation took effect on January 1, 1863. One practical result of emancipation was that black enlistment in the Union Army rose dramatically. Almost 200,000 African Americans served in the Union Army (about ten percent of the total force) and about 38,000 died in the conflict. Some northerners feared that liberated slaves would move north and want to integrate their society. It was the more common experience, however, for the freedmen and their families to move to cities in the South. There they were protected by Union troops. The cities were safer than rural areas, which were plagued by lawlessness.

The northern attitude toward the southern states' relation to the Union was conveniently inconsistent. Article IV, Section 3 of the U.S. Constitution says that no state may be formed within the jurisdiction of another state without approval from Congress and the state's legislature. The creation of West Virginia in June of 1863 was a clear violation of this clause unless Virginia was considered no longer a part of the Union. However, Lincoln's Emancipation Proclamation applied to the southern states that he considered still a part of the Union.

Early 1863

In the West, U.S. Grant, who had been in charge of the Union forces controlling Memphis, moved down the Mississippi River to finish the job of dividing the Confederacy. His target was Vicksburg, Mississippi, which is positioned on a high bluff overlooking the river. Union attempts to dislodge the Confederates from the city failed for several weeks. Grant then decided to change tactics. He went further down river on the west bank, crossed to the east side, and headed toward Vicksburg overland. En route, he captured Jackson, Mississippi; and then Grant's forces headed west toward Vicksburg. He trapped the Confederate forces inside the city and began a siege on May 18. The city eventually fell to Grant on July 4, 1863. This gave the Union control of the entire Mississippi River.

While Vicksburg was under siege, Lee proposed another invasion of the North. He thought this

General Stonewall Jackson was accidentally shot by his own Confederate troops after the first day of the Battle of Chancellorsville (Virginia) in May of 1863. He died a few days later.

The 54th Massachusetts Volunteer Infantry Regiment led the attack against the Confederate Fort Wagner in South Carolina in 1863. Sgt. William Carney carried the U.S. flag to the fort and safely carried it away when the regiment withdrew, even though he was wounded. Carney received the Medal of Honor in 1900. Rick Reeves painted this image of the attack for the National Guard.

might relieve pressure on Vicksburg, give renewed legitimacy to the Confederate cause, and perhaps even end the war. Lee moved north through Maryland and entered south central Pennsylvania. A Union army shadowed Lee, staying between the Confederates and Washington, D.C. Small units on each side came upon one other in the little town of Gettysburg, and the main armies converged there.

The Confederates pushed the Federal troops out of town on July 1, but the Union soldiers regrouped on higher ground to the south. Lee attacked on July 2, but the Federal troops held. The next day, Lee planned an all-out assault on the Union position on Cemetery Ridge. Confederate General George Pickett led his 15,000 men in a charge across open fields toward the Union line. The Federals' fire was accurate and merciless. Only about half of Pickett's men returned from the failed assault. The remnants of Lee's army retreated south on July 4, the very day that Grant took Vicksburg far to the southwest. This double blow made the defeat of the South only a matter of time.

Late 1863

The next major fighting took place once again in Tennessee. Union General Rosecrans continued his push from Stones River in Middle Tennessee southeast toward the major railroad city of Chattanooga. Rosecrans took the city and

Unit 13 - The Terrible Conflict

A delegation of Native American leaders visited Washington, D.C., in 1863.

pursued the Confederates, led by Braxton Bragg, to Chickamauga in northern Georgia. Bragg held firm at Chickamauga, however, and the Federals retreated to Chattanooga. Union reinforcements arrived, led by Joe Hooker, William Sherman, and U.S. Grant, who had been given command of all Union troops in the West.

In late November, the Federal troops broke out of the city and attacked the Confederate position on Lookout Mountain, south of Chattanooga. Union troops scaled the nearly-sheer cliffs and gained control of the mountain. They also took nearby Missionary Ridge. A few days later, a Confederate attempt to retake Knoxville, Tennessee, from Union forces failed. Federal troops thus had control of all of East Tennessee, which was already full of Union sympathizers.

On November 19, 1863, a ceremony was held to dedicate the national cemetery at the Gettysburg battlefield. Edward Everett, one of the best-known orators of the time, delivered a two-hour speech that has been largely forgotten. President Lincoln then presented his address that consisted of ten sentences. What he said has become one of the most famous speeches in the world.

For the Lord your God is the God of gods and the Lord of lords, the great, the mighty, and the awesome God who does not show partiality.
Deuteronomy 10:17

★ Assignments for Lesson 62 ★

American Voices — Read the Emancipation Proclamation (pages 214-215), the Gettysburg Address (page 232), and "The Man Without a Country" by Edward Everett Hale (pages 216-231).

Literature — Continue reading *Co. Aytch*.

Bible — Read Luke 23:44-47. How did this centurion show that he was convicted by the crucifixion of Jesus?

Work on memorizing Ephesians 6:10-13.

Project — Work on your project.

Student Review — Optional: Answer the questions for Lesson 62.

Officers on the USS Mahopac, *1864*

Lesson 63

1864-1865

In U.S. Grant, President Lincoln had finally found a commander who could win. In March of 1864, he named Grant as general-in-chief of Union forces. Grant pursued Lee in Virginia for another year before the Federals were finally able to wear down the Confederate Army of Northern Virginia and for all practical purposes end the conflict.

Lee, meanwhile, was now hampered by a severe shortage of troops. Grant pursued flanking maneuvers to the west, forcing Lee also to move west and extend his thin line of soldiers. Lee still had fight, however, and Grant's forces suffered heavy losses in the battles of the Wilderness and Cold Harbor in May and June of 1864. Grant then moved toward Richmond, pinning Lee's forces into a defensive position.

In the West, Union General William Sherman left Chattanooga and headed for Atlanta, another major rail center for the South. Sherman was dogged by troops under Confederate General John B. Hood, but despite a series of battles in northern Georgia, Hood was not able to stop the Union advance. Sherman took Atlanta on September 2, 1864, and destroyed the city on November 15. He then led his troops on a seventy-mile wide path of destruction for 250 miles through Georgia to Savannah. On Christmas Eve, Sherman telegraphed the President that he wished to present the city of Savannah to him as a present.

Meanwhile, the autumn of 1864 brought a presidential election in the Union. Lincoln replaced Hannibal Hamlin with Andrew Johnson of Tennessee as his running mate. Johnson was an East Tennessee Democrat and Unionist who was the only southern Senator to remain in Washington when the southern states seceded. After Union troops took Nashville in early 1862, Lincoln named Johnson as military governor of the state.

The President thought that he might well be defeated in the election because of the large number of northerners who opposed him. Lincoln hoped that having Johnson on the ticket would increase his chances of winning re-election. They ran officially as the National Union ticket rather than as the Republican candidates. Meanwhile, northern Democrats nominated George McClellan on a platform that called for an immediate armistice and a peace conference to end the war.

Sherman's success in Atlanta and David Farragut's taking of Mobile Bay just before the election helped Lincoln's re-election bid. The President received 55% of the popular vote (2.2 million to 1.8 million) and a resounding 212-21 victory in the electoral college.

The Confederates made one last desperate attempt in the West to weaken Union control of

Coins of Lincoln and Johnson were used to promote their 1864 campaign and to commemorate their victory. When Abraham Lincoln and Andrew Johnson were inaugurated on March 4, 1865, Johnson had over-medicated himself with brandy while recovering from an illness and was obviously intoxicated. He delivered an embarrassing and irrational speech. Opponents of the Administration took this as further proof of Lincoln's poor judgment in selecting Johnson.

the region. Confederate General John Hood pulled away from his contest with Sherman in Georgia and swung back into Middle Tennessee. He hoped to continue north and invade Kentucky. However, Hood was defeated in a series of engagements in Middle Tennessee, most notably at Franklin on November 30 and at Nashville on December 15-16. This was the final defeat for Confederate forces between the Appalachians and the Mississippi River.

1865

Sherman moved his troops up the Atlantic coast with the goal of joining Grant in Virginia. On February 17, 1865, Columbia, South Carolina, fell to Union forces. In Virginia Lee held out as long as he could, but Petersburg was taken by Union troops and Richmond was evacuated. On April 9, 1865, Lee met Grant in a farmhouse near the village of Appomattox Court House and surrendered his army. Grant allowed the Confederate troops to keep their sidearms and to take their horses and mules home to help with spring plowing. He ordered the Union troops not to cheer because the southerners were now their countrymen once again. Confederate General Joseph Johnston surrendered in North Carolina later in April. The Confederate government dissolved and its leaders fled. Jefferson Davis was captured in Georgia on May 10.

The Beginning of Reconstruction

Even before the final Confederate surrender, leaders in Washington debated how to readmit southern states into the Union. Lincoln had set forth a plan in 1863 that called for the readmission of a state when a number equal to ten percent of that state's voters in 1860 took an oath of allegiance to the Union and promised to obey laws dealing with emancipation. High ranking Confederate officers and officials of the Confederacy were excluded from

Surrender of General Lee, Currier & Ives (1865)

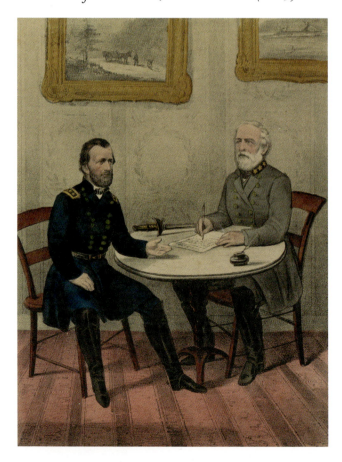

the new state governments. Provisional governments were created under these terms by Unionists in Tennessee, Arkansas, and Louisiana; but Congress refused to recognize them.

The resistance by Congress was a symptom of the growing division in Washington between moderate and radical Republicans. Lincoln believed that Confederate states were simply "out of their proper practical relation with the Union," and he wanted to readmit them with as little disruption and controversy as possible. The President believed that he had the power to oversee reconstruction of state governments under the presidential power to grant pardons.

Radical Republicans in Congress, however, wanted to make southern leaders pay dearly for their rebellion; and northern Radicals wanted to reform southern society so that the planter class was not in control. The Radicals claimed that Congress should guide the reconstruction process because of Congress' power to admit states. The readmission plan put forth by Congress was more stringent than Lincoln's proposal. It required a majority of white males in a state to swear allegiance to the Union, and only those who took an "ironclad" oath that they had always been loyal to the Union could vote or help write the new state constitution. This would severely limit the number of voters who could participate, and they would all be Unionists. A state also had to forbid high-ranking Confederate officers and political leaders from participating in a new government, and it had to repudiate Confederate war debts (Congress did not want investors profiting from the rebellion). This more demanding plan was passed by Congress late in 1864, but Lincoln refused to sign it before Congress adjourned. This use of the pocket veto killed the plan and made Republican leaders in Congress furious at Lincoln.

In April of 1865, Lincoln was hoping that new governments could be formed in the former Confederate states before Congress met in December of that year because he assumed that Congress would again pass a more severe plan.

John Wilkes, Edwin, and Junius Jr. were the American-born sons of British actor Junius Brutus Booth. The three brothers appeared together in Julius Caesar *in New York in 1864. The one-night performance raised money to place a statue of Shakespeare in Central Park.*

April 14, 1865

Federal troops reoccupied Fort Sumter in the Charleston harbor on April 14. The former commander, Robert Anderson, oversaw the raising of the Stars and Stripes. The ceremony brought a sense of completion to the struggle to reunite the nation.

That evening, President and Mrs. Lincoln attended a performance of the play "Our American Cousin" at Ford's Theater in Washington. It was one of the few times that the President had allowed himself time for pleasure during the prosecution of the war. During the play, crazed actor and Confederate sympathizer John Wilkes Booth entered Lincoln's balcony box and shot the

This is the box at Ford's Theatre where President Lincoln was shot.

President in the back of the head with a small pistol. He stepped to the front of the box, shouted, "*Sic Semper Tyrannis*" ("Thus always to tyrants") and jumped to the stage. As he jumped, his spur caught in the bunting on the front of the presidential box. The way Booth landed on the stage caused him to break his ankle. He limped off the stage to a waiting horse. Gradually everyone in the theater realized what had happened.

Booth was part of a plot to attack several leaders of the Federal government in the hopes of giving new life to the Confederate cause. Secretary of State William Seward was stabbed the same night, but he recovered from his wounds. Vice President Johnson was to be another target, but his assassin talked himself out of it over drinks in the lobby of the hotel where Johnson was staying.

The President was taken to a house across the street from the theater. He died the next day without ever regaining consciousness. Booth rode off into the Virginia countryside. He stopped at the home of Dr. Samuel Mudd to have his broken leg set. The assassin was finally trapped in a barn that was set on fire by pursuing Federal troops, and Booth was shot to death on April 26. Some believe that he took his own life. Other members of the conspiracy were arrested and tried. Three were convicted and hanged, along with Mary Surratt, the owner of the boarding house where Booth and others were staying. Dr. Mudd and two others received life sentences. Many years later, Mudd was exonerated of any involvement in the conspiracy.

The nation was in shock at this turn of events. Just as the war was ending, Lincoln was killed by a half-mad Confederate sympathizer. Lincoln's funeral train made a long, slow trip across the country to his final resting place in Springfield, Illinois.

What Else Was Happening?

1860   *The Pony Express begins making runs between St. Joseph, Missouri, and San Francisco, California. Each rider covers about 200 miles per day for ten days, changing horses every ten miles or so. The service does not last long because it is so expensive to use.*

1860   *Linoleum is invented in France as a floor covering.*

1861   *Nationalist fighters led by Giuseppe Garibaldi help bring about a unified Italy.*

1861   *Prince Albert, husband of Britain's Queen Victoria, dies. The queen will remain in mourning for the rest of her life, until she dies in 1901.*

1861   *Czar Nicholas II ends serfdom in Russia, freeing about 40 million serfs (peasants tied to the land owned by nobles).*

1862   *Otto von Bismarck becomes prime minister of Prussia and hopes to unify Germany under his leadership.*

1862   *Louis Pasteur disproves the idea of spontaneous generation of life.*

1863   *Leo Tolstoy finishes the first draft of* War and Peace, *his epic novel about Russia during the Napoleonic War. The final work was published in 1869.*

1863   *Ebenezer Butterick begins production of dress-making patterns. By 1871 six million are sold each year.*

1863   *An underground railroad begins service in London. Steam railroad engines carry passengers along tracks in the world's first subway.*

1864   *British and French workers organize the International Working Men's Association, often called the First International. The ideas of Karl Marx are influential in the group.*

1864   *William Cummings of the Brooklyn Stars throws the first curveball in baseball. Skeptics claim it is an optical illusion.*

1864   *Representatives at an international conference adopt the first Geneva Convention, which deals with the treatment of wounded soldiers on the battlefield. Original signatures and seals from the governmental representatives are shown below. The Convention will be revised in 1904.*

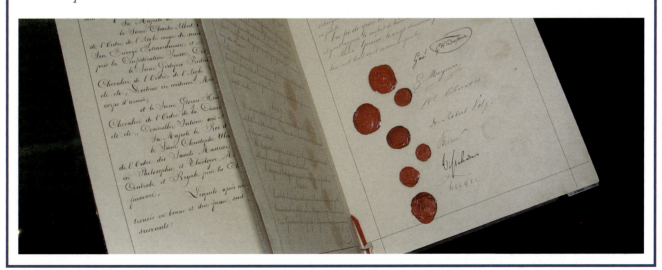

Unit 13 - The Terrible Conflict

In May of 1865, an estimated fifty thousand spectators turned out in Washington, D.C., to watch a Grand Review of the U.S. armies, as seen in this contemporary illustration by E. Sachse & Co., Boston. Some two hundred thousand Union veterans marched from the Capitol to the White House. The parade took several hours over two days.

But you, why do you judge your brother?
Or you again, why do you regard your brother with contempt?
For we will all stand before the judgment seat of God.
Romans 14:10

★ Assignments for Lesson 63 ★

American Voices — Read Abraham Lincoln's Thanksgiving Proclamation and Second Inaugural Address (pages 233-235).

Read "O Captain! My Captain!" by Walt Whitman (page 187).

Literature — Continue reading *Co. Aytch*.

Bible — Read Acts 10:1-48. List three positive attributes of Cornelius.

Work on memorizing Ephesians 6:10-13.

Project — Work on your project.

Student Review — Optional: Answer the questions for Lesson 63.

Andersonville National Cemetery in Georgia, Decorated for Memorial Day

Lesson 64

Costs of the Conflict

The Civil War was not fought by impersonal armies in distant lands. It was fought on American soil by fellow-citizens and brothers, your ancestors and mine. It was not just two armies or even just two governments at war; it involved two societies which were caught up in a military conflict that reflected deeply held but conflicting beliefs and traditions. Both of those two societies were transformed by the realities of war.

Men and Women at War

One out of every twelve American males served in the conflict. A total of almost three million men eventually served in either the Union or Confederate Army. Since military companies were usually organized by localities, the men with whom a soldier fought shoulder to shoulder were often people he knew personally.

The United States had a strong tradition of volunteer military service. Therefore, when both the Federal and Confederate governments resorted to drafting men for service, the actions were met with strong resistance. Many southerners resisted the Confederate draft as an unauthorized action of a central government, which was exactly why they had left the Union.

In the North, New York City endured a week of riots in July of 1863 when the Union draft began. The rioting was mostly carried on by immigrants. Their main target was blacks, whom they thought of as causing the war and whom they saw as potentially taking their jobs if the immigrants had to go into the Army. The rioting caused over one hundred deaths and cost about $2 million in property damage. In the end, the Union draft only supplied about 6% of the North's soldiers.

Fighting that took place west of the Mississippi primarily consisted of small skirmishes, most notably along the Kansas-Missouri border. The Confederate raider William Quantrill led his band of young men against anti-slavery settlements, and anti-slavery Jayhawkers responded in kind. Their fighting was on a small scale, but it was still brutal. Native Americans were also involved in the war. Some tribes fought for the Union, others joined the Confederacy, and still others sought to remain neutral.

Women were involved in the war effort in significant ways. While the men were away, women ran their homes, farms, and plantations. Many women went to work in factories and a large number became schoolteachers.

Mary Edwards Walker worked as a physician for the Union Army. She was captured in 1864 and held as a prisoner of war in Virginia for a few months. In 1865 she became the first and only woman to receive the Medal of Honor. Walker promoted women's rights until her death in 1919.

About 20,000 women worked as nurses or in other health-related positions. They were vital to the work of the U.S. Sanitation Commission, which was charged with caring for wounded soldiers. Two well-known Union health workers were Dorothea Dix, the first Superintendent of Women Nurses, and Clara Barton, who served bravely in field hospitals. Sally Tompkins ran a hospital for Confederate soldiers in a large Richmond, Virginia, home. Her staff tended to over 1,300 wounded men and lost fewer than eighty patients, an unparalleled record of success. When the Confederate government took over the operation of all hospitals, Tompkins was commissioned a captain in the Confederate Army so that she could continue her work. She was the only female officer the South ever had. At her funeral in 1916, she received full military honors.

Still other women served as spies. After Nashville was taken by Union forces, for instance, some women befriended the Union troops and lured military information out of them, which they then passed on to Confederate troops. In addition, an estimated 400 women dressed as men and served as soldiers.

Sam Davis was a Confederate scout captured in 1863 with information about Union troop placements. Davis was sentenced to die. As he stood on the gallows, he was given one last chance to reveal the identity of his informant. He said, "If I had a thousand lives, I would lose them all here before I would betray my friends or the confidence of my informer." Many Union soldiers wept as Davis was hanged at the age of 21. The Davis family home in Smyrna, Tennessee, was opened for tours in 1930.

Northern and Southern Economies

The Civil War brought into conflict two opposing economies: the agrarian economy of the South and the increasingly industrial-based economy of the North. The effect of the war on the two regional economies was profound, though opposite. The southern economy was decimated while the northern economy prospered.

Northern industry was stimulated by wartime production of both military supplies and regular consumer goods. Higher tariffs enacted by Congress gave American manufacturers additional protection from foreign competition. Midwestern farms experienced booming production rates as population growth and Army needs created a larger market.

The southern economy, on the other hand, was devastated. During the war the South had the problem of not enough goods and too much money that was worth little. The Union blockade of the southern coastline interrupted regular commerce. The South's largest cotton customer, Great Britain, found other sources for the fiber. Southern farms and cities were ruined by the fighting. Southerners lost their wealth through war costs, plummeting property values, and the loss of their investment in slaves. Railways in the South were damaged or destroyed. Many southerners who were able to do so (that is, many of the wealthier ones) gave up living in the South and moved to Canada, Mexico, England, or the western U.S. This robbed the South of resources and talent that would have helped the rebuilding process.

Financing the War

Wars cost money: for munitions, food, uniforms, and other expenses. Neither side in the Civil War had the money available to finance their efforts, so they raised it as best they could. The Union tried placing taxes on agricultural and manufactured goods as well as imports, but these did not provide revenue quickly enough. The Federal government then printed more paper money. The notes were called greenbacks because of the color of the ink that was used. This action increased the amount of money in circulation, but it made the money less valuable since the amount of gold backing the greenbacks did not increase. Taxes and the printing of greenbacks provided about two-thirds of the money that the Federal government needed; for the rest, it issued bonds. With bonds, investors loan money to the government for a period of time; and investors receive their money back later with interest.

Private citizens loaned the Confederate government about $100 million, and another $15 million in loans were secured from foreign sources. The Confederacy tried to raise money by imposing taxes, but the collection process was ineffective.

1862 Currency of the Confederate States of America

The Civil War saw many innovations put into use for the first time, such as the repeating Gatling gun (shown above), ironclad ships, and observation balloons.

Only about $100 million was raised through taxes. The southern government tried to impose import tariffs; but few imports made it through the Union blockade, and the revenue thus generated was a tiny amount. Finally the southern government resorted to printing about one billion dollars in paper money. The bills were little more than promissory notes, because they could only be redeemed for gold after a peace treaty was signed between the Union and the Confederacy. By 1865 a Confederate dollar was worth only about 1.6 cents in gold. No peace treaty was ever signed; and after the southern government collapsed, its money was worthless.

Northern and Southern Governments

Behind the battle lines, northern and southern politicians had their own conflicts throughout the war. President Jefferson Davis and Vice President Alexander Stephens were elected to their positions by a convention of delegates representing the seven seceded Confederate states in February of 1861. The Confederate constitution only allowed one six-year term; so the Confederate leaders never had to face the voters.

Davis was rigid and dogmatic in his leadership, and Stephens was a constant critic of Davis' policies. Stephens, however, was not alone. In the 1863 Confederate congressional elections, about one-third of those elected opposed Davis' Administration. The southern government constantly had to battle food shortages and other commodity shortages as well as rampant inflation. Bread riots broke out more than once, and many times women were the demonstrators. Poor transportation compounded the South's problems. Southern rail lines already lagged behind the North, and the war made things even more difficult. At times the tracks for smaller railroads and spur lines were pulled up to use on lines that were in greater demand.

Confederate diplomats were not successful in securing recognition for their government from Great Britain or France. Both of those countries were officially neutral, although the Union did obtain some help with war supplies from Britain. Neither France nor Britain wanted to be seen as supporting slavery. The Confederacy did purchase some ships from Britain and then, in order not to violate Britain's neutrality, outfitted them for war when they were on the high seas.

Partisan politics were not suspended for the war in the North, either. Lincoln was admired by

"The Soldier's Song—Unionism vs. Copperheadism" was published in 1864 against "Home Traitors."

Private William Sargent of Co. E, 53rd Pennsylvania Infantry Regiment, lost both arms at the Battle of Seven Pines, Virginia, in 1862.

many northerners, but not all of them. He was criticized by those who thought he did not do enough and by those who thought he did too much. He was constantly under pressure from Radical Republicans, who wanted quicker emancipation of slaves, the confiscation of southern property, and a more vigorous prosecution of the war.

On the other hand, some northern Democrats pressed for an armistice in the fighting. They were called Peace Democrats and were given the nickname Copperheads because they wore copper coins as symbols of their stance. Since Copperheads were perceived as being sympathetic to the South, Republicans thought of them as dangerous snakes in the grass. Probably the best known Copperhead was Clement Vallandigham, an Ohio Congressman. Vallandigham let it be known that he didn't wish to live under the Lincoln Administration. He was arrested in 1863 and found guilty of obstructing the war effort. Lincoln ordered him deported to the South, but Vallandigham escaped to Canada. He was nominated in exile for governor of Ohio, but he lost the election.

Lincoln invoked martial law during the war and had about 14,000 Confederate sympathizers in the North jailed without bringing formal charges against them (this is called suspending the writ of habeas corpus).

In the fall of 1862, many in the North were tired of what looked like an ineffective war effort. Democrats picked up several seats in Congress, although not enough to give them a majority. Lincoln genuinely feared that he would not be re-elected in 1864. He did, after all, only receive 39% of the vote in 1860. Even with the war going better for the North in late 1864, Lincoln only received 55% of the popular vote.

Some 618,000 men died during the war, the highest number of American casualties of any war in our history. That was about two percent of the population, the equivalent of six million people today. About one soldier in five died during the war—a tremendous loss from that generation.

Cherokee Confederate Reunion in New Orleans, 1903

A Hold on Our Hearts

The Civil War holds a unique place in American history and in American hearts. Historians and novelists continue to churn out books about the war, adding to an already immense library on the subject. A PBS mini-series on the war was widely watched, and the video recordings of the series have been huge sellers. Emotions ran high on both sides in the 1860s; and people continue to have strong ideas on the subject. Even in the 21st century, people in southern states have debated whether symbols from the Confederate flag should appear on state flags and license plates.

The Civil War has this hold on the American mind for several reasons. Both sides believed deeply in the causes for which they fought, and each side believed that their principles were supported by American history and blessed by God. Few elected leaders and few in the population as a whole showed any willingness to compromise on their beliefs. Perhaps above all else, the war was such a huge tragedy for the country, affecting so many people, that its effects have run deep in many ways, including economically, socially, and racially.

U.S. Marines honor Civil War soldiers by placing flags on their graves for Memorial Day in New York in 2012.

For it is better, if God should will it so, that you suffer for doing what is right rather than for doing what is wrong.
1 Peter 3:17

★ Assignments for Lesson 64 ★

Literature — Continue reading *Co. Aytch*.

Bible — Work on memorizing Ephesians 6:10-13.

Project — Work on your project.

Student Review — Optional: Answer the questions for Lesson 64.

P. P. Cooney, Irish Catholic Chaplain of the 35th Indiana Regiment

Lesson 65 - Bible Study

Faith on the Front Lines

World War II chaplain William Thomas Cummings, who died in the Pacific theater in 1944 at the age of 41, is credited with creating the phrase, "There are no atheists in the foxholes." The harsh conditions of war, including the reality of death, lead many of those involved in war to turn to God. At the same time, some soldiers give in to the vices that tempt them during military service. In war you can find men of great faith and men who live as pagans. As with the rest of life, military service has a mixture of all kinds of people.

Leading Examples

Generally speaking the Confederate Army had a more active religious life than the Union forces did. Several Confederate leaders had strong Christian convictions. President Jefferson Davis ordered days of fasting several times during the war. Robert E. Lee was widely respected as a man with strong Christian beliefs. High-ranking officers such as Stonewall Jackson and P. G. T. Beauregard were also known as being deeply devout.

General Leonidas Polk was Episcopal bishop of Louisiana before entering military service. He was called the Fighting Bishop. During the war, General Polk baptized fellow Generals W. J. Hardee, John B. Hood, and Joseph E. Johnston. Braxton Bragg made a confession of faith to a minister serving the Confederate forces. Sometimes the examples of the commanding officers had a positive effect on the men they commanded.

Among the Soldiers

Religious activity among the rank and file soldiers was not widespread at the first of the war. Chaplains were few and not well organized. One successful effort that changed this was the distribution of Bibles, New Testaments, and religious literature. The American Bible Society (based in the North) devoted considerable resources to providing printed materials to southern soldiers. The tracts distributed included examples of Christian faith in wartime (such as the faith of George Washington) and teachings against such sins as swearing, gambling, and drinking.

Prayer meetings and revivals were held regularly where soldiers were camped. As the war progressed, these became more common and generated more responses. Again, these were better attended by Confederate soldiers, perhaps because they were used to attending prayer meetings and revivals in their home towns. As has long been the case, when men

Members of the Young Men's Christian Association (YMCA) formed the United States Christian Commission in 1861 to look after the physical and spiritual welfare of soldiers. USCC workers, called delegates, visited soldiers in camp and after battles to distribute food, medical supplies, and Bibles and religious literature.

know that a battle is looming, many give themselves to serious Bible reading and prayer.

The story was told of a Confederate private being baptized in a Virginia river. As the baptism was taking place, Confederate troops were on one side of the river and Federal soldiers lined the opposite bank. They watched the baptism and sang songs together.

Local ministers sometimes accompanied troops from their community. Some became discouraged at the lack of religious interest and returned home. Many chaplains served sacrificially, receiving low pay, enduring harsh camp life, and circulating among the troops even in battle. Some chaplains lost their lives in the war.

The faith of Abraham Lincoln has been a subject of much discussion and speculation. He did not fit easily into any category within organized Christian churches, but he did attend church services while in Washington. His Second Inaugural Address was filled with quotations from the Bible and ideas about how he thought God might be working through the war. In some ways it was more of a sermon than a political speech.

The Influence of Sin

The evils of life were certainly present among soldiers. Men engaged in all kinds of gambling, including card games, raffles, horse racing, and dice games. An effective revival would sometimes reduce the involvement in such activity, but it never went away. The use of profanity was widespread. Men commonly did not want their wives to visit them in camp because of the foul language they would have to hear. Soldiers were known to plunder farms and houses for anything they could find as spoils of war.

Lesson 65 - Bible Study: Faith on the Front Lines

One Soldier's Story

Sam Watkins, the Confederate soldier who shared his memoirs in *Co. Aytch*, is a good example of faith triumphing over the difficult circumstances of war. He wrote of a friend who was killed during a tornado: "I loved Berry. He was my friend—as true as the needle to the pole. But God, who doeth all things well, took his spirit in the midst of the storm to that beautiful home beyond the skies. I thank God I am no infidel. We shall meet again."

When Watkins' unit came across some wild blackberries, Sam enjoyed the fruit and remembered, "I felt, then, like David in one of his psalms—'The Lord is good, the Lord is good, for his mercy endureth forever.'" One night outside of Atlanta, Watkins was on guard duty. He noticed the pale moon and the twinkling stars. "I thought of God, of heaven, of home, and I thought of Jennie. . . . I had Jennie's picture in my pocket Bible, alongside of a braid of her beautiful hair."

The Religion of the Lost Cause

When the war began, the South believed that they would win because their cause was just and right. When the South lost the war, many in the South did not give up their beliefs; they just adapted

Charles A. Fischer from Kentucky was a chaplain and physician in the Union Army.

their worldview to the new reality. A new idea, which has been called the religion of the lost cause, gained popularity. It compared the experience of the South to the suffering and death of Jesus Christ. Just as Christ died even though He was righteous and good, the South lost even though (in the eyes of many southerners) her principles were righteous and good.

Instead of southern beliefs being vindicated through victory, some saw their ideas as being vindicated through defeat. This idea circulated at the end of the war and resurfaced near the end of the nineteenth century, as Confederate veterans were dying off and many southerners looked back longingly at the civilization they had lost.

Robert Bean Sutton of Virginia was a chaplain in the Confederate Army. The photos below show him during the war and afterward.

Unit 13 - The Terrible Conflict

Charles Todd Quintard was born in Connecticut in 1824. He became a doctor and then an Episcopal priest. During the Civil War, he provided the 1st Tennessee Regiment with medical care and spiritual instruction, as described by Sam Watkins in Co. Aytch. *After the war, he was made a bishop in the Episcopal Church and became a leader at the University of the South in Sewanee, Tennessee. He encouraged service to the poor and opposed segregation in the Church. He died in 1898.*

*Therefore, take up the full armor of God,
so that you will be able to resist in the evil day,
and having done everything, to stand firm.
Ephesians 6:13*

★ Assignments for Lesson 65 ★

Literature — Finish reading *Co. Aytch*. Literary analysis available in *Student Review*.

Bible — Recite or write Ephesians 6:10-13 from memory.

Project — Complete your project for the unit.

Student Review — Optional: Answer the questions for Lesson 65 and for *Co. Aytch* and take the quiz for Unit 13.

A Visit from the Old Mistress, *Winslow Homer (American, 1876)*

14 Reconstruction

Continuing conflicts of opinion brought about the bitter period of Reconstruction after the Civil War. The conflict between congressional leaders and President Andrew Johnson led to Johnson being impeached by the House and having to endure an impeachment trial in the Senate. Despite the all-encompassing nature of the Civil War, other significant events took place during and after the war. An example of reconstruction is found in the Old Testament book of Nehemiah.

Lesson 66 - Off to a Rocky Start
Lesson 67 - Congressional Reconstruction
Lesson 68 - The Impeachment and Trial of Andrew Johnson
Lesson 69 - Life Goes On
Lesson 70 - Bible Study: Nehemiah's Reconstruction

Memory Work Memorize Matthew 5:43-45 by the end of this unit.

Books Used The Bible
American Voices

Project (choose one)

1) Write 300 to 500 words on one of the following topics:

- Research and write about one of the reforms passed by Congress during the Civil War: the Homestead Act, the beginning of land grant colleges, or the National Bank Act. Tell how the reform makes a difference in everyday life for people today. See Lesson 69.

- Describe what you admire in Nehemiah's example of leadership and what lessons you learn from his story that are needed today. See Lesson 70.

2) Make a video "public service announcement" as if made during Reconstruction that encourages forgiveness and cooperation between northerners and southerners or slaves and slave owners, opponents in Congress, other opposing groups that saw conflict, or for the divided country in general. Your video should be at least three minutes long.

3) Make a strategy board game that concerns former slaves building a new life after the Civil War. Think about and incorporate into the game what former slaves needed to make a new start, what challenges they faced, what help was available to them, and their likely interactions with fellow former slaves and others. Choose a goal or goals toward which the game's players are working to "win." Make the events of your game as realistic as possible. Play the game with your family. See Lesson 66.

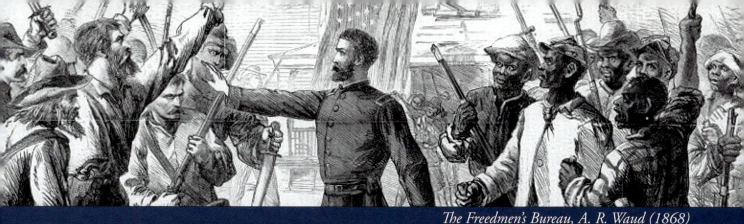

The Freedmen's Bureau, A. R. Waud (1868)

Lesson 66

Off to a Rocky Start

The outcome of the war answered some questions, but then new dilemmas confronted the war-weary nation. America had to find a way to rebuild from the devastation caused by the war. The eleven former Confederate states had ruined economies. They were filled with hundreds of thousands of former Confederate soldiers who had fought against the Union. Almost four million former slaves now had their freedom; but they had no jobs, no land, and no education. Who would govern the southern states? What would be the rights and the roles of former slaves in postwar America? Could whites and blacks live together in harmony?

The economy and society of the northern states were largely intact, but all was not peaceful there either. In addition to the division between Republicans and Democrats, the Republicans were divided between moderates and radicals. Politicians debated what the Federal government's policy should be toward the once-rebellious states. What was the best way for those states to be made fully part of the Union again?

Moreover, whites and blacks did not live together in harmony in the North; many whites did not believe they ever could. Strong racial prejudice existed in the minds of many northerners. As late as 1864, the House of Representatives (with no members from the South present) defeated a proposed constitutional amendment banning slavery. The 13th Amendment that did outlaw slavery finally passed Congress and was sent to the states for ratification in January of 1865. The war settled the question of slavery, but it had not eradicated racism and prejudice from American society.

New Life for Former Slaves

To help former slaves with their transition into new lives of freedom Congress created the Freedmen's Bureau in March of 1865 as an agency of the War Department (former slaves were called freedmen). The bureau was charged with helping former slaves get basic provisions, such as food, clothing, shelter, and medical supplies. It also oversaw abandoned and confiscated southern land and gave it to freedmen.

In addition, the bureau set up schools for former slaves to attend. Public schools were not common as yet, and black children would not have been allowed to attend with whites anyway. Many in the South had frowned on educating slaves before the war, fearing that they would develop a desire to rebel against the slaveowning system. In building the schools, the Bureau worked with several Christian mission agencies that were also helping former slaves. The Freedmen's Bureau accomplished a great deal of good, but its success was limited because it faced a huge job with insufficient funds while having to deal with opposition from white southerners and inconsistent support from northerners and Congress.

Another way that blacks were helped was by the military service that thousands of former slaves gave during the war. Many learned to read and write while in the Army. They learned skills that helped them after the war. Those who became officers learned about filling leadership roles. They also developed a strong sense of nationalism that helped them to be loyal to the country despite the treatment they had received before being freed.

Since blacks were segregated from white society, they created their own society. One of the first and most common moves was to establish black churches. There they gained an important sense of identity as people loved by God whether or not those around them cared about them. Black men also served in roles of leadership in the churches that gave them experience in carrying out responsibilities to others. One of the deficiencies of the slave system was that it created a dependency among blacks. Slaves had known that, however talented, hardworking, or intelligent they were, they would always be subservient to whites. In their new roles, blacks learned how to be responsible leaders. Blacks also began fraternal organizations and other groups in which they had meetings and took on service projects. Slave families that had been separated during the time of slavery were reunited. New homes were begun now that marriage between former slaves was legal and expected. As blacks were given the right to vote, they learned how to be involved in the political process.

Defining Ways People Mistreat Others

Four common terms used in describing race relations are prejudice, racism, discrimination, and segregation.

- *Prejudice is having preconceived ideas about certain people or groups—such as blacks, women, or southerners—that are not based on evidence.*

- *Racism, strictly defined, is using the power of official governmental policy against certain people based on their race; for example, forbidding black people from voting or forcing Japanese-Americans to live in detention camps.*

Clinic in Mississippi with Entrance "For Colored" (c. 1966)

- *Discrimination is the policy of treating races differently, such as not allowing blacks to use the same public facilities as whites.*

- *Segregation is keeping different races separate. An example of legal segregation was not allowing whites and blacks to attend the same school. An example of social segregation was the informal practice of not allowing blacks to live in white neighborhoods. Such social segregation was a practice that might not have been based on law but was enforced by social pressure.*

Sharecropping

Former slaves now faced the necessity of providing for their families. In doing so they had to deal with several important issues. If the men simply went to work for someone else, they could become victims of their employers' pay scales, demands for overtime, and decisions to fire them. Because jobs offered to blacks paid so little, every family member who could hold a job usually would have to work, which could weaken family structure. Because of these pressures, and because of the economic pressures of the South, many former slaves became sharecroppers. A sharecropper family lived on the land owned by someone else, worked in the owner's fields, and received a share of the crop as pay. Sharecropping had the advantages of keeping a family together, allowing the wife to stay at home, and giving the family some control over their lives. The disadvantage was that they were still largely dependent on others for their material well-being. Sharecroppers were often in debt. They bought their necessities during the year on credit, anticipating the value of the crop share they received once a year. If that share was less than anticipated, they started the next year still in debt. Tenant farmers, by contrast, were usually a little better off than sharecroppers.

Officials met with Freedmen in their church at the Trent River Settlement in North Carolina in 1866.

Former slaves Joseph and Mary Province received this marriage certificate in 1866. They had lived together as husband and wife for twenty-one years, but did not as slaves have legal recognition of their marriage.

Tenants often owned their own equipment and were able to rent land from an owner.

Progress was difficult for the freedmen. As the former Confederate states re-established their governments in 1865, whites were still in control. One issue the new state governments addressed was regulating the lives of the former slaves. Before the war, slave states had laws called slave codes, which regulated what slaves could and could not do and how they could be treated. Now, states passed black codes, which were laws regulating what blacks could and could not do. Some improvements were made, such as the right to own property and testify in court. However, blacks still could not vote, own guns, assemble without whites present, travel without a pass, or marry a non-black. In South Carolina, blacks were not permitted to own city property; in Mississippi, they could not own rural property.

Lincoln/Johnson Reconstruction, 1865

The process of readmitting the former Confederate states to the Union was called Reconstruction. This referred to the process of reconstructing the Union and reconstructing state governments in states that had seceded. Two crucial issues in the national debate over Reconstruction were how to do it and who was to oversee it. One factor in making these decisions was determining the nature of the war.

President Lincoln believed that the rebellion was carried out by individuals, not states. To him the Union could not be dissolved. Because of the actions of individuals, the Confederate states were simply out of their proper relation to the Union and needed to be restored quickly. Lincoln believed that the President should oversee reconstruction because of the constitutional power the President has of granting pardons to individuals. He proposed a relatively mild plan for bringing the states back into the Union. When Andrew Johnson became President, he supported Lincoln's ideas with only a few minor changes. Johnson required that a state repudiate secession and any Confederate war debt and also ratify the 13th Amendment. Those in Congress who backed this plan were called moderate Republicans.

This 1865 cartoon mocked the Lincoln-Johnson plan to restore the Union. Johnson had worked as a tailor, and Lincoln was known as "The Rail Splitter" because of his frontier background.

THE "RAIL SPLITTER" AT WORK REPAIRING THE UNION.

Lesson 66 - Off to a Rocky Start

Radical Republican Ideas

However, many Republicans in Congress had a different view. They sharply opposed Lincoln and Johnson even though they were of the same political party (before the war, the Democrats had divided; now it was the Republicans' turn to divide). Those who wanted to lay down harsh terms for the readmission of former Confederate states were called Radical Republicans. The Radical plan was also outlined in Lesson 63.

Charles Sumner, Republican leader in the Senate (and once the victim of Preston Brooks' cane) said that the Confederate states had committed "state suicide" and now had the status of unorganized territories. This put them under the authority of Congress. House Republican leader Thaddeus Stevens went even further. He considered the Confederate states to be conquered provinces, without even the rights of territories. The effect of Stevens' view was the same as that of Sumner, since Stevens believed Congress should oversee Reconstruction. The theories of Sumner and Stevens supported what they wanted to do anyway, which was to control the readmission of southern states and to keep the process out of the hands of the President.

Congress, however, was not in session during the summer and fall of 1865. All of the former Confederate states except Texas reorganized themselves under the milder terms of the Johnson Administration, and the President readmitted them to the Union. During the year, Johnson granted over 13,000 pardons to former Confederates who took the required loyalty oath. The 13th Amendment outlawing slavery was ratified by enough states for it to become part of the Constitution by December of 1865.

Confrontation in Congress

The new session of Congress convened in December of 1865. This was the first session for Congressmen and Senators from the North who had

Thaddeus Stevens (1792-1868)

been elected in the fall of 1864 and for members from the former Confederate states who had been elected after the war had ended in April of 1865. When the delegations from the former Confederate states presented themselves, they included former Confederate vice president Alexander Stephens, four former Confederate generals, five former Confederate colonels, six former Confederate cabinet officers, and fifty-eight men who had served in the Confederate Congress.

The Radical Republican leaders of Congress refused to accept the credentials of any southern state's delegation and did not allow them to be seated. When Congress investigated what had gone on in the southern states since the end of the war, they found that the southern states had enacted black codes, had put many former Confederates in positions of leadership, and were under the control of the Democratic Party. In political terms, the Radicals feared that Democrats (northern and southern) might combine with moderate Republicans in Congress to lower tariffs and to repeal other actions

Unit 14 - Reconstruction

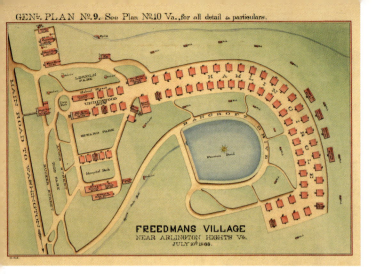

During the Civil War, many escaped slaves sought refuge in Washington, D.C. The government established Freedman's Village in nearby Virginia. The community eventually had over 1,000 residents living in dozens of two-story duplex houses. They had two churches, a school, a meeting hall, a hospital, and a home for the infirm and aged. Intended to be temporary, the community continued to exist until the 1890s.

that had taken place under Radical rule. The Radicals wanted to change southern society, but they didn't see much that had changed. The Radicals wanted to restrict the political power of former Confederates, and they wanted to see that blacks were given the right to vote. Some Radicals wanted these changes out of principle, but many Radicals simply believed that these actions would make it more likely that Republicans would be elected to office in the South.

Congress has the right to pass judgment on the credentials of those elected to it. In exercising this right to refuse the southern congressional delegations, the Radical Republicans in Congress made a statement about their desire to control Reconstruction. They thus began a confrontation with President Johnson that continued for the remainder of his term.

*Be kind to one another, tender-hearted, forgiving each other,
just as God in Christ also has forgiven you.
Ephesians 4:32*

★ Assignments for Lesson 66 ★

Bible As we study Reconstruction after the Civil War in this unit, you will read the Old Testament book of Nehemiah in preparation for Lesson 70. Concentrate on what Nehemiah did to lead the reconstruction of Jerusalem. Read Nehemiah 1-4 today.

Start memorizing Matthew 5:43-45.

Project Choose your project for this unit and start working on it.

Student Review Optional: Answer the questions for Lesson 66.

Proposed 14th Amendment to the Constitution in the Records of the U.S. House, 1866

Lesson 67

Congressional Reconstruction

The Radical Republican-led Congress began to assert itself in December of 1865 when it refused to seat the men elected in the former Confederate states. It continued to take Reconstruction into its own hands in 1866. During that year, Congress passed two important bills that gave former slaves more legal rights. One measure expanded the powers of the Freedmen's Bureau by allowing it to prosecute in military courts (as opposed to civil courts) anyone accused of denying a former slave his civil rights. Johnson vetoed the bill as a violation of the due process clause of the Fifth Amendment, but Congress passed it over the veto. The second measure, called the Civil Rights Bill, was designed to give blacks full rights of citizenship. Johnson vetoed this bill on the grounds that it was an unconstitutional invasion of states' rights, but again Congress overrode his veto.

The 14th Amendment

Congress also created the Joint Committee on Reconstruction. The Committee was made up of Senators and members of the House, but it was dominated by Congressman Thaddeus Stevens. The Joint Committee was charged with developing a plan for readmitting the former Confederate states.

The Joint Committee drew up a proposed constitutional amendment which, when modified by Congress, was submitted to the states. The amendment served as the foundation for Radical Republican Reconstruction. It embodied many of the provisions of the Civil Rights Bill; as part of the Constitution it could not be vetoed by the President or changed by later congressional action.

The 14th Amendment has five clauses:

1. The amendment grants citizenship to all those born or naturalized in the United States. It says that no state can abridge the rights of any citizen or deny a citizen due process of law or equal protection under the law. This was an attempt to prevent states from limiting the rights of any of its citizens, including former slaves.

2. The three-fifths clause of the Constitution was repealed. The amendment said that congressional representation would be based on the total population of a state. If a state denied the right to vote in Federal elections to any male 21 or older, other than those persons having participated in a rebellion or other crime, that state's representation would be reduced proportionally. For example, if twenty percent of a state's adult

male population were not allowed to vote, that state would lose twenty percent of its representation in the House. This clause was intended to guarantee that blacks could vote.

3. The amendment forbade anyone from holding any state or Federal office who had served in the Federal government or in a state government and then participated in the rebellion. This section was intended to take most former Confederate officials out of the political process.

4. The fourth clause declared Confederate debts null and void. Congress did not want to be obligated to repay debts incurred by the Confederacy, nor did it want any investors to profit from the rebellion.

5. Congress was empowered to enforce the amendment with appropriate legislation. Basically this provision gave Congress a blank check to pass whatever laws it considered to be needed.

Tennessee, whose government was in the hands of Radical Republicans, ratified the 14th Amendment in July of 1866 and was readmitted to the Union. All of the other former Confederate states, however, rejected the amendment overwhelmingly. This brought Reconstruction to a halt as Congress considered what to do next.

Freedmen Voting in New Orleans, 1867

1866 Congressional Election

As congressional mid-term elections approached in the fall of 1866, people wondered whether the Radicals could maintain control of Congress. Some Radical Republicans feared that a combination of moderate Republicans and Democrats might be elected that would thwart the Radical program. The Radicals were helped, however, by three factors. First, race riots broke out in Memphis and New Orleans. In those cities, when problems arose in black sections, white mobs and policemen cruelly and indiscriminately attacked blacks. This made many northerners fear what might happen if the Radical program to restructure the South were abandoned.

Second, President Johnson went on a speaking tour across the Midwest in the late summer attacking the Radicals. When he was heckled by some listeners, Johnson got into an angry shouting match with them. This caused him to lose respect with many voters. Third, the memory of the war was still too fresh for people to ignore. They believed that the issues that caused the war had to be addressed and that the Union had to be re-established on a firm foundation.

In the election, the Radical Republicans gained strength in both houses of Congress. In fact, they had more than a two-thirds majority in each house. This meant that, if all of the Radicals voted together, they could override any veto that Johnson might issue on legislation passed by Congress.

Congressional Reconstruction Begins

Even before the new representatives took their seats, the Radicals began implementing their program. In March of 1867, Congress passed and then overrode Johnson's vetoes on a number of laws that further defined the Radical plan for Reconstruction.

"The Misses Cooke's school room, Freedman's Bureau, Richmond, Va." (1866)

First, the Military Reconstruction Act divided the ten remaining former Confederate states into five military districts, each overseen by a military governor with troops stationed there to maintain order and to protect the rights of blacks while states rewrote their constitutions. Second, Congress took away the right to vote from former Confederate officials and gave freedmen the right to vote and hold office. Third, Congress required that the states' new constitutions guarantee all adult males, including blacks, the right to vote. Fourth, Congress required that each state ratify the 14th Amendment. Seven of the southern states submitted to these requirements and were readmitted by the summer of 1868. Texas, Mississippi, and Virginia were readmitted in 1870.

It was during the period of 1867-1868 that Republicans came into power in the southern states. This happened primarily because former Confederates were excluded from government and newly-enfranchised blacks overwhelmingly voted for the party they credited with giving them their freedom. White southern Democrats saw two kinds of people as being mainly responsible for stealing their political power. Southern whites called these people carpetbaggers and scalawags.

Carpetbaggers were northerners who supposedly packed their carpetbags (a common form of luggage) and came south. Some of these were political opportunists who obtained government positions by going along with those in power. Other northerners, however, came south to teach school and to render other legitimate service. The second group that infuriated white southern Democrats were called scalawags. These were southerners who cooperated with the Republicans and who were seen by southern Democrats as traitors to the South. Many of those called scalawags had been opposed to secession.

This was also the time when many blacks were elected to office for the first time. Six hundred state legislators, fourteen members of the U.S. House of Representatives, and two U.S. Senators (elected by state legislatures) were African American. No blacks were elected governor, but the black lieutenant-governor of Louisiana served as acting governor while the governor was under indictment. Resentful southerners called this period Black Reconstruction, even though the most powerful positions were predominantly held by white Republicans. Although blacks made some social and economic gains during this period, no serious effort was made to end racial segregation anywhere in American society.

The first black U.S. Senator elected by popular vote was Republican Edward Brooke of Massachusetts, who was elected in 1966. Shown below with President Lyndon Johnson, he was the first African American to serve in the Senate after the Reconstruction period. Democrat Douglas Wilder, elected governor of Virginia in 1990, was the first black governor of any state.

Problems in the South

During Reconstruction considerable corruption existed in southern state governments, although it was present in northern states as well. For instance, some government officials pocketed money from the sale of state government bonds which were sold to finance rebuilding projects. Money that was donated to a fund to buy homesteads for black families was stolen by the fund's organizers. Not every official was corrupt, but the states saw plenty of people taking advantage of the system for personal gain.

Extremist white southerners began reacting to their loss of power and to the increasing number of blacks in positions of authority. In addition, although the actual number of Federal troops was relatively small (1,000 in Virginia, 700 in Mississippi, for instance), their presence was a bitter pill for unreconstructed southerners to swallow. This resentment lasted for many years after Reconstruction came to an end, and some southerners carry the resentment even today. Some southern whites became hostile to the changing social arrangement and the increased role of blacks. Several localities across the South saw violence and threats of violence against white Republicans and against blacks. Victims were subjected to whippings, nighttime acts of terror, and lynchings.

In 1866 in Pulaski, Tennessee, the Ku Klux Klan was organized ostensibly as a social club to preserve traditional white southern society. (The name "Ku Klux" came from the Greek word for circle, *kyklos*.) However, it soon began to take part in acts of violence and intimidation to scare blacks away from voting. Congress eventually passed laws to break the Klan's power, and President Grant executed those laws forcefully in 1871. The Klan lost power for many years, but it gained renewed strength in the twentieth century. Former Confederate General Nathan Bedford Forrest took part in organizing the Klan, but he withdrew when it became violent.

Congress was exerting its power over the southern states in Reconstruction, but congressional leaders also wanted to limit the power of the President. Their attempts to do so led to the confrontation with President Johnson that brought about the first impeachment trial of a United States President.

This Ku Klux Klan disguise was displayed at the National Underground Railroad Freedom Center in Cincinnati, Ohio.

George W. Ashburn of Georgia served in the Union Army. After the war, he promoted the rights of African Americans in Georgia. Ashburn was shot and killed in 1868, and involvement by the Ku Klux Klan was suspected. After Georgia ratified the 14th Amendment, all suspects were released.

> And the seed whose fruit is righteousness
> is sown in peace by those who make peace.
> James 3:18

★ Assignments for Lesson 67 ★

American Voices — Read the 14th Amendment to the U.S. Constitution (pages 67-68).

Bible — Read Nehemiah 5-7.

Work on memorizing Matthew 5:43-45.

Project — Work on your project.

Student Review — Optional: Answer the questions for Lesson 67.

The Ladies' Gallery of the Senate During the Impeachment Trial, Harper's Weekly (1868)

Lesson 68

The Impeachment and Trial of Andrew Johnson

Andrew Johnson was born to a poor family in Raleigh, North Carolina, in 1808. His father died when Andrew was three years old. The boy never had any formal schooling.

While he was apprenticed to a tailor, young Andrew got into trouble. He and a friend threw some pebbles against a window at the home of a young girl, and her father threatened to have them arrested; so Andrew ran away. Throwing pebbles was no big deal, but violating the terms of an apprenticeship by running away was a serious problem. Andrew secretly came back and persuaded his family to leave town. The Johnsons settled in Greeneville, Tennessee. Johnson went into the tailoring business and married the daughter of a shoemaker. Historians disagree on whether Johnson was able to read and write by this time or whether his wife helped to teach him these skills.

Johnson became interested in politics. He was considered a good political speaker, although he was somewhat harsh in his style. He was elected to the town council and then, at age 21, became mayor of Greeneville. Johnson later was elected to the state legislature and then to the U.S. House of Representatives. After serving four years as governor of Tennessee, Johnson was selected by the state legislature as a U.S. Senator in 1857.

Andrew Johnson was a slave owner and a Democrat who hated the southern aristocracy and supported the common man. He was also devoted to the Union. When the southern states seceded, Johnson was the only southern Senator to remain in Washington. While there, he helped Congress pass the Homestead Act that enabled thousands of average citizens to acquire property. After the Union Army captured Nashville in February of 1862, President Lincoln named Johnson as military governor of Tennessee. In that role he pushed for the abolition of slavery in the state. He was put on the Republican/National Union ticket as the vice presidential candidate in 1864. When Lincoln was assassinated, Johnson became the seventeenth President of the United States of America.

Confrontation with Congress

At first congressional Republicans thought that Johnson would go along with them in their desire to change southern society and reconstruct southern governments; but Johnson did not agree with their extreme views, and he began to resist their efforts. His vetoes of congressional bills and the wholesale pardons he issued to former Confederates (most of whom were his fellow Democrats) increased the tension between Johnson and the Radical Republicans.

Congress created a confrontation with Johnson with two laws that it passed in 1867 and then sustained over the President's veto. The Command of the Army Act said that all orders from the commander-in-chief (that is, the President) had to go through the General of the Army, who had to stay in Washington, D.C., unless Congress consented for him to leave. The General of the Army at the time was U.S. Grant, who was leaning toward the Radical position and who was seen by the Radicals as someone they could trust. The effect of this law was to take away the President's power as commander-in-chief and put it in the hands of Congress.

The second and even more confrontational law was the Tenure of Office Act. This law required the Senate's approval for the President to remove from office anyone who had been confirmed by the Senate. The purpose of the law was to keep in office Secretary of War Edwin Stanton, who was the lone Radical sympathizer in Johnson's Cabinet. The question of whether a President could fire a Cabinet member was an old one, dating back at least to the Jackson Administration. Congress attempted to settle the question by saying that the President could not do so, thus once again limiting the President's powers.

Years later the Supreme Court declared the Tenure of Office Act to be unconstitutional, but at the time the law served as the primary grounds for the impeachment of Johnson by Congress. In August of 1867, when Congress was in recess, Johnson suspended Stanton and replaced him with Grant. When Congress came back into session, it refused to confirm Johnson's action, and Grant gave the office back to Stanton. Johnson then fired Stanton and named Lorenzo Thomas as Secretary of War.

The Supreme Court After the Civil War

In 1864 the U.S. Supreme Court had ten members, as shown at right. President Lincoln had nominated Salmon P. Chase to be Chief Justice after the death of Roger Taney. Congress wanted to limit President Johnson's power to appoint new justices to the Court, so it passed a law stating that the next three vacancies on the Court would not be filled. Two vacancies occurred while Johnson was in office, and this reduced the Court's membership to eight. Then in 1869, after Johnson was out of office, Congress passed a law which set the court's membership at nine. The Court has had nine members ever since that time.

After limiting the President's powers, Congress also acted against the Supreme Court. In March of 1868, Congress removed the right of the Supreme Court to hear appeals of cases based on the Military Reconstruction Act, something it had the constitutional power to do. That same month, the Court issued a decision in the case of Texas v. White, *which dealt with whether the postwar Texas state government had the right to recover U.S. bonds sold off by the Confederate government during the war. Chief Justice Chase held that secession was not a legitimate action by a state. The Confederate states could not legitimately secede, Chase said, since the Articles of Confederation declared the Union to be perpetual and the Constitution made the Union more perfect. In Chase's words, the Union was "indissoluble." The decision of the Court was that Texas and the other Confederate states continued to be in the Union but had governments that were out of their proper relation to the Union. This was the position that Lincoln had maintained.*

Impeachment and Trial

To impeach means to accuse, not to find guilty. An impeached person is an accused person; he then has to stand trial to determine his guilt or innocence. On February 24, 1868, the House of Representatives voted eleven articles of impeachment against Johnson. Eight of them had to do with his alleged violations of the Tenure of Office Act. One accused him of violating the Command of the Army Act, and another cited Johnson's supposed contrivance to ignore Reconstruction laws. A final article of impeachment accused the President of "intemperate, inflammatory and scandalous harangues" against Congress. This last was obviously not an impeachable offense but was simply a political statement against Johnson.

The impeachment trial began in the Senate on March 5 and continued for five weeks. Chief Justice Salmon P. Chase presided before packed galleries. The accusers quickly focused on the Tenure of Office Act and Johnson's firing of Stanton. Johnson's attorneys argued (1) the law did not apply to Johnson, since it said that the firing could not take place during the term of the President who appointed the official, and Stanton had been appointed by Lincoln, not Johnson; (2) the law was unconstitutional (which was later proved to be true); and (3) the entire matter was a political dispute, and Johnson had done nothing for which he would be indicted in any court of law.

Individual tickets were issued for each day of Johnson's trial. They were issued to Senators, Representatives, Justices, and Cabinet members. The President received twenty tickets. The President Pro Tempore of the Senate received sixty tickets to give to reporters. (Compare with the tickets on page 853 in Part 2.)

As the trial dragged on, the Senators leading the impeachment process decided to ask for a vote on the article dealing with the Command of the Army Act. On May 16, seven Republican Senators joined the twelve Democrats in voting to acquit Johnson. The vote was 35 for conviction to 19 against, thus the article failed to receive the necessary two-thirds majority by one vote. When the same vote totals were recorded ten days later on two other articles, the Senate dissolved the trial.

Moderate Republicans saw the trial for the political vendetta that it was and refused to go along. They did not want to cripple the presidency and make the office subservient to Congress. Should Johnson be removed, Senator Ben Wade of Ohio, who was Senate President Pro Tempore, was next in line for the presidency. Moderates worried that since he was one of the most radical of the Republicans, he would be extremely hard to deal with as President. During the impeachment trial, Wade was said to be

The Senate as a Court of Impeachment for the Trial of Andrew Johnson, Harper's Weekly *(1868)*

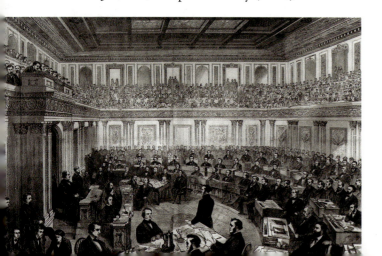

Lesson 68 - The Impeachment and Trial of Andrew Johnson

writing his inaugural address and considering people to put in his Cabinet.

The Senate's failure to convict Johnson insured that a President would not be removed from office merely for having political differences with Congress. Such a drastic step would be reserved for the gravest offenses.

Aftermath of Impeachment

The impeachment trial did political damage to both Johnson and Congress. The President did not try to block any other congressional action for the remainder of his term. Johnson hoped that the Democratic Party might nominate him for re-election in 1868, but his national reputation was ruined and he was passed over by both parties. Johnson's last act as President was to grant a pardon to former Confederate president Jefferson Davis.

The Radical Republicans in Congress also lost favor with the public for their harsh attacks against the President, but their control over the Reconstruction process was firm. In practical terms, however, this hold weakened as Democrats regained power in the South in the 1870s.

Of the seven Republicans who voted for acquittal, one died in 1869 while another suffered a serious stroke the same year. Two retired from politics at the end of their terms. Two became Democrats with long and successful careers. The final member, even though he lost favor with the Radicals at the time, regained enough respect from his fellow Republicans to preside over the 1884 Republican National Convention.

Andrew Johnson's Home in Greeneville, Tennessee

Andrew Johnson returned to Tennessee after his term as President ended in March of 1869. He refused even to attend the inauguration of his successor, Ulysses S. Grant. Johnson ran for Congress twice, in 1870 and 1872, but was defeated both times.

Finally in 1874, the Tennessee legislature elected Johnson to be a U.S. Senator from Tennessee. Johnson is the only man elected to the Senate after leaving the presidency. When he returned to the Senate chamber where he had endured the impeachment trial, he saw it as a measure of personal vindication. While in the Senate, Johnson gave a strongly-worded speech against the Grant Administration. He died of a stroke in 1875 while in Tennessee.

*The fear of the Lord is clean, enduring forever;
The judgments of the Lord are true;
they are righteous altogether.
Psalm 19:9*

★ Assignments for Lesson 68 ★

Bible   Read Nehemiah 8-10.

Work on memorizing Matthew 5:43-45.

Project   Work on your project.

Student Review   Optional: Answer the questions for Lesson 68.

Kansas State Agricultural College (Now University), Established in 1863

Lesson 69

Life Goes On

As all-consuming as the Civil War and Reconstruction were, other things were happening in the country during the 1860s. This lesson highlights some of these non-war developments.

Tariff

In 1862 Congress passed the Morrill Tariff, which set higher rates for imported goods. This protected American business and began the trend that continued for many years of the government giving assistance to business through tariff protection and other indirect ways.

Homestead Act

Another important piece of legislation in 1862 was the Homestead Act, which encouraged the settlement of the West. This law enabled Americans (or immigrants who had declared their intention to become citizens) to acquire 160 acres of land from the government. A person could do this simply by living on the land for a minimum number of days per year for five years, or by cultivating the land for five years. Alternatively, after six months' residence the homesteader could buy the land outright for $1.25 an acre.

The collection of tariffs was overseen by government officials working in custom houses around the country. The Customs office in San Francisco was located in this building, constructed in 1855. This photograph shows the building after extensive repairs following an 1865 earthquake. Another earthquake in 1868 caused relatively minor damage. The building was torn down in 1905 to prepare for construction of a new customs house. The devastating 1906 earthquake delayed completion of the new building until 1911.

381

Lives After the War

Robert E. Lee

After the war, Robert E. Lee became president of Washington University in Lexington, Virginia. Lee served in that role until he died in 1870. He continued to be revered for his character and bravery by many southerners and northerners alike. The photo at right shows Lee (seated, second from left) at a gathering with other former Confederate officers in 1869.

Lee requested a pardon from the Federal government, but the oath he signed was misplaced. It was not found until 1920. Full citizenship was restored to Lee posthumously in 1975. His son, George Washington Custis Lee, had also been a Confederate general. The younger Lee succeeded his father as president of what became Washington and Lee University.

Jefferson Davis

Jefferson Davis, who had been born in Kentucky not far from the birthplace of Abraham Lincoln, fled from Richmond at the end of the war and was captured in Georgia. He was held for two years and indicted for treason, but he was released on bail and never tried. President Johnson granted him a pardon in 1869.

Davis lived out his life in Biloxi, Mississippi, and wrote his memoirs, *The Rise and Fall of the Confederate Government.* He often attended reunions of Confederate veterans. Davis died in 1889. His funeral procession in New Orleans is shown at left. Jefferson Davis is still remembered with state holidays in several southern states.

The Lincolns

After President Lincoln's death, Mary Todd Lincoln received notes of condolence from around the world. She replied to Queen Victoria, also a widow, that she was "deeply grateful for the expressions of tender sympathy, coming as they do, from a heart which from its own sorrow, can appreciate the intense grief I now endure." Mrs. Lincoln suffered through much family sadness, as only one of her four sons, Robert, lived to manhood. She spent time in a mental institution in 1875 and died in 1882.

Robert Todd Lincoln (pictured at right) was a corporate lawyer, Secretary of War from 1881 to 1885, and minister to England from 1889 to 1893. He also served as president of the Pullman Railroad Car Company. Robert Lincoln died in 1926. The last direct descendant of Abraham and Mary Todd Lincoln, great-grandson Robert Beckwith, died in 1985.

Lesson 69 - Life Goes On

The Morrill Tariff and the Morrill Land Grant Act were named for Justin S. Morrill (1810-1898), a Republican who represented Vermont in the U.S. Congress for forty years, thirty of those in the Senate. Another Morrill Act in 1890 gave universities direct Federal appropriations.

The Homestead Act was intended to help the average family own their own land. By the end of the war, 15,000 families had begun to homestead 2.5 million acres. Many more families moved west and claimed homesteads after the war. However, many fraudulent claims were filed on behalf of lumber and mining companies and speculators who profited illegally from the homesteading process.

Morrill Land Grant Act

The final major legislation enacted by Congress in 1862 was the Morrill Land Grant Act, designed to create agricultural and engineering colleges. Congress gave states 30,000 acres of Federally-owned land for each Senator and Congressman they had. A state could then sell or rent the land (to homesteaders, for example), and the proceeds went to establish colleges that would emphasize studies in the agricultural and mechanical arts.

State universities in California, Illinois, Ohio, Pennsylvania, and many other states, as well as Purdue University in Indiana and the private Cornell University in New York, were designated as land grant institutions.

National Bank Act

After the Bank of the United States closed during the Jackson Administration, the United States had a loose and poorly regulated monetary system. The Federal government operated an Independent Treasury that did not engage in banking but merely held Federal deposits and paid government debts.

Daniel Freeman filed one of the first homestead claims in 1863. Five years later, he received the certificate below left confirming his ownership of the land. The photo below right shows the Freeman homestead in Nebraska in 1904.

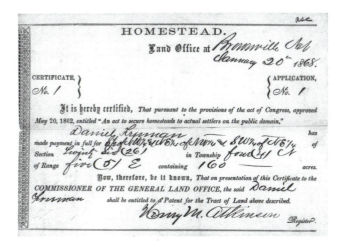

The central government operated on a hard money policy, issuing only coins and bills backed by the face value amount of gold or silver held by the government. This kept the value of money under control, but it slowed economic growth. The only banks were those chartered under state regulations. Those regulations varied from state to state, which meant that some banks were not as reliable as others. State bank notes varied in value and reliability and provided an unstable currency supply.

The National Bank Act of 1863 attempted a long-term solution for the national monetary system while dealing with the short-term need for huge amounts of money to finance the Union war effort. The law allowed for banks to be chartered by the Federal government under strict regulations. A Federally-chartered bank had to use at least one-third of its assets to buy U.S. bonds (thus providing the government with short-term cash). The bank then received Federal bank notes equivalent to 90 percent of its bond holdings. The notes, which had the bonds to back them, were used as currency and could also be used for making loans. This meant that the Federal banks could earn interest on the bonds and on the notes as well. In addition, the law placed a tax on state bank notes, which made them less attractive and eventually drove them out of circulation.

The new law gave the country a sound, uniform currency and a regulated national banking system. It also established the principle of a national monetary system overseen by the Federal government. The negative side was that it made the amount of money available in the economy dependent on Federal debt, which is not the healthiest way to run the economy. The notes issued under the law were the principle currency used in the country until the Federal Reserve System was created in 1913.

Louisa May Alcott

Louisa May Alcott was born in 1832, the daughter of a Transcendentalist teacher who knew Ralph Waldo Emerson and others in that circle. Alcott published a few stories and poems before the Civil War. During the war she worked as a nurse in a Union hospital. From her experiences she wrote Hospital Sketches, *which enjoyed mild success.*

Alcott wrote some stories for children, and her publisher encouraged her to write a book for young women. Little Women, *published in 1868, was the hugely successful result. It gives a warm portrayal of middle-class American family life in the mid-nineteenth century and is based in great measure on her own experiences.*

Alcott wrote several other novels, including An Old-Fashioned Girl *(1869),* Little Men *(1871), and* Jo's Boys *(1886). She cared for her invalid parents in their home and adopted the children of two of her sisters who died relatively young. Alcott never married. Her mother died in 1877 and her father died in 1888. Alcott died two days after her father's passing.*

What Else Was Happening?

1865 Louis Pasteur develops the germ theory of disease, showing that disease is caused by the spread of infectious germs.

1865 William Booth begins a ministry in London that eventually becomes the Salvation Army.

1865 Charles Dogson publishes Alice's Adventures in Wonderland under the pen name Lewis Carroll.

1866 The monk Gregor Mendel publishes his studies in breeding peas. His research was largely ignored until 1900, but it eventually became the basis for studies in heredity.

1867 The U.S. buys Alaska from Russia for $7.2 million in a deal spearheaded by Secretary of State William Seward. The deal is ridiculed as "Seward's Folly" and "Seward's Icebox." The first page of the Russian version of the Treaty of Cession is shown at right.

1867 Karl Marx publishes Das Kapital in Berlin, Germany. The book discusses historic trends in economics and predicts that a Communist revolution is inevitable and will soon take place, overthrowing capitalism and creating a worker-led system of government and economics.

1867 Alfred Nobel of Sweden patents dynamite, which revolutionizes mining and railroad construction. His sorrow at its use in war prompts him to leave instructions in his will that the bulk of his estate is to be used for Nobel prizes in several fields of scientific research as well as world peace.

1867 A discovery in South Africa leads to a major diamond rush. From 1871 to 1914, thousands of workers dig The Big Hole, by hand, looking for diamonds. The city of Kimberley grows up nearby, as seen at left.

1868 Railroad construction workers find skeletons in the Cro-Magnon caves of southern France. They come to be called "Cro-Magnon Man."

1868 – The element helium is discovered in the spectra of the sun. It will be discovered on earth in 1895.

1868 – The stapler is patented. Used first in making shoes, it spreads to the printing industry in the 1890s.

Laura Ingalls Wilder was born near Lake Pepin, Wisconsin, (shown above) in 1867. Her Little House *series of books provide an excellent record of what life was like for homesteading families in the late 1800s. The books tell the story of Laura's growing up years, though a few elements were fictionalized. These are usually considered to be children's books, but they tell dramatic stories in a wonderfully descriptive writing style that people of any age can enjoy.*

Make sure that your character is free from the love of money, being content with what you have; for He Himself has said, "I will never desert you, nor will I ever forsake you."
Hebrews 13:5

★ Assignments for Lesson 69 ★

Bible Read Nehemiah 11-13.

Work on memorizing Matthew 5:43-45.

Project Work on your project.

Student Review Optional: Answer the questions for Lesson 69.

Portion of Wall Discovered in Jerusalem in 2007, Thought to Be That Built by Nehemiah

Lesson 70 - Bible Study

Nehemiah's Reconstruction

The United States had a major rebuilding job to do after the Civil War. This involved not only the physical rebuilding of the South but also the social and emotional rebuilding that was needed throughout the country. Centuries earlier the Jews had to undergo a period of rebuilding following their exile in Babylon. Their experience under the leadership of Nehemiah teaches several important lessons for us today.

Background

Babylon conquered Judah in a series of invasions around 600 BC. The invading armies destroyed Jerusalem and the temple. Thousands of Jews were taken into captivity. Seventy years later, after Babylon itself had been conquered, the Persian king allowed the Jews and other captives to return to their homelands. Many more years passed before the story of Nehemiah begins.

In 445 BC, the Jew Nehemiah was cupbearer to the king (Nehemiah 1:11). This was more than just being a waiter. The cupbearer was charged with making sure that the king's wine was not poisoned. Because of this responsibility, a cupbearer had to be one of the king's most trusted servants. Nehemiah heard that the Jews who had returned to Israel were distressed and that the walls of Jerusalem had not yet been rebuilt (1:3). At the time Nehemiah lived, the Jews had been in captivity for several generations. Nehemiah himself had never even been to Jerusalem; but he still considered it to be a special city for himself and for his people because it was the place where God had chosen for His glory to dwell.

Nehemiah Goes to Jerusalem

Nehemiah wept, prayed, and fasted for the difficulties of his people. An essential step for Nehemiah involved confessing the sins of the Jews. He knew that this was the basic reason why they had endured such troubles (1:4-11). The king, noting Nehemiah's distress, asked what was wrong; and Nehemiah told him. The king granted Nehemiah's request to go to Jerusalem to rebuild it (2:1-6). Nehemiah knew that the king's permission was given in response to Nehemiah's prayers, but Nehemiah also took the practical step of getting letters of passage from the king for his trip home (2:7-8). This was the first of many occasions when Nehemiah prayed and knew that God responded, but he also took practical action.

As Nehemiah was returning, Sanballat and Tobiah heard about it and began to formulate their opposition to Nehemiah's project (2:10). This reveals another basic principle of life: whenever someone

Unit 14 - Reconstruction

Gustav Doré was a French artist. His well-known Bible illustrations were published in 1866. This one depicts Nehemiah surveying the ruined walls of Jerusalem.

attempts to do something good, others will arise to oppose it.

Nehemiah arrived in Jerusalem and surveyed the walls by himself at night (2:11-16). Both distress and determination mounted within him as he saw the ruined defenses of the once-proud city. Then Nehemiah called together the Jewish leaders and said, "Let us rebuild the wall of Jerusalem" (2:17). When he explained how God had led him to come there, the leaders responded, "Let us arise and build" (2:18). Nehemiah shared his vision for the project with other people, and it became their project also. Nehemiah did not say, "I'm going to rebuild this wall"; instead, he described the project in such a way that others wanted to join him. Once again Sanballat and Tobiah expressed their opposition, but Nehemiah declared his trust in God and said that the naysayers would have no portion in the project (2:19-20).

The Building Begins

Nehemiah then described how the rebuilding project took place. Families worked next to each other rebuilding the wall (3:1-32). This was a community project in which all who worked were encouraged by seeing others working on it, too. Verse 10 indicates that at least some Jews worked near their own homes. This gave their work special meaning because they knew that they had a personal stake in it.

Everyone worked on the project, even those who were not stonemasons. One section was built by a goldsmith and a perfumer and their families (3:8). Another was built by a man and his daughters (3:12). These sections might not have looked as good as the parts that were built by experts, but that didn't matter. Each person and each family gave their best, and they all worked on the project together.

Opposition and Dissension

Then the opposition arose again. Sanballat and Tobiah mocked and ridiculed the Jews' efforts (4:1-3). Nehemiah's response was to turn it over to God in prayer and to keep working. He did not let the critics win the day because "the people had a mind to work" (4:6). Once again Nehemiah combined the spiritual and the practical. He prayed about it and set up a guard (4:9). From then on, half the people worked and the other half stood guard (4:16). Even those who were building carried their weapons in one hand and worked with the other (4:17). In other words, they did what they had to do in order to get the work done. The plan of action was that if trouble arose at any one spot, everyone would go to that place to defend the city (4:20). The people showed dedication to the project, being willing even to sacrifice their comfort for the work (4:22).

No project is so important that it cannot be threatened by internal dissension. The wall-rebuilding project was no exception. The people and their wives cried out against their Jewish brothers

(5:1). The dedicated workers were being taken advantage of by those wanting to make a profit from the situation. People were having to mortgage their property to buy food (5:3). They had to borrow money to pay their taxes (5:4). They were facing the prospect of selling their children into slavery and were being victimized by the profiteers (5:5). Nehemiah spoke to those who were forcing the people into these situations, and he convicted them of their wrong. They repented and the crisis passed (5:6-13).

Nehemiah's Leadership

Nehemiah was appointed governor of Judah by the king (5:14). He had a large staff and had to entertain official visitors (5:17). Yet Nehemiah did not eat the food allotted to him, nor did he lord it over the people (5:14-15). In addition, he continued working on the wall project and did not hide behind a desk (5:16). In these ways Nehemiah showed himself to be a good leader. He did not use his position for personal gain or comfort, and he got his hands dirty in the project that needed to be done.

Nehemiah also showed wise leadership in the next crisis. Sanballat, Tobiah, and other opponents said that they wanted to meet with Nehemiah to discuss the project. What they really wanted to do was to harm Nehemiah (6:1-2). Nehemiah replied that he was just too busy to meet (6:3). Nehemiah didn't need to take time for a meeting, especially a meeting with his enemies; he needed to work. Sanballat then tried to threaten Nehemiah with rumors he had heard (or made up). Sanballat said that the talk he had heard indicated that Nehemiah was going to declare himself king, which would be treason and rebellion against the real king (6:5-7). Nehemiah was not intimidated. He simply replied that it was all a fabrication and absolutely not true, and again he prayed to God about it (6:8-9).

Someone told Nehemiah that he ought to go hide in the temple to escape the murderous plot of Sanballat and Tobiah. Nehemiah refused, saying that he was not afraid of them. If his enemies could intimidate him and make him react out of a desire for his own self-preservation, that would be the first step toward their defeating him. Instead, Nehemiah trusted God to protect him and once more prayed that God would deal with the opposition (6:10-14).

Completion of the Project

Finally the wall was completed (6:15). When the enemies heard about it, they lost heart because they knew that the project had been completed by God's help (6:16). Even as the wall was completed, some within the ranks opposed Nehemiah (6:17-19). Nehemiah then listed the families of those who had returned from exile (7:6-73). In listing the families, Nehemiah once again showed that this was a shared project. He honored all who were living in the province. Everyone and every family was important, not just Nehemiah.

Then the people were gathered together, and they asked Ezra to read aloud from the Law. As he opened the book, the people stood up, showing their respect for God's Word (8:1-5). Ezra blessed God, and all the people worshiped Him (8:6). As Ezra read, he translated as needed, since some people only knew Aramaic and not Hebrew (8:8). As Ezra read from the Law, the people wept (8:9). They were convicted by how much they had failed to obey God's Word.

Rebuilding the Wall Illustration by Jim Padgett (1984)

Nehemiah, Ezra, and the Levites told the people that this was not a day to weep but to rejoice. They had finished the task of rebuilding the wall, they were listening to the words of God, and they were rededicating themselves to following the Law. Conviction about the past is necessary, but the time comes when people need to count their blessings and move forward. The people heard about the Feast of Booths and set about celebrating it (8:13-18). The book notes that Israel had not celebrated the festival in this way since the time of Joshua (8:17).

Chapter 9 records the national day of repentance. The Levites led the people in prayer, recalling Israel's history, especially what God had done and how the people had alternately followed and disobeyed Him. They committed themselves in writing to following the Lord (9:38). Chapter 10 records who signed the document and what it said.

After giving other lists of people and officials, Nehemiah recorded the joyous day when the wall was dedicated (12:27-47). As the Jews did this, they found that the process of restoration was not complete. They learned that they were to exclude foreigners from the assembly. Nehemiah recalled that they had expelled Tobiah from the temple, where he had been given a room. Tithing and Sabbath observance were restored (13:10-22). Nehemiah also had to address the issue of Jewish men marrying foreign wives in violation of the Law. These foreign influences were pulling the Jews away from the Lord and even away from the language of Israel (13:23-31).

The restoration of the wall was a great accomplishment, but it was only a one-time event. Restoring the hearts of the people to the Lord was an ongoing project that required continuing vigilance. In the same way, the physical rebuilding of the South was finished long before the social and emotional healing was done; and in some ways that more difficult project is still taking place.

> *I told them how the hand of my God had been favorable to me and also about the king's words which he had spoken to me. Then they said, "Let us arise and build." So they put their hands to the good work.*
> Nehemiah 2:18

★ Assignments for Lesson 70 ★

Bible — Recite or write Matthew 5:43-45 from memory.

Project — Complete your project for the unit.

Student Review — Optional: Answer the questions for Lesson 70 and take the quiz for Unit 14.

La Crosse, Wisconsin, 1873

15 Moving Forward

During the post-Civil War period the United States witnessed tremendous growth and change as well as serious failings. Slaves were free, but corruption in government was rampant. The transcontinental railroad was an engineering triumph, but the financial mismanagement associated with it was astounding. A back-room political deal finally brought about the end of Reconstruction. The contrasts of the period raise the question of how we should define progress.

Lesson 71 - The Grant Presidency
Lesson 72 - Postwar Life in the United States
Lesson 73 - The Transcontinental Railroad
Lesson 74 - The Election of 1876
Lesson 75 - Bible Study: What Is Progress?

Memory Work Memorize Proverbs 16:1-3 by the end of this unit.

Books Used The Bible
American Voices
Humorous Stories and Sketches

Project (choose one)

1) Write 300 to 500 words on one of the following topics:
   - Look through the lessons in this unit and select a leading figure that is discussed. Write a biography of him or her.
   - Write an essay on contrasts present in the United States after the Civil War. Consider, for instance, the end of slavery and the bondage of discrimination; the power of corporate leaders and the dependency of people who worked for them; material wealth and spiritual poverty. You might concentrate on one contrast or list as many contrasts as you can think of. Discuss what we in America today have learned and failed to learn from these experiences.
2) Create a sculpture related to the Transcontinental Railroad. Be creative in determining your subject: it could relate to the railroad itself, a train, the regions of the country impacted, the workers involved, or something else. You can use any combination of media your choice (e.g., paper, wire, wood, cardboard, clay, STYROFOAM™, LEGO® bricks). See Lesson 73.
3) Make a video about "progress" as discussed in Lesson 75. You can choose the style of your video: a story, documentary style, or artistic/poetic. Your video should be at least five minutes long.

Literature

Humorous Stories and Sketches

Samuel Langhorne Clemens (1835-1910) was one of the most important and popular American writers during the late 1800s. He grew up in Hannibal, Missouri, on the Mississippi River. His father died when he was young, and Sam was apprenticed to a printer. He later worked as a riverboat captain and, later still, as a reporter in Nevada and California. He eventually settled in Connecticut. Mark Twain (the pen name he adopted) had a great sense of humor, but he was also a cynic with regard to religion and human nature. Twain's life was touched by tragedy, including the deaths of his wife and two daughters and serious financial reversals.

Twain's numerous books were popular during his lifetime and many are still read today. You will enjoy the short stories and comic essays by Twain in the brief volume of *Humorous Stories and Sketches* published by Dover. If you want to find these pieces in other books, the works included are "The Notorious Jumping Frog of Calaveras County," "Journalism in Tennessee," "About Barbers," "A Literary Nightmare," "The Stolen White Elephant," "The Private History of a Campaign That Failed," "Fenimore Cooper's Literary Offences," and "How to Tell a Story." Plan to finish them by the end of this unit.

Grant Home, Galena, Illinois

Lesson 71

The Grant Presidency

Hiram Ulysses Grant was born in Ohio in 1822. When he enrolled in West Point, he registered as Ulysses Simpson Grant, keeping the given name he preferred, adding his mother's maiden name, and acquiring the initials U.S. After graduating twenty-first out of a class of thirty-nine, Grant went on to serve in the Mexican War and at various military posts in the U.S. He had a problem with drinking, however, and eventually resigned his commission as an Army officer. Grant attempted to go into business but failed. In 1860 his younger brothers offered him a job as a clerk in their store in Galena, Illinois.

When the Civil War began, Grant applied for and was given command over a state militia group. He quickly rose to the rank of brigadier general in the United States Army. We have recounted his leadership of Union troops at Forts Henry and Donelson, Shiloh, Vicksburg, and Chattanooga. Eventually Grant was named General of the Army and brought about the surrender of Lee's forces and the end of the war. The victorious general became a national hero. The people of Philadelphia and New York gave him a house in Galena and over $100,000.

Because of his war record and his leaning toward the Radical position, the Republican Party nominated him for President in 1868. He defeated the Democratic candidate, former New York governor Horatio Seymour. Grant received a large electoral vote landslide, but had only about a 300,000 popular vote majority. It has been estimated that newly-enfranchised blacks gave Grant at least a 500,000 majority of their votes, making the black vote the key to Grant's victory. The former general was 46 when he was inaugurated. He was thus the youngest man ever to become President up to that time. Republicans continued to control Congress.

After the 1868 election, Republicans in Congress saw that the black vote had helped to bring about their party's victory. As a result, Congress passed and sent to the states the 15th Amendment, which outlawed denying the right to vote because of "race, color, or previous condition of servitude." The amendment became part of the Constitution in 1870.

Scandals

Grant was President during a period of terrible corruption in American government and business. Grant himself was apparently not directly involved in the scandals, but his poor leadership made corruption possible. He appointed weak men to important positions, he stood by while his friends took advantage of him, and he failed to exercise the leadership that could possibly have stopped the practices. The scandals described below are just some of the incidents that can be cited.

In 1869 two wealthy railroad executives, Jim Fisk and Jay Gould, schemed with Grant's brother-in-law to gain control of the buying and selling of gold. Gould used his influence to keep the government from selling gold in the open market. Less gold on the market meant that the price of gold would rise. Meanwhile, Fisk and Gould invested heavily in the precious metal; this activity caused the price to rise even more because of increased demand. Apparently Grant knew something was wrong because on September 24, 1869, he ordered the Treasury Department to sell a large amount of gold, which lowered its value in the marketplace. Fisk lost money, but he refused to pay his debts and he intimidated the people to whom he owed money. He is reported to have said, "Nothing is lost save honor."

Grant's Secretary of War was found to have taken a bribe in order to give a certain businessman the contract for selling goods to Fort Sill in Oklahoma. The Cabinet member resigned when Congress began impeachment proceedings against him. A whiskey-producing ring in St. Louis used bribes and blackmail to avoid paying liquor taxes to the United States government. The director of the Internal Revenue office in St. Louis went to jail for a year because of the scandal, and Grant's personal secretary was found to have been involved.

Tammany Hall in New York hosted the Democratic National Convention in 1868.

The biggest scandal during Grant's tenure involved the construction of the transcontinental railroad. One company involved in the project, the Union Pacific Railroad, created its own construction company, Credit Mobilier, to do the work. The railroad company got huge amounts of money from the government to build the railroad. It then awarded the construction contract to its own Credit Mobilier company. The railroad company and the construction company had the same board of directors, and the directors skimmed off large amounts of money into their own pockets during the transactions. It was later learned that some Congressmen had been bribed to refrain from investigating the deal.

The Tweed Ring

Corruption extended into state and local governments also. The worst example was the control of New York City politics held by Boss William Tweed and his Tammany Hall machine in the 1860s and 1870s. The corruption took several forms. Tweed's group got their candidates elected, and these office-holders then used their position to give Tammany men and their friends public money. When immigrants got off the boat, Tammany Hall men helped many of the new arrivals find housing and jobs; Tammany men did other favors for the immigrants as well. When election time came, the political party representatives went back to these immigrants and made sure that they voted for Tammany Hall candidates. If their candidate wasn't winning, Tweed's men simply stuffed ballot boxes with phony votes.

Tammany Hall men sold jobs to people who were willing to give back part of their salary to the party operatives. They sold licenses for a high price to people wanting to operate businesses in the city and kept some of the fees for themselves. Political bosses awarded contracts for projects such as street and sidewalk construction to companies who agreed to give back part of the money to the people in

Lesson 71 - The Grant Presidency

Ely Parker (1828-1895), a member of the Seneca tribe, met Ulysses S. Grant in Illinois, and Parker became part of Grant's staff during the Civil War. Parker was present at Lee's surrender, and Lee remarked, "I am glad to see one real American here." Parker shook Lee's hand and said, "We are all Americans." President Grant appointed Parker to be Commissioner of Indian Affairs, the first American Indian to hold that position. The U.S. government gave peace medals to Native American leaders who signed treaties or visited Washington, D.C. The medal shown above was created in 1871.

---

authority who helped them get the contract (called a kickback). Companies that were in the "Tweed Ring" were paid much more than the legitimate cost of the projects. All of this corruption was financed with taxpayer dollars. Estimates are that the Tweed insiders stole $20 million and cost the city $100 million in bloated contracts and other mismanagement. The Tammany Hall operation was eventually broken by an investigation that was led by attorney Samuel J. Tilden, who was later elected governor of New York. Many other cities and states had similar stories of corruption.

Abuse of the public trust was a sad pattern during this time. It had been a problem during the Civil War, when some companies selling goods to the government were not above making a huge profit at the expense of the country. The rapid expansion of the economy after the war made more money available. Unprincipled men took advantage of the system. The laws of the system, moreover, hadn't caught up to the ingenuity of criminals wanting to take advantage of it. In addition, the companies involved were often large corporations, not small family businesses. The increased impersonalization and the many layers of responsibility in corporations made stealing easier and accountability harder.

Liberal Republicans React

A portion of the Republican Party called Liberals reacted to the corruption of the Grant Administration and what they saw as imposed Republican control of several southern state governments. For the 1872 presidential election, Liberal Republicans held a separate convention and nominated Horace Greeley, editor of the

Horace Greeley

New York Tribune and supporter of several reform causes. Although Greeley had previously expressed hostility toward Democrats, the Democratic Party also nominated Greeley as their only hope to defeat Grant. The incumbent President, however, still had the loyalty of the majority of the Republican Party in the North, the support of carpetbagger governments in the South, and the backing of business leaders.

Greeley campaigned actively around the country, an unusual move for a presidential candidate. The tradition that most candidates followed was to let others do the campaigning for them. Grant won an impressive 286-66 victory in the electoral college and had a 56-44 percent majority in the popular vote (a 750,000 vote margin out of 6.4 million cast). Greeley's wife died during the campaign, and Greeley himself was so exhausted that he entered a mental institution and died three weeks after the election was decided.

Greenbacks

Grant and the Republicans carried the election of 1872, but their power was beginning to weaken. More scandals were uncovered during Grant's second term, and a severe economic downturn began in 1873 and lasted for six years. This recession was related to the government's monetary policy.

During the Civil War, the U.S. Treasury had issued $432 million in paper money (greenbacks) to increase the supply of available cash beyond the government's gold reserve. In 1866 Congress gave the Treasury Department the right gradually to withdraw the greenbacks and return to a hard money currency consisting of gold coins and paper notes backed by gold; the Treasury began doing so.

However, many farmers and those with debts opposed this move because it meant that less money would be available. They feared that this would mean lower farm prices and that they

Thomas Nast (1840-1902) was a political cartoonist whose stinging portrayal of the Tammany machine helped end their grip on political power in New York City. He created the elephant as a symbol of the Republican Party and popularized the donkey as a symbol of the Democratic Party. The cartoon below is a self-portrait of Nast sharpening his pencil in preparation for work.

Lesson 71 - The Grant Presidency

1861 Greenback (Front and Back)

would have to repay debts with money that was worth more than the money they had borrowed. In addition, some Radical Republicans believed that inflation, caused by a larger money supply, would help stimulate economic growth. Influenced by these pressures, Congress halted the retirement of greenbacks in 1868.

With fewer dollars available, debtors had difficulty paying their loans. In 1873 twenty-five railroad companies were unable to pay the interest on loans that had been made to them because their revenue did not support the debt they had. A large investment company went bankrupt in September of that year. Many investors wanted to sell their stocks to avoid losing more money, and the rush to sell caused the stock market to close for ten days. Bankruptcies, unemployment, and a slower pace of railroad construction followed. The Panic of 1873 was the most serious economic downturn the country had seen to date. As a result of these widespread economic problems, the Democrats gained control of the U.S. House in the 1874 election.

The Treasury reissued $26 million in greenbacks to help the economy, but in 1874 Grant urged that the government return to the policy of withdrawing paper money. The next year, Congress passed the Resumption Act, which called for the payment of gold for greenbacks turned in to the government starting in January of 1879. This angered those who supported a larger money supply and led to the formation of the Greenback Party. The party fielded a presidential candidate in 1876. Two years later, it elected a few members of Congress and its candidates received a total of one million votes nationwide. However, its 1880 presidential candidate received only 300,000 votes. The party soon folded, but the issue it highlighted continued to be a matter of concern for many Americans for the rest of the century.

The Fall of Republican Rule in the South

Republican control continued in some southern states but it weakened during Grant's term as Democrats regained power. Most states were back in Democratic hands by the end of 1872. Several factors influenced the changes taking place in the South.

First, former slaves were not, as a rule, politically active. Many of them deferred to the whites who did want to exercise political power. Most blacks were more interested in using their energies to obtain land and economic security than in gaining political clout. Second, whites were determined to regain control; and they were willing to intimidate blacks and Republicans to get it. Third, white southerners still controlled the southern economy. They owned the land, the banks, and the factories; and whites were the ones who handed out most of the available jobs. If blacks wanted to work, they had to go along with what the white power structure wanted. Strengthening the whites' position was the 1872 Amnesty Act passed by Congress. This law pardoned 160,000 former Confederates, leaving only about 500 former rebels still outside of the political process.

Despite the desire of some Radical Republicans to transform southern society, in reality the fabric of southern life was not significantly changed beyond the ending of slavery. Most white southerners felt that the results of the war had been imposed upon them, and they resisted change as much as they could. Before the war, the whites had power and most of the blacks were slaves. Now, the whites believed that they deserved to be in power again and were willing to keep blacks subjugated as much as possible. Ex-slaves and reformers were not unified on what they wanted to see happen for the former slaves or on how to bring about what they did want, and this lack of unity weakened their efforts to accomplish reform.

Most northerners did not help the situation. Strong prejudice existed in the North against blacks. Some northern states had laws forbidding free blacks from moving into the state. One motive of some free-soilers in wanting to keep slavery out of the territories before the war had been simply to keep blacks out of those regions altogether. Congress took no significant action to provide land or education for former slaves.

Southern blacks were given the right to vote, but the primary reason was not out of a belief in racial equality; it was out of a desire to keep former Confederates from getting back into power. The 1868 Republican platform, for instance, urged that blacks be given the vote in southern states, but it said that northern states should be allowed to decide the question for themselves.

In economic terms, the weak southern economy that languished under Republican rule was bad for business on a national scale. The growing industrial sector wanted to develop more of a market in the South, and the weak economy there hindered that. If Democratic control and its resulting discrimination against blacks would bring a stronger southern economy, many northern business leaders were content to let it happen.

Leaving Office

President Grant had helped to win the war, but unfortunately his Administration did not do much to help win the peace. He considered running for a third term in 1876, but he decided against it because the scandals and economic depression made him increasingly unpopular. After he left office, Grant and his wife went abroad for two years, where he was welcomed warmly as "Savior of the Union." This helped him regain some of his stature in the United States—so much so that his name was put in nomination at the 1880 Republican convention. However, the deadlocked convention turned to James Garfield as its consensus candidate.

The Grants settled in New York City, where the former President invested heavily in a bank of which his son was a partner. However, the head of the bank turned out to be a crook and Grant lost all of his

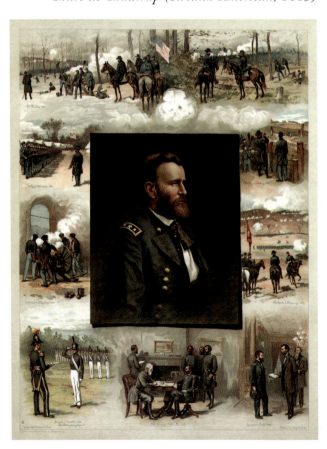

Grant from West Point to Appomattox
Thure de Thulstrup (Swedish-American, 1885)

Lesson 71 - The Grant Presidency

money. About this time, Grant was diagnosed with cancer. He worked day and night, often in intense pain, to finish his memoirs so that their publication would provide income for his family. He completed the memoirs four days before he died in 1885. Grant was born fifteen years later than Robert E. Lee and died fifteen years later than Lee.

Grant's memoirs appeared first in serialization, and then Mark Twain arranged to have them published in book form. This brought the family about a half million dollars in royalties. The memoirs give a brief survey of Grant's early life, concentrate on the war years, and only briefly touch on his presidency. They are considered an excellent volume of military recollections.

The General Grant National Memorial in New York City, commonly called Grant's Tomb, was dedicated in 1897. It is the largest mausoleum in North America.

A false balance is an abomination to the Lord, but a just weight is His delight.
Proverbs 11:1

★ Assignments for Lesson 71 ★

American Voices — Read "O Little Town of Bethlehem" by Phillips Brooks (page 236).

Literature — Begin reading *Humorous Stories and Sketches*. Finish it by the end of this unit.

Bible — In the Bible study lesson this week, we will examine the subject of progress: how the world defines it and how God defines it. List three ways in which the world commonly defines progress.

Start memorizing Proverbs 16:1-3.

Project — Choose your project for this unit and start working on it.

Student Review — Optional: Answer the questions for Lesson 71.

Pikes Peak, Colorado

Lesson 72

Postwar Life in the United States

Most Americans wanted to put the bitterness of the Civil War behind them and move on. They believed that they had good reason to be optimistic about the future of America. The American dream was not shared by everyone to the same degree; but the general mood of the country was definitely one of a desire to move forward.

First, slavery had been ended and the country had been reunited. Second, the end of the war had brought a greater degree of equality for more people, at least in theory. Third, the nation saw that the vast stretches of the West offered cheap land and the opportunity for millions of Americans to succeed. Fourth, advances in technology opened up new possibilities in transportation and communication. Finally, many Americans were enjoying a rising standard of living; they believed that opportunities for a still better life lay before them.

Western Migration

The United States experienced two great people movements in the years following the Civil War. One was the movement into the western part of the country. Horace Greeley encouraged westward migration in his article, "To Aspiring Young Men," published in the *New York Tribune*:

The best business you can go into you will find on your father's farm or in his workshop. If you have no family or friends to aid you, and no prospect opened to you there, turn your face to the great West, and there build up a home and fortune.

The saying "Go west, young man" became popular. (Some give Horace Greeley credit for the phrase and others believe John Babsone Soul coined the phrase in 1851 in the Terre Haute, Indiana, *Express*.) Thousands of young men, families, and immigrants did just that. In the years between 1870 and 1900, settlers established about one million farms. Americans and new immigrants settled more square miles on the continent than had been settled in the previous 250 years. The main attraction was the land on the plains that could be claimed by homesteaders. People moved west, staked their claims, endured the elements, and carved out an existence. Towns developed along rail lines. American civilization came to the Great Plains.

Gold and Silver Mines

Another attraction that the West held was mining activity. Ten years after the discovery of gold in California, another gold strike was made near Pikes Peak in Colorado. Over 100,000 Fifty-Niners said "Pikes Peak or Bust" and headed west. The population boom enabled Colorado to become the 38th state in 1876. Also in 1859, the Comstock Lode was discovered in the Utah Territory (in the area that became Nevada). This mineral deposit yielded about $340 million in gold and silver by 1890. Nevada became a state in 1864.

Gold was discovered in 1874 in the Black Hills of the Dakota Territory, in what became South Dakota. The land on which gold was discovered was actually the Sioux Reservation, but the United States government gave in to pressure from miners and declared the region open to white settlement. Between 1860 and 1900, western mines yielded about $1.2 billion in gold and $901 million worth of silver. This made more hard money available in the economy. Copper, an element important in the transmission of electricity, was discovered in Montana, Utah, Nevada, and Arizona.

The lawless life of mining towns has been portrayed—and stereotyped—in many short stories, books, and movies. These towns grew up quickly and were populated mostly by men. Local citizens usually developed their own system of law enforcement to maintain order. Many of the original prospectors stayed in a town only as long as the chance for quick wealth remained. When mining activity slowed, they moved on to other places. The mining towns that were eventually abandoned became the ghost towns of western lore. Some people stayed where they were, however. Families moved in to work for mining companies or to establish farms and businesses. Schools and churches were built, and a real sense of community developed in many former rough-and-tumble mining towns.

Cattle Drives

Yet another economic activity unique to the West was the open range cattle drive. Most drives involved herding cattle from the vast expanses of Texas northward to the railroad town of Abilene, Kansas. From there the herds were shipped by rail car to meat processing plants further east. In 1868 Abilene received 75,000 head of cattle. By 1871 the number had grown to approximately 700,000. Over the next dozen years, some four million head were driven to Abilene and other railroad and meat processing towns. A typical cattle drive involved about 2,300 head of cattle and sixteen to eighteen cowhands.

Restoring the Union

Radical Republican leader Charles Sumner of Massachusetts died in March of 1874. He was the man who had verbally attacked South Carolina Senator Andrew Butler and then was physically attacked by Butler's nephew. Before his death, Sumner asked Mississippi Congressman Lucius Quintus Cincinnatus Lamar to deliver a eulogy at his funeral. Lamar (pictured at right) had been a strong advocate for secession and had served in the Confederate Army.

In his funeral address, Lamar said that Sumner had come to believe that all reason for division between North and South had passed. "Is not that the common sentiment—or if it is not, ought it not to be—of the great mass of our people, North and South?" Lamar asked. He said that if Sumner could speak from the grave, he would say, "My countrymen! Know one another, and you will love one another!" Lamar went on to serve as a U.S. Senator, as Secretary of the Interior, and as an Associate Justice on the Supreme Court.

Conflict with Native Americans

The huge western migration of Americans and immigrants created conflict with Native American tribes living in the region, including the Sioux, Blackfoot, Crow, Cheyenne, Comanche, and Apache. About 250,000 Indians lived on the Plains and in the upper Midwest. The U.S. government had signed treaties recognizing Native American ownership of their lands. The tribes usually let whites travel through their land without incident, but they fought fiercely against whites who tried to settle there. Between 1869 and 1875, over two hundred battles took place between native warriors and the U.S. Army. Americans met any Indian attack with fierce reprisal.

Perhaps the best known battle occurred in what is now Montana. As gold seekers invaded the region, they wanted the U.S. Army to protect them from Indian attacks. Lt. Col. George Armstrong Custer led an attachment of about 260 troops as part of a larger force. Custer's men discovered the main Sioux encampment along the Little Bighorn River and decided to attack on June 25, 1876. The

Geronimo (1905)

U.S. troops were badly outnumbered, and all of the soldiers under Custer's command were killed, as well as Custer himself. The leader of the Indians was Sitting Bull, who fled to Canada but eventually returned to the U.S. and toured the country with Buffalo Bill Cody's Wild West Show. In 1890 Sitting Bull was killed during an attempt by authorities to arrest him in order to limit his influence among Native Americans.

Apache leader Geronimo led raids against Americans until he was captured in 1886. He eventually came to believe in Jesus. Geronimo participated in the inaugural parade of Theodore Roosevelt in 1905 and died in captivity at Fort Sill, Oklahoma, in 1909.

The last resistance by the Sioux ended in 1890, when a group of Native Americans assembled to surrender to U.S. troops at Wounded Knee in

Susan La Flesche Picotte (1865-1915) was the first Native American woman to earn a medical degree. She traveled on horseback to serve tribes around her home in Nebraska and later became a missionary and a prohibitionist.

South Dakota. An accidental rifle discharge caused nervous troops to fire into the group. About 200 Indians and 25 soldiers died in what was called the Battle of Wounded Knee.

Movement to the Cities

The second major people movement of the period was to the nation's cities. Between 1830 and 1870, rural population in America grew two and a half times, from 11 million to 28 million people. During the same period, however, urban population increased nine times, growing from 1.1 million to 9.9 million. More people still lived on farms and in small towns, but the pace of urban growth increased dramatically. The rate of increase in the number of farms slowed during the period as more people left rural areas for larger towns and cities.

Another big reason for the growth in the cities was a new wave of immigration from other countries. Between 1860 and 1900, fourteen million immigrants came to America's shores, and most of these settled in the cities. In 1870 33% of the people in New England and 42% of the population in the Middle Atlantic states were either foreign born or the children of foreign-born residents. By 1900 those percentages had increased to 54% in New England and 50% in the Middle Atlantic states.

Most of the immigrants came from Southern or Eastern Europe, primarily Italy, Poland, the Balkan countries, and Russia. Most were poor and either Catholic or Jewish. They tended to live together in the same section of a city. Urban areas came to be separated into ethnic groupings and identifiable neighborhoods. For these immigrants, family and community meant a great deal.

The sections of the city where they lived were separate from where the wealthy lived, which enabled the well-to-do to ignore the poor easily. The immigrants were often victims of prejudice by Americans who felt threatened by their presence. Many of the newcomers became wage earners in factories or shops. They were better off than they had been in their native lands, but by American standards they were poor.

Even as Americans moved west or moved to the cities, the nautical tradition remained strong. Below is Winslow Homer's painting Breezing Up (A Fair Wind), *finished in 1876.*

City Life

The swelling population of the cities challenged the public services that were available to the residents and led to huge changes in city life. Public transportation, such as streetcars (first pulled by horses, then by steam-powered engines, and finally by electricity), was offered to help people travel the long distances from their homes to work or to shopping districts. Street lights were installed for convenience and safety. Gas arc street lights in the 1870s were replaced by electric lights in the 1880s. Police departments modernized to deal with increases in crime. Wood-burning steam streetcar engines and wood stoves in the rapidly-multiplying apartments and homes led to the need for professional fire departments.

Public health became a major issue, and cities made efforts to improve sanitation. One great fear of the times was yellow fever, caused by mosquitoes that bred in standing water or open sewage pools (although the cause was not fully understood until 1900). Numerous occurrences of yellow fever occurred during this period. Memphis, Tennessee, had a series of outbreaks of the disease, probably caused by ships from the Caribbean or the West Indies coming up the Mississippi River and docking there. Two thousand people died in the yellow fever outbreak in Memphis in 1873. Five years later, 5,100 died and 25,000 people fled the city (when its population was less than 100,000). Some of those who left Memphis escaped the city by going to nearby small towns, but they inadvertently carried the disease to the towns in which they took refuge. A third, smaller outbreak occurred in 1879.

Labor and Management

The period after the Civil War was a favorable time for business. Congress had enacted a protective tariff that allowed domestic producers to sell goods at prices higher than they could have charged on the open market. The more stable national banking system helped creditors to collect their debts and encouraged business investment. Government assistance to railroads was commonplace. At the same time, legal authorities undertook few investigations of questionable business practices. Businesses had little accountability for what they did.

As the power of big business grew, workers and farmers tried to organize themselves to protect their interests. Small attempts at organizing labor had taken place before the war; and in the decades after the war, labor movements still were not strong. The

A huge fire burned about one-third of the city of Chicago during October 8-10, 1871. Tradition attributes the cause to an oil lantern kicked over by a cow belonging to Mrs. O'Leary. The fire took 250 lives and left 90,000 people homeless. Below is part of a panorama photograph of the city after the fire. The city recovered well, however, and hosted the 1893 World's Fair.

efforts of wage-earners to organize eventually led to powerful national unions in the twentieth century, but, in the late 1800s, organized labor had little clout. The National Labor Union was formed in 1866, primarily as a reform group urging the eight-hour work day and the abolition of slums. It was a short-lived effort. The Knights of Labor group was organized in 1869 as a secret brotherhood; even its name was not known publicly until 1881. Farmers were not successful in building and maintaining a unified and effective power base during this period.

The Black Experience

About ten percent of the American population had little hope of enjoying the American dream simply because of their race. Negroes or colored people, as they were called then, were kept separate from the mainstream of American life. Slavery had ended, but prejudice had not. Equal rights for blacks was not a cause promoted by either national political party or by any influential special interest group. Americans for the most part rejected the idea of equality for the Negro.

After the 13th, 14th, and 15th Amendments were passed (but not well enforced), blacks did not receive further protection of their rights. Instead, they were downtrodden in the South and stereotyped throughout America as inferior, unintelligent, and lazy. They lived in segregated neighborhoods and, where schools were available, their children attended segregated schools. For the most part, the situation of the Negro was an issue that most Americans did not want to address. Blacks made up a large part of America's rural poor, and those who lived in the cities were not much better off.

Former slave Benjamin "Pap" Singleton of Tennessee encouraged blacks to leave the poverty and discrimination of the South and go west to establish their own homestead farms. He visited various camps of displaced freedmen to encourage them to move. About 25,000 former slaves made the journey from the South to Kansas. Others started the

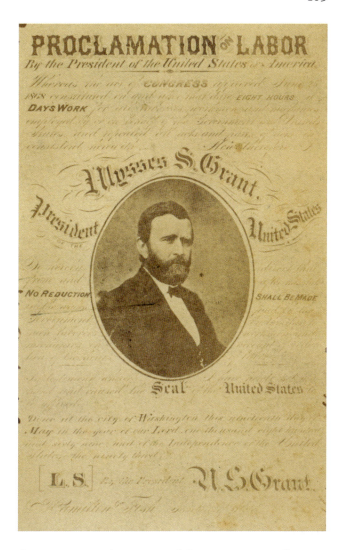

In response to the growing labor movement, Congress passed and President Grant signed legislation that the work day for people employed by the Federal government would be limited to eight hours.

trip but ran out of money and supplies. Those who went became known as Exodusters, a term coined by combining the word exodus from the Bible with the dusty plains of Kansas. Singleton called himself the father of the Black Exodus and made his own move to Kansas in 1879.

A Changing Nation Once Again

America was becoming an industrial nation that still maintained its traditional agrarian values of freedom, individualism, personal dignity and worth, and hope for a better future. Most

Unit 15 - Moving Forward

A group of students from Fisk University in Nashville, Tennessee, began touring as the Jubilee Singers in 1871. President Grant invited the group to perform at the White House, and they went on a successful tour of Europe. The Fisk Jubilee Singers continue to inspire audiences today.

Americans believed that these values were being achieved despite evidence to the contrary for blacks, Native Americans, and first- and second-generation immigrants. A great disparity was growing between the lives of the rich and the poor; racial prejudice and discrimination were commonplace; and the rich (not the poor) received special treatment from the government.

The identity of the typical American was changing from that of an independent farmer or businessman to that of a hired worker in a factory or shop. Most people of the day believed that this was the right path for people to take, but they did not clearly see the cost of such a change. Many Americans lost the initiative that comes from working on one's own, and family life suffered as well because men spent less time at home. The new economic system might have been a step up for immigrants, but it was a step down for Americans in general. As has often been the case, America was facing the difficult question of how to define progress and what price its people would be willing to pay for progress. Often the cost was paid in intangible factors beyond money and things.

*It is vain for you to rise up early, to retire late,
to eat the bread of painful labors;
for He gives to His beloved even in his sleep.
Psalm 127:2*

★ Assignments for Lesson 72 ★

American Voices — Read "Dear Lord and Father of Mankind" by John Greenleaf Whittier (page 239).

Literature — Continue reading *Humorous Stories and Sketches*.

Bible — Work on memorizing Proverbs 16:1-3.

Project — Work on your project.

Student Review — Optional: Answer the questions for Lesson 72.

This Plaque Reads: "The last tie laid on the completion of the Pacific Railroad, May, 1869"

Lesson 73

The Transcontinental Railroad

Transportation is important to human life and interaction. Throughout history people have developed new ways to get from here to there faster, cheaper, and more safely. Inventions such as the wheel and the steamboat as well as the development of better road systems have led to new horizons and new possibilities for mankind.

The Need

The fact that the United States spanned a continent three thousand miles wide brought challenges and exciting opportunities for the people, the states, and the national government. In the mid-1800s, the railroad held the greatest potential for bringing the nation together. The nation had no cross-country water or road transportation system. Going from the East Coast to the West Coast required a long, slow, and sometimes dangerous trek across the vast plains by a combination of railroads and stagecoaches. Travel on foot or on horseback was even slower. An ocean voyage around Cape Horn on the tip of South America took six months. The Panama Canal did not exist.

Railroad companies were the first large corporations. Local, state, and Federal governments eagerly assisted those companies in building rail lines because of the possibilities for increased commerce. The nation had about 35,000 miles of railroad track at the end of the Civil War. Thirty years later, almost 200,000 miles of rail lines were in use, which was about forty percent of the world's total railroad mileage. However, the growth of rail lines was not without problems. Companies went into debt to build the lines, and this caused difficulties. The bankruptcies of small lines helped bring about the Panic of 1873, and further insolvency contributed to the Panic of 1893 and the depression that followed.

The Plans

Serious discussion of a transcontinental railroad line began taking place in the early 1850s. Stephen Douglas' desire for the line to originate in Chicago led to his advocacy of the Kansas-Nebraska Act so that those areas might be organized as Federal territories. Territorial status would provide greater protection by the national government for the proposed rail line. Douglas' fellow Illinoisan, Abraham Lincoln, was also a proponent of a transcontinental line. Southerners wanted to see a line built from New Orleans across Texas and through the desert southwest. Northern politicians, however, never seriously considered a route that might benefit the slaveholding South or encourage the spread of slavery.

Chinese Workers on the Central Pacific Railroad

The crisis of secession and war slowed the development of a transcontinental railroad but did not stop it entirely. In 1862 Congress passed the Pacific Railway Bill. The law chartered the Union Pacific Railroad to build a line west from Omaha, Nebraska, and the Central Pacific Railroad to build a line east from Sacramento. Sacramento was the capital of California and the home of the Central Pacific's largest investors. In other words, the two companies were commissioned to build rail lines toward each other. When they met, the transcontinental railroad would be a reality.

The Work

Work began during the war, but relatively little was accomplished. It was only after the war that the two companies made significant progress on each end of the project. The work on the line was an engineering marvel. First the surveyors had to map out the best route. The towns that the railroads connected were few and far between. More often, the railroad created towns as it moved across the plains. The project would have been amazing enough had it simply covered level ground. The fact that they had to deal with mountains, rivers, canyons, Indian reservations, and weather problems made it even more difficult.

The construction process used the best technology of the day: steam engines, earth-moving explosives, and railcar construction. America's abundant trees, minerals, and other natural resources, as well as iron and steel production, aided the project. All supplies had to be carried to the construction sites and moved along as work progressed. The moving work camps attracted peddlers, gamblers, and other opportunists. Telegraph lines were strung above the railroad lines to report to both coasts on the progress being made (the first transcontinental telegraph line had gone into use in 1861).

As many as 15,000 workers were employed by each company. Union Pacific used mostly Irish immigrants and ex-Civil War soldiers. They had to deal with water shortages and bad weather as they built west. Central Pacific relied mostly on Chinese workers as it moved east. One estimate is that ninety percent of the CP work force was Chinese. For the most part, the Chinese were men who were already living in California. Many of them hoped to earn enough to go back to China, buy some land, and start a family. Relatively few people came from China specifically to work on the railroad. The adult male Chinese population of California grew from 7,500 in 1850 to 105,000 in 1880; but this increase was the result of general migration to the U.S. and not specifically because of work on the railroad. When the lines reached the Utah Territory, thousands of Mormons were hired to help get the job completed.

The project was hard work. Most of the construction was done by hand: loading wheelbarrows of dirt from tunnel excavations or in building a level roadbed, putting ties and rails in place, driving stakes with sledgehammers, shoveling snow. The heat was merciless in the summer and the cold was bitter in the winter. Some workers died from the weather, sickness, or excavation accidents.

Financing the Project

Private companies built the transcontinental railroad but most of the funding came from the Federal government. The government gave each company twenty sections of land (about ten square

Lesson 73 - The Transcontinental Railroad

miles) along the route for every mile of track laid. These land grants alternated with blocks of land that the Federal government retained. The companies were able to sell the land later to private speculators and make huge profits. The government also made loans to the companies: $16,000 to $48,000 per mile, depending on the difficulty of the terrain. In addition, the companies received tax breaks from local, state, and national governments. Communities often made grants to rail construction companies during this period to try to get the company to build a line through those towns. The more track that the companies built, the more they received. This made it into a race between the two crews, which encouraged their work but also led to some shoddy construction that had to be redone later.

The Federal government was the main investor in the project; the companies themselves carried little risk for its success or failure. Since the government basically offered the railroads a blank check to do the work, profiteering by the companies was enormous. When the Central Pacific hired its own construction company to do the work, profits increased all the more. The directors of the companies became fabulously wealthy, especially the "Big Four" of the Central Pacific: Charles Crocker, Collis Huntington, Mark Hopkins, and Leland Stanford. Stanford was governor of California when the project began and later endowed Stanford University.

The Last Spike, *Thomas Hill (American, 1881)*

This guide, published in 1870, promised to tell readers "what is worth seeing—where to see it—where to go—how to go—and whom to stop with" along the Transcontinental Railroad.

Completion

The Union Pacific covered more ground than the Central Pacific: 1,086 miles by UP compared to 689 miles by CP. This was because building the line on the plains was easier than building it through the mountains of eastern California, Nevada, and Utah. Finally on May 10, 1869, Leland Stanford drove a gold spike the last few inches into the combined rails at Promontory Point, Utah; and the transcontinental railroad was a reality.

Completion of the project had many benefits. A person could now travel from coast to coast in seven days. The railroad opened the West for more rapid settlement. It connected raw materials and products with manufacturers and markets.

It created a national market for goods and increased the market for iron, steel, and lumber by the growth in the railroad industry itself. The Federal government got back what it invested in the project plus additional benefits. The land that the government owned along the line rose in value. The railroads carried government workers, supplies, and the mails at reduced rates or for free. The economic growth stimulated by the railroad brought in increased tax revenues.

The success of this project encouraged other transcontinental lines to be built. The general trend in railroading became the consolidation of smaller lines into larger companies, which is what Cornelius Vanderbilt (called "Commodore" because of his previous success in the shipping industry) did in creating the New York Central Railroad.

The project had its negative aspects as well. Because of corruption and overbilling, the government paid about $100 million for work that actually cost about $45 million. The encroachment

The Influence of the Railroad

Railroads have contributed many phrases to the English language that we use in everyday life. For instance, if someone messes up his life, he is said to have gone off the rails. If someone believes that he has been pushed into an unfavorable situation against his will, he might say that he was railroaded into it. The track bed is called the grade, and an incline of the track up a mountain is also called a grade. If someone completes a task or meets the required qualifications, he is said to have made the grade. Railroad steam engines have to work extra hard to get up an incline, so someone working as hard as he can on a project is said to have built up a full head of steam.

The railroads, and especially the transcontinental railroad, had a major effect on the way we tell time. A solar day is understood to be the 24 hours between the times when the sun is highest in the sky each day. Before the day of railroads, each individual community kept its own time. It could have been 9:00 in one town and 9:05 just down the road. It was not crucial for different communities to have exactly the same time. Railroads, however, had to develop a reliable and understandable schedule for their arrivals and departures. A passenger wanted to be able to know when a train was arriving or leaving. Different methods of time-keeping by different railroad companies also led to fatal accidents.

In 1883 railroad companies in the United States and Canada divided the two countries into four time zones. Most people began to use the railroad time for their zone, but Congress did not officially adopt the time zones as a Federal standard until 1918. World standard time was established through international agreement in 1884. The world was divided into 24 zones, each 15 degrees of longitude or an average of just over 1,000 miles wide at the equator, with the zero meridian of longitude that passes through the Royal Observatory in Greenwich, England, being the starting point. In practice, time zone boundaries are not straight lines of longitude; political considerations have led to many unusual deviations in the lines.

Road Sign in Kentucky

Lesson 73 - The Transcontinental Railroad

of white men almost wiped out the bison population on the plains. Men shot bison (commonly called buffalo) for sport as trains moved along. Some bison were used for hides when they became fashionable in the East, but it is estimated that four out of five bison killed were left on the ground. Between 1871 and 1874, about three million bison were killed each year. Because of the impact on bison herds, the life of the Indians on the plains was also decimated. Native Americans relied on bison meat for food and on the hides for clothing and shelter. White men were already coming onto their lands, but the senseless slaughter of bison hastened the end of their way of life.

The U.S. government established the National Bison Range in Montana in 1908 to preserve the American bison in its natural habitat.

*As far as the east is from the west,
so far has He removed our transgressions from us.
Psalm 103:12*

★ Assignments for Lesson 73 ★

Literature — Continue reading *Humorous Stories and Sketches*.

Bible — Jesus said, "From everyone who has been given much, much will be demanded" (Luke 12:48). How are we under obligation to use well these blessings of progress?

- transportation and travel
- communication
- medical and agricultural technology
- American churches and Christians

Work on memorizing Proverbs 16:1-3.

Project — Work on your project.

Student Review — Optional: Answer the questions for Lesson 73.

Thomas Nast Cartoon (1877)

Lesson 74

The Election of 1876

Republicans gained control of the Federal government with the inauguration of Abraham Lincoln in 1861. However, the scandals of the Grant Administration and the Panic of 1873 caused many people to question the leadership of the Republican Party. The lingering presence of Federal troops in a few southern states more than ten years after the end of the Civil War was a bitter remnant of Republican Reconstruction and an unpleasant reminder of something most people were ready to put behind them. After Democrats won a majority of seats in the U.S. House of Representatives in 1874, they believed that they had a good chance to capture the White House in 1876.

H. H. Lloyd & Co. of New York printed educational posters during the 1876 campaign. Portraits of the candidates were surrounded by images of each of the preceding Presidents. Also included were the party platforms, short biographies of the candidates, and statistical details about past elections.

412

Lesson 74 - The Election of 1876

What Else Was Happening?

1869   The first professional baseball team, the Cincinnati Red Stockings, is organized. It is later known as the Redlegs and today as the Reds.

1869   Thomas Edison invents the stock ticker, which transmitted stock prices by telegraph lines. Prices were printed out on a long, continuous strip of paper. It became common for people to throw used strips of the paper out of windows at passing parades, leading to the term "ticker tape parade."

1869   Mendeleyev devises a table that arranges the elements according to their periodically recurring properties; hence it is called the periodic table.

1870   France declares war on Prussia, which starts the Franco-Prussian War. France surrenders in early 1871 and is forced to cede Alsace-Lorraine and accept an occupation army.

1870   Charles Dickens dies.

1870   The first Vatican Council declares papal infallibility in ex cathedra pronouncements.

1871   James Abbott McNeill Whistler paints "Arrangement in Grey and Black No. 1," which becomes better known by its subject, "Whistler's Mother."

1871   Henry Stanley of the New York Herald finds missionary David Livingstone in Africa.

1871   Phineas Taylor (P. T.) Barnum begins his circus called "The Greatest Show on Earth" in Brooklyn. He merges with the James Bailey Circus in 1881 and sells out to the Ringling Brothers in 1907. A poster from 1900 is shown at right.

1872   Retailer Montgomery Ward sends out the first mail-order catalog, a one-page list. The 1884 edition has 240 pages. Sears, Roebuck and Company begins a catalog in 1888.

1873   The typewriter is invented, using the QWERTY keyboard arrangement still employed today to prevent the most-used keys from jamming together.

1874   The painting "Impression: Sunrise" by Claude Monet at a Paris exhibition leads an art critic to coin the term Impressionism to describe the works on display.

1874   The ice cream soda is invented in Philadelphia.

1875   Tchaikovsky's ballet Swan Lake debuts in Moscow; the opera Carmen by George Bizet opens in Paris.

1876   Eight baseball teams form the National League.

1876   Alexander Graham Bell invents the telephone.

Nominations

The Democrats nominated New York governor Samuel J. Tilden. Tilden had gained prominence as the attorney who led the crackdown on the Tammany Hall political machine in New York City. His successes in that effort led to his being elected governor. The Democratic platform called for an end to corruption by public officials and reform of the civil service system for hiring government workers. Meanwhile, although the Republican Party was still powerful, they were concerned. They nominated Civil War veteran and Ohio governor Rutherford B. Hayes. Hayes had improved the civil service system in Ohio and advocated an end to Reconstruction. Both candidates were able and honest men, well-to-do, and associated with successful businessmen.

Hayes/Wheeler Campaign Banner

Tilden/Hendricks Campaign Paper Lantern

A Dirty Campaign

During the campaign, Democrats reminded voters of the Republicans' record of scandals. The Republicans, on the other hand, called on voters to remember the horrors of the Civil War. They blamed Democrats for the South's secession, Lincoln's assassination, and most other ills that the nation faced.

In the election, both the popular vote and the electoral vote were close. Tilden had a 250,000 vote lead and stood one electoral vote shy of winning. However, the election was filled with fraud on both sides. Voters (especially blacks) were intimidated away from voting. In some states rival sets of returns were submitted by competing election boards. Serious questions were raised about the returns from Oregon, Louisiana, South Carolina, and Florida. Hayes had clearly won Oregon; and if all the disputed votes of the remaining three states went to Hayes, he would win by one electoral vote.

Lesson 74 - The Election of 1876

Tilden's 250,000 popular vote margin was out of 8.3 million votes cast. Just under 82 percent of eligible voters participated in the election. This was slightly more than the 1860 turnout rate, and no election since has surpassed that percentage. In recent presidential elections, the turnout has been about 60 percent of eligible voters.

Congress Decides

The Constitution did not provide for a clear solution to the vote count dilemma. If the Republican-controlled Senate decided the controversy, it would favor Hayes; if the Democratic House decided, it would go for Tilden. In January of 1877, Congress set up a fifteen-member commission to investigate the election. Five members of the Senate, five from the House, and five from the Supreme Court were to decide the issue. Seven were Democrats, seven were Republicans, and Associate Supreme Court Justice David Davis from Illinois was selected as a non-partisan member of the commission.

At the last minute, however, the Illinois legislature elected Davis to be a U.S. Senator. Davis resigned from the commission, and his place was taken by Republican Justice Joseph Bradley. By a straight 8-7 party vote, the commission decided that Hayes had won all three states. This gave Hayes the election, 185 electoral votes to 184. The House accepted the commission's report on March 2, two days before the inauguration.

The United States celebrated its 100th birthday in 1876. This image shows Independence Hall in Philadelphia that year. For six months, Philadelphia hosted a Centennial Exposition, officially titled the International Exhibition of Arts, Manufactures and Products of the Soil and Mine. Ten million visitors viewed exhibits from around the world and learned of exciting new technological developments such as the telephone, the typewriter, and Heinz ketchup.

The Compromise of 1877

Apparently a meeting at a Washington hotel in late February (which might have been the culmination of several earlier meetings) between leading Republicans and southern Democrats set the stage for the outcome. Republicans promised that if Hayes were elected, he would withdraw the remaining Reconstruction troops from the South. This pleased the Democrats, who wanted to be able to go their own way in southern state governments. On that condition, Democrats agreed to accept Hayes and not to continue partisan bickering. Other, more general promises from Hayes relating to Federal aid for a southern transcontinental railroad and the naming of a southerner as Postmaster General were also mentioned. The position of Postmaster General was important because he was able to give out many government jobs as political favors. Democrats also said that they would not oppose Republican James Garfield as Speaker of the House.

After Hayes was inaugurated, he did remove the last Federal troops from Louisiana and South Carolina and he did name former Confederate general David Key of Tennessee as postmaster general. However, southern Democrats opposed Garfield for House Speaker and all of the other promises made in the negotiations were forgotten. Republican-led governments in Louisiana and South Carolina soon collapsed without the support of Federal troops. This meant that Democrats once again controlled all eleven former Confederate state governments. In the South, Republican Reconstruction was over and the Democrats were back in charge.

Appraisal of the Election

Both sides almost certainly cheated in the 1876 election. If a fair count of votes cast had been taken, Democrat Tilden probably would have been declared the winner. The party leaders who decided the outcome of the election determined that their interests would be better served by compromise instead of continued conflict. Reconstruction might have ended soon anyway, so Hayes' agreement to remove troops was largely symbolic. Both parties could see themselves as winners in the melee.

The main losers in the arrangement were southern blacks. The Republican Party abandoned them because they were no longer needed for the party to achieve its goals, and southern Democrats had no interest in protecting or extending the rights

While powerful men in Washington, D.C., made political deals, regular people across the United States went about their daily lives. After two years of grasshoppers destroying their crops in Minnesota, the Ingalls family moved to Burr Oak, Iowa, in the fall of 1876. They lived and worked briefly at a hotel (kitchen pictured at left) before Pa Ingalls started a feed mill. The youngest Ingalls daughter, Grace, was born in Burr Oak in 1877.

of blacks. The civil rights of blacks were limited or removed by southern Democratic state governments in the years that followed.

Republican Domination?

The last half of the nineteenth century is often seen as a period of complete Republican domination, but their control was actually not as firm as it might appear at first glance. Grant apparently received a minority of votes cast by whites in 1868, and Democrat Tilden received a majority of popular votes in 1876. Democrat Grover Cleveland won the 1884 and 1892 elections and had a plurality of the popular vote in 1888.

The Republicans controlled both Congress and the presidency for only eight years (1881-1883, 1889-1891 and 1897-1901), while the Democrats controlled both for two years (1893-1895). Moreover, Democrats were in complete control of southern state politics. The parties differed only in emphasis on most important national issues except tariff laws. Both parties wanted to see the economy continue to grow, and neither party had much interest in promoting the civil rights of blacks.

*There is no wisdom and no understanding
and no counsel against the Lord.
Proverbs 21:30*

★ Assignments for Lesson 74 ★

American Voices — Read "God of Our Fathers" by Daniel Roberts (page 243).

Literature — Continue reading *Humorous Stories and Sketches*.

Bible — Work on memorizing Proverbs 16:1-3.

Project — Work on your project.

Student Review — Optional: Answer the questions for Lesson 74.

Portland Star Match Company, Portland, Maine (c. 1870)

Lesson 75 - Bible Study

What Is Progress?

In our centennial year of 1876, the United States had to deal with the scandal of the Hayes-Tilden presidential election. In our bicentennial year of 1976, we were recovering from the Watergate scandal and had a President (Gerald Ford) who had not been elected by the people. This comparison illustrates that "progress" of the American experiment does not move in a consistently positive direction.

Talking about how busy we are and how rapidly things change has become commonplace. We can now communicate instantaneously around the world, whereas getting a message across the United States once took several days. Medical technology has alleviated much suffering and has enabled us to live longer, more productive lives. With new technology being introduced all the time, we have come to think that leaving the old ways behind is always good (which is exactly what advertisers want us to think). Nobody wants to be seen as being against progress. When a liberal wants to scare an audience about conservatives, he or she will sometimes say that conservatives want to turn back the clock, at which thought the audience is supposed to draw back in horror.

However, progress in material terms as people usually define it is not always a good thing, especially if God's moral principles are left behind. Sometimes what appears to be progress is really only making something go faster, and going faster does not necessarily mean doing things better. The Philistine culture in Biblical times, for instance, was advanced in terms of technology. They developed the use of iron before the Israelites did (1 Samuel 13:19-22). The Philistines were pagan, however, and from God's perspective that technologically advanced culture was evil.

After the Civil War, the United States acquired a momentum that, as one observer noted, was commonly mistaken for progress. Some things were indeed better: the end of slavery, improved agricultural technology, and advances in medicine and science. However, racial prejudice still existed and was widely accepted. Workers in factories suffered under poor conditions in the name of economic expansion. Government seemed more interested in helping the rich than in helping the poor (if the government needed to be helping anybody in this direct way). As we study the beginnings of modern America, it is good to consider the spiritual issues involved in what we call progress. We will consider two specific areas of human activity.

Lesson 75 - Bible Study: What Is Progress?

Medical Technology

Advances in medical technology have raised major issues concerning the quality of human life. For instance, a baby born with certain birth defects would have died in previous generations; but now the child will likely survive. However, the child's survival will often require enormous resources from the parents and from health care providers. At the other end of life, the elderly can remain alive much longer than was previously the case, though sometimes their last years are spent with little quality of life.

This is not to say that we should oppose medical advances or that people should not give the best care possible to their ailing loved ones. We should be thankful that such advances are available. But modern medical technology raises issues of faith and the meaning of human life that did not have to be considered in previous generations. Are we willing to give the time, energy, and expense that loved ones will need? As individuals and as a nation, we must consider with the eyes of faith the ethical questions that confront us.

Another example of so-called progress is stem cell research. Advocates say that tissue from unwanted embryos should be available for research and should be used to help others who are suffering from a variety of diseases. Opponents of this research maintain that allowing such use might encourage the creation of embryos for the purpose of harvesting tissue. Just because we can do something does not necessarily mean that we should do it. Stem cell research is still in its early stages. The claims made for embryonic stem cells by advocates of this procedure appear to be rosier than what we actually know. Medical advances can be made without using tissue from embryos. Even if stem cells from embryos could help people, should we use such tissue in the name of medical progress? We have to consider whether human life is indeed sacred before God and whether some areas of activity are simply off limits (such as killing people in the name of medical research).

The City

The glamor of the city has attracted people from small towns for centuries. Small-town residents lament the lack of opportunities that their children face if they continue to live in the town. Yet the city is not altogether a good thing. Traffic, pollution, crime, evil influences, and impersonal existence detract from quality of life in the city. Sometimes what appears to be progress is only momentum.

In addition, it is easy to forget God in the city. Once when I was visiting a large city, I was in a rail station transferring from a commuter train to the subway. The place was a bustle of human activity, human advertisements, and praise for human achievements. I could see little that directly pointed to God or gave Him glory. Walking or driving through the canyons formed by skyscrapers in a major city is vastly different from seeing the canyons of God's created world. You get different perspectives on Creation when your contact with

Benjamin Rush, a Philadelphia physician, signed the Declaration of Independence. He worked to establish Dickinson College in Carlisle, Pennsylvania, in 1783. Rush emphasized the important of religion and education. Laboratory equipment from the college is shown below about 1876.

The City of New York, Currier & Ives (1876)

nature is a potted plant in the midst of an asphalt jungle and when you can see a forest or a field of colorful wildflowers. The mission of believers who live in the city must be to make sure that people see God in their lives if their fellow urban dwellers are not able to appreciate much of His created world.

A Mixed Blessing

Progress as the world defines it is a mixed bag. Our ability to save lives has increased, as has our ability to take lives. The September 11, 2001, terrorist attacks, for example, would not have been possible one hundred years earlier. We can communicate more information to more people in a shorter time, but much of that information is worthless and degrading. We no longer watch men killing each other for entertainment as the ancient Romans did, but we have digressed from the path of godliness in other ways. People in our culture do not have to spend huge amounts of their time merely surviving (growing food, building their own shelter, etc.), but we do not always use our time for good purposes. We have grown in what we are able to do, but what are we doing with that capability?

How God Defines Progress

From God's point of view, progress means getting closer to the goal we ought to be pursuing. To God, the main question is not whether something is new or old but whether it is right. Sometimes pursuing the right way involves leaving what is currently being done and going back to former ways. The prophets often called people to repent and return to God. God's message through Jeremiah, for instance, was, "Stand by the ways and see and ask for the ancient paths, where the good way is, and walk in it; and you will find rest for your souls" (Jeremiah 6:16). The people of Jeremiah's day refused to do this, however. Going back to the ancient paths would have been real progress for them, while continuing on their current path was going to result in loss.

The writer of Hebrews appealed to his readers to "remember the former days" when they had joyfully endured suffering and persecution (Hebrews 10:32-34). He was writing to his readers to admonish them not to give up on the Lord, which they were being tempted to do (Hebrews 2:1). For them, going back to the former days would be making progress. In

Lesson 75 - Bible Study: What Is Progress?

another example, the Christians in Colossae had moved beyond the simple gospel of Christ and had accepted what they thought was more enlightened thinking about worldly philosophies. Paul warned them not to continue in that direction but to return to the basic truths of Christ (Colossians 2:4-8).

The Lord condemned the church at Ephesus because they had left their first love (Revelation 2:4). What they needed to do to make spiritual progress was to go back to what they had done previously. Making progress on the wrong path is not real progress. When you are on the wrong path, the most positive thing you can do is to go back to the right path. The Bible calls this repentance, and repentance from sin is one of the best ways to make spiritual progress.

Identifying the Real Issues

The purpose of this lesson is not to say that we should go back to the good old days of the 1950s or the 1800s or any other supposedly idyllic time. Following God has been difficult in every generation from the Garden of Eden on. I doubt that any of us would want everything the way it was in the 1950s or the 1800s if that included racial segregation, less medical knowledge, shorter life expectancies, and dangerous work places. Many simple or plain folk of today avoid technological advances because they

North Carolina's Cape Hatteras Light Station, pictured above, is the tallest brick lighthouse in North America. It was lit for the first time in 1870 and received its distinctive black and white stripes in 1873 so that sailors could recognize it during the day.

fear the evil influences that such advances bring. They are right about the kind of temptations that technology puts before us; but a person can sin easily enough dressed in plain clothing and without owning a television.

Detail from Opening of the Midwest, *Robert White (American, 1937)*

Unit 15 - Moving Forward

This "Symbolical Centenary Chart of American History" illustrates American history from 1492 to 1872. The central pictures highlight key developments and events while portraits of political and military leaders, explorers, writers, and other individuals are around the outside.

The purpose of this lesson is to remind us not to be seduced by the world into thinking that material progress automatically makes us better people. All material possessions and advances have to be used for God's purposes and governed by His eternal principles. Real history is not straight line progress, however one defines the line. To know what is real progress requires looking at history and life through the eyes of faith.

Then He said to them, "Beware, and be on your guard against every form of greed; for not even when one has an abundance does his life consist of his possessions."
Luke 12:15

★ Assignments for Lesson 75 ★

American Voices — Read "It Is Well With My Soul" by Horatio Spafford (page 240).

Literature — Finish reading *Humorous Stories and Sketches*. Literary analysis available in *Student Review*.

Bible — Recite or write Proverbs 16:1-3 from memory.

Project — Complete your project for the unit.

Student Review — Optional: Answer the questions for Lesson 75 and for *Humorous Stories and Sketches* and take the quiz for Unit 15. Take the third history exam, English exam, and Bible exam.

Detail from The Boat Builders, *Winslow Homer (American, 1873)*

Image Credits

Images marked with one of these codes are used with the permission of a Creative Commons Attribution or Attribution-Share Alike License. See the websites listed for details.

CC-BY-2.0	creativecommons.org/licenses/by/2.0/
CC-BY-3.0	creativecommons.org/licenses/by/3.0/
CC-BY-SA-2.0	creativecommons.org/licenses/by-sa/2.0/
CC-BY-SA-2.5	creativecommons.org/licenses/by-sa/2.5/
CC-BY-SA-3.0	creativecommons.org/licenses/by-sa/3.0/

Uncredited images are in the public domain in the United States, taken from Wikimedia Commons and other sources.

iii	Ted Kerwin / Flickr / CC-BY-2.0
iv	National Archives and Records Administration
v	Library of Congress
vi	Yale Collection of Western Americana, Beinecke Rare Book and Manuscript Library
vii	Notgrass Family Collection
x	User:Kroton / Wikimedia Commons / CC-BY-3.0
xvi	Mark Clifton / Flickr / CC-BY-2.0
1	Dwight Sipler / Flickr / CC-BY-2.0
3	Bernt Rostad / Flickr / CC-BY-2.0
4	National Archives and Records Administration
5	Medill DC / Flickr / CC-BY-2.0
7	Carol M. Highsmith's America, Library of Congress
8	Library of Congress
9	Library of Congress
11	W. Lloyd MacKenzie / http://www.flickr.com/photos/saffron_blaze / CC-BY-SA-3.0
12	Wikimedia Commons
13	Liz Jamieson (diywebmastery) / Flickr / CC-BY-2.0
14t	User:AlejandroLinaresGarcia / Wikimedia Commons / CC-BY-SA-3.0
14b	Charlene Notgrass
15	Charlene Notgrass
16	User:Daderot / Wikimedia Commons
17	User:Lencer / Wikimedia Commons / CC-BY-SA-3.0
18t	Wikimedia Commons
18b	National Park Service
19	Wikimedia Commons
21	Library of Congress
22	National Archives and Records Administration
23	Nicolas Vollmer Project 1080 / Flickr / CC-BY-2.0
25	Timothy Valentine / Flickr / CC-BY-SA-2.0
27t	Hamner_Fotos / Flickr / CC-BY-2.0
29	Library of Congress
32t	Megan Allen (tudor-rose) / Flickr / CC-BY-2.0
32b	Ben Salter (Capt' Gorgeous) / Flickr / CC-BY-2.0
36	rickpilot_2000 / Flickr / CC-BY-2.0
38	Yuri Long / Flickr / CC-BY-2.0
44	Vix_B / Flickr / CC-BY-2.0
45	English Wikipedia User Daniel Case / CC-BY-SA-3.0
46	Yale Collection of American Literature, Beinecke Rare Book and Manuscript Library
47	Wereon, Ilmari Karonen / Wikimedia Commons
48b	Library of Congress
49	John Carter Brown Library
50	Swampyank at en.wikipedia / CC-BY-3.0
51	AlbertHerring / Wikimedia Commons / CC-BY-SA-3.0
52b	U.S. Senate
53	Charlesdrakew / Wikimedia Commons
55	InAweofGod'sCreation / Flickr / CC-BY-2.0
58	Photograph © Andrew Dunn, 5 November 2004. Website http://www.andrewdunnphoto.com / CC-BY-SA-2.0
62	Rafaelgarcia / Wikimedia Commons
63	Library of Congress
64	Library of Congress
66	Fred Benenson (mecredis) / Flickr / CC-BY-2.0
67	Hoodinski / Wikimedia Commons / CC-BY-SA-3.0
68	User:PRA / Wikimedia Commons / CC-BY-SA-3.0
69	Photograph Ad Meskens / Wikimedia Commons / CC-BY-SA-3.0

74t	Library of Congress
74b	Daderot / Wikimedia Commons
75t	Library of Congress
75b	User:Kooma / Wikimedia Commons / Based on National Atlas of the United States
78	Library of Congress
81	CycloKitty / Flickr / CC-BY-2.0
84	New York Public Library
85	National Park Service
88	Library of Congress
89t	Library of Congress
89b	User:Rdsmith4 / Wikimedia Commons / CC-BY-SA-2.5
90	Library of Congress
91	Architect of the Capitol
92	Manuscripts & Archives, Yale University
93	National Archives and Records Administration
97	Doug Francis / Flickr / CC-BY-2.0
101	Library of Congress
103	National Archives and Records Administration
105	National Archives and Records Administration
107	National Archives and Records Administration
108	U.S. Geological Survey Map-It / John Notgrass
110	Library of Congress
111b	State Library and Archives of Florida
114	Bill Koplitz / FEMA
117	Timothy Tolle / Flickr / CC-BY-2.0
118t	Library of Congress
118b	U.S. Senate Historical Office
119	Shayan Sanyal / Flickr / CC-BY-2.0
121	W Nowicki / Wikimedia Commons / CC-BY-3.0
122	Library of Congress
123	National Archives and Records Administration
124t	Postdlf from w / Wikimedia Commons / CC-BY-SA-3.0
124b	Adrian Sulc / Wikimedia Commons / CC-BY-SA-3.0
126	National Archives and Records Administration
127	Eli Christman (Gamma Man) / Flickr / CC-BY-2.0
128	Library of Congress
129	Library of Congress
132	Library of Congress
133	Library of Congress
135	National Gallery of Art, Washington
137	Library of Congress
138	National Gallery of Art, Washington
139	Metropolitan Museum of Art
143	Library of Congress
145	U.S. Navy
146	Library of Congress
147	National Gallery of Art, Washington
149	National Park Service
150	Library of Congress
151	Library of Congress
152	Bibliothèque Nationale de France
153	English Wikipedia User Daniel Case / CC-BY-SA-3.0
154	User:Patrickneil / Wikimedia Commons / CC-BY-SA-3.0
155	User:Magicpiano / Wikimedia Commons / CC-BY-SA-3.0
156	Swampyank at en.wikipedia / CC-BY-SA-3.0
157	Library of Congress
159	Library of Congress
161	Martin Falbisoner / Wikimedia Commons / CC-BY-SA-3.0
163	U.S. Navy
167	University of Pennsylvania
168	NuclearWarfare / Wikimedia Commons
170	Tony Fischer Photography / Flickr / CC-BY-2.0
172	Library of Congress
173	Library of Congress
174	Villy Fink Isaksen / Wikimedia Commons
176b	Natalie Maynor / Flickr / CC-BY-2.0
177b	Library of Congress
180	The George F. Landegger Collection of District of Columbia Photographs in Carol M. Highsmith's America, Library of Congress
181	© Jeremy Atherton, 2001 / Wikimedia Commons / CC-BY-SA-2.5
183	Library of Congress
185	Library of Congress
186	Library of Congress
187	Library of Congress
189	Charlene Notgrass
191	aimee castenell (aimeeorleans) / Flickr / CC-BY-SA-2.0
192	Daderot / Wikimedia Commons
193	Nyttend / Wikimedia Commons
195	Architect of the Capitol
196t	U.S. Environmental Protection Agency
199	National Numismatic Collection at the Smithsonian Institution / CC-BY-SA-3.0
200	National Atlas of the United States
202	Library of Congress
204	Library of Congress
205	Maureen (amerune) / Flickr / CC-BY-2.0
206	Tennessee Portrait Project
209	John Notgrass
210	Library of Congress
212	Photo by DAVID ILIFF / Wikimedia Commons / CC-BY-SA-3.0
213t	Library of Congress
213b	Charlene Notgrass
215	Architect of the Capitol
217	Library of Congress
218	User:blahedo / Wikimedia Commons CC-BY-SA-2.5
220	Library of Congress
221	Nikater / Wikimedia Commons
223t	Library of Congress
223b	Jim Bowen (jimbowen0306) / Flickr / CC-BY-2.0
224	Aashish Lamichhane / Wikimedia Commons / CC-BY-SA-3.0
227	Library of Congress
230t	Elizabeth Albert / Flickr / CC-BY-2.0
232	Library of Congress
233	Library of Congress
234t	Robert Nunnally (gurdonark) / Flickr / CC-BY-2.0

Image Credits

234b	Library of Congress
235b	Lutz Fischer-Lamprecht / Wikimedia Commons / CC-BY-SA-3.0
236	Library of Congress
237	Library of Congress
239	Library of Congress
240	Library of Congress
241t	National Archives and Records Administration
241b	Library of Congress
242t	Beinecke Rare Book & Manuscript Library, Yale University
242b	Library of Congress
244	Ryan Bavetta / Flickr / CC-BY-2.0
245	Library of Congress
252t	TheLeopards / Wikimedia Commons
252b	Library of Congress
253b	Library of Congress
254t	Dieter Weinelt / Flickr / CC-BY-2.0
255b	Library of Congress
257	Library of Congress
258t	Library of Congress
259t	cliff1066™ / Flickr / CC-BY-2.0
260	Freddie Phillips (summonedbyfells) / Flickr / CC-BY-2.0
261t	cliff1066™ / Flickr / CC-BY-2.0
262	Library of Congress
264	National Archives and Records Administration
265	Library of Congress
266	Library of Congress
269	TravelingOtter / Flickr / CC-BY-2.0
270t	Seaman Michael Achterling / U.S. Navy
270b	Library of Congress
272	Library of Congress
274t	Library of Congress
274b	Lidia Kozenitzky, available from http://commons.wikimedia.org/wiki/User:Effib
275	Shoshanah / Flickr / CC-BY-2.0
277	Library of Congress
279	butforthesky.com (fabulousfabs) / Flickr / CC-BY-2.0
281	Carol M. Highsmith Archive, Library of Congress
282	Library of Congress
283	Library of Congress
284	Library of Congress
287	Library of Congress
290	Library of Congress
291	Library of Congress
292t	Library of Congress
294	Library of Congress
295	Library of Congress
296	cliff1066™ / Flickr / CC-BY-2.0
297	cliff1066™ / Flickr / CC-BY-2.0
299	Architect of the Capitol
300t	Library of Congress
300b	National Archives and Records Administration
301	Carolyn Cuskey (DogLovr) / Flickr / CC-BY-2.0
303t	cliff1066™ / Flickr / CC-BY-2.0
304	tornintwo2011 / Flickr / CC-BY-2.0
305	The Jon B. Lovelace Collection of California Photographs in Carol M. Highsmith's America Project, Library of Congress
306	The Jon B. Lovelace Collection of California Photographs in Carol M. Highsmith's America Project, Library of Congress
307	The George F. Landegger Collection of Alabama Photographs in Carol M. Highsmith's America, Library of Congress
309	Library of Congress
311t	Matt Turner (MT_Image) / Flickr / CC-BY-2.0
312	Library of Congress
313	Library of Congress
314	Library of Congress
315	Library of Congress
316t	Methaz / Wikimedia Commons / CC-BY-SA-3.0
317t	Library of Congress
317b	Brian Stansberry / Wikimedia Commons / CC-BY-3.0
318t	Library of Congress
318b	Ron Cogswell / Flickr / CC-BY-2.0
319t	Boston Public Library / Flickr / CC-BY-2.0
320	The George F. Landegger Collection of Alabama Photographs in Carol M. Highsmith's America, Library of Congress
321t	Carol M. Highsmith Archive, Library of Congress
322t	Library of Congress
322b	Southern Methodist University, Central University Libraries, DeGolyer Library
323	Library of Congress
325	David (dbking) / Flickr / CC-BY-2.0
326	Library of Congress
327t	Library of Congress
327b	Jim Bowen (jimbowen0306) / Flickr / CC-BY-2.0
328t	Charlene Notgrass
332t	Library of Congress
332b	Jason Dickert (japedi) / Flickr / CC-BY-2.0
334	Library of Congress
335	Accurizer / Wikimedia Commons
336	Carol M. Highsmith Archive, Library of Congress
337	David (dbking) / Flickr / CC-BY-2.0
339	Library of Congress
340t	Shiloh National Military Park / Flickr / CC-BY-2.0
340b	Library of Congress
341t	Library of Congress
343	U.S. Army
344t	Library of Congress
345	National Guard
346	Library of Congress
347	National Archives and Records Administration
348t	Cornell University Collection of Political Americana, Cornell University Library
348b	Library of Congress
350	Carol M. Highsmith's America, Library of Congress
351	Kevin T. Quinn (kevinq2000) / Flickr / CC-BY-2.0
353	Charlene Notgrass
354t	TradingCardsNational Park Service / Flickr / CC-BY-2.0

354b	Robert Claypool / Wikimedia Commons / CC-BY-SA-3.0	391	Library of Congress
356t	Ryo Chijiiwa / Flickr / CC-BY-2.0	393	Teemu008 CC-BY-SA-2.0 / Flickr / CC-BY-2.0
356b	Library of Congress	394	Library of Congress
357t	Library of Congress	395l	Cliff (cliff1066™) / Flickr / CC-BY-2.0
358	Cpl. Tyler Bolken / U.S. Marine Corps	395r	National Archives and Records Administration
359	Library of Congress	396	Library of Congress
360	National Archives and Records Administration	397	National Numismatic Collection at the Smithsonian Institution
361	Library of Congress	398	Library of Congress
362	Library of Congress	399	Neal Stimler / Flickr / CC-BY-2.0
365	Library of Congress	400	Alan Sandercock (alans 1948) / Flickr / CC-BY-2.0
366	Tom Hilton / Flickr / CC-BY-2.0	401	Library of Congress
367t	National Archives and Records Administration	402t	Northwestern University Library, The North American Indian the Photographic Images, 2001
367b	Library of Congress	402b	Nebraska State Historical Society
369	Library of Congress	403	National Gallery of Art, Washington
370	National Archives and Records Administration	405	Library of Congress
371	National Archives and Records Administration	406	Library of Congress
373t	Library of Congress	407	Mike Renlund (deltaMike) / Flickr / CC-BY-2.0
373b	U.S. Senate	410	User:Kevinraleigh / Wikimedia Commons / CC-BY-SA-3.0
374	Charlene Notgrass	411	U.S. Fish & Wildlife Service
376	Library of Congress	412	Library of Congress
378b	Library of Congress	413	Library of Congress
379	Brian Stansberry / Wikimedia Commons / CC-BY-3.0	414	Cornell University Collection of Political Americana, Cornell University Library
381t	Architect of the Capitol	415	Library of Congress
381b	National Archives and Records Administration	416	Charlene Notgrass
382b	Library of Congress	418	Library of Congress
383t	Library of Congress	420	Library of Congress
383bl	National Archives and Records Administration	421t	Charlene Notgrass
383br	Library of Congress	421b	Carol M. Highsmith Archive, Library of Congress
385t	National Archives and Records Administration	422	Library of Congress
385b	User:NJR ZA / Wikimedia Commons / CC-BY-SA-3.0		
386	Charlene Notgrass		
387	Jason Thomas (jathomas222) / Flickr / CC-BY-2.0		
389	Jim Padgett / Sweet Publishing http://sweetpublishing.com		

Also Available from Notgrass

Exploring World History by Ray Notgrass

Engaging lessons, combined with primary sources, survey history from Creation to the present. Your child can earn one year of credit in world history, English (literature and composition), and Bible. High school.

Exploring Government by Ray Notgrass

With a special emphasis on the U.S. Constitution, lessons cover Federal, state, and local government and also contemporary issues in American government. This one-semester course provides a half-year credit. High school.

Exploring Economics by Ray Notgrass

This one-semester course gives a practical overview of economic terms and concepts to help the student understand how our economy works and grasp contemporary economic issues from a free market perspective. High school.

America the Beautiful by Charlene Notgrass

This one-year American history, geography, and literature course combines the flexibility and richness of a unit study with the simplicity of a textbook-based approach to history. Ages 10-14.

Uncle Sam and You by Ray and Charlene Notgrass

This one-year civics and government course teaches your student about the foundations of American government, the election process, and how Federal, state, and local governments work. Ages 10-14.

For more information about our homeschool curriculum,
call 1-800-211-8793 or visit www.notgrass.com.